THE LOW COUNTRIES IN THE EARLY MODERN WORLD

To Monique — with love

THE LOW COUNTRIES
IN THE
EARLY MODERN WORLD

Herman Van der Wee

translated by Lizabeth Fackelman

VARIORUM
1993

Copyright   © 1993 Herman Van der Wee.

All rights reserved. No part of this publication may be reproduced, stored in a retrieval system, or transmitted in any form or by any means, electronic, mechanical, photocopied, recorded, or otherwise without the prior permission of the publisher.

Published by   VARIORUM
Ashgate Publishing Limited
Gower House, Croft Road
Aldershot, Hampshire GU11 3HR
Great Britain

Ashgate Publishing Company
Old Post Road
Brookfield, Vermont 05036
USA

British Library Cataloguing in Publication Data

Wee, Herman Van der
Low Countries in the Early Modern World
I. Title II. Fackelman, Lisabeth
ISBN 0-86078-384-7

Library of Congress Cataloging in Publication Data

Wee, Herman Van der
The Low Countries in the Early Modern World/
Herman Van der Wee.
    p. cm. Includes bibliographical references and index.
ISBN 0-86078-384-7
1. Netherlands - History - To 1384   2. Netherlands - History - 1648–1795   3. Belgium - History - To 1555   4. Belgium - History - 1555–1648   5. Netherlands - Economic conditions   6. Belgium - Economic conditions   7. Netherlands - Commerce - History   8. Belgium - Commerce - History   I. Title
DH162.W44   1993
949.2 - dc20   93-34829
                                                        CIP

This book is printed on acid free paper.

Typeset by   JL & GA Wheatley Design, Aldershot

Printed in Great Britain at the University Press, Cambridge

Contents

Preface   vii

Acknowledgements   xi

I GENERAL

1 The Low Countries in Transition: From the Middle Ages to Early Modern Times   3

2 The Low Countries in Transition: From Commercial Capitalism to the Industrial Revolution   29

II AGRICULTURE

3 Agricultural Development of the Low Countries as revealed by Tithe and Rent Statistics, 1250–1800   47

4 Agrarian History and Public Finances in Flanders, 14th to 17th Century   69

III TRADE

5 Trade in the Southern Netherlands, 1493–1587   87

6 Economic Activity and International Trade in the Southern Netherlands, 1538–1544   115

7 Trade Relations between Antwerp and the Northern Netherlands, 14th to 16th Century   126

IV MONEY AND FINANCE

8	Antwerp and the New Financial Methods of the 16th and 17th Centuries	145
9	Monetary Policy in the Duchy of Brabant, Late Middle Ages to Early Modern Times	167
10	Credit in Brabant, Late Middle Ages to Early Modern Times	183

V INDUSTRY

11	Structural Changes and Specialization in Southern Netherlands Industry, 1100–1600	201
12	Prices and Wages as Development Variables: A Comparison between England and the Southern Netherlands, 1400–1700	223

VI SOCIAL HISTORY

13	Typology of Crises and Structural Changes in the Netherlands, 15th to 16th Century	245
14	The Economy as a Factor in the Revolt in the Southern Netherlands	264
15	Nutrition and Diet in the Ancien Régime	279

Index		289

Preface

When Variorum publishers kindly proposed the publication of a volume of some of the essays I had written I welcomed the idea, but at the same time felt myself faced with a difficult dilemma. If I decided to publish these essays in their original version, I knew that I could not expect to be entirely happy with some of the hypotheses which had been formulated, since my own subsequent researches – and those of many other scholars – had generated new insights and fresh ideas about the problems involved. On the contrary, if I decided to revise and update the essays, I would have ended up re-writing the articles, which was not in any case the publisher's intention. The decision I made was a compromise between the two options mentioned above. I decided not to update the essays which were selected, in other words to respect the original version of each essay as much as possible. However, when I had the feeling that the original version lacked clarity, I altered the text slightly, sometimes by eliminating a few lines.

A second problem to be solved was the selection of articles as such. Fortunately, the publishers made my task easier in this respect by suggesting that I select those essays which referred to the period of the late Middle Ages and Early Modern times. Within this chronological framework I tried, in making the final choices, to cover the main themes in which I had been interested during many years of research: economic growth in general in the Low Countries; agricultural development; medium- and long-distance trade; industrial dynamics; mintage and monetary policy; innovations in banking and finance; and standards of living, income distribution and social relations. Most of the essays were written within the geographical context of the Low Countries, although it has always been my aim to study this region in a European pespective.

In the general section, the essays chosen refer to two periods of crucial change in the economic history of the Low Countries: first, the era of structural change at the end of the Middle Ages and the beginning of Early Modern times; second, the period of structural transition from commercial to industrial capitalism. In both essays, the problem of institutional rigidity versus institutional flexibility is discussed as the main fundamental issue. In the section of this book devoted to agriculture, the specific aspects of agricultural development in the Low Countries at the end of the Middle Ages are studied as compared to the general situation in Europe during the same period. In more detailed fashion, I have considered the contributions to the public finances, which were made by the royal domains, and also the question of how to define the 'agricultural revolution' in the Low Countries, when the phenomenon is placed in a European context.

In the section relating to trade, a first essay analyses the nature of commercial expansion in the Low Countries during the sixteenth century; another essay examines in greater depth the evolution of long-distance trade between Italy and the Low Countries in the middle years of the sixteenth century; and a similar in-depth analysis is focused on the evolution of trading relations between the Northern and Southern Low Countries during the fifteenth and sixteenth centuries. The section entitled industry focuses on the product-life-cycle theory, which I have applied in several studies on the development of the urban textile industries in the Low Countries at the end of the Middle Ages and at the beginning of Early Modern times.

In the section devoted to money and finance, one essay presents the monetary policies of the Dukes of the Burgundian Netherlands: this study seeks to demonstrate in particular the impact of those policies on the monetary situation in neighbouring countries, whilst a second essay explores the development of credit in the Duchy of Brabant during the fifteenth century. My third study in this section goes into the crucial impact of the Antwerp money and capital market on innovations in European financial and banking techniques in the course of the sixteenth century.

The final section, society, examines social and political aspects of economic development in the Low Countries. The studies include, *inter alia*, the effects of economic growth on the emergence of an attitude of resistance, even revolt, against the Habsburg government; the effects of harvest failures and the resulting sharp rises in prices on the incomes of independent craftsman and of dependant wage-earners, as well as their effect on consumption patterns and health; and the effect of a primitive agricultural economy on the diet of middle income groups.

The selection made for this volume does not, of course, cover all aspects of social and economic development in the Low Countries during the late Middle Ages and Early Modern times. In fact they overemphasise the fifteenth and sixteenth centuries at the expense of earlier and later centuries. The studies also give too much priority to the economic aspects of development at the expense of the social ones and they finally have a bias towards institutional aspects of development at the expense of other variables determining economic growth. However, the themes treated in the volume do fairly represent the spectrum of problems I have studied during my career as a researcher in Early Modern history.

* * *

I am in debt to many people who assisted me in realising this volume. First of all I want to thank Dr John Smedley of Variorum for launching this idea and in particular Dr Mark Steele for his wise advice and valuable editorial help during the preparation of this volume. I am very grateful to Dr Jan Blomme and to Simone Verbreyt, Martine Goossens and Anne Henau for their much-appreciated assistance in the copy-editing of the text. I would also like to thank Lizabeth Fackelman for translating several of the essays from French and Dutch into English, Karl Keenan for translating an essay from German into English and Emeritus Professor Peter H. Ramsey for his care in reading the final manuscript.

Last, but not least, my warmest thanks to my wife Monique for her inspiring comments and her patience with a husband who has abused her time and dedication too much.

"De Hettinghe"
25th April 1993.

HERMAN VAN DER WEE

Acknowledgements

The author and publisher wish to thank the following for permission to use the material reprinted in this volume.

Chapters 1 & 2: Dr L.C.M. Röst, Winkler Prins Redactie and Uitgeversmaatschappij Argus B.V. for the articles, 'The Low Countries in Transition: From the Middle Ages to Early Modern Times' and 'The Low Countries in Transition: From Commercial Capitalism to the Industrial Revolution', in *The Low Countries from 1500 to 1780*, I. Schöffer, H. Van der Wee, J.A. Bornewasser (eds), II of: *Winkler Prins Geschiedenis van de Nederlanden*, J.A. Bornewasser, H.P.H. Jansen, I. Schöffer, R.C. Van Caenegem, H. Van der Wee (eds), (Amsterdam–Brussels: 1977), (2nd ed. 1983, 3rd ed. 1985, 4th ed. 1988), pp. 11–37 and pp. 425–38.

Chapter 3: Leuven University Press for 'The Agricultural Development of the Low Countries as Revealed by the Tithe and Rent Statistics, 1250–1800', in *Productivity of Land and Agricultural Innovation in the Low Countries, 1250–1800*, H. Van der Wee and E. Van Cauwenberghe (eds), (Louvain: 1978), pp. 1–23.

Chapters 4, 8 & 13: *Annales, Economies, Sociétés, Civilisations* for 'Agrarian History and Public Finances in Flanders, 14th to 17th century', E. Van Cauwenberghe (co-author), 28, 1973, pp. 1051–64; 'Antwerp and the New Financial Methods of the 16th and 17th centuries', 22, 1967, pp. 1067–89; 'Typology of Crises and Structural Changes in the Netherlands, 15th to 16th centuries', 18, 1963, pp. 209–25.

Chapter 5: *Algemene Geschiedenis der Nederlanden* for 'Trade in the Southern Netherlands, 1493–1587', VI, (Haarlem: 1979), pp. 75–97.

Chapter 6: Prof. Dr Schneider, Otto-Friedrich-University of Bamberg for 'Economic Activity and International Trade in the Southern Netherlands, 1538–1544', in: *Wirtschaftsgeschichte und Wirtschaftswege. Festschrift für Hermann Kellenbenz: Beiträge zur Wirtschaftsgeschichte 5*, 2, (Bamberg: 1978), pp. 133–44.

Chapter 7: *Bijdragen voor de Geschiedenis der Nederlanden* for 'Trade Relations between Antwerp and the Northern Netherlands, 14th to 16th century', 4, (The Hague-Antwerp: 1965–1966), pp. 267–285.

Chapters 9 & 10: H. Van den Eerenbeemt, Catholic University of Brabant for 'Monetary Policy in the Duchy of Brabant: Late Middle Ages to Early Modern Times' and 'Credit in Brabant: Late Middle Ages to Early Modern Times' in *Het geld zoekt zijn weg, Van Lanschot-Lectures on Banking in Brabant, Bijdragen tot de Geschiedenis van het Zuiden van Nederland*, H. Van den Eerenbeemt (ed.), (Tilburg, 1987), pp. 37–58 and pp. 59–78.

Chapter 11: C. Dyer, *The Economic History Review* for 'Structural Changes and Specialization in the Industry of the Southern Netherlands, 1100–1600', 2nd series, 28, 1975, pp. 203–221.

Chapters 12 & 14: *Acta Historiae Neerlandicae* for 'Prices and Wages as Development Variables: A Comparison between England and the Southern Netherlands, 1400–1700', 10, 1978, pp. 58–78 and 'The Economy as a Factor in the Revolt in the Southern Netherlands', 5, 1971, pp. 52–67.

Chapter 15: *Spiegel Historiael* for 'Nutrition and Diet in the Ancien Régime', 1, 1966, pp. 94–101.

Every effort has been made to trace all copyright holders, but if any have been inadvertently overlooked the publishers will be pleased to make the necessary arrangement at the first opportunity.

I

GENERAL

1

The Low Countries in Transition: from the Middle Ages to Early Modern Times[*]

The Conceptual Background: Continuity in Movement

In European historiography the Middle Ages and the Early Modern period are usually considered two separate periods, with the transition between them characterized by profound structural changes. In this work we have retained these categories. Such a division between the medieval and modern periods is broadly justified, since significant changes did indeed occur around 1500 in the Low Countries as well as in the rest of Europe. Nevertheless, it would be erroneous to interpret these changes as a real and generalized break between the two periods. The tension and discontinuity present in the Low Countries around 1500 are better understood as elements of creativity, emerging from the 'historical mass' of the late Middle Ages and injecting their own specific vitality into the fundamental continuity of commercial capitalism. From an economic standpoint the true chronological divisions in the history of the Low Countries are different: the start of a new era stemmed from the revival, creation and expansion of the cities beginning in the 11th century and led to the development of commercial capitalism; the end of that era coincided with the collapse of the Ancien Régime and the beginning of the Industrial Revolution.

A civilization can only realize large-scale structural changes if innovation leads to the production of a significant surplus of material goods. Such a surplus makes a reorganization of human activities possible that can bring about new patterns in the division of labour, in institutions, and in mentality. The innovations that characterized the European economy at the beginning of the 11th century were of precisely that nature. Productivity on the great estates had seriously declined in the course of the 9th and 10th centuries owing to depopulation, presumably as a result

---

[*] For a bibliography, see the end of Chapter 2.

of Malthusian factors aggravated by institutional rigidity, military unrest and primitive agricultural methods. Ultimately, this threat acted as a challenge. In the castles, and in the abbeys and collegiate churches in particular, the idea gained ground that new approaches should be applied to counteract declining estate revenues. Labour was the most responsive variable in the production process. Therefore an attempt was made to provide added incentive to peasant labour by modifying the relationship between lord and serf, offering the prospect of greater recompense for individual performance and more attractive material and social conditions. This gradually led to an altered distribution of agricultural income, giving rise in turn to a pattern of increasing productivity destined to make a profound impression on the general development of Western Europe.

Rising agrarian income stimulated the growth of the peasant population through better nutrition. As soon as the population began to rise too sharply, European agriculture took on the characteristics of a frontier movement: land reclamation was undertaken on a large scale, either within the region by winning land from the sea, or by colonizing Central and Eastern Europe, and the territories on the Iberian Peninsula re-conquered from the Muslims. Such a geographical broadening of agrarian horizons brought out clear differences in climate and in soil composition that increased the potential for agricultural specialization and for the interregional distribution of agricultural production. Colonization also frequently brought more fertile land under cultivation and this naturally increased productivity. It was precisely these gains in productivity which made possible a long period of little or no decline in *per capita* income from agriculture.

The rural population also gradually abandoned the autarkic production pattern and devoted itself more and more to purely agricultural pursuits. Greater attention could thus be paid to a more intensive exploitation of the soil during the growing seasons and to improvements in the rural infrastructure in the intervals between them. Moreover, all sorts of craft products that had formerly been manufactured on the farms themselves during the winter months could now be purchased from specialized craftsmen working in nearby urban centres. Consequently the agricultural surplus encouraged a growing concentration of industry and services in the urban agglomerates. With this growing redistribution of labour between town and country, the European economy took a further step towards increased productivity.

Finally, the growing surpluses were applied to the production of capital goods. With this we reach the heart of the European revival. We have just touched upon the major investments made in the agricultural infrastructure: they were by no means limited to the proliferation of dikes and dams, farms and roads, but also involved the introduction of new rural codes of behaviour and institutions, leading to the penetration of the market and money economy into agriculture.

The importance of investment in infrastructure was even clearer in the towns. Urban expansion in itself, as it developed from the 11th century onwards, represented what was for that time an essentially new and profitable investment: a thorough modernization of the economic infrastructure. Together the markets, halls, ports and warehouses, the merchants' guilds, the urban and central administrations, the aldermen's benches and other courts, the craft organizations, schools and apprenticeship arrangements, formed an economic structure made available by collective savings and possessing colossal potential for gains in organizational productivity. The merchants in particular made good use of this enormous potential: they utilized the new infrastructure as a basis for the expansion of their regional activities and the extension of their trade to distant lands. They reinvested their commercial profits in their own enterprises to finance the renewal of their stock, for advance payments to manufacturers, or to advance credit to their customers. This was the dawn of a new era of growth for commercial capitalism, based on the private utilization of a collectively financed infrastructure and on the investment of private floating capital.

Technological innovations also contributed substantially to increased productivity in agriculture, industry and trade, and it was in part such innovations that made improvements in the infrastructure possible. In the era of commercial capitalism, however, the accent lay not so much on technological as on organizational progress. The gains made in productivity were primarily the result of a more efficient organization of agricultural, industrial, commercial, cultural and political activities.

Our point of departure in the following demonstration is that the fundamental movement in European history shows a clear image of increasing civilization from the 11th century onwards up to the present. Moreover, it has been assumed that this fundamental upward development was characterized by a phenomenon of acceleration: during the era of commercial capitalism growth was significantly slower than during the subsequent phase of industrial capitalism from the 18th century onwards, when technological progress predominated. Finally, looking at the economic history of Europe from the point of view of its long-term growth neglects the social aspects of cyclical economic fluctuations. The long waves in the development of commercial capitalism between the 11th and 18th centuries are in fact chiefly examined as a function of the structural changes they provoked, in other words only in so far as they influenced the fundamental upwards movement. Furthermore, the shorter cyclical fluctuations – as far as they led to famines and to commercial or industrial crises with a dramatic effect on the real income of the lower classes – are not treated specifically here. The social dimension of famine as such, however real and important we consider it, is not relevant to the argument developed in this essay.

The Low Countries as a Hub of European Development in the High Middle Ages

During the new period of expansion in Europe that began in the 11th century two poles of development arose, characterized by a rapid increase in urban population density and dominated by the marked growth of commercial capitalism. On the one hand there was Northern Italy and on the other the Low Countries on the mouths of the Meuse, Rhine and Scheldt. The recent historiography on the Low Countries contains a great deal of data that can provide a direct answer to the question of why development in the Low Countries was so much more intense and progressive than in the other regions north of the Alps. However, two aspects of this problem merit particular attention. The Low Countries did not develop as one homogeneous area of growth: some regions, like Artois, Flanders, Hainault, and the Meuse valley, were clearly in advance of the others. They were soon joined by Brabant, with Zeeland, Holland and Overijssel following rapidly. Moreover, the Mediterranean area was the original centre of gravity for this new world economy: territories to the north of the Alps were only gradually integrated into the southern expansion.

The inhabitants of the Low Countries were the most successful at integrating Northwestern Europe into the new economic dynamics of the Mediterranean region. Climatological factors, such as the end of the Dunkirk II Transgression in the 8th–9th centuries, had opened up the prospect of an agrarian 'frontier' in the Low Countries while at the same time obliging land reclaimers to specialize, in sheep breeding, for example, on the silty coastal lands, and this in turn would further urban industrialization. Geographical factors played an important complementary role. The Low Countries were located not far from the North of France, where numerous agricultural innovations, such as the three-course rotation of crops, had been implemented from the 8th century onwards. Moreover, the low elevation and the dense network of waterways, facilitating transportation within the region, furthered the exchange of agricultural surpluses between one region and another.

The invasions of the Vikings left a demographical and political vacuum in their wake. The local lords attempted to fill the political vacuum by legitimizing their assumption of power within a framework of smaller geographical units. They also took dynamic action in response to the prevailing shortage of labour relative to the quantity of agricultural land available. By establishing military strongholds they were able to ensure the security of the peasants; they stimulated the foundation of new abbeys, placing large tracts of wasteland at their disposal and granting them all sorts of advantages to encourage them to bring these lands under cultivation; they sought the cooperation of the local population through the amelioration of working conditions and supported the growth of urban activity.

The commercial traditions of the delta region along the great rivers were a second and no less essential factor. Already in the early Middle Ages the region of the Meuse, Rhine and Scheldt had served as an operational base for the Frisians in their long-distance trade between Western Europe and Scandinavia. Both craft activity and local trade were closely linked to this trade. In the 10th and 11th centuries the economic revival of the Mediterranean region became tangible, stimulated by the expansion of the North Italian cities and soon consolidated by the Spanish Reconquista, the crusades, and the colonization of the coasts of the Black Sea. The Frisian traders were ill-equipped to take advantage of this revival in the south of Europe. The merchants of the Meuse and Scheldt valleys on the other hand, who as city-dwellers had developed more modern trading techniques and who had always maintained their age-old ties with the continental interior, seized the opportunity. They established a systematic link between Northwestern Europe and the Mediterranean area. It became an overland trade route based on the exchange of luxury products from Italy, North Africa, the Levant, and the Far East on the one hand, and the industrial products of their own region on the other. Thus a northern centre of development was added to the existing commercial triangle Venice–Genoa–Florence; it was concentrated on the expansion of the industrial export cities in the Low Countries which gradually began to function as staple markets for Northern and Northwestern Europe. Industrial expansion was the first crucial factor in the rise of the Low Countries as the leading economy of the north. The urban textile industry was systematically oriented toward export to distant regions. Weaving equipment was modernized. A systematic division of labour was applied: this not only cut costs, but also, thanks to greater specialization, improved the quality of manufactured goods. Wool was originally supplied by the nearby coastal areas and by the abbeys of the interior. Within a short time, however, the investment of urban capital made possible the organized importation of better-quality wools from England.

Beginning in the 12th, but especially in the 13th century, Flemish cloth penetrated the Levant and North Africa by way of Italy. There was also a steady increase in demand both in Italy itself and in France, England and Germany, where Flemish cloth often supplanted local production of luxury textiles. Moreover, the urban export industry of the Low Countries was continually on the move. The technology in use remained simple, and the division of labour facilitated imitation or adoption of processing methods. The mobility of capital also kept the merchant-entrepreneur from being tied to a particular centre of production. If successful export caused the cost of labour to rise too steeply in one centre, production could easily be shifted to another centre elsewhere. The older textile cities usually reacted by further diversifying their products, by concentrating on the production of the best fabrics or, in view of their established infrastructure, by expanding the range of services offered relative to the textile production in younger, developing centres. The result was a gradual multiplication of the number of export towns in the Low Countries, giving rise not only to an increasing density of urbanization as such, but at the same time causing industrial activity to shift towards the northeast. Originally the most dynamic textile towns were those located close to the Ile-de-France and the annual fairs of Saint-Denis, like Saint-Omer and Arras. From the 12th century onwards Cambrai, Lille, Douai, Tournai and Valenciennes grew in importance. They were rapidly followed by the Flemish cloth-producing cities of Ghent, Bruges, Ypres and Diximuide, which were more closely linked to wool imports from the coastal regions and from England, and in the 13th century by the Brabantine cloth-producing towns of Mechlin, Brussels and Louvain, more favourably located with respect to the trade route to Cologne and Germany. In the course of the 14th century numerous smaller export centres arose, especially in Flanders, for example along the Lys and in the southern part of the county. A similar evolution took place in the 'small' towns of the duchy of Brabant, such as Geldenaken, Zoutleeuw, Diest, Tienen, Vilvoorde, Lier, Aarschot and Herentals. In the 15th century it was Holland's turn, since it was better situated for trade with the Hanseatic territories: flourishing textile centres developed in Amsterdam, Naarden, Leyden and Haarlem, among others.

The increasing lead of the Low Countries' economy over that of the rest of Northern and Northwestern Europe was also due to the expansion of their function as staple markets. Originally the economic revival had been closely linked to the expansion of overland traffic to Italy via France and to Germany and Italy via the Rhine: the merchants of Flanders, Brabant and the Meuse valley were active everywhere, often dominating the new long-distance trade. The main staple markets associated with this expansion, however, were located outside the Low Countries, namely in London, in the towns along the Rhine, and foremost at the annual trade fairs of Champagne. The Low Countries first established staple markets of their own in a purely local or purely regional context, that is to say from the inside out. The rapid growth in the number of cities and city-dwellers in the Low Countries stimulated a more systematic organization for the exchange of goods between town and countryside and between the various towns among themselves, with the latter gradually developing into staple markets for their own regions. These staple markets gradually extended their sphere of influence: in the first place to England and the Rhineland, later also to the Hanseatic area in Northern Europe. The colonization of Eastern Europe had multiplied the contacts between the Rhineland and the Low Countries on the one hand, and Central Europe and the Baltic on the other. The German Hanse was primarily responsible for integrating the Northern regions into the Western European economy. Soon the Bruges and London offices of the Hanse proved the most important vehicles of this dynamic development. Bruges functioned more and more as the primary staple market both for the whole Hanseatic area, and in part, by way of Cologne, for Central Germany. Shortly before 1300 Italian galleys established a direct sea link between the Italian trade cities and Bruges–London, thanks to technological progress in seamanship and to innovations in entrepreneurial organization. The annual trade fairs of Champagne gradually faded away. Bruges was the primary heir to this commerical legacy, redistributing South European and Asian goods in the north and becoming the dominant staple market for the whole of Northern and Northwestern Europe. The international trade of Bruges and its satellites, especially the cities of the Ijssel, Middelburg, Dordrecht, and the annual Brabant trade fairs, contributed greatly to the economic pre-eminence of the Low Countries in Europe outside Italy.

A third decisive element in the leading position of the Low Countries was political and institutional. The disintegration of imperial centralized power in the Low Countries after the death of Charlemagne in 811 led to the rise of a number of well-administered small territorial units, within which modern political systems evolved. The county of Flanders (10th–11th centuries) was the great leader in this respect, but it was soon followed by the prince-bishopric of Liège, the duchy of Brabant, the Sticht Utrecht, the counties of Hainault, Zeeland and Holland, and by others. Territorial expansion and administrative reorganization assured the growth of a new central authority, albeit on a smaller geographical scale, and provided economic development with the support necessary for further success. On the one hand the urbanization of the Low Countries substantially increased the revenues of their rulers: demesnial revenues received in kind could be sold for good prices on many local markets; the collection of common rights for the use of mills, weighing houses, halls for cloth, meat, bread and other products provided an attractive source of new income during the first stage of urban expansion. Before long the finances of the counts, dukes and prince-bishops were appreciably augmented by the extraordinary aids and exceptional subsidies that the cities granted the ruler in exchange for privileges or protection. Finally, the cities also functioned as financial centres where the ruler had access to credit when necessary. On the other hand the ruler was able to establish, thanks to the presence and support of the cities, an institutional framework forming a basis for the better organization of social and economic life in his territory: the cities made use of this framework to achieve substantial gains in productivity, ensuring their own further growth.

The Low Countries During the European Depression of the 14th and 15th Centuries

The deep wave of depression which engulfed the rest of Europe during the 14th and 15th centuries did not have the same paralysing effect on the economic, political and cultural life of the Low Countries. In the 14th and the beginning of the 15th centuries the urban agglomerations in particular fought successfully against the threat of economic stagnation. The direct sea link between Italy and the North, and the growth of the German Hanse were of commercial and industrial benefit primarily to Bruges and the Low Countries. What they lost in long-distance overland trade and foreign demand was more than compensated by increased domestic demand, so that at first the transfer of labour from the countryside to the cities could be sustained. The demographic decline and ensuing stagnation in the rest of Europe which began in the 14th century caused a world-wide drop in the price of foodstuffs, expressed in silver currency. Thus the maritime location of the Low Countries ensured that supplies could be imported cheaply. Famines, the Plague (the Black Death) and other contagious diseases all passed our lands by without occasioning drastic demographic collapse. The more favourable employment situation in many sectors of the economy and the declining trend in grain prices, during periods when the decline was not neutralized by currency devaluation, increased the real income of large numbers of salaried employees, wage earners, and of those who made their living from trade and finance. The increased purchasing power of money relative to foodstuffs was particularly advantageous for persons of private means. These groups taken all together formed a fairly extensive middle-income group which was able to create a substantial demand for non-essential foodstuffs and manufactured goods. In this way the foundations were laid for a remarkable broadening of the internal market in the Low Countries.

The unfortunate effects of the European depression first made themselves felt in the Low Countries among the rural farming population. Declining prices for foodstuffs formed a threat to the income of both the farmers and the great landowners. The latter strove in vain to compensate for dwindling ground rents at the expense of their tenants; but the emancipation of the peasant population was already so far advanced, and contact between the countryside and the ever-present urban economy had increased so much, that the process had become irreversible and a return to dependent serfdom was out of the question. In this light the peasant uprisings of the 14th and 15th centuries in the Low Countries can be seen as crucial moments in the relationship of peasant and lord, as the violent reaction of a dynamic group which, when confronted with a serious threat to their income posed by the political and seigneurial authorities, was able to counter the threat in an organized fashion. The resilience of the peasant population also expressed itself in a more positive manner through the search for technical solutions to bolster agrarian income. Precisely because of the prevailing mentality and the former high degree of development, the serious European depression operated more as a challenge to agriculture in the Low Countries and proved a direct stimulus to innovation. Specifically, the peasants experimented with three different methods of increasing their productivity to compensate for declining grain prices. First of all they strove to increase their yield per acre through new cultivation methods. Starting in the 14th–15th centuries, crop rotation in Flanders and Brabant was improved by no longer allowing land to lie fallow, introducing instead a system permitting the harvest of two crops per year from the same field. More efficient soil fertilization was attained by increasing the quantity of livestock and above all by systematic organization of a trade in urban waste.

A second means of increasing agricultural productivity was through greater specialization. In the many urban conglomerates the rise in real income had increased the demand for non-essential foodstuffs like butter, cheese, fish, meat and beer. Consequently, prices for these products had decreased less sharply than had grain prices, encouraging specialization in dairy products, meat and beer. Flanders began concentrating on the production of butter and cheese in the 14th to 15th centuries; Holland and Frisia followed suit in the 15th to 16th centuries. Groningen, Drenthe and Overijssel became the chief producers of beef cattle, and sheep breeding rose in the Campine. Starting at the end of the 14th and at the beginning of the 15th century the herring fishery of Holland laid the foundations for the establishment of a major fish-processing industry in the cities. The substantial increase in the brewing of beer in Holland during the 14th to 15th centuries was based on the extension of the use of Dutch summer grain and on the importation of foreign grain, particularly from the Baltic; it was also linked to the spread of specialized hop cultivation in several regions of the Low Countries. Specialization brought about a magnification in the scale and scope of production: it allowed, through the introduction of new products in related product lines, a differentiation of supply (economies of scope); it also allowed, through the rationalization of production, for an increase in the productivity of land and labour (economies of scale). Consequently its advantages were based, on the one hand, not only on the difference in decline between grain prices and the prices of non-grain agricultural products, and on the other hand, on enhanced productivity, which substantially improved the input–output ratio in terms of yields or in terms of labour costs.

The rise of rural industry provided the third and final means for the rural population to maintain its income level. Originally supplementary activities to be engaged in during the dead periods of winter – wool spinning and later on flax spinning to support the growth of the urban textile industries – soon expanded to include production of standardized articles, based on a systematic division of labour and organized through the intermediary of merchant-entrepreneurs. The incentive for the latter to transfer their activities from town to countryside lay in the lower wages prevalent in the countryside and in the absence of corporative organizations and of restrictive regulations. In the 15th century some towns and rural areas in Flanders began producing cheaper textiles of Spanish and Scottish wool, which met with a certain degree of success both at home and abroad under the name 'new drapery'. The area around Weert, Maaseik and Hoorn began processing domestic wool from the Campine into cheap cloth. From the 14th century onwards a rural serge industry (*sayetterie*) developed as 'light drapery' in the vicinity of Hondschoote in West Flanders. Some of the rural areas grew during the 16th century into important production centres increasingly oriented towards the export market. Meanwhile the rural linen industry in Flanders and Hainault had also developed into a strong export sector.

A second group whose income was threatened by the European depression consisted of those involved in the traditional urban export industries. Both workers engaged in actual production and exporters whose activities were oriented towards long-distance trade met with difficulties. The demographic decline and stagnation in the rest of Europe, and the consequent weakening of agriculture, local commerce, and transcontinental trade totally disrupted the market system throughout the vast area of the European continent, so crucial for the export industries of the Low Countries. The older textile-producing towns did attempt to reach new markets, particularly by reorienting their export towards the flourishing maritime region of the German Hanse. However, they faced increasing competition from the cheaper goods produced in the smaller Flemish textile centres, in the Flemish countryside, and in the growing cloth towns of Holland. Shortly afterwards English cloth also penetrated the Baltic and gradually succeeded in dominating the new market. The smaller Brabantine cloth towns were able to maintain their export to the Mediterranean area for a time, until Italian imitations, and particularly English competition, forced them to abandon these traditional markets.

The disruption of the continental market system and the stiff competition, especially from the English, forced the cloth cities to reorient their industry. A good number of them remained committed to the traditional industrial structures and strove to solve the problem by switching to high-quality products. This made them dependent on the importation of raw materials from England, since it was the only source of the top-quality wool they needed. The English king, in need of money to finance the Hundred Years' War, took advantage of the English monopoly and of the inelastic Flemish demand to impose heavy tariffs on the export of English wool. At the same time he took measures favourable to the export dynamics of English cloth.

Other cities hoped to rescue their traditional cloth manufacture by reducing export prices. The urban government and the patrician merchant guilds acted in concert to establish lower wage scales at the expense of the textile workers. The urban textile workers, however, reacted violently. Riots broke out, and in some cities the craft guilds were even able to seize power temporarily. Under pressure of these circumstances the workers' organizations often came to be more directly involved in the government of the cities. Their demand for higher wages could no longer be simply refused. But higher wages led to higher prices, closing many more markets to the traditional urban export industry: losses due to higher unemployment thus outstripped the gains made by higher wages, precipitating urban decline. Sooner or later many of the cities reacted with a remarkable degree of creativity to the loss of their traditional industry. The larger cities in particular were able to restructure their industries and by doing so ensured that the Low Countries actually increased their economic lead over the other territories of Northern Europe.

The revival of the urban economy was based essentially on the development of a specialized and diversified fashion and luxury industry, together with the vigorous expansion of the service sector. These new activities drew their vitality from highly skilled labour, the craftsmen's creativity, intellectual ingenuity and artistic refinement. The relatively high wages and salaries current in the cities of the Low Countries could be sustained since they were remuneration for exceptional skills, the price paid for particularly valuable achievements. Thus progress in physical productivity (production of a greater quantity of goods or services per unit of labour input) no longer dominated urban prosperity in the Burgundian era, but rather gains made in economic productivity (production of better, more valuable goods or services per unit of labour input). This was a decisive structural change, which had far-reaching consequences not only for the economy, but also from a political, cultural, institutional and religious point of view.

As far as the economy is concerned, one can summarize the change by saying that to the crucial commercial capital assets created by the actions of towns and princes from the 11th century onwards, a new and important capital asset had now been added: human capital, based on education and the learning of special skills. This new structural progress enabled first the Southern, and afterwards the Northern, Netherlands to maintain their leading position in Northwestern Europe until far into the 18th century. The flourishing art of the Flemish Primitive painters was the most illustrious fruit of the revival of the urban economy in the Low Countries. There were, however, many other noteworthy artistic contributions: altar-pieces, furniture, tapestries, embroidery and the fashion industry. The structural changes were also evident in the service sector, in education and literature, in music and entertainment, in finance and credit, in trade and banking methods, and in other fields.

The revival of the urban economy of the Low Countries would not have been possible if the structural shifts in the supply of goods and services had not been stimulated by demand. This demand presupposed a substantial high- and middle-income group in the cities of the Low Countries. The Burgundian court and the establishment of a strong central authority created a first source of higher incomes. The rise of maritime trade moreover brought numerous wealthy Italian merchants to Bruges, Mechlin, and the annual fairs of Brabant. These merchants naturally kept up their opulent pattern of consumption and set a demonstrative example similar to that of the magnificent court held by the Burgundian dukes. On the other hand there were also not inconsiderable numbers of idle rich – native merchant-entrepreneurs who had retired from business to live on the private income derived from the proceeds – who also began to show more interest in 'l'art de vivre'. The declining trend in food prices increased their real income, as it also increased that of all the wage-earners and salaried employees in the cities, particularly in the sector of goods not normally traded and in the sector of the new tradables. Thus demand for non-essential consumer goods rose for a broad spectrum of society. At the same time the broadening of urban education laid the foundations for a more refined life-style for these groups.

The structural progress which the Low Countries and a few other maritime regions so successfully maintained throughout the whole of the European depression was by no means exclusively determined by socio-economic factors. Political and religious–cultural developments were also of decisive importance. Under the influence of the Burgundian dukes a strong central authority was established over the various territories of the Low Countries and attempts to establish a unitary state took concrete form (the era of the Burgundian Netherlands started in 1384, when Philip the Fair, Duke of Burgundy, inherited through his wife Margaret of Male the first territories in the Low Countries, soon to be enlarged by new acquisitions). The interaction between the strengthening of central authority and structural change was important because the latter tended to favour government intervention, which was regularly called upon for help in resolving temporary problems in particular places or regions. Given the framework of late medieval power structures, the personality of rulers and counsellors cannot be ignored in the success of government interventions. In this context the establishment of a subtle complex of new institutions was of the utmost importance. Without healthy government finances, however, both the dukes and their institutions were entirely powerless.

The Burgundian rulers also made decisive improvements in this area. Before the Burgundians had firmly consolidated their authority over the Low Countries, the budget deficit in the various territories had often been financed by successive currency devaluations and by expensive short-term loans. In the first case the weight or percentage of silver in the basic coinage was lowered slightly and the new, less valuable, coin was brought into circulation at the original face value. The Flemish counts had so frequently resorted to such practices that the silver content of the Flemish denier, and later of the Flemish groat, had drastically diminished during the 13th and 14th centuries. Originally, the business community had been relatively unperturbed by this practice, because its transactions were carried out in gold currency, which was more stable in its value (Italian gold coins from the 13th century onwards, and gold coins from the Low Countries or elsewhere from the 14th century onwards). Thus devaluation of the silver coinage caused it little hardship. Moreover such silver devaluations meant an increase in the value of gold coins in terms of Flemish (silver) groats, that is to say in local monetary units, so that the devaluation did not adversely affect the personal fortunes of the wealthy, who kept their savings mainly in gold. At the same time wages were paid out according to the official rates in the devalued silver coins, thus reducing the real production costs for the merchant-entrepreneurs and increasing profits, at least as long as the final price could be maintained at the same level in stable gold currency. For his part the ruler made instant profit through the extra revenues generated by the minting of new silver groats. In the long term, however, the practice represented a loss for the ruler since his fixed revenues were usually collected in silver money, and were thus unfavourably influenced by the currency devaluation. People of modest private means and creditors were of course the greatest losers in currency devaluations. Eventually, business people also suffered from the uncertain climate created by monetary chaos.

The Burgundian rulers clearly pursued a monetary policy of recovery and stability. From the end of the 14th century onwards they even attempted to increase the silver content of the basic monetary unit, sometimes successfully and sometimes in vain. In any case they were able to ensure the stability of the basic currency for a long period and managed to integrate all the territorial diversity into a single monetary system, based on the silver stiver (= one double Flemish silver groat). Finally they lent a powerful stimulus to the minting and circulation of their own Burgundian–Flemish gold coins: the gold coins were assigned an official exchange rate in stivers, more favourable than the current gold–silver ratio on the free market. Later on, the Habsburg rulers faithfully continued to pursue a policy of monetary stability, Maximilian of Austria being the sole great exception.

The Burgundian rulers reorganized government finances as well as currency. They upheld the notion that: *le prince doit vivre du sien* (*dat ons genadich heere synen staet onderhoudt op syn eygen domeynen*) as the guiding principle of their financial administration. In exploiting the ruler's domains great care was devoted to the leasing of the fields, meadows and woods, as well as to the collection of rents, tolls, and other seigneurial or common rights. As a result of this special attention the revenues derived from the domains increased significantly and remained an important part of Burgundian governmental revenues throughout the whole of the 15th century. Financially sound princely domains offered numerous advantages: first and foremost the ruler thus obtained greater freedom of action with respect to the provincial estates; the sovereign was now less dependent on whether or not they would grant new aids. A second great advantage pertained to credit. The collection of aids had always been a cumbersome process organized by the territories themselves. If the ruler needed money at once he was obliged to seek loans at high interest from bankers on the strength of revenues expected from the aids. The domanial stewards on the other hand were ducal officials, and as such they could be called upon to give interest-free advances on the revenues they were to receive during the current or coming year. With the ruler's stewards also acting as his bankers, the government's revenues could now be better adjusted to the timing of expenses, without incurring the high interest payments. Philip the Good in particular made use of this method of financing.

Aside from the demesnial revenues and the receipts from aids granted them, the dukes also developed an extensive system of long-term credit: they allowed the cities to sell, for the benefit of the central government, both life annuities and hereditary annuities, guaranteed by the public domain and by the urban community; and to finance these annuities they assigned certain governmental revenues to the cities involved. In this way the dukes obtained long-term credit on quite reasonable terms (the cities had already been applying this system of long-term credit for some time to achieve their own goals). It was still true that in extreme circumstances the Burgundian dukes, especially Charles the Bold, were obliged to resort to the money market of Bruges, negotiating short-term loans at high interest from the Italian merchant bankers or from the Lombards. These remained, however, exceptional measures: in general the Burgundian dukes pursued a sound, if conservative, policy of budgetary equilibrium.

The Low Countries and the Global Economy in the 16th Century

The vigorous economic expansion that the Low Countries experienced during the 16th century was closely linked to the structural evolution of the preceding centuries; indeed in a sense it represented the culmination of that evolution. The changes occurring in the industrial structure of the area during the 14th and 15th centuries served to consolidate and strengthen the region's political, cultural and socio-economic lead over the rest of Northern Europe. The rise of the Habsburg Empire should be seen in this context. In the course of the 15th century the Burgundians had succeeded in their attempt to give more substance to the expansion of a unitary state by transferring economic surpluses to the public sector. An analogous transfer was discernible in the Habsburg Empire, but was now organized on a global scale. To this end the Habsburgs appealed first to the Low Countries because of their wealth and economic strength, but soon for the same reasons they also appealed to Spain, Italy and the New World. The new situation had a favourable influence on the economy of the Low Countries as the Antwerp money market functioned as the central base of financial operations for the whole system.

During the 16th century the Low Countries climbed the economic ladder to become the dominant growth pole of the West. Viewed in its entirety this development was spectacular, and can be perceived as two great waves of expansion. The first phase (1495–1520) was dominated by a remarkable revitalization of European world trade, characterized by an intensification of maritime traffic and by a simultaneous growth of overland and river transport.

The three monthly Brabant fairs at Antwerp and Bergen-op-Zoom played a prominent role therein. They first became the great staple markets for the export of English cloth to Central and Southern Europe. The concentration of England's foreign trade in these markets had begun spontaneously because of the qualitative excellence of the processing industry that had developed at Antwerp. It was soon to be officially consolidated by the English crown and by the London merchants, who saw in it a means of effectively controlling cloth export and export prices.

Around 1500 the Portuguese also made Antwerp the nucleus of their trading activities in Northwestern Europe. For some time they had been conducting exploratory voyages in the Atlantic Ocean and along the coasts of West Africa. They had introduced sugar production on the Atlantic islands (on the Canary Islands and the Azores, among others), they had found certain spices (notably malaguetta pepper) on the African coast and last but not least they discovered a direct access route to Sudanese gold. The prosperous territories of the Burgundian Low Countries proved an appropriate market for such products as sugar and spices. They were also a profitable market for Sudanese gold, because the policy of the Burgundian dukes favoured minting gold coin, enabling the masters of the mint to offer high prices for gold. The Portuguese also encountered merchants from Holland and Zeeland at the Brabant fairs: the latter had specialized in maritime transport in the Northern European waters and were engaged in sharp competition with the Hanseatic League, whose trade was still, in accordance with tradition, oriented towards Bruges. Finally, the Portuguese also found at Antwerp an abundant supply of the bronze, copper and brass products of Mechlin, Dinant, Aachen and Southern Germany that were in such very great demand for their trade with West Africa.

Around 1450 the spread of the *Saigerungs* technique (a method of separating silver from copper by the addition of lead to silver-rich copper ore) in Central Europe greatly increased copper and silver production in the Alps (Tyrol), in Hungary (Banska Bystrica) and in Saxony (Mansfeld). The town of Nuremberg, closely concerned in the spread of this technology since it had financed the requisite new investment, became the main export centre of silver and copper metal as well as a dominant centre of the copper processing industry.

The Southern Germans, who had traditionally marketed their products (chiefly fustian cloth made from wool and cotton) northwards via the Frankfurter Messen, through the intermediary of Cologne merchants, gradually eliminated these Cologne distributors. Not only did the Southern Germans wish to circumvent the expensive staple monopoly Cologne held over Rhenish river traffic and to avoid the numerous Rhine tolls, but also to offer an extended range of merchandise, which included not only their own metal products but also Italian and Oriental wares, directly for sale at the Brabant fairs, especially at Antwerp. Becoming in their turn active merchants in Antwerp, the Southern Germans hoped to gain better control over the continental English cloth trade in view of strengthening their own sales monopoly in Central, Southern and Eastern Europe. These new factors had contributed to the revival of overland traffic from the second half of the 15th century onwards. A climax was reached at the beginning of the 16th century. Other factors also contributed to the expansion, such as the integration of the fairs of Castile and of Lyons into the re-established system of intracontinental trade in Central and Northwestern Europe, and the organization of regular transport services between Italy and the Low Countries via Germany and France. Meanwhile the Portuguese had reached

India and had begun to import spices from the Far East as well. When at the beginning of the 16th century the Portuguese king granted Antwerp a monopoly on the distribution of spices throughout Europe, the Southern Germans had an even greater interest in consolidating their trading position on the Scheldt.

The expansion of overland and river trade in Europe was undoubtedly a stimulating factor in the growth of the global economy during the 16th century. The Low Countries, and the Brabant fairs in particular, had a decisive transit function in this: they formed the heart of a new and complex network of intensive contacts that encompassed the whole of Europe. Apart from this revival of transcontinental trade under the leadership of the Brabant fairs, there was also a revitalization of maritime traffic. In this context we have already highlighted the strategic role played by the Portuguese. The Spaniards, who opened up the Atlantic routes to the West Indies, also closely involved the Low Countries in the discoveries made to the west. Here the political union with Spain in 1494 was naturally a prominent factor. Commercial contacts were, however, even more decisive: the Basque region, the Castilian fairs, Seville itself, and soon the whole of Spain supplied themselves in the Low Countries in exchange for the wool of the Spanish *Mesta* (national association of the owners and shepherds of sheep flocks) and for the gold and silver imported from the New World. The traders of Brittany, the Hanse, England, Flanders, Brabant, Zeeland and Holland also chose the Low Countries as the hub of their expanded maritime traffic in the North Sea region.

Wine and salt were shipped in from the Atlantic coasts. Tin, lead, wool and textiles arrived from the British Isles. Zeeland and Holland, with the most important herring fisheries in the North Sea region, established successful salt refineries and further expanded their herring processing industry, making it the strongest in Europe. Increasingly, they began to dominate shipping in the Baltic and the ports of the great German rivers. It was largely due to the active intervention of the Habsburg rulers that the resultant struggle between Holland and the German Hanse ended in favour of Holland. The copper that the Southern Germans were exporting northwards even travelled in part to Antwerp via Gdansk and Amsterdam aboard Dutch vessels. Shipping by Zeeland and especially by Holland of grains from the Baltic region was of still greater importance: Amsterdam made itself the veritable granary of the West, to the point that even the Southern Low Countries gradually replaced their traditional grain imports from Northern France with the massive importation of Baltic grain. Scandinavian timber, Northern European pitch, wax, tar and talc were also shipped in by vessels from Zeeland and Holland and formed the raw materials for the rapidly expanding ship-building industry of the Dutch.

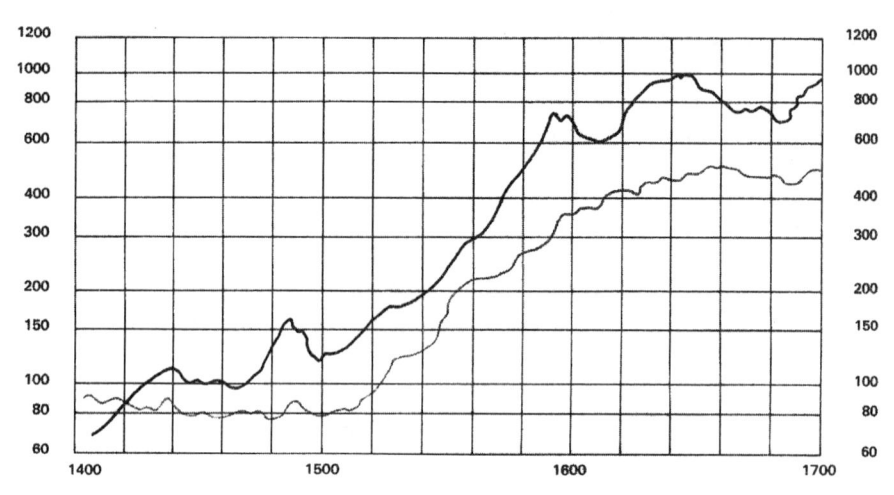

Figure 1.1: *Comparison between the weighted index figures for the prices of essential consumer goods in Antwerp and Southern England (trend calculated according to a moving median over 13 years). The solid line represents Antwerp, the dotted line is Southern England (semi-logarithmic scale).*

Although the new success of the international transit trade of the Low Countries extended over a period from approximately 1450 to 1570, the most explosive growth occurred between 1495 and 1520. During these 25 years of expansion Antwerp grew into the greatest trade metropolis of the West and the fate of Bruges as the leading international market of the North in the 14th–15th centuries was sealed. Bruges did, however, sustain its importance for a time as a secondary port, and Italian, Spanish and Hanseatic merchants continued to reside there. The wars between the Valois and the Habsburgs in the 1520s caused a serious breakdown of the transit function of the Low Countries, so that a number of Flemish and Brabant towns dependent on it were badly affected. The regularly recurring international conflicts of the subsequent decades prolonged this situation of insecurity, and posed a threat to the further growth of these centres. The Low Countries as a whole, however, were sufficiently resilient to survive such difficulties. The industrial reorganization of the region, achieved during the 14th and 15th centuries, had been integrated into the broader complex of the European economy, thanks to the expanding transit function so highly developed in the beginning of the 16th century. Thenceforth the refined products of the skilled craftsmen in the towns were not only better serving the domestic market, but were also exported throughout Europe. In the end this development provided stronger and more stable foundations for the commercial development of the Low Countries. European demand for specialized manufactured goods and luxury articles had greatly risen, especially in Spain and Portugal after the discoveries brought the massive importation of precious metals from the New World. The demand for finer consumer goods also increased noticeably in France and England, in the mercantile circles of Germany and the Baltic region, and even among the great East and Central European landowners, now producing grain and meat on a large scale for export to the West.

In all of Northwestern Europe only the Low Countries had, thanks to the structural adjustment of the preceding centuries, sufficient flexibility in their supply of luxury products and differentiated manufactured goods to meet the increased consumer demand on the international market. The specialized industries of the towns in the Low Countries therefore became increasingly oriented towards European export. They were primarily inspired by the example of Italy, where during the two previous centuries the blossoming Renaissance had generated a variety of crafts and specialized industries that already produced for the European market. First, some techniques of the Italian luxury industry, among others in silk-weaving, in the glass-, crystal- and mirror-making industries, and in majolica processing, were systematically integrated into the production system of the Low Countries in order to substitute for imports, soon becoming export sectors themselves. Second, tapestries, furniture, bells, musical instruments, altar-pieces, paintings, fashion articles, embroidery and many other fine fabrics produced in Flanders, Brabant and Hainault were distributed on a large scale throughout the whole of Northwestern Europe. The metal-working industry in the cities of Wallonia also became more export-oriented, the weapons industry being the most important example. Finally, rural industry decisively attuned itself to export: in Wallonia this meant primarily the manufacture of nails and other simple ironware; in Flanders and Limburg it chiefly concerned mass-produced textiles. The light Hondschoote serges became famed throughout the whole of the Mediterranean area. The coarser fabrics produced in the countryside around Weert and Hoorn and in the West Quarter of Flanders were sold on the international market too, but it was the growth of linen exports, based on domestic flax production, on rural spinning and weaving in Flanders, Hainault and Brabant, with further processing in some towns of Flanders, Brabant and Holland, that was most spectacular.

By the middle of the 16th century the transit trade was, owing to these developments, no longer the only pillar of the prosperity of the Low Countries. The structural progress achieved over a broad arch of the domestic economy, including both agriculture and industry, had now become the most dynamic factor, and so were laid the foundations for a second period of impressive economic expansion, running from the late 1530s to the middle 1560s.

The demographic consequences of 16th-century prosperity are reflected in a rapidly rising population curve. At the same time the degree of urbanization also increased: in the duchy of Brabant (in so far as it lies within modern-day Belgium) 32% of the population was already living in towns with 5,000 or more inhabitants in 1437; by 1480 this proportion had risen to 39%; and by 1565 it had reached as much as 47% (based on P.M.M. Klep's calculations). Analogous increases are observable for Flanders, Hainault, Liège and Holland. This demographic development did not immediately lead to a decrease in *per capita* income, since substantial productivity gains and higher levels of employment neutralized for a time the negative effects of population growth. Again impressive gains were made in agricultural production: the methods of intensified cultivation which had appeared only sporadically in the preceding centuries spread through numerous regions of the Low Countries; in places agriculture became more commercialized and industrialized by an expanded use of monoculture or by the introduction of industrial crops on a larger scale; trade in urban fertilizers was more efficiently organized; improvements were made in dikes and irrigation ditches.

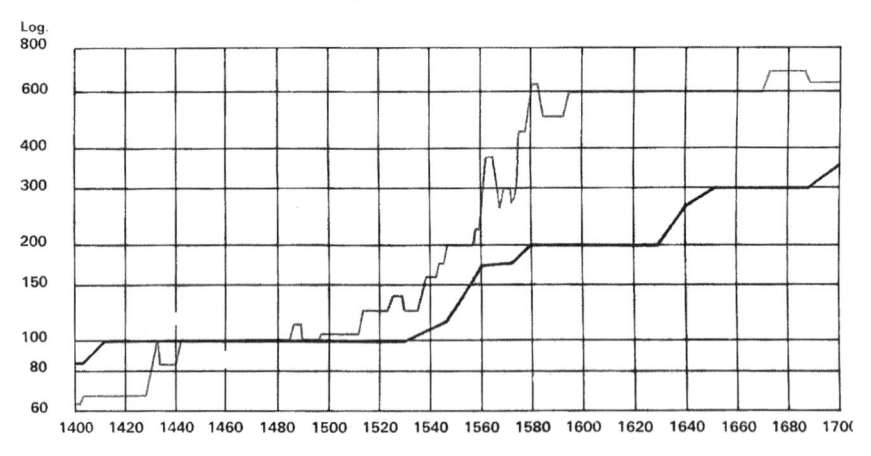

Figure 1.2: *Comparison between the nominal daily wage rates (summer) of a master-mason at Antwerp and in Southern England between 1400 and 1700 (semi-logarithmic scale). The dotted line is Antwerp, the solid line is Southern England (semi-logarithmic scale).*

In the agricultural regions of the Southern Netherlands it was primarily more intensive methods of cultivation and higher employment in rural industries that sustained the prosperity of the growing population. Although there was a clear tendency towards further division into smaller land parcels, income in many cases continued to rise. In the Northern Netherlands, and particularly in the coastal provinces, a gradual concentration of cultivated land became noticeable, providing an adequate surface area for agricultural specialization. At the same time an important group of non-agricultural skilled crafts developed in the countryside, furnishing special services to the rural communities or to the towns: fishing, peat digging, land reclamation, maintenance of dikes, construction and maintenance of windmills, and internal and maritime transportation were some of the most striking examples. Here, too, a rising population and prosperity still went hand in hand for a while. Only in the eastern agricultural regions did development take a less favourable turn, and the growth of productivity came much more slowly: there the population increase was more rapid than the growth of global production and global income, with all the negative consequences associated with this phenomenon. Owing to the more extensive use of monoculture in agriculture and to the expansion of trade and industry in the countryside, the Low Countries were obliged to import huge quantities of certain foodstuffs, notably grain and meat. They thus gave impetus to a broadening of the international division of labour. Long-distance trade was no longer exclusively in small articles of high added value, but now included large or heavy articles and bulk goods. A large Dutch maritime fleet brought grain in quantity from the Baltic region to Amsterdam warehouses, whence it was distributed to other parts of the country and beyond. This trade necessitated the construction of hundreds of new vessels, which could be built only with increased importation of timber from Scandinavia. The rise of the ship-building industry in Holland in turn stimulated the expansion of the herring fleet and the construction of ships for Levantine and Far Eastern trade. The expansion of the great trade in oxen from Denmark, Schleswig-Holstein, Frisia, Groningen, Drenthe and Overijssel was also related to the rise of international trade in bulk goods. Finally, the growing export of coal from Liège and Hainault to Flanders and Brabant for industrial and domestic use worked in the same direction.

The role played by the Low Countries in the broadening of international trade cannot be overemphasized. It involved crossing a structural threshold, allowing the Low Countries to bypass the Malthusian dilemma in their own territories for a time. A breakthrough, at least temporary, in the vicious circle of relative overpopulation was made possible by substantial innovations in the various agricultural regions of the Low Countries and by the importation of bulk foodstuffs. It was thus that a growing population and increasing prosperity could coexist. Is this not perfect proof of the economic vitality of the Low Countries, at a time when the rest of Europe was powerless in the face of the threat posed by relative overpopulation?

The economic vitality of the Low Countries in the middle of the 16th century manifested itself to the fullest in the urban sector. During the second third of the 16th century full employment was attained, or the situation had at least evolved in that direction, not only in Antwerp but also in some other towns and in centres of rural industry. Nominal urban and rural wages rose to such an extent in some parts of the South that they counteracted the negative effects of the European price revolution. Occasionally the increase was even more than proportional. In the North the peak of this increase in wages was reached later, between 1580 and 1650. The Low Countries were virtually the only region north of the Alps where many wage-earners clearly did not always suffer from the price revolution, and where real earned income, taking into account increased employment and improving skills, actually rose. The Low Countries were thus able to achieve a unique degree of prosperity through their export industry, both in the towns and in the countryside, with all the consequences for production for the domestic market this entailed. Consolidation of the substantial gains in physical and economic productivity, achieved during the 14th and 15th century renovation of the industrial structure, made it possible to sustain a favourable real wage level for industrial and craft sectors in several centres and for extended periods during the 16th century.

Commercial income followed much the same pattern of development. The revival of overland traffic and the spread of efficient trading techniques, such as commission selling and temporary participation in international trading ventures, democratized long-distance trade and worked to the advantage of the Low Countries. The multiplication of active trading cities had substantially raised the cost of maintaining agencies for the large Italian, Iberian and Southern German merchant and banking houses. The revival of the Flemish and Brabant small merchant in international trade, now working with the system of commission and participating as temporary partner in international ventures, proved both flexible and particularly appropriate in a region where world trade had become concentrated. An additional advantage, especially for the merchants from the northern coastal territories, was control over an internal shipping network. Such an alliance between shipper and merchant held enormous new promise and was to become an essential factor in the world leadership of the North in the course of the 17th century.

Finance and Commercial Capitalism During the 16th Century

The commercial successes of the Southern and Northern Netherlands in the 16th century also had a marked effect on the development of financial and monetary practices. In effect it was primarily progress in the financial techniques of the Low Countries which formed the decisive link between the Italian financial revolution of the late Middle Ages and the English one of the 18th century. In montary matters the tradition established by the

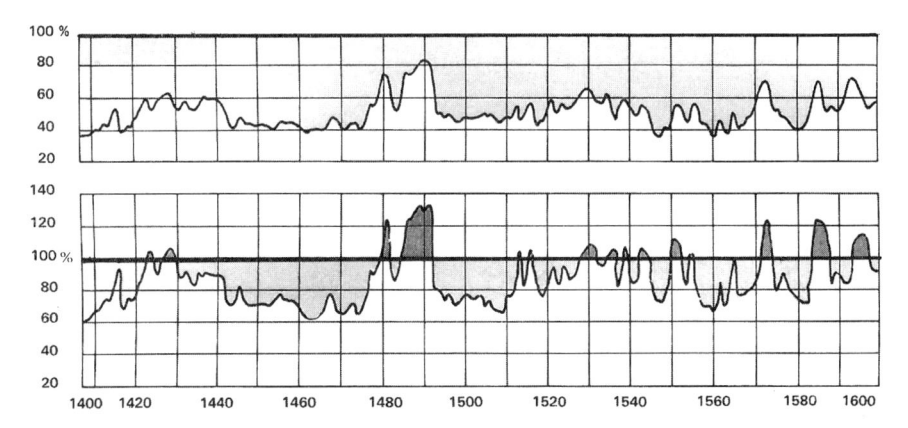

Figure 1.3: *Comparison of real income of wage-earners in Antwerp, 1407–1600 (master-mason, above; journeyman mason, below) and the cost of living of a family of five (represented by the curved line).*
The light shaded area of the curved line below the 100% line represents the margin of the yearly income of the masons available for consumption of goods other than essential food stuffs by a typical family of five persons (father, mother and three children).
The dark shaded area of the curved line above the 100% line represents the periods during which the yearly income of the father was insufficient to meet the consumption of essential foodstuffs by a typical family of five persons.

Burgundian rulers was further upheld by the Habsburg monarchy and by the Dutch republic. Monetary stability remained a high priority: the official silver ratio was adjusted only with the greatest reluctance to the weakening of the value of silver relative to gold, resulting from increased importation of silver from Central Europe and, later, from the New World. The government only very exceptionally resorted to a devaluation of the monetary unit through a reduction in the silver content of the basic coin (the stiver). The Emperor Charles V further strove, in the footsteps of his grandfather Maximilian, to introduce a stable bimetallic standard (as opposed to the monometallic silver standard of the preceding centuries); he issued a gold Carolus guilder officially valued at 20 silver stivers. However, the price of gold relative to silver rose continually on the free market, so that the golden guilder soon developed a higher exchange rate in silver stivers and the attempt to stabilize the value of gold relative to silver failed yet again. The guilder did, however, continue to function for centuries as a theoretical accounting multiple of the real silver stiver (1 guilder = 20 stivers).

With the commercial rise of Antwerp starting in the second half of the 15th century, the economic centre of gravity in the Low Countries shifted gradually from Flanders to Brabant. In the 16th century the whole of the

Low Countries would become a virtual suburb of the trading metropolis of Antwerp, where the products of town and countryside found a global market. For a while Bruges could sustain a leading position in financial matters, but it lost even this position to Antwerp from the second decade of the 16th century onwards. By the election of Emperor Charles V in 1519, the South German merchant bankers, especially the Fuggers and the Welsers, had come to the fore as pre-eminent financiers; and they chose Antwerp as their base of operations. The money market of Antwerp soon became the leading European centre for short-term commercial and government credit. Antwerp became the primary destination of the gold and silver transfers from Spain to Northern Europe for the purposes of Habsburg world politics. In these years Antwerp also grew into a significant capital market, where loans in the form of redeemable life annuities or consols were systematically issued and traded. During this spectacular expansion numerous new formulas and techniques were introduced that exercised a decisive influence over later developments in public finance and upon the creation of the public debt.

There were yet more far-reaching innovations in the field of commercial finance. It could even be postulated that the Antwerp money market would never have been able to play such a vital role in government finance, had it not already become 'the world trade financier of the age'. Such financing was arranged chiefly by means of bills of exchange, and even more often by means of letters obligatory with the clause 'to bearer', a document in use in Northwestern Europe for some time. In Antwerp commercial credit techniques were greatly improved by changes in the use of these two commercial documents. Application of the practice of assignment on the transfer of letters obligatory with a bearer's clause strengthened guarantees for the possessors of such documents so effectively that they began to circulate intensively from hand to hand as payment for commercial debts. The introduction of endorsement at Antwerp around 1600 in order to better identify the successive assignors was also the starting signal for a new, vigorous expansion in the transfer of paper, now extending its practice fully to bills of exchange as well. Moreover, bills of exchange were used not only in international trade, but increasingly in financing regional trade: bills from Antwerp to Lille, Amsterdam or Middelburg were now in routine use. On the other hand the intensified circulation from hand to hand of letters obligatory to bearer laid the foundations for the later success of the bank note, a success that became established during the 17th century, in part through its use in Sweden, but chiefly in England and Scotland.

The modern notion of discount also originated in the 16th century money market of Antwerp. Initially discounts were applied only to the long-term letters obligatory to bearer, but the new technique was soon integrated into a more widespread usage of the bill of exchange. Further development took place in the fields of marine insurance, futures dealing, and many others which had made their first appearance in Italy and Spain, but were now improved and more generally disseminated, stimulated by the expansion of Antwerp's world trade.

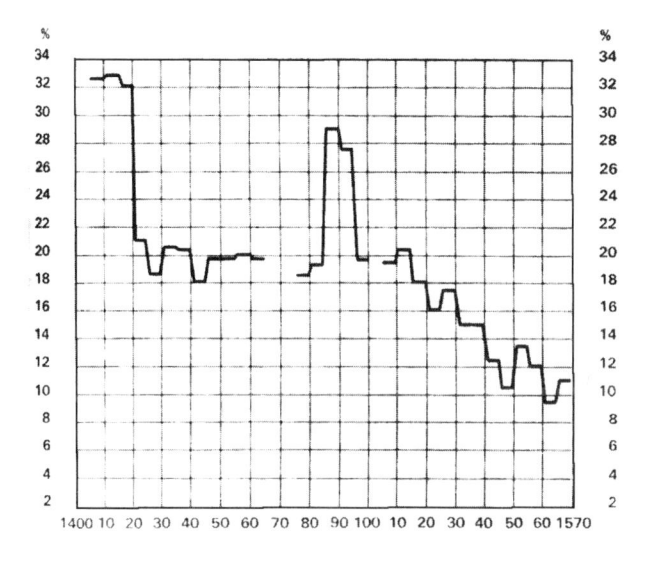

Figure 1.4: *Short-term interest rates for loans made to the government in the Southern Netherlands (on the money markets of Bruges and Antwerp). The breaks in the line indicate a lack of data.*

The progress in financial techniques achieved at Antwerp unquestionably owed much of its success to the opening of the Exchange (Bourse) in 1531. The idea of an exchange for commodities, payments and other financial transactions was already present in embryonic form both in Italy and in Bruges, but it was at Antwerp that it was first systematically worked out in the form of a specific building and a specific organization wherein all transactions relative to international trade and finance were concentrated.

The improved financial techniques constituted a decisive factor in the successful rise of European commercial capitalism in the 16th century. According to our interpretation the birth of commercial capitalism dated from an earlier period, during the rise of the cities. However, from around 1500 onwards an acceleration became apparent in the growth of European capitalism. However, the progress in financial techniques was as yet insufficient to meet the enormous demands made by the Habsburg Empire and by the other European monarchies. The infrastructure still remained too weak for the absorption of a massive public debt. Long-term credit for the government, achieved through large-scale sales of annuities by the cities and by central institutions, therefore had to be supplemented by short-term loans on the Antwerp money market.

The financial tensions mounted during the wars of the 1550s. They led to the first moratorium by the governments of Spain and the Low Countries in 1557. The bankruptcy was a heavy blow to the South German merchant bankers, who lost their hegemony over the Antwerp money market to the Genoese. The Antwerp money market itself suffered grievous losses and never regained its earlier position as the dominant European money centre. From the 1560s onwards the financial fairs of Besançon, and later of Piacenza, established and controlled by the Genoese, assumed in large measure the role of Antwerp in financing Habsburg power politics.

Increasing fiscal revenue was one effective means of restoring government finances. The Habsburgs did not hesitate to make use of this means, but in doing so they were confronted with the system of aids, which implied the consent of the provincial states for each tax. When Philip II attempted to reorganize the existing tax system by replacing the principle of occasional aids with a system of permanent taxation, he threatened not only the income of the population of the Low Countries, but also their dearest-held and holiest principles of regional sovereignty. The new legislation, along with a tightening of the Inquisition and certain ecclesiastical reforms – notably the profound changes in the organization of the bishoprics – became a thorn in the flesh for a region where economic advantage and material prosperity had whetted the appetite of both the elite and the masses for spiritual and political emancipation. Fiscal and religious factors thus combined to exacerbate the tensions between two opposing social and political ideas of societal order: that of Habsburg imperialism and that of the more popular-oriented particularism of the Low Countries, causing them to flare up into a violent and fanatical conflict. The resulting Eighty Years' War became the tragic scenario of that conflict. It ripped the Low Countries asunder. More tragic still was the fact that by the end of the struggle the principles behind such violent strife were no longer relevant. Europe's political structure was indeed already evolving in the direction of the national, mercantilist power state. One thing was crystal clear: neither the Spanish dominion in the South nor the United Provinces fulfilled this rising political ideal.

2

The Low Countries in Transition: from Commercial Capitalism to the Industrial Revolution

Malthusian Theory and the Development of the Southern Netherlands, 17th and 18th Centuries

The path travelled by the Northern and Southern Netherlands during the 16th, 17th and 18th centuries was both long and eventful. Both regions had shown signs of impressive and dynamic expansion during the 16th century. The South made substantial contributions at that time to the accelerated growth of European commercial capitalism. The two phases of the Revolt or the Eighty Years' War (1568–1648), however, brought an end to the economic predominance of the South. The balance of economic power between the North and South shifted in favour of the North. Soon the balance of political power between Europe and the Netherlands would change also: the power of mercantilistic states, such as France, England, Sweden and Prussia was rising; that of the Netherlands was weakening.

During the 17th century the growth path of North and South diverged. The South had been greatly affected by the military operations of the first Revolt period (1565–1609): misery, insecurity and unrest dominated the region for many years. Though decades of recovery followed, the revival was halted by the dramatic decline of the Spanish Empire into which the Southern Netherlands had been reintegrated after the reconquest. From a political point of view the Southern Netherlands had now become a conquered territory of secondary importance, and moreover, from the Spanish point of view, a mere peripheral territory. Culturally the influence of the Counter-Reformation was positive during the first half of the 17th century; in particular it stimulated an active renewal of the religious and artistic heritage, but later in the century the fires of creativity were smothered under the weight of the strict formalism which characterized the later Counter-Reformation. The remarkable flowering of the plastic arts reached its height chiefly during the period from 1600 to 1650, afterwards producing only lesser talents and imitators. Economic recovery proved to be more difficult: commercial activity had been crippled during the war, to the advantage of the Northern provinces. Furthermore, there were substantial losses in human capital due to emigration for religious, economic or political reasons. Nevertheless the economic recovery of the Southern Netherlands during the 17th century could, in the light of all these paralysing effects, still be called remarkable: it reached and in some sectors even surpassed the peak levels of the 16th century. But seen in a more global perspective it was a recovery only, not an expansion; and it ended about 1660.

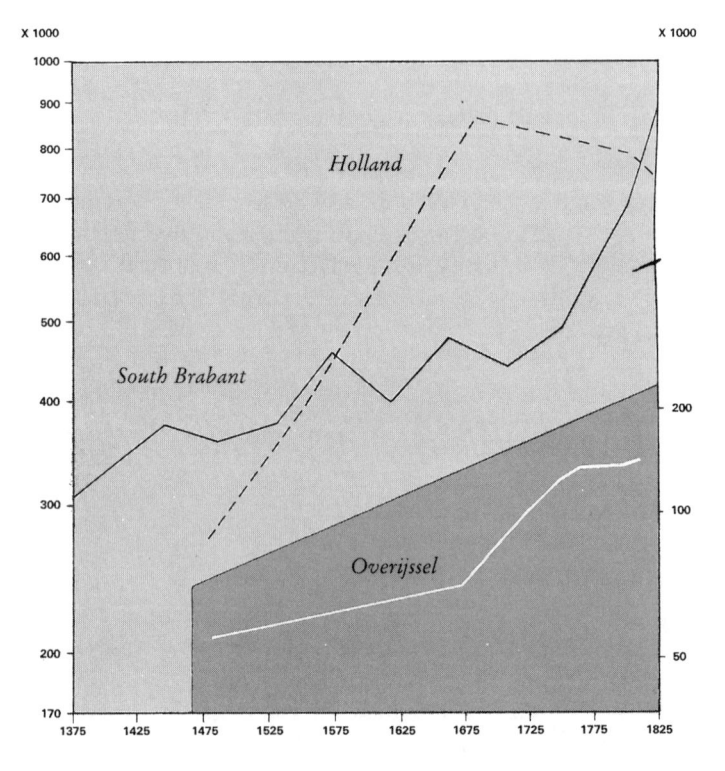

Figure 2.1: *Population growth in South Brabant, Holland (urbanized region) and Overijssel (rural region) between the 14th and 19th centuries; semi-logarithmic scale.*

The declining trend of the economy of the Southern Netherlands is clearly reflected in the demographic evolution. During the early Revolt period and again during the wars of Louis XIV, between 1665 and 1715, the population diminished drastically. Moreover, the towns were more greatly depopulated than the countryside: in 1565, 47% of the Brabantine population lived in cities with 5,000 or more inhabitants; by 1665 this percentage had declined to 42%; and by 1765 to 34% (according to P.M.M. Klep). The Southern Netherlands were reverting to an economy dominated to an increasing extent by rural activity. The economic evolution of the South became once again more clearly influenced by demographic factors; in other words threats to income no longer automatically provoked a powerful reaction which would safeguard economic growth through new initiatives and creativity. On the contrary, the weakening of the urban infrastructure had turned the Southern Netherlands into a region of straitened means and limited wealth. A demographic recovery such as the one which occurred in the course of the 17th century led at first to relative overpopulation, rendering a new and substantial economic adjustment downwards inescapable in the face of the unfavourable climatological, political and military circumstances prevalent at the end of that century. After the end of the War of the Spanish Succession (1701–15), however, the population had declined to such an extent that a new growth in *per capita* income could be expected. The relative underpopulation now allowed a better organization of the agricultural economy in the Southern Netherlands: demographic factors again took a hand in the rural economy and lent a powerful impetus to the revival of the South.

The Triumph of the Northern Netherlands

In the Northern Netherlands the Revolt and the war effort that followed it were no impediment to further progress. On the contrary they advanced the political emancipation of the region and led to the establishment of an original, republican form of government. Moreover, it was precisely during the Eighty Years' War that the North converted its economic expansion of the 16th century into a commercial hegemony over the world.

The rise of the North was not only remarkable considering its own lengthy war effort; in the context of the overall European situation at that time it was extraordinary. The growth of the European population, the price revolution and the collapse of real wages, and the Wars of Religion in France and Germany, had combined to totally undermine the European expansion of the 16th century. During the 17th century the continental economy sank into stagnation, in Central Europe in particular, which suffered greatly from the Thirty Years' War (1618–1648) and from the Ottoman conquests. Italy, Spain and the other territories in the Mediterranean region stagnated as well. Overland traffic from all these areas to the North waned: the crisis underlines the maritime character of the 'Golden Century' of the Northern Netherlands.

Holland's maritime glory rested upon four great pillars. The enormous expansion of the Baltic trade (the *moedernegotie*), prompted by population pressures in Western Europe in the 16th century, made Amsterdam the granary of Western and, from the end of the century, also of Southern Europe (the *Straatvaart*). The profits of the Eastern European agricultural surplus, which the local great landowners had appropriated thanks to a return to feudal practices in that area, had to be shared with Dutch shippers and merchants. Soon the Dutch shippers and merchants appropriated the Levant trade too, and expanded it to a second maritime pillar. They also began to take a hand in transporting cargoes of Italian and Spanish manufactured goods to the Levant. As manufacture in Holland had become both more diversified and more competitive, primarily under the influence of emigrés from the Southern Netherlands, the Dutch shippers and merchants gradually replaced the Italian and Spanish wares formerly used in their trade with the Levant with home-produced textiles, even in the face of heavy competition from the English, and later from the French. Rather as happened in the 14th century the direct maritime link between the North Sea and the Mediterranean region took over a substantial portion of transcontinental overland trade. There was, however, more to it than that: this time the direct link eliminated Italian exports from the Levant and crippled the Italians in their traditional role as intermediaries between Europe and the Middle East.

A third essential component of the maritime prosperity of the Northern Netherlands in the 17th century was the closure of the Scheldt. The world port of Antwerp was almost entirely sealed off, whereas the transfer of capital and the inflow of commercial talent from the South significantly strengthened the basis of overseas trade in the North. Finally, the spectacular success of Zeeland and Holland on the ocean routes should be mentioned as a fourth factor in maritime expansion: the penetration of the East and West Indies indeed lent momentum to the rise of the United Provinces during the 17th century. Quantitatively, colonial expansion in the 17th century was undoubtedly not so decisive for economic growth in the North as the other three factors: however, it afforded the entrepreneurial spirit of Holland a global field of action, it provided exceptional returns on investment, and – becoming more important in the 18th and 19th centuries – it helped to compensate for the weakening of other sectors in the Dutch economy.

The booming maritime trade of the North during the 17th century was further enhanced by vigorous progress in fishing, agriculture, industry and finance. Herring, cod and whale fishing became leading sectors, as did fish processing and ship building. In the towns, division of labour and mass production formed the basis for an expanding export industry in woollen and linen textiles; more extensive processing of colonial wares, sugar refining in particular, expanded in the ports; an urban luxury industry developed, based on highly skilled labour and gradually producing more for export. Specialized non-agrarian crafts were growing in the countryside also, providing skilled services for agriculture, such as drainage of the polders, upkeep of dikes and waterways, maintenance of windmills, and services for the nearby towns, such as barge transportation and peat digging. Agriculture itself made substantial improvements in productivity, especially in the coastal provinces, by increasing specialization and by the commercialization of agrarian activity. Monetary reorganization was completed towards the end of the 17th century. The success of the guilder of the Amsterdam Exchange Bank had made the monetary unit of Holland the dominant currency of the world. With respect to financial techniques the progress realized by the Amsterdam Exchange Bank represented a peak in the evolution of the international clearing system. Its role in the organization of a stable world trade in precious metals was crucial. The contribution of private bankers to the modernization of money and credit was also very significant: the private bankers of Amsterdam, for example, introduced the technique of acceptance credit; they created a world market in futures dealing with stock and commodities; and they reorganized long-term government credit on a new basis.

The maritime regions of the North were able to escape for a while the dilemma described in Malthusian theory. Vigorous forces responded to any threat to prosperity with structural adaptations. A population increase did not destroy the rise in income, because it stimulated creative reactions leading to improved physical and economic productivity.

Elements of Stagnation in the Northern Netherlands

Towards the end of the 18th century the tide of fate turned against the North. Its economy grew gradually more fossilized, whereas in the South the effects of renewal and creativity were manifest once again. Why this reversal in the development of the two regions? What factors were most decisive in this process?

The rigidity which gradually undermined the society of the North, beginning in the late 17th century and reaching its climax in the 18th century, is at first glance difficult to comprehend within the framework of the institutional interpretation of economic growth as it was presented to explain the dynamism of the previous centuries. Nevertheless the paradox can be solved with this theory. The progress which spontaneously perpetuated itself in a region possessing such an advanced economic and cultural infrastructure as the North was the result of organizational improvements within the potentialities of the existing system. The rise of the North indeed took place within the framework of commercial capitalism: it even represented its peak, which meant that the Golden Age of Holland represented the limits of what could be attained through commercial capitalism. More precisely, the potential for organizational advances within the system of European commercial capitalism was progressively exhausted during the period of Holland's glory.

The atrophy is particularly clear in the case of industry. The urban export industry, based on mass production and a far-reaching division of labour, could from the second half of the 17th century onwards no longer sustain itself owing to the high taxes needed to finance the world politics of the North, to rising wages and the rising cost of living. As a result, urban industry concentrated more and more on the production of craft products and specialized services requiring highly skilled labour and consequently better able to support the higher costs of production. Moreover, these products and services were marketed mainly to the Dutch urban and rural middle classes, their specifically local character protecting them from foreign competition. Production of many of these luxury articles and services tended to require highly specialized labour; in other words the industrial structure, as developed in the North, progressed toward high quality craftsmanship and began to entrench itself deeply into a production pattern that was more likely to hinder than to encourage the shift towards mechanization.

Attempts to reorganize the production of textiles for export in rural areas encountered serious difficulties. The great success of commercialized agriculture in the coastal regions of the North had created a stratification which tended to check the establishment of a textile rural-industry as an ancillary occupation. The prosperous farmers had so organized themselves as to prevent any further division of their acreage; the other groups supported themselves by providing specialized goods and services to the farmers and the urban population. There was thus little leeway, real or psychological, for the introduction on a large scale of a new industrial activity based on a new, specific, division of labour and providing by the absorption of disguised unemployment a supplementary source of income. Therefore rural industry did not develop in the maritime provinces of Holland, but in the less advanced regions of the republic such as Twenthe and North Brabant. It was precisely due to the less advanced character of agriculture in these regions that rural industry became successful there, gradually developing into an export sector. For the same reason it would be relatively late in converting to mechanization.

In the coastal regions commercial agriculture itself continued to prosper. However, little new organizational progress was to be expected within this model of agrarian specialization. The agricultural regions of the North merely profited from the lead in productivity they had earlier attained, and from the favourable agricultural climate of rising prices in Europe during the 18th century. The prosperity arising from this climate in the agrarian sector was sufficient to sustain rural employment at a reasonable level through demand for goods and services; at least if these goods and services were produced in the countryside, which was frequently the case. Still, the lasting prosperity of the Dutch countryside in the 18th century must be placed in perspective, since the dynamic expansion of the preceding century had gradually waned and no growth sectors of any significance were added to compensate for the decline manifesting itself here and there in other sectors for technological or demographic reasons. For example, the decline of peat digging in favour of importing coal and the reduced number of new drainage projects must have led to unemployment in the countryside and must also have adversely affected the activities of the other non-agrarian skilled workers.

The stagnation of Dutch trade has been highlighted by numerous historians. The merchants have been generally blamed: they had transferred their investments from trade to the financial sector. Peter Klein has correctly pointed out that the fault should in fact be attributed to the much-lauded trade pioneers of the 17th century. These founders of Holland's Golden Age had opted for an extension of commercial capitalism. Within the limits of this capitalism they had indeed achieved amazing organizational progress, but by realizing it they had consolidated the structures of the system in depth, rendering them less open to renewal and adaptation. Holland's long-distance trade consequently became a prisoner of the chosen system and was no longer capable of disentangling itself. The development of Holland's attempted westward expansion is a clear illustration of this. By creating the West Indian Company in 1623 Holland tried to take an active, if not a leading part, in the colonization of America. Herein lay the enormous promise of a frontier, of opening up a whole new world, potentially the cornerstone of a new system: industrial capitalism. During several decades the North did indeed take important steps in this direction, as demonstrated by ventures in Brazil, in the West Indies, and on the east coast of North America. Holland's efforts, however, failed: it had in fact committed itself too much to commercial capitalism. Holland was strengthening its colonial expansion more in the direction of the Far East. Here, however, there was no question of a true 'frontier' – only of a colonial empire that could be commercially exploited. It long remained a great success because the venture was so perfectly suited to the Dutch system of commerical capitalism.

Nor was the Amsterdam money and capital market entirely free from stagnation. The Amsterdam Bank, apart from its innovative role in the sphere of trade in precious metals, had entrenched itself in clearing operations and become a sideliner in the development of issue banking. The private merchants, on the contrary, further refined their financial methods, and in such a way that large-scale investment outside the system of Dutch commercial capitalism became possible and profitable. England proved especially attractive to Dutch investors: the money and capital market of Amsterdam now started financing England's transition from commercial to industrial capitalism.

Political institutions and social relations in the North also fell victim to increasing rigidity. In the 17th century republican ideology and the decentralized nature of institutions had stimulated the initiative and entrepreneurial spirit of the middle classes in town and countryside; however, as entrepreneurial spirit led to economic power, it was used to bend social and political institutions to preserve acquired wealth. The stagnation of the 18th century tended to reinforce the conservative reflexes of the well-to-do classes. The political changes that marked the beginning of the 19th century did not fundamentally change this characteristic. Even the farming system organized on Java (the so-called *cultuurstelsel*) was concentrated in the hands of those who dominated the traditional commercial capitalism of Holland.

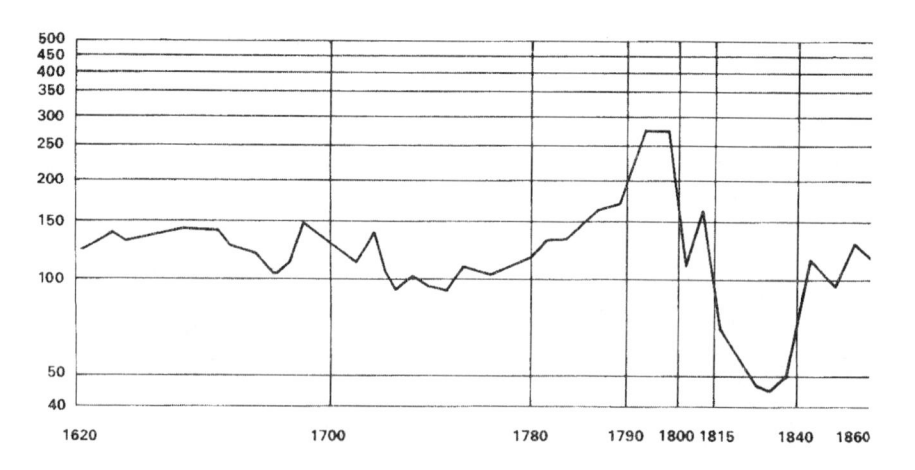

Figure 2.2: *Weighted price index figures (five-year averages) (quantity × price of 44 products) for the Northern Netherlands between 1620 and 1860; semi-logarithmic scale.*

Demographic evolution reflected the structural changes taking place in the North. From the end of the 17th century onwards the urban population in the coastal regions stagnated, or even declined. On the other hand the population began slowly to grow in the agriculturally less advanced regions in the eastern and southern parts of the republic under the influence of the expanding rural industry.

The Structural Renovation of the Southern Netherlands

The development of the South diverged sharply from that of the North during the 18th and 19th centuries. The weakening of the South in the 17th century had a structural impact as well as an immediate effect on the economic situation: in addition to extending urban poverty it gradually destroyed the traditional structures of commercial capitalism. Whereas in the North the economic successes of the 17th century had consolidated commercial capitalism and by doing so had increased its rigidity, the South underwent the reverse of this evolution. The economic weakness of the South in fact contributed to a decline in the rigidity of its economic system, allowing the forces of innovation to re-emerge. This is one of the reasons why the South was able to become the first region on the European continent to imitate England's Industrial Revolution.

The industrial modernization of the South presupposed profound cultural, political and economic changes during the 18th and 19th centuries. Political developments in the 18th century were favourable to the South. The transition from Spanish to Austrian domination in 1713 had numerous positive aspects. The Southern Netherlands escaped the tutelage of a languishing, dying empire and were integrated into an empire that was in full expansion. Austria's vitality, together with analogous developments in Prussia and tsarist Russia, had a decisive effect upon the economy of East and Central Europe. This economic revival provided new stimulus for transcontinental trade in the direction of the North Sea. Thanks to its special political ties with Vienna, the South benefited substantially from the new situation: it became a strategic bridgehead for long-distance overland trade from Southern and Central Europe. Overland traffic revived in France as well, as demonstrated by the building of the Pavé du Roi. The impressive increase in the exportation of coal from Hainault to Paris, of Liège metal-wares and textiles from Verviers to Southern and Central Europe during the 18th century was undeniably due in large measure to the revival of transcontinental trade. Thanks to this new development the economy of the South was able to escape from the commercial paralysis brought on by the North's blockade of the Scheldt since 1585. In particular, the revival stimulated the growth of Ostend as a port: among others, smugglers desirous of evading the constraints of the English staple market sought direct contact with Ostend, then emerging as a terminus for European overland traffic.

The mercantilist Austrian monarchy energetically supported these shifts in commercial development. There was a systematic extension of the road and canal network, great encouragement of transit trade, improvements in customs administration and an active policy of promoting exports. The policy of further encouraging the modernization of communications and trade continued under French rule (1795–1814), greatly increasing the integration of the Southern Netherlands into the great French market. King William I of Holland, ruler of these territories during the period of the United Kingdom (1815–30), and the Belgian governments after 1830 also devoted considerable attention to the modernization of the transportation system, the monetary and banking systems, administration and transit trade. The influence of liberalism and of the Enlightenment on the mentality and life-style of the upper classes, including progressive elements within the nobility and the clergy, was also a factor of great importance. The French-speaking élite had always been open to new liberal ideas sweeping in from nearby Paris. Moreover, the reforms carried out during the annexation of the Belgian provinces by France had a lasting impact on the institutional infrastructure of the territory. The emergence of the Belgian state in 1830 should also be seen against this background. The new constitution provided a solid ideological basis for the foundation of an industrialized society, the guarantee of a working compromise between conservative and progressive forces in the country.

The establishment of a modern infrastructure in the South through the intervention of the government was, however, insufficient to achieve an Industrial Revolution. Innovation had to take root within the various economic sectors themselves. This was clearly the case with agriculture. There was a further intensification and commercialization of agriculture through extension of the cultivation of clover and of flax. Another important factor was the spread of the potato, which gathered momentum during the 18th century and had favourable effects well into the 19th century. The per acre yield in calories was so greatly augmented that the export of agricultural products begun in the 17th century could be sustained for a considerable time despite the demographic growth of the 18th century.

Rising productivity of land was accompanied by a substantial increase in labour productivity. The further expansion of rural industry in the 18th century, absorbing more disguised unemployment from the countryside, was primarily responsible for this increase. Other important factors were the commercialization of the agricultural economy as a whole, and its attendant specialization in skills. In the 18th century all these elements combined to shape a climate of rural prosperity and optimism that could not but stimulate initiative and entrepreneurship in the agrarian regions. This 18th century development undeniably had its negative aspects: the resistance of the traditional rural sectors to the mechanization process was strengthened by its earlier success, as in the case of the 19th-century Flemish linen weavers.

In the towns of the Southern Netherlands, industry developed in the direction of mechanization. Domestic and foreign demand for the highly specialized articles formerly produced there had gradually waned: the higher income groups at home had been noticeably thinned, while in the rest of Europe the products of highly specialized craftsmanship were produced locally with increasing success, due to the stimulus of mercantilist policies and often with the help of emigrants from the Netherlands. As a result the towns of the Southern Netherlands had again oriented their industry towards textiles, which could be mass-produced by the application of a division of cheap, semi-skilled labour. At the same time there were attempts to increase the value of the products through differentiation: for example experimenting with new kinds of woollen or cotton fabrics or new combinations of wool, flax and cotton. Special efforts were also made in processing: various towns for example developed into centres for the printing of cotton cloth, or for bleaching cotton cloth and linens. Merchant-entrepreneurs in Flanders and at Verviers gathered the workers together under a single roof to improve quality control and to increase processing efficiency. They were the pioneers of the modern factory. New tools were introduced, soon to be followed by machines.

The Walloon territories derived extra advantages from their wealth of coal and iron ore. The demand for coal for home heating and to supply industrial energy was sharply on the rise throughout Europe, as was the demand for iron ore. The industrial tradition of Liège and Hainault was well suited to meeting this increasing demand. Moreover, the geographical situation of both regions was more favourable than that of their greatest rival, England, in responding to demand from Germany, France and the Northern Netherlands. However, access to long-term financing was an essential prerequisite for taking full advantage of opportunities in the heavy industry sectors. The South had the necessary infrastructure for this. Antwerp had remained a significant money and capital market during the 17th and 18th centuries, even if only as a satellite of Amsterdam. In the course of the 18th century, Brussels also set up a flourishing money market. Thus the expansion of the 18th century export trade from Flanders and Wallonia was easily managed. The reopening of the Scheldt by Napoleon around 1800 also attracted many merchants, financiers and insurance specialists, from Germany in particular, to the support of the reviving maritime industries. The founding of the Société Générale (1822) and of the Banque de Belgique (1835) finally completed the organization of industrial financing. Industrial capitalism was now able to forge full steam ahead in Belgium.

Two Routes Towards an Industrial Economy

The closure of the Scheldt in 1585 lent a peculiar twist to the development of North and South. Its triumph over Spain enabled the North gradually to monopolize the extension of commercial capitalism. This monopoly

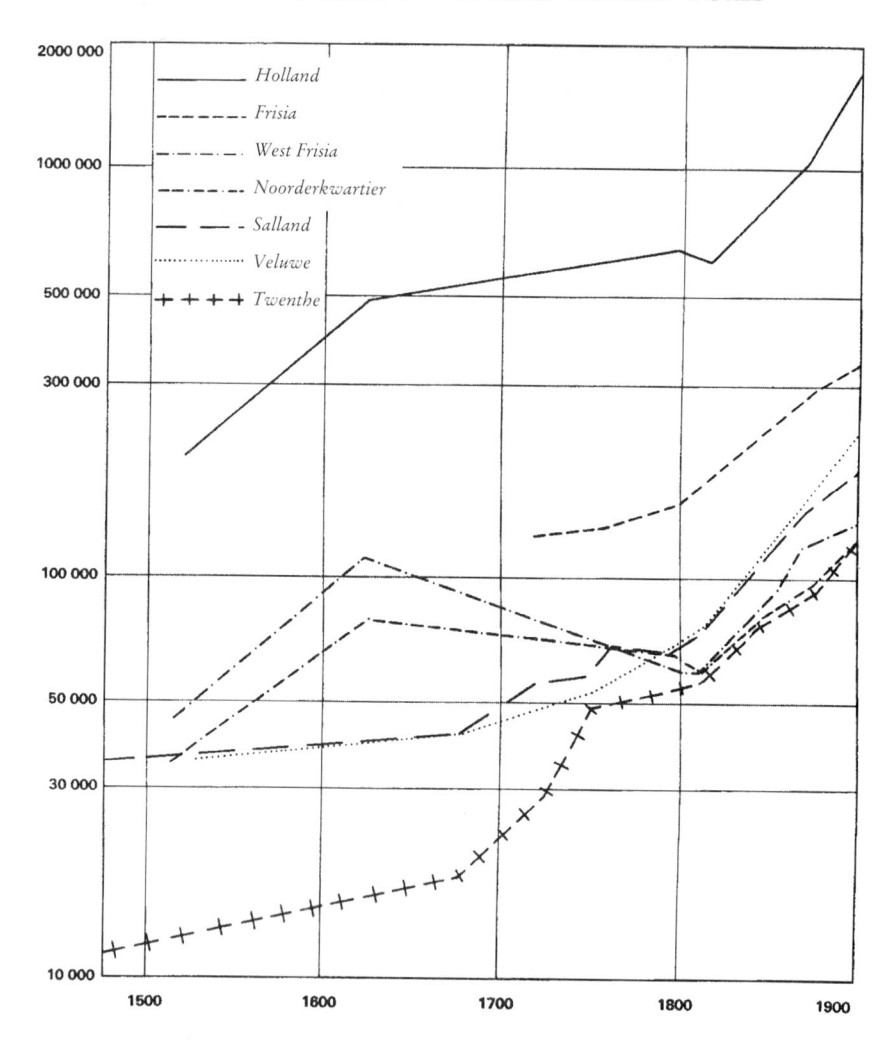

Figure 2.3: *The population curve for Holland, Frisia, Salland, Twenthe and the Veluwe in the period 1475–1899; semi-logarithmic scale.*

brought the North a golden 17th century, with the organizational progress of commercial capitalism reaching unparalleled heights. The merchants of Holland were able to call upon the commercial infrastructure, which they and the Dutch government had extended over the entire world, as a kind of fixed capital for the production of their commercial and financial services. This original combination of Dutch entrepreneurship with Dutch merchants' floating capital and a worldwide network of Dutch fixed commercial capital enabled the Dutch to achieve impressive productivity gains, guaranteeing an enormous lead over the rest of Europe. The success was in the long run fatal to the North: its organization grew rigid, leading to a stagnating commercial capitalism, which no longer held opportunities for further progress.

The Southern Netherlands by contrast had lost through their defeat at the hands of the Spanish all possibility of further tapping the commercial infrastructure of the world as a fixed capital asset for the production of commercial and financial services, which they had earlier done. As a result they rapidly lost their international supremacy. The extinction of commercial capitalism in the South, however, heightened interest in various new forms of industrial production, investment in capital goods becoming more central. As conditions for such investment became more attractive, the South could proceed with the realization of an Industrial Revolution.

Economic growth was now determined in large measure by the rapid accumulation of capital goods in the industrial sector: substantial productivity gains were achieved by substituting labour for capital. On the other hand, the price for the modern industrialization of the economy was exceedingly high: structural unemployment and the difficulty of reallocating labour led to social upheaval, misery and poverty. In the long run, however, modern industrial civilization brought about greater material prosperity, the democratization of political life and the cultural elevation of the entire community. For the South this process was already noticeable by the middle of the 19th century, first in Wallonia, and later in Flanders. In the North, where the Industrial Revolution took place rather late, at the end of the 19th century, the beneficial effects of industrialization on prosperity and culture were experienced more slowly. However, the bourgeois society formed in the 17th and 18th centuries provided considerable compensations. Higher wages for craftsmen and a more equitable income distribution in comparison to the South served substantially to cushion the structural upheaval invariably associated with industrialization, when it took place.

Bibliography for Chapters 1 and 2

H. Van der Wee, *Historische aspecten van de economische groei. Tien studies over de economische ontwikkeling van West-Europa en van de Nederlanden in het bijzonder, 12de–19de eeuw* (Antwerp–Utrecht: 1972); H. Van der Wee, 'Monetary Credit and Banking Systems in Western Europe, 1400–1750', Chapter V in: E.E. Rich and C.H. Wilson (eds), *The Cambridge Economic History of Europe* V (Cambridge: 1977), pp. 291–392, 653–71. With regard to the transition from an agrarian, self-sufficient economy to a market system under the leadership of the towns, see, among others, J. Hicks, *A Theory of Economic History* (Oxford: 1969); A. Gerschenkron, *Mercator Gloriosus. Kritische essays over economische ontwikkeling, Europees socialisme en Sovjet-problematiek* (Antwerp–Utrecht: 1973); D.C. North and R.B. Thomas, *The Rise of the Western World. A New Economic History* (Cambridge: 1973).

For the medieval economy and society in general, see especially G. Duby, *L'économie rurale et la vie des campagnes dans l'Occident médiéval* (Paris: 1962), 2 vols, English edition *The Rural Economy and Country Life in the Medieval West* (London: 1968); M.M. Postan, *The Medieval Economy and Society. An Economic History of Britain in the Middle Ages* (London: 1972); G. Fourquin, *Histoire économique de l'Occident médiéval* (Paris: 1969); R. Fossier, *Histoire sociale de l'Occident médiéval* (Paris: 1970); R.S. Lopez, *The Commercial Revolution of the Middle Ages, 950–1350* (Englewood Cliffs, N.J.: 1971); P. Dollinger, *La Hanse, XIIe–XVII siècles* (Paris: 1964); W. Abel, *Die Wüstungen des ausgehenden Mittelalters* (Stuttgart: 1976), 3rd edition. Here are three excellent studies on medieval towns: F. Rörig, *The Medieval Town* (London: 1967); E. Ennen, *Die Europäische Stadt des Mittelalters* (Göttingen: 1975); H. Van Werveke, 'The Rise of the Towns', Chapter 1 in M.M. Postan, E.E. Rich and E. Miller (eds), *The Cambridge Economic History of Europe* III (Cambridge: 1963), pp. 3–41. For the problem of structural change in history and of structural analysis in general, see the controversial book, I. Wallerstein, *The Modern World-System. Capitalist Agriculture and the Origins of the European World-Economy in the Sixteenth Century* (New York: 1974). On the question of the interdependence between population and material civilization, see E. Boserup, *Evolution agraire et pression démographique* (Paris: 1970); E.A. Wrigley, *Population and History* (London: 1969); P. Laslett, *The World We Have Lost* (New York: 1965); C.M. Cipolla, *The Economic History of World Population* (Harmondsworth: 1962); P. Goubert, *Beauvais et le Beauvaisis de 1600 à 1730. Contribution à l'histoire sociale de la France du XVIIe siècle* (Paris: 1960); E. Le Roy Ladurie, *Les paysans du Languedoc* (Paris: 1965), abridged English translation *The Peasants of Languedoc* (London: 1974); J.D. Chambers, *Population, Economy and Society in Pre-Industrial England* (London–Oxford: 1972). In this context special mention should be made of: F.F. Mendels, 'Agriculture and Peasant Industry in Eighteenth-Century Flanders', in W.N. Parker and E.L. Jones (eds), *European Peasants and their Markets. Essays in Agrarian Economic History* (Princeton: 1975), pp. 179–204; P.M.M. Klep, 'Urbanization in a Pre-Industrial Economy. The Case of Brabant, 1374–1930', in: *Belgisch Tijdschrift voor Nieuwste Geschiedenis* VII, (1976), 1–2, pp. 153–68; and P.M.M. Klep, *Bevolking en arbeid in transformatie. Een onderzoek in Brabant, 1700–1900*, (Nijmegen, 1981).

The expansion of European civilization in modern times is treated in F. Braudel, *La Méditerranée et le monde méditerranéen à l'époque de Philippe II* (Paris: 1966), 2nd edition, English translation *The Mediterranean and the Mediterranean World in the Age of Philip II* (London: 1972–73); F. Braudel, *Civilisation matérielle et capitalisme (XVe–XVIIIe siècle)* I (Paris: 1967), 2nd edition, (Paris: 1979), English translation *The Structures of Everyday Life* (London: 1981). Also J. Meuvret, *Etudes d'histoire économique. Recueil d'articles* (Paris: 1971); M. Malowist,

Croissance et régression en Europe, XIVe–XVIIe siècles (Paris: 1972); Tr. Aston (ed.), *Crisis in Europe, 1560–1660* (London: 1965); W. Abel, *Massenarmut und Hungerkrisen im vorindustiellen Europa. Versuch einer Synopsis* (Hamburg–Berlin: 1974); C.M. Cipolla (ed.), *The Economic Decline of Empires* (London: 1970); V. Vives, *An Economic History of Spain* (Princeton: 1969); C.M. Cipolla, *Guns and Sails in the Early Phase of European Expansion, 1400–1700* (London: 1965); P. Jeannin, *L'Europe du Nord-Ouest et du Nord aux XVIIe et XVIIIe siècles* (Paris: 1969); A. Attman, *The Russian and Polish Markets in International Trade, 1500–1650* (Göteborg: 1973); F. Mauro, *L'expansion européenne, 1600–1870* (Paris: 1967); P. Chaunu, *La civilisation de l'Europe classique* (Paris: 1966); R. Mousnier and E. Labrousse, *Le XVIIIe siècle. L'époque des 'Lumières', 1715–1815* (Paris: 1959). On the subject of the second wave of feudalism in Eastern Europe there is for example an interesting work on the subject of Poland: W. Kula, *An Economic Theory of the Feudal System: towards a Model of the Polish Economy, 1500–1800* (London: 1976).

Regarding mercantilism, see especially an important book, if open to discussion: E.F. Heckscher, *Mercantilism* (London: 1955), 2nd edition. Also: P. Deyon, *Le mercantilisme* (Paris: 1969); C.H. Wilson, 'Trade, Society and the State', Chapter VIII in: E.E. Rich and C.H. Wilson (eds), *The Cambridge Economic History of Europe* IV (Cambridge: 1967), pp. 487–575, 615–6; A. Gerschenkron, *Europe in the Russian Mirror. Four Lectures in Economic History* (Cambridge: 1970).

II

AGRICULTURE

3

Agricultural Development of the Low Countries as revealed by Tithe and Rent Statistics 1250–1800[1]

The Methodological Problem

The survey of very long-term trends in the agriculture of the Low Countries offered in this study concerns principally the development of land productivity and is essentially based on a quantitative analysis of sources. The most important series comprises the income from tithes which were payable in kind and which were changed into money or were leased beforehand to the highest bidder. Large numbers of land or farm leases, in which not only the sums agreed between parties were featured, but also what was in fact paid, were used in this research. Finally, a number of specific statistics were included, namely sale prices of farm land, population figures, frequency distribution of the sizes of farms, land taxes and so on. Part of the material from these sources has already been published in separate monographs and articles, while the rest, which is extensive, is based on new research and is analysed and published here for the first time.

As a rule simple descriptive statistics have been used to organize and explain the figures. Analytical statistical techniques have rarely been employed. Furthermore it was not possible to include all regions of the Low Countries in the survey. However, when applying tests for randomness, the geographical spread of individual pieces of evidence seems to be sufficient to guarantee a representative picture of the developments as a whole. The statistics produced by our investigations cover the following regions: Flanders, Brabant, Namur, Liège, Southern Limburg, Holland, Frisia and Overijssel.

---

[1] This article comes from a collection entitled *Productivity of Land and Agricultural Innovation in the Low Countries (1250–1800)*, edited by Herman Van der Wee and Eddy Van Cauwenberghe (Leuven University Press: 1978). The author wishes to acknowledge with thanks extensive use of the contributions to the collection. Use was also made of the data and conclusions from studies which treat the same problems, and these are noted at the end of the chapter.

Unfortunately, representative geographical coverage was only realized for the period 1500–1800. The sources for the late Middle Ages (1250–1500) were much more restricted: for the 14th and 15th centuries, there were only data for Flanders, Brabant, Southern Limburg and Namur, and only for Southern Limburg in the 13th. On the basis of qualitative information, however, it was possible to make a number of reasonable extrapolations, from which more general conclusions could be drawn.

The quantitative analysis of the growth of land productivity in the Low Countries is of course of vital importance for the agrarian and, more generally, for the economic history of the region. It is, however, also very important for the history of Europe: changes in land productivity in the Low Countries during the period 1250–1800 deviated quite markedly from the Western European pattern, as was shown by J. Goy and E. Le Roy Ladurie on the basis of French data. Analysing these differences should certainly give us a better insight into the mechanisms which determined agrarian development in preindustrial Western Europe. J. Goy and E. Le Roy Ladurie formulated the following hypothesis for France: land productivity showed a trend increase from the 11th till the early 14th century under the influence of the increase in population. The peak, which was reached around 1300, was not maintained but was, on the contrary, followed by a catastrophic decline, which was only reversed again about the middle of the 15th century.

This second increase, however, did not reach the earlier peak of 1300 and during the religious wars and the crisis of the end of the 16th century a further fall could be identified. The 17th century was characterized by a strong revival, which was again spoiled by the wars of Louis XIV. During the 18th century land productivity increased again: as a rule the increase reached the high level of the beginning of the 14th century. In some regions, as for example Cambrésis, however, the historical peak was surpassed so that the first phase of the Agrarian Revolution was already realized there in the course of the 18th century. This point is denied by Morineau, Vandenbroeke and Vanderpijpen, who maintain that even in these progressive regions the Agrarian Revolution only started in the 19th century.

The productivity in the Low Countries developed differently. It did not collapse catastrophically from the high level reached at the beginning of the 14th century, but was maintained, generally speaking, on a reasonable level during the whole of the European depression of the 14th–15th centuries. During the 16th century a new trend of growth which even surpassed the peak of the 1300s could be noted. This improvement continued during the 17th century, especially in the coastal areas of the Northern Netherlands. The 18th century brought new successes, this time especially in the South, thanks to the fast and vigorous increase of crop diversification. Consequently, the Agrarian Revolution in the Low Countries was born in the 16th century: and there the growth of land productivity was maintained practically continuously from that date.

The Slowing Down of the Increase in Land Productivity (1250–1350) and the Stabilization of Growth at a High Level (1350–1437)

In contrast to the French data for income from tithes, which between 1284 and 1342 tended towards stabilization at a high level, those concerning the Low Countries for the same period still revealed further increases. Indeed, the scarce information available on tithes and agricultural rents in kind for the Low Countries in some regions shows increasing rather than stable returns between 1250 and 1350. The rate of growth, however, slowed down, so that the situation in the Low Countries cannot be said to be substantially different from that in the Paris region. For the land of the abbey of Saint-Truiden, the only locality for which we have explicit figures, an increase from 10 to 20% for the period from 1250 to 1350 was apparent. The agricultural area in Flanders and Namur around 1300 was moreover already exceptionally subdivided: this splitting up of peasant holdings after 1300 increased even more, which should normally have led to higher land productivity. The extension of agriculturally useful land by reclamation and the changing of saltings into fields and pastures during the same period must have had a similar growth effect. Finally, the strong expansion of trade and industry, as well as the growing urbanization in this region, undoubtedly had a stimulating influence on the intensification of agriculture. Under the circumstances, land productivity especially in Flanders, Artois, Hainault, Brabant, Holland, Zeeland and the valley of the Meuse must have risen further, although more slowly, between 1250 and 1350.

From the middle of the 14th century onwards productivity in the Netherlands underwent a very special development, which this time contrasted sharply with what was happening in the rest of Western Europe. Western Europe underwent a severe agricultural depression, which reached its peak in the middle of the 14th century and led to dramatic mortality, a sharp decline in profits from tithes, decreasing agricultural rents and lower land productivity. The Black Death was also rampant in the Low Countries as is indicated by the figures for Hainault; between 1350 and 1437 there were also frequent wars in the area and land remained temporarily untilled, but there was no question of a real lasting catastrophe anywhere. On the contrary, there was a tendency towards stabilization of yields at the high level which was reached around 1350–70. It is now possible, thanks to quantitative source material which is more abundantly available, to give more precise information about the specific development of each separate region. In Flanders stabilization at a high level was clearly present, although the region went through a serious, though short, crisis in this period. The Revolt of Ghent of 1379-85, which betrayed the growing conflict between the old textile industry in Ghent, Ypres, Bruges and the new textile activities of the smaller towns and the countryside, ravaged the whole county, and the temporary fall in rents and land productivity was the result. The curve, however, soon recovered, although there was an important revaluation of Flemish money of account in 1389-90 and a resulting long deflation, which hindered rather than encouraged revival.

It is also important for the quick revival that the subdivision of peasant holdings in the ducal domains of Flanders continued unabated during the first half of the 15th century in spite of the fact that peasant holdings in Flanders were already highly divided during the preceding century. If we accept the conclusions concerning productivity in the domain of Ninove (1394-1444), i.e. the smaller the size of the holding, the higher the land productivity, it is possible to state that in some parts of Flanders there was not only a quick revival but a further intensification of agriculture which led to still higher land productivity.

In Brabant and Limburg the general tendency towards stabilization of returns from land at a high level is also evident: in some parts of both regions a further increase of productivity was even more prominent than in Flanders. It is possible that about the middle of the 14th century there was a slight overall decline in Brabant, but this possible loss was undoubtedly compensated afterwards: the income from tithes in Leerbeek and Pepingen in Southwest Brabant, the income from temporary leases in the ducal domains of Turnhout, Tienen, Lier and Meldert near Tienen indicate a generally upward movement, with a tendency towards stabilization only during the last quarter of the 14th and first third of the 15th century. In the agricultural region between Saint-Truiden and Maastricht the increase clearly continued during the third quarter of the 14th century, after which the curves stabilized. The grain trade along the Meuse with the prosperous areas of Holland and Zeeland was certainly an important element in this favourable development. In Holland and Zeeland the economic expansion during the same period was so strong, partly under the influence of navigation and the expansion of the brewing industry, that an increase rather than a stabilization of productivity can be assumed. In the county of Namur military operations, temporary reductions of leases and rents, even temporary abandonment of cultivation on certain tracts of land during the years 1368-74 and especially during 1395-1413 and 1430, imply a fall in the effective yield per acre. The long term increase of grain prices from 1365 till 1437 and of rents due indicates, however, that there was no definite decrease of the population in Namur: on the contrary, it went on increasing, which inevitably resulted in a further intensification of agriculture.

The maintenance of a favourably high level of land productivity in the Low Countries throughout the 14th century until the early 15th, cannot be accounted for by agrarian factors only. Urban growth also played a crucial role. Under the impetus of industrial development and the expansion of world trade during the preceding centuries population density in the towns of the Low Countries had increased enormously. This specific structure encouraged further intensification of agriculture. Farmers were encouraged by better marketing opportunities in the urban markets to achieve more efficient combinations of factors of production. Intensification of farming was also encouraged by urban investment. Moreover, marginal crops could be shed because of the growth of trade. Finally, during harvest time the towns provided, when necessary, extra workers for the surrounding countryside, which again led to more intense exploitation of land.

More intensive farming increased the productivity of the land, which in turn, because of the higher agrarian incomes, caused further subdivision of peasant holdings and more intensive agriculture. Of course, in the end diminishing returns with a tendency towards zero could not be avoided because agricultural techniques were developing only slowly. Under such conditions, the trend of land productivity showed a tendency towards stabilization, and further divisions of peasant holdings would lead to a decrease in agricultural income *per capita*. As long as urbanization progressed – which was the case in Brabant, Holland, Zeeland, Limburg and Flanders at least until about 1430 – the possible decrease of agricultural output *per capita* in physical terms could be neutralized by an increase in the prices of essential food products and agrarian raw materials, reflected in an increase in the rent of land in money terms. Retaining a favourable income level in the agricultural sector therefore implied a transfer of money from the towns to the countryside. As long as textile exports were maintained, the costs of this transfer could be passed on abroad. Already in the 14th century, however, it was becoming more and more difficult for the oldest cloth towns to transfer the rising production costs to foreign buyers: such towns tried to solve the problem by depressing wages which resulted in the proletarisation of large numbers of textile workers and a decline in the demand for agricultural products from this sector. The dynamic expansion of the many small cloth centres in Flanders, Hainault, Brabant, Limburg and Holland and the successful development of Dutch maritime world trade fortunately offered important compensations in the Low Countries after 1350: cost savings by a simpler production structure and more rational trade and transport organization made it possible to absorb rising costs for essential foodstuffs without necessitating a parallel rise in selling prices of industrial products or a decrease in wages.

In conclusion one can say that the maintenance of a high level of agricultural income in the Low Countries was partly financed by the proletarisation of certain urban textile workers and partly by improvements in the organization of urban textile production. It is against this background, enhanced by the gradual improvement of agricultural methods, that the unique development of land productivity in the Low Countries until circa 1437 must be seen.

The Difficult 15th Century (1437-95)

The favourable, or less unfavourable, development of agricultural productivity in the Low Countries after 1350, compared with the other rural areas in Western Europe, was not maintained after the first third of the 15th century. From the 1420s to 1430s onwards, the decline of the traditional textile industry also affected the smaller cloth towns in Flanders and Brabant. Hanseatic sea trade underwent internal difficulties which led to serious tension between the Hanse and its rival, Holland, which also threatened Bruges's position. There were commercial difficulties with England, culminating in the import prohibition on English cloth in 1434. Finally, the military side-effects of the unification policy of Philip the Good were also damaging.

Increasing industrial unemployment in the towns, which most severely hit the traditional textile sectors, was not immediately compensated by a reallocation of labour to new, more promising urban sectors of industrial activity. Slowly a movement began of town workers back to the countryside: immigration in the opposite direction was, for the moment, at an end. This demographic change caused a further sub-division of small holdings in Flanders and Brabant during the first half of the 15th century. Moreover, the rural cloth industry in Flanders and Limburg, in comparison with the cloth industry of the greater and even of the smaller textile towns, could defend itself better against foreign competition, which must have proved attractive for the impoverished urban textile workers seeking employment.

Subdivision of peasant holdings – which went on all the time – in a region where development of the physical productivity of the land was already showing a tendency towards stabilization, could only result in a serious undermining of agricultural income *per capita*. There were a great number of victims of the famine and the epidemic of 1437-39, not only in the towns, where there was high unemployment, but also in the now overpopulated countryside. The resulting agrarian confusion often led to a fall in the total physical product which, in relation to income, was not compensated by an immediate increase in the size of holdings. Furthermore, under the influence of the decline in population in the towns and of the expansion of maritime trade, grain prices in the Low Countries moved more towards the lower European price level, so that money returns from land also declined. When falling money returns from land were not immediately followed by an adjustment in the rent level in leases – and such inertia often happened – the lag resulted in a loss of disposable income for the tenants.

Economic factors were not only responsible for the tendency of land productivity to decline in the Low Countries. Military operations within the national boundaries, especially in Holland, Liège and Namur but also in Flanders during the revolt of Bruges in 1436–37 and of Ghent in 1450–53, were the result of the Burgundian policy of unification and expansion of Philip the Good. During the rule of his son, Charles the Bold, the political and military effects became even more important: the clash of arms became louder as a result of the expansion of the Burgundian Empire and the suppression of internal revolts, while a systematic rise in taxation endangered incomes even more. The climax of military operations in the countryside was reached during the Flemish War (1483–92), which brought unrest to many regions of the Southern Netherlands.

The agricultural rents actually paid on the ducal domains in Flanders underwent two short but serious relapses, one about the middle and one about the end of the 15th century. This movement is confirmed by the aggregate money rent returns from the domains of Ninove and Petegem in Flanders and of Turnhout and Tienen in Brabant, and by the rent returns in kind from the farms of the Poor Relief in Lier, near Antwerp. The rent which the farm of Meldert paid to the Poor Relief fund in Louvain also diminished during these years, but only minutely. The same can be said of the incomes from tithes in Leerbeek and Pepingen in Southwestern Brabant, while those in the region of Namur on the contrary were much more reduced. In Limburg, incomes from tithes in the western part suffered some difficulties while those in the east remained almost stationary and even rose in some places.

Negative tendencies in land productivity are also confirmed by the development of population and the size of holdings. During the second half of the 15th century the number of tenants of small holdings on the ducal domains of Flanders decreased substantially, while at the same time the number of tenants of bigger holdings increased. There was, therefore, obviously a process of reconcentration of cultivated land in Flemish farming. In Brabant there was also, between 1437 and 1496, serious depopulation of the countryside, especially in the southern part of the duchy. Both phenomena implied a deintensification of agriculture in the relevant regions, which in conjunction with unchanging techniques signified falling land productivity. Under these circumstances it is surprising that some nominal agricultural money rents, due annually, show on the whole a more or less positive trend. In Meldert near Tienen, around Lier and Antwerp, and even on the Flemish domains the curves of some rents were still rising slightly (in real terms the rise even lasted a little longer). But the agricultural money rents actually paid during the same period were much lower than the agreed sum. Owners thus obviously tried to make the tenants bear the burden of decreasing land productivity as much as possible. Instead of lowering the money rents, due annually, they kept them high in agreement with the tenants, while being prepared to allow for delay or reduction of payment when too sharp a fall in production occurred. Such a policy could help explain the evolution of agriculture in the Low Countries during the 15th century: relative overpopulation of the countryside had reduced the income *per capita* of the inhabitants through higher rents and diminishing returns and had caused higher mortality rates, which – with a time lag – had resulted in a tendency towards reconcentration of farming units. When this concentration had occurred, the owners of the bigger farm units once again could demand higher rents per hectare, as the total product per farm unit increased and because the higher rents per hectare did not absorb entirely the increase in the total income per farm.

Although the general trend of development of land productivity was certainly negative during the second and last third of the 15th century in the Low Countries, it was far from catastrophic. There was no question of a brutal decline, of a continuing depression, or of permanent *Wüstungen*. On the contrary, in a progressive area like the Low Countries, the difficulties turned out rather as a stimulus for the introduction of important innovations. It was in this period particularly that new techniques for crop rotation were introduced, that more effective tools were invented and that specialization became more important. Flemish cheese and butter were a much sold product at the Brabant fairs, hop growing became widespread, the sale of cattle from Frisia, Groningen, Drenthe and Overijssel became important just at this moment. The revival of urbanization, which was favourably influenced by structural changes and by the growth of new more diversified industries in the bigger towns, gradually produced a positive effect on the rural economy and also on land productivity. At the same time this tended to induce a renewal of migration from the countryside to the towns, and in this way also substantially improved rural incomes.

The Effective Growth of the 16th Century

During the 16th and 17th centuries in the Low Countries, agrarian progress reached a new peak. This favourable development, however, was interrupted by the dramatic Revolt against Spain, which caused the centre of gravity of agrarian progress to shift from the south to the north of the Low Countries. Neither circumstance affected the increase in land productivity, not only in comparison with the 15th, but also with the 13th–14th centuries.

After the peace of 1492–93, rental values of land revived extraordinarily rapidly. Nominal agricultural money rents, due annually or actually paid, rose substantially everywhere: the increase around Antwerp, in Holland and in Flanders was most obvious. The total receipts from leases in money and in kind on the royal domains of Ninove and Petegem in Flanders and of Turnhout in Brabant, the total receipts from leases which the Poor Relief authority of Lier realized in kind from its many farms, and the income from tithes in the region of Namur and in Leerbeek and Pepingen in Southwestern Brabant all rose. While the average annual rent returns in kind of the Poor Relief authority in Lier were 15.8% higher during the period 1530–50 than during the 1430–54 period, the difference between the period 1501–50 and the period 1401–30 in the domain of Turnhout was as high as 51.2%. The annual receipts from tithe rents in Southwestern Brabant during the period 1530–60 were, on average, 13.3% higher than during the period 1424–45 and as much as 40% higher than at the beginning of the 15th century.

Yield ratios in the region of Bruges (Flanders) and in Lier and Louvain indicate analogous increases in land productivity. The yield ratios in Louvain, for example, during the 15th century for rye, barley and oats respectively were 1:6.2, 1:7.2, 1:4.2; during the period 1502–1726 they were respectively 1:6.9, 1:9.4, and 1:7.2; implying a rise of 11%, 32% and 71%. For wheat, an average ratio of 1:11 was even reached in this last period. Moreover, if only the favourable years of the 16th century were taken into account, the rise would be even more pronounced.

The real advance in agrarian productivity in physical terms came from different causes. The substantial population growth of the 16th century was undoubtedly an important element. This not only led to more intensive production techniques in agriculture but also to the diffusion of such techniques, inter alia, as the improved rotation system, which allowed two crops per year per unit of land and which led to the gradual disappearance of fallow land. The high rate of urban growth at this time was also an essential factor, allowing an even more intense integration of agriculture in the market economy. During the 16th century the urban population in the provinces of Holland, Brabant, Flanders, Hainault,

Overijssel and Gelderland reached 30 to 55% of total population. Not only did a systematic trade in urban dung, rubbish and suchlike come into being, which favourably influenced the physical productivity of land, but the increasing urban contacts also made the dissemination of new techniques easier. The proximity of the urban market and the fact of being included in a money economy encouraged the search for higher real returns.

It is important to note, however, that not all available statistics show favourable results. In the first place there are the data for the regions which had concentrated only on the production of grain, i.e. the old established agricultural areas of Walloon–Brabant and Hesbaye and of Cambrésis and Picardy. Round Cambrai the increase in incomes from tithes in kind had reached its peak between 1520 and 1540, and after that it fell to a slightly lower level. In Hesbaye and Condroz the peaks occurred even earlier and already just after 1520 a stabilization or a slow decline could be traced: the trends for the incomes from tithes in South Limburg, i.e. in the region of Saint-Truiden, Hannut, Tongeren, Maaseik, Weert and Meerssen, are clearest in this respect but they are complemented by those concerning the total money income from leases on the royal domain of Tienen and those concerning the agricultural rents in Meldert near Tienen.

The principal reason for early stabilization in these regions was the fact that they maintained a monoculture of grain: because of this imbalance the shock caused by massive imports of foreign grain could not be resisted. Thanks to the vigorous expansion of navigation in Zeeland and especially in Holland, the urbanized coastal areas of the Low Countries were invaded by the massive importation of Northern French and soon, principally, Baltic grain. The effect of this change was first felt in Holland: the grain trade (i.e. in bearded wheat) along the Meuse towards the towns in Holland fell away rapidly from the beginning of the 16th century onwards. Soon the expanding urbanized regions in Flanders and Brabant were also reached: from about 1540 onwards grain imports from Picardy, Cambrésis, Walloon–Brabant and Hesbaye had given way more and more to the import of Baltic grain. The unbalanced grain production in these regions did not seem to have enough flexibility to allow thorough structural change. This structural change was, moreover, not helped by the decline of the cloth towns in South Brabant: as a result there was less urban dung available at hand and a reorientation of demand by the towns could not be expected. In this way Walloon–Brabant and Hesbaye seemed to be evolving into a more or less extensive grain production area, partly in view of industrial beer brewing in a number of towns in the vicinity such as Louvain and Hoegaarden. The pays de Herve, on the other hand, which was nearer flourishing Liège, switched over successfully to cattle breeding and dairy production.

Walloon–Brabant, Hesbaye, Picardy and Cambrésis were not the only regions to have divergent statistics with respect to the further successful growth of the physical productivity of land. Even in the highly urbanized areas of Holland, Brabant, Flanders, Hainault, Overijssel and Gelderland not all series of agricultural money rents (when deflated by the market prices of cereals) continued to rise until the Revolt at the end of the 16th century. If, for example, the annual agricultural money rents per unit of land on the Flemish royal domains are deflated by the market grain prices, the rising trend had already reached a ceiling around 1535. However, an important correction has to be made here. For the Low Countries, the price of grain is a particularly bad deflator. Because of the rapid population increase and changing prices on the European market, grain prices in the Low Countries rose much faster than prices for non-essential agricultural produce. In comparison with the rest of Europe, therefore, exclusive use of the grain index as deflator for the nominal rental rates in the Low Countries leads inevitably to an unrepresentative result. If a general price index is applied, the series of agricultural rents in terms of constant prices shows a protracted rise that extends much further than to the period circa 1535.[2]

Another observation is more fundamental. During the 16th century, the population increase and the sweeping urbanization of the Low Countries contributed to the progress of productivity, not only in physical terms, but also in value terms. These advances relative to economic productivity form a crucial point that is often neglected. The massive importation of Baltic grain via Holland allowed agriculture in the urbanized coastal regions to concentrate on specialized and diversified crops that, because of urban demand and the better use of available land and labour, ensured higher incomes. Holland and Frisia concentrated particularly on dairy production and Groningen, Overijssel and Drenthe on cattle breeding. In Northern and Western Brabant and in Flanders hop growing and horticulture were very widespread; in Flanders and Zeeland, flax growing increased markedly. The production of flax in particular, with the attendant processing spinning and weaving, enabled large amounts of hidden unemployment in rural areas to be absorbed. It is precisely because of such optimal combination possibilities of land and labour with respect to flax and

---

[2] It can be asked why farmers in the Low Countries during the 16th century reduced grain growing in favour of other agricultural products given that grain prices increased much more quickly than those of other crops. This noticeable preference for non-grain output probably was connected with the fact that the labour-intensive character and the industrial processing potential of these crops enabled much hidden unemployment in agrarian areas to be absorbed. At the same time, this increase in non-grain production was accompanied by important scale effects, causing in turn higher productivity and more attractive selling prices.

linen that rents and sale prices of agricultural land in Zele (South-east Flanders) went on rising perceptibly until about 1580. In South and West Flanders and in Hainault tapestry and wool crafts expanded notably.

As a result of the expansion of the wool and flax industries in the countryside the number of tenants of small holdings (between about 3.00 and 7.50 acres) in Flanders increased greatly during the whole of the 16th century; after 1550 the number of tenants of typical submarginal holdings (between about 1.50 and 3.00 acres) also increased. In fact, the rural wool and linen industries in Flanders and Hainault along with horticulture in Brabant induced, through crop specialization, a striking increase in the economic productivity of the land. At the same time, they made a reduction in the scale of agricultural exploitation possible. This led to further intensification of cultivation, thus favouring where still technically possible the physical productivity of the land. In Holland and Frisia specialization in dairy production was mainly responsible for the increase in the economic productivity of land: accompanying this transition was a tendency toward larger farms which made possible, again within the framework of specialization, an increase in the physical productivity of the area. Presumably this was also the case with cattle breeding in the Northern and Northeastern parts of the Netherlands.

It is undeniable that within the confines of traditional agriculture, principally based on grain cultivation, there was not much more room for spectacular increases in the physical productivity of land during the 16th century. The Low Countries did, however, probably realize some advances in this area too, because in some regions the holdings could still be reduced considerably thanks to rural industry and to extreme urbanization: in this way further intensification of grain cultivation could be obtained, albeit on a rather limited scale. In fact, the import of grain from the Baltic was a much more important though indirect factor in rising agrarian productivity, as it allowed specialization of agriculture in a whole series of other crops in the Low Countries which, as a result, increased land productivity in value terms.

The Revolt and the Different Types of Revival in the North and the South, 1568–1648

The Revolt of the Low Countries against Spain, which started around 1568 and resulted, chiefly from the 1570s onwards, in large-scale military campaigns and extensive misery, had a brutal influence on agriculture in nearly all regions. The armies lived off the land for years and continuously plundered villages and hamlets.

Originally, military operations were concentrated in the North. In 1573 and 1574 the provinces of Zeeland, Holland and Gelderland were ravaged by the armies of the duke of Alva. Under the short rule of Requesens, Holland and Zeeland were most affected. From 1576 onwards, however, the centre of the war moved for a long time to the south. In Brabant rents and incomes from tithes had already collapsed in 1576–77, while Namur, Flanders, Hainault and Limburg followed in 1577–78. Even the neutral prince-bishopric of Liège did not escape troop movements and garrisons, with lower incomes from tithes as a result.

It is difficult to give a correct evaluation of production and productivity losses in agriculture during the war. In many places farms were burned and the fields stayed untilled for years because of the death or flight of the farmers or tenants; in other places the looting was of shorter duration and the fugitive farmers returned quite soon. Generally speaking, however, it may be concluded that losses during the last quarter of the 16th century, especially in the Southern Netherlands, were enormous. This point is illustrated by all available statistics.

Later, all statistical data also illustrate the revival, but the precise timing and extent were different for each region, and even for each locality. The military factor played an important role, as well as the fact that the Northern Netherlands became independent and were moving towards the 'Golden Age', while the southern regions stayed under Spanish rule. The southern provinces underwent an enormous emigration of skilled workers and came out of the war economically weakened.

The revival of agricultural rents, land prices, aggregate returns from leases in money and in kind, and yields from tithes in the South often started at the end of the 1580s. In most statistics an acceleration of the revival can be noted during the Twelve Years' Truce (1609–21). After the resumption of hostilities in 1621 the revival again weakened in places like Meldert near Tienen, in the county of Namur, in Maastricht and in the rest of the prince-bishopric of Liège which during this period became involved in both the Eighty and the Thirty Years' Wars. Elsewhere the revival continued, as for example in Eastern Flanders, where flax growing and processing guaranteed a very favourable development of agriculture, and also in Southwestern Brabant, where the growth of the capital Brussels and probably hop growing created favourable circumstances. This was also noticeable in Louvain where the agrarian revival was maintained and average harvests increased during that period.

The favourable development associated with agricultural revival in the South, however, had a serious disadvantage. In many regions it materialized at a lower level, and the record figures of the 16th century were generally not reached. This failure to attain the earlier level is very noticeable in the income from tithes in the county of Namur. The same can be said for the evolution of agricultural rents in Meldert near Tienen (Brabant), and for the tithe returns in Southwestern Brabant, in Southern Limburg and seemingly also in the prince-bishopric of Liège. Only rent and sale prices (in nominal money terms) of farm land in Zele (Eastern Flanders) showed an increase in comparison with the 16th century: this is probably due to the successful flax culture.

The surprising aspect of revival in the South is the fact that it was accompanied by important demographic growth and, if Brussels is not taken into account, by clear deurbanization. In Brabant, excluding the region of 's Hertogenbosch, the population density as a whole, which was about 76 inhabitants per km^2 in 1565, had fallen dramatically at the end of the 16th century, and had then increased again to 66 inhabitants per km^2 in 1615 and even to 79 per km^2 in 1665. At the same time the urban population in Brabant had fallen from 47% in 1565 to 42% in 1665. This implied an important increase in the rural population.

In view of this demographic development the limited character of the agrarian revival created a serious problem. The revival, as such, no doubt was connected with the important increase of the rural population, which in the middle of the 17th century was considerably higher than the peak reached before the Revolt. Therefore revival in grain production and land productivity seemed to have been determined by the intensification of agriculture, which in turn was a consequence of the remarkable demographic growth in the countryside. Deurbanization and ruralization, however, had a double effect; while they encouraged the intensification of agriculture once more, at the same time they induced rural autarky and stimulated a further weakening of the urban market economy, which had already suffered badly from the emigration in great numbers of merchants and highly skilled workers around 1600. Both factors, i.e. the weakening of the urban market economy and the increasing self-sufficiency of the countryside, were probably responsible for reducing the level of the revival of the land productivity in Brabant in value terms, and even in physical terms. There was only partial compensation from the economic and demographic growth of Brussels, which can be explained in view of the rise of capital cities for political reasons in Europe during the era of triumphant mercantilism.

It is probable that an analogous hypothesis about agrarian productivity can be formulated for the other regions in the Southern Netherlands, in so far as they evolved towards increasing ruralization and self-sufficiency. Only the rural parts of Flanders, on the contrary, which concentrated on the growing and processing of flax or on linen weaving, and as a result retained strong links with urban markets and international trade, appeared to undergo a revival of production and productivity, which rose above the level of the 16th century. Even with the assumption of deurbanization in Flanders, which is not yet proven, the hypothesis of land productivity rising again above the maxima of the 16th century remains plausible, because the export of linen was a sufficient substitute for stagnating urban consumption. Probably the growth potential of a more intensive agriculture based on integrated flax growing and linen processing had not yet been fully exploited in the 16th century and could now be realized more completely after the interlude of the Revolt and thanks to further demographic growth. Flanders would thus be the only region in the Southern Netherlands which progressed during the first half of the 17th century as far as land productivity was concerned: the combination of growth in physical and value terms was again essential.

The situation in the Northern Low Countries was, on the whole, considerably more favourable. Military operations there were shorter and less extensive, and they had no catastrophic effect on agricultural rents in money terms, which continued to rise vigorously after 1580 until about 1650–70. The data also indicate a marked increase of rents in real terms, when we take into account the obviously slower rise in the price of dairy produce and grain after 1600. The increase was especially spectacular in the urbanized regions of Holland, Utrecht and Zeeland. In Frisia and Groningen, it was less pronounced after 1600, while in the eastern regions the Thirty Years' War (1618–48) and the more traditional agricultural structure of the area tended to slow down the pace of advance during the first half of the 17th century.

It can consequently be stated as a valid hypothesis that, especially in the flourishing, urbanized coastal areas of the Northern Netherlands, the rising trend of land productivity, which had already been noted in the 16th century, clearly continued until about 1650–70. An effective increase in productivity in physical as well as in value terms was maintained. This improvement was principally the result of pronounced specialization: grain was imported *en masse* from the Baltic so that the coastal areas could concentrate on dairy produce, horticulture and industrial crops for the rapidly increasing affluent population of the growing towns. Specialization was further stimulated by substantial investments in agriculture: there were large-scale polder reclamation projects; drainage systems were improved in an exemplary manner by a whole series of technical innovations; new types of farm buildings came into being and new techniques of intensification were introduced into horticulture; the construction of a whole network of efficient waterways encouraged the sale of agricultural produce in the urban markets and the purchase of urban dung, better seeds, and so on. Finally, a trend towards a reconcentration of agricultural holdings, and the multiplication of specialized commercial and industrial handicrafts in the countryside, led to important improvements in organization. To this new peak in the rise of land productivity in physical and in value terms the name 'Dutch husbandry' was given. Together with what had been achieved during the same period in the flax and linen areas of Flanders, it was another cause of the effective progress of agrarian productivity beyond the maxima reached during the 16th century. It must, however, once again be underlined that this progress can only be understood if a combination of physical and economic productivity gains is taken into account.

Frisia, Groningen, Overijssel and Drenthe, which during the 16th century had concentrated with more success on cattle breeding, could not achieve similar progress. The reason was probably the loss of the important meat markets in Germany and in the Southern Netherlands during both the Eighty and Thirty Years' Wars: this could not be adequately compensated by the urbanization of the coastal areas in the Northern Netherlands. That was probably the reason why Frisia and Groningen gradually changed their specialization to dairy production.

The Delayed Depression of 1650–1750

The lower level at which the revival took place was not the only gloomy aspect of the agrarian economy in the Southern Netherlands and in the prince-bishopric of Liège during the 17th century. The revival did not endure. Already at the outbreak of the Thirty Years' War in 1618 and especially when hostilities were resumed in the Low Countries at the end of the Twelve Years' Truce in 1621, the returns from tithes in the border areas decreased. Afterwards, in the region of Maastricht and Liège, they fluctuated round a low and unstable level and again reached a nadir soon after the middle of the century and especially round 1700.

In the county of Namur the revival of income from tithes was already stabilized during the 1620s and 1630s; a first serious collapse occurred during the 1640s, and there was another dramatic one during the wars of the last third of the century. The situation in the duchy of Brabant was no better: in Louvain and Meldert, near Tienen, the revival had already stabilized around 1630; this stabilization was followed by a serious depression at the end of the 1630s and by a dramatic collapse of incomes during the last quarter of the century. The revival of tithe returns in Southwestern Brabant reached a peak around 1640, and was followed by gradual decline, resulting in spectacular losses in 1680. The same trend could be noted in the county of Flanders. The peak of the revival of agricultural rents was reached in Zele and Nevele (East Flanders) around 1640, whereupon rents declined continuously until the end of the 17th century, although there was a short revival in the 1650s. The physical yields of the harvests in the region of Alost (Southeast Flanders) reached their maximum during the 1630s, after which they diminished gradually until in the decade 1686–95 the annual produce was on average nearly 30% lower than during the 1631–40 period. Agricultural rents in nominal money terms for cultivated land and pasture in the Franc de Bruges and in the Castellany of Furnes (Western Flanders) also decreased from the 1640s onwards: here the decline was especially pronounced in the beginning phase of the downward movement, weakening slowly towards the end.

The wars of the second quarter of the 17th century, those of Louis XIV in 1667–68, 1672–78 and 1688–97 and finally the Spanish War of Succession, 1701–14, undoubtedly had a disastrous effect on the agrarian economy of the Southern Netherlands, and must therefore be taken into account when explaining the difficulties of the rural economy after 1630–50. The fear and destruction resulting from the war certainly prejudiced the development of agrarian productivity. It would, however, be wrong to claim that war was the only explanatory variable. Demographic and organizational factors also played an important role. In Brabant the growth of population, the impoverished urban economy, the process of deurbanization and of ruralization all encouraged a return to a self-sufficient, traditional agriculture. This sort of agriculture at first produced increasing returns, i.e. rising physical productivity of land, because of more intensive labour made possible by the greater number of countrymen. The increasing returns, however, soon started to decline again, because of a lack of expanding and differentiated demand from the towns: soon the marginal product would reach zero. The disruption caused by the wars during the second and particularly during the last quarter of the 17th century and the beginning of the 18th century finished it off completely.

Probably the same explanation is also valid for many other regions of the Southern Netherlands. In this context it must not be forgotten that export industries in the Southern Netherlands, especially the urban-based ones, were increasingly hindered by the inception of state mercantilism and by the economic decline of Central and Southern Europe. Mercantilism also, of course, harmed Flemish rural industry: here, however, the main variable explaining the stagnation was the collapse of colonial trade which was a direct result of the wars and only indirectly a consequence of mercantilistic policy.

The situation in the Northern Netherlands was not basically different. The rise of agricultural rents in nominal money terms, a rise which was vigorous in the coastal regions of the area during the 16th century and the beginning of the 17th century, gave way to stabilization around 1650 and even to a drastic decline around 1670 which continued until about 1750. The European depression of the 17th century therefore also had an influence on the North, although with some time lag in comparison with the rest of Europe and the Southern Netherlands. New agricultural specialisms, i.e. dairy production, horticulture and industrial crops, were particularly affected, in other words precisely those elements which had determined the favourable growth of agrarian productivity in the Northern Netherlands until about 1650.

The weakening urban economy in the coastal areas, which was, moreover, accompanied by considerable urban depopulation, was undoubtedly an important reason for the consolidation and even the decline of 'Dutch husbandry'. The weakening of the urban economy was the result of very high wages which in their turn were the consequence of successful industrial corporatism during the period of urban expansion. It was also partly determined by the dominance of state mercantilism in Europe, which hindered the import of artisanal luxuries and of industrial products from the Dutch market. Finally it resulted from the traditional structure of the commercial and colonial hegemony of Holland, which had reached saturation point. Urban demand for Dutch specialized foodstuffs thus decreased. The weakening of the urban economy and the creation of a bourgeois oligarchy implied also a shift of fiscal pressure from the towns towards the countryside: the expanding rural economy during the previous decades had created an economic surplus which was now a good subject of taxation. On the other hand, the overhead expenses of maintaining an expanded agrarian infrastructure increased costs relative to the smaller urban demand. This was also true in absolute terms: the dikes especially had suffered a great deal from the wars of Louis XIV. Their timbers were subject to attack by the so-called 'shipworms' and in urgent need of repair. The investment required for their replacement was considerably greater because the wooden dikes had to be rebuilt in stone.

Rural expansion and incomes fell sharply and soon land productivity also started to fall as a result of increasing neglect. During the 18th century the economic decline of the Dutch republic and the serious cattle epidemics (1714-20, 1744-54, 1769-84), consolidated the difficulties of agriculture in the coastal areas of the Northern Netherlands and decreased land productivity. The close connection between the development of agricultural productivity in progressive agrarian areas and the fortunes of the urban economy is thus once again fully illustrated by the example of 'Dutch husbandry'. Consequently, institutional as well as demographic factors had a strong influence on the success or lack of success of agriculture in process of modernization. The latter of course had a significant influence on the development of the urban economy too. Interdependency has to be acknowledged.

The development pattern of the Dutch coastal areas was not followed on the eastern and southern edges of the Republic, which had remained faithful to traditional agriculture. The demographic decline in population in North Holland, Frisia and Overijssel was indeed complemented by an increase in the population of Salland, Twente, the Veluwe and the bailiwick of 's Hertogenbosch. Intensification of agriculture in these traditional areas was undoubtedly encouraged by the increase of population and by the rise of rural industry there. Moreover, successful rural industry, which was the result of high wages in the Dutch coastal areas and of lower wages in this area, led to an increase in contacts with commercial Holland. It encouraged the transfer of modern agrarian know-how and is well illustrated by the expansion of tobacco growing in the eastern part of Utrecht and in Gelderland after 1650. At the same time the growth of the towns in the same periphery stimulated local market demand for essential foodstuffs. From this a rise in productivity of land in the east and south of the country can be assumed. The increase, however, remained mostly within narrow traditional limits, so that the threat of a Malthusian trap was inevitable, as illustrated by the case of Twente.

The Inception of the 'Agrarian Revolution', 1750–1800

The installation of Austrian rule over the Southern Netherlands brought a period of strong agrarian revival, and soon also a noticeable increase in land productivity. In the prince-bishopric of Liège, particularly round Liège and Maastricht, the revival was already underway before 1700, remaining hesitant for some time, and even suffering a relapse before becoming a confirmed trend from 1735–50 onwards: the expanding industrial area of Liège–Verviers–Aachen nearby must have played a dynamic role here too.

In Brabant some agrarian revival was already noticeable from the end of the Spanish War of Succession (1713), but only from the end of the Austrian War of Succession about the middle of the 18th century can a new and definite rise of agrarian productivity be traced; even then it is possible that some rises of agricultural rents and of sale prices of farm land were the result of the vigorous increase of the Brabant population rather than of higher land productivity. The counties of Namur and Hainault, and also East Flanders experienced the same process of development as Brabant. In the polders of the Franc de Bruges, of the Castellany of Furnes and of Antwerp, on the contrary, leases went on decreasing until after 1750 and only started to increase slowly after that date: in some areas the losses of the first decade of the century had not yet been made up by 1800.

Morineau, Vandenbroeke and Vanderpijpen have claimed, on the basis of yield ratios of grain, that the 18th-century revival of agricultural productivity should not be overrated, because the 13th and 14th century maxima were only just reached. These authors maintain that the record figures of the late Middle Ages were only surpassed during the 19th century and consequently that only then did the 'Agrarian Revolution' begin.

In our view this hypothesis is not completely acceptable. It has already been indicated that further subdivision of peasant holdings, growth of population, and increasing urbanization occurred in the Low Countries after 1350: they encouraged the geographical diffusion and the intensification of traditional grain growing to such an extent that there was not only a further rise in the physical productivity of land in certain areas but also of the average productivity in whole regions. Strong diversification of agriculture in the Low Countries after 1350 was no less important: dairy produce and horticulture were much expanded and there was a general diffusion of fodder and industrial crops. While such diversification also encouraged in some ways the physical productivity of the land, it was in the first place favourable for productivity in value terms. It is precisely this diversification which must be taken into account when assessing the 18th century.

The theory of Vandenbroeke–Vanderpijpen that during the 18th century there was not much room left within traditional grain growing in the Southern Netherlands for higher productivity is of course correct. Their data for the region of Alost (East Flanders) confirm this completely. The new tension between rising population and a limited supply of land, however, was in fact solved by new diversification in agriculture. The large-scale introduction of potatoes in the 18th century was the most important innovation in this respect. It soon increased the productivity of agricultural land in terms of calories and even in terms of money. This process of diversification extended rapidly. Moreover, the industrial expansion in the Flemish flax, linen and cotton areas and in the Walloon coal, metal and textile regions quickly created more demand for dairy produce and horticulture. In Brabant, there was no such industrial revival but here the specialization of artisan activities in the countryside induced the process of diversification. In Brabant the rapid increase in the population (74 inhabitants per km^2 in 1709, 82 in 1755 and 117 in 1806) was accompanied by relative deurbanization (42% of inhabitants of Brabant lived in towns in 1709 and only 34% in 1755 and 30% in 1806). Here, the real expansion of trade and crafts in the villages was initially responsible for the diversification of agriculture.

The different degree of adaptation to agricultural renewal is rather well illustrated by the important time lag between the rise of agricultural rents in the polders of Flanders and of Antwerp and their earlier increase in more developed agrarian areas. Farmers in the polders stayed faithful to traditional crops longer, so that productivity only increased very slowly. On the contrary, the expanding agricultural areas in the Southern Netherlands exemplified the earliest stages of the Agricultural Revolution during the 18th century, thanks to new crops and further diversification: thus in these areas an accelerated growth of productivity, although not within the framework of traditional grain growing, cannot be denied. On the other hand the Agricultural Revolution in its strict sense was only extended to traditional grain growing in the 19th–20th centuries, thanks to machines and natural and chemical manures.

In the Northern Netherlands the preliminary stages of the Agricultural Revolution during the 18th century were much less noticeable. In the coastal areas agricultural rents only recovered from the long malaise, which reached its trough around 1750, during the second half of the 18th century. It was, moreover, only a slow improvement which by 1800 was far from reaching the maxima of the middle of the 17th century. Against a background of weakened trade and industry, stagnating population, cattle epidemics and suchlike, the development of specialized agriculture in the coastal areas did not make a very dynamic impression: here productivity certainly did not reveal an Agricultural Revolution in the strict sense, which overshadowed the achievements of the 17th century.

In the rest of the Dutch republic, especially in the regions where rural industry allowed a further increase in population, the introduction of new crops, especially potatoes, gave rise to increases in land productivity. Here, as in the Southern Netherlands, the early phases of the Agricultural Revolution were noticeable during the second half of the 18th century. However, these preliminaries were decidedly weaker, as the expansion of industrial activities in the eastern and southern border regions of the Dutch republic was not as dynamic and progressive as in the Southern Netherlands and because the development of trade and of handicraft industry was not comparable to that in Brabant. Consequently in the 18th century the Agricultural Revolution of the Northern Netherlands was on the whole much slower than in the South. Only the completion of this Agricultural Revolution during the 19th–20th centuries would give the North the opportunity to achieve again an advance in the primary sector.

Further Reading

J. De Vries, *The Dutch Rural Economy in the Golden Age, 1500–1700* (New Haven: 1974).

P. Deyon, 'La production agricole et les communautés paysannes de Flandre et d'Artois du XVIe au XIXe siècle', in *Bulletin de la Société d'Histoire Moderne*, (1974), 1, pp. 2–5.

P. Deyon, *Contribution à l'étude des revenus fonciers en Picardie. Les fermages de l'hôtel Dieu d'Amiens et leurs variations de 1515 à 1789* (Lille: n.d.)

J.A. Faber, et al., 'Population Changes and Economic Developments in the Netherlands: a Historical Survey', in: *A.A.G.-Bijdragen* (Wageningen: 1965), 12, pp. 47–113.

J.A. Faber, *Drie eeuwen Friesland, Economische en Sociale Ontwikkelingen van 1500 tot 1800* (Wageningen: 1972), 2 vols.

L. Genicot, et al., *La crise agricole du bas Moyen-Age dans le Namurois* (Louvain: 1970).

J. Goy and E. Le Roy Ladurie (eds), *Les fluctuations du produit de la dîme* (Paris–The Hague: 1972).

P.M.M. Klep, *Groeidynamiek en stagnatie in een agrarisch grensgebied. De economische ontwikkeling in de Noordantwerpse Kempen en de Baronie van Breda, 1750–1850*, (Tilburg: 1973).

P.M.M. Klep, 'Urbanization in a Pre-industrial Economy. The Case of Brabant, 1374–1930', in: *Revue Belge d'Histoire Contemporaine*, VII, (1976), 1–2, pp. 153–68.

J. Meuvret, *Le problème des subsistances à l'époque de Louis XIV. La production des céréales dans la France du XVIIe et du XVIIIe siècle* (Paris: 1977).

M. Morineau, *Les faux-semblants d'un démarrage économique: agriculture et démographie* (Paris: 1971).

H. Neveux, *Les grains du Cambrésis (fin du XIVe–début du XVIIe siècle). Vie et déclin d'une structure économique*, (Lille (service de reproduction des thèses): 1974).

H.K. Roessingh, *Inlandse tabak. Expansie en contractie van een handelsgewas in de 17de en 18de eeuw in Nederland* (Wageningen: 1976).

J. Ruwet, 'Mesure de la production agricole sous l'Ancien Régime. Le blé en pays mosan', in: *Annales, E.S.C.* (1964), 19, 4, pp. 625–42.

J. Ruwet, 'Pour un indice de la production céréalière à l'époque moderne: la région de Namur', in *Les fluctuations du produit de la dîme*, ed. by J. Goy and E. Le Roy Ladurie (Paris–The Hague: 1972), pp. 67–82.

B.H. Slicher van Bath, *Een samenleving onder spanning. Geschiedenis van het platteland in Overijssel* (Assen: 1957).

B.H. Slicher van Bath, 'Yield Ratios, 810–1820', in: *A.A.G.-Bijdragen*, 10 (1963), pp. 1–264.

B.H. Slicher van Bath, *De agrarische geschiedenis van West-Europa, 500–1850* (Utrecht–Antwerp: 1960).

G. Sivery, *Structures agraires et vie rurale dans le Hainault à la fin du Moyen-Age* (Lille (Service de reproduction des thèses): 1973).

C. Vandenbroeke and W. Vanderpijpen, 'The Problem of the "Agricultural Revolution" in Flanders and in Belgium: Myth or Reality?', in: *Productivity of Land and Agricultural Innovation in the Low Countries (1250–1800)*, ed. by H. Van der Wee and E. Van Cauwenberghe (Leuven, 1978), pp. 163–170.

H. Van der Wee, *The Growth of the Antwerp Market and the European Economy (Fourteenth–Sixteenth Centuries)* (Paris–The Hague: 1963), 3 vols.

A.M. Van der Woude, *Het Noorderkwartier. Een regionaal historisch onderzoek in de demografische en economische geschiedenis van westelijk Nederland van de late middeleeuwen tot het begin van de negentiende eeuw* (Wageningen: 1972), 3 vols.

C. Verlinden, *et al.*, *Documents pour l'histoire des prix et salaires en Flandre et en Brabant, XIVe–XIXe siècle* (Bruges: 1959–73), 4 vols.

4

Agrarian History and Public Finances in Flanders, 14th to 17th Century[*]

In collaboration with E. Van Cauwenberghe

The domains of the counts of Flanders merit more attention from Belgian economic historians. To be sure, the domanial accounts have often been examined for information on institutions and administration, or to compile series of prices,[1] but the economic information in them has never been the subject of systematic study or in-depth statistical analysis. Nevertheless, the demesnial estates represent an invaluable source for the history of public finance in general, and are equally valuable for the agrarian and economic history of numerous specific regions. The relative importance of demesnial revenues to public finance declined materially towards the end of the Middle Ages, and throughout Western Europe the principle that '*le prince doit vivre du sien*' ceased to carry its former weight. Still, the dukes of Burgundy seem to have remained substantially unaffected by this development: around 1419–20 the Burgundian domains still provided a solid basis for public finances[2] and retained their importance well into the 16th century.[3]

Moreover, the detailed information in the accounts can furnish us with a dynamic overview of the economy of an estate or of a number of estates over a period of centuries. Consequently, if an estate sufficiently rich in agricultural information is chosen, such a study could be considered

---

[*] Interpretation of a provisional statistical analysis of the accounts of a domanial estate (1329–1604). The data used in this article are those used in E. Van Cauwenberghe, *Het vorstelijk domein van Deinze–Petegem–Astene–Drongen, 1329–1604. Beheer en financiën* M.A. thesis, K.U. Leuven, Louvain: 1969). The authors are indebted to the suggestions made by Professor J.A. Van Houtte upon reading the thesis, and are very grateful to him.

[1] H. Van der Wee, *The Growth of the Antwerp Market and the European Economy (Fourteenth–Sixteenth Centuries)* I (Paris–The Hague: 1963), pp. 173 ff.

[2] M. Mollat, 'Recherches sur les finances des ducs Valois de Bourgogne', in: *Revue Historique*, CCXIX (1958), pp. 311–2.

[3] See the accounts of the general receipts of Flanders (Archives départementales du Nord, Lille, Série B, pp. 1878–2706).

representative of the evolution of the rural economy of an entire region where, along with evidence of agricultural methods and yields, or together with that of seigneurial and peasant incomes, the commercial and industrial resources of the rural world appear in their proper setting.

Examination and Evaluation of the Source

The accounts of the estate of Deinze-Tronchiennes[4] were the subject of our first survey. This choice was determined by a variety of factors. First, these accounts show remarkable continuity.[5] Moreover, the estate was a large one, disposing of a sufficient variety of resources to make it representative of the rural economy. The period examined in our study was necessarily limited by the dates for which the estate's accounts have been preserved: from 1329 to 1604.[6] This has made possible an overview spanning several centuries, when these estates were of crucial importance to both public finance and the rural economy of the Low Countries as a whole.

The income derived from the estate of Deinze-Tronchiennes falls into two main categories: ordinary and extraordinary revenues.[7] The ordinary revenues consisted of fixed monetary income derived most often from old ground rents (*erfcijnsen*) on the one hand, and on the other from the profits of direct exploitation and fixed revenues in kind. Both, by their sale on the market or by their conversion to money at the market rate, could be annually adjusted to the current economic situation. Finally, there was also the income from farm rents in money. We have classified as extraordinary income all those revenues that fail to fit into these categories.

Compared to receipts, expenses were less regular and continuous. Nevertheless, here too it is possible to distinguish between ordinary and extraordinary expenses. Ground rents and annuities encumbering the estate belong to the first categorey, as do administrative costs, and the cost of maintaining the infrastructure of the estate (buildings, bridges, roads, and so on). We have classified among the extraordinary expenses the levies of the general receiver of Flanders, the general receiver of Finance, and all remittances to the central authorities, as well as new

---

[4] Deinze-Tronchiennes: province of East Flanders (Belgium), Ghent arrondissement. Administratively the estate belonged to the castellany of Courtrai for the region Deinze–Petegem–Astene and to that of Vieuxbourg of Ghent for the Tronchiennes region.

[5] Brussels, General Archives, Chambre des Comptes, comptes en rouleaux, nos 50–67; comptes en registres, nos 7149–60.

[6] The estate of Deinze-Tronchiennes was sold by the sovereign at the beginning of the 17th century.

[7] For a more detailed analysis of the administration and accounting of the Deinze-Tronchiennes estate we refer the reader to the above-mentioned thesis by E. Van Cauwenberghe.

pensions and annuities assigned '*sur le domaine*' to third parties by the count.

Receipts and expenses have been consistently calculated using the criterion of the '*somme due*'. In those instances where the receiver later granted a reduction to a debtor, recording the fact as a reimbursement in his accounts, we have systematically corrected the original sum. For the rest we have not taken account of deferred payment: before 1500 such delays were in any case exceptional and even after that date, when deferment of payment had become more common, the arrears were usually paid soon after their due date. It was only towards the end of the period studied (toward the end of the 16th century) that payments became more irregular because of the war. At that time, reductions in arrears became more frequent, and then of course we corrected, as mentioned before, the original sum.

Statistical Methods

The statistical processing of our quantitative data was done by computer. The computer was primarily used for simple statistical calculations: calculating trends in the various categories of receipts and expenses over a century (making use of moving interquartile medians over 13 years); calculating the distribution of these categories over whole systems and its evolution over time (for example the relative annual distribution of the different categories of variable revenues within the total variable revenues and within the total revenues; and the relative annual distribution of the various categories of ordinary and extraordinary expenses against total expenses).

The quantity and variety of data available regarding revenues derived from farm rents are sufficient for more sophisticated statistical analysis. The following information is available for each farm unit: the name of the farmer, the object of farming (seven categories: forests, fields, meadows, farms, tolls, mills, fisheries), the length of the farm lease, the price of the lease, and (for the first three categories) the area of the land leased.

Using this information the computer made a whole series of cross tabulations for the whole of the available information, at the same time calculating their relative distribution. In addition, the computer grouped the information by 50-year period (roughly) (1329–99, 1400–49, 1450–99, 1500–49, 1550–1604), making similar calculations and graphs and thus simplifying comparisons over time.[8]

---

[8] For fuller details on the use of the computer we refer the reader to the above-mentioned thesis. See also: H. Van der Wee and E. Van Cauwenberghe, 'L'utilisation de l'ordinateur pour l'étude des domaines royaux aux Pays-Bas (XIVe–XVIIe siècle)', in: *Actes du Ve Congrès International d'Histoire Economique* (Leningrad: August 10–14, 1970), pp. 1–12.

We intend to pursue further this operational research in historical statistics. Many other series of domanial accounts are currently being examined. We hope to apply these calculations of correlations to the various chronological series available. If this research and analysis yields satisfactory results, we also intend to venture into cliometrics. We shall also undertake the construction of specific quantitative models in a quest for functional relationships among the different variables of the rural economy, verifying these relationships by the regression method.[9]

The goals of this article are, however, much more modest: it is confined to a statistical analysis of the accounts of the first estate examined, Deinze-Tronchiennes, with a tentative effort at qualitative interpretation.

Rural Demography, Technical Progress, and Size of Holdings

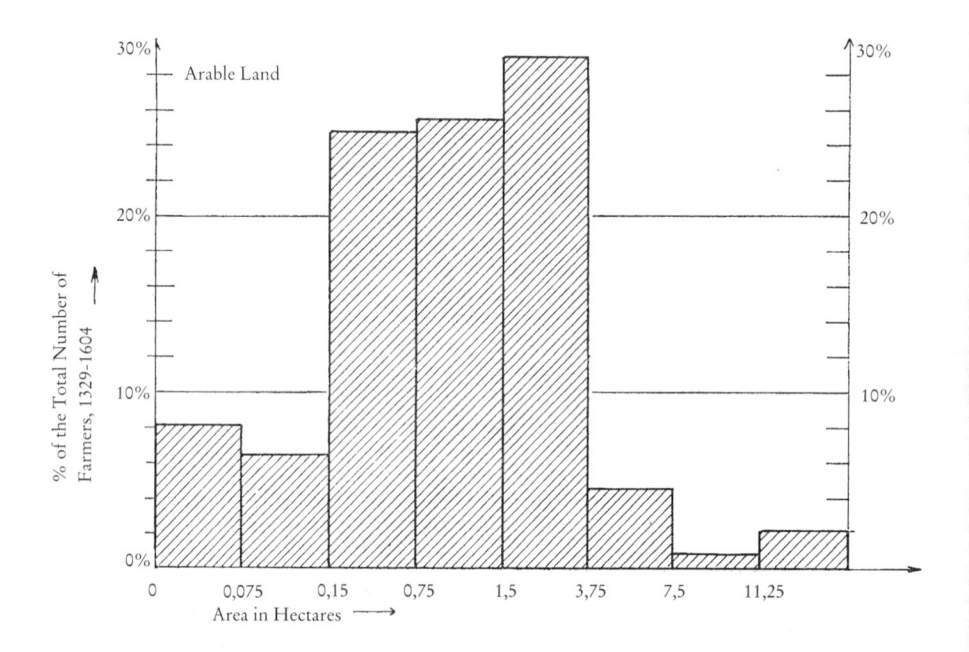

Figure 4.1: *Relative distribution of agricultural holdings in Flanders, 1329–1604.*

---

[9] H. Van der Wee, H. Daems, E. Van Cauwenberghe, 'Some New Methodological Concepts and the Use of the Computer', in: *Quantitative Economic History, Actes du colloque sur l'ordinateur et les sciences sociales. Brussels: February 25–27, 1971* (Brussels: 1972), *passim.*

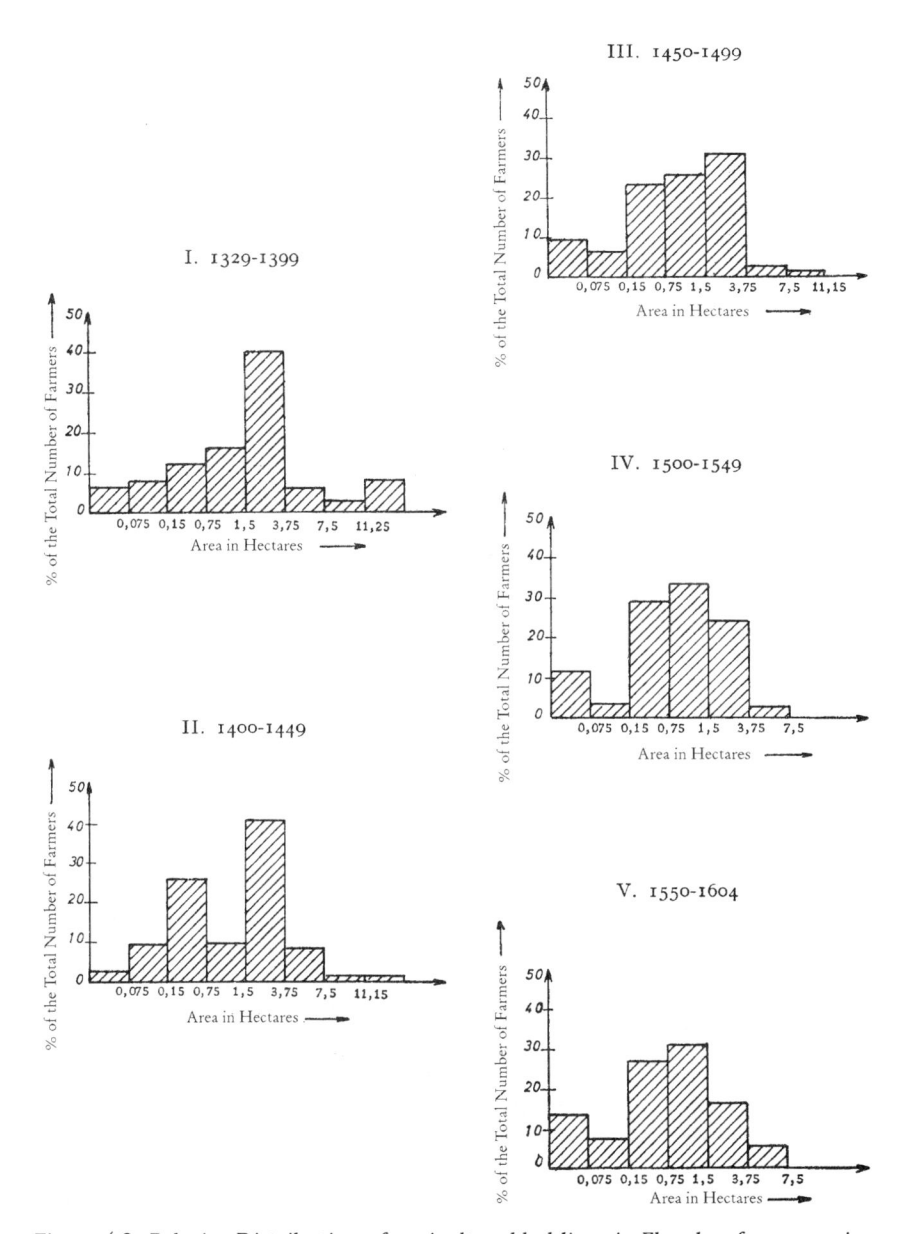

AGRARIAN HISTORY AND PUBLIC FINANCES IN FLANDERS 73

I. 1329-1399

II. 1400-1449

III. 1450-1499

IV. 1500-1549

V. 1550-1604

Figure 4.2: *Relative Distribution of agricultural holdings in Flanders for successive 50-year periods, 1329–1604.*

Figures 4.1 and 4.2 show the intriguing results of a cross tabulation of the area of leased fields. The total area of the leased fields was first divided into the holdings of a given farmer, that is to say all the fields rented by a single farmer in a given year were grouped together and their respective areas totalled.[10] Then, in function of the number of farmers, we calculated the frequency distribution of holdings, classifying them by area, for example what percentage of farmers leased holdings with an area between 0.075 and 0.15 hectares, what percentage of farmers leased holdings with an area between 0.15 and 0.75 hectares, and so on.

Based on annual data for the entire period examined, from 1329 to 1604, the frequency table shows the overwhelming preponderance of holdings between 0.15 and 3.75 hectares in area: half of the holdings consisted of from 0.15 to 1.50 hectares, 29% of 1.50 to 3.75 hectares. Figure 4.1 thus clearly confirms the further subdivision of peasant holdings and it can be deduced that Flemish agriculture was extremely intensive in the region of Ghent during the period from the 14th to the 16th centuries.[11] A more profound analysis of the data, making the same calculations for successive 50-year periods, enables us to detect important changes in relative distribution over time by means of the frequency tables (Figure 4.2). During the first period, from 1329 to 1399, holdings of 1.5 to 3.75 hectares were clearly predominant, representing some 40% of all farmers. The other categories did not yet include a substantial number of farmers. However, the number of farmers renting more than 11.25 hectares of land was relatively large, accounting for 8% of the total. These large holdings represented a total area greater than that rented by the entire category of farmers holding between 1.5 and 3.75 hectares.

The 15th century brought many changes. At first holdings between 1.5 and 3.75 hectares continued to grow slightly relative to the others. On the other hand the number of large holdings decreased noticeably, whereas those between 0.15 and 0.75 hectares increased, now representing 26% of the total. From 1450 onwards this tendency towards smaller parcels was accentuated, eroding the number of holdings between 1.5 and 3.75 hectares and progressively increasing the relative share of holdings between 0.15 and 0.75 and between 0.75 and 1.5 hectares. During the second half of the 16th century the relative share of holdings between 1.5 and 3.75 hectares had already declined to 16.35% of the total, whereas larger holdings were virtually extinct.

What conclusions can be drawn from this shift towards smaller farms? First of all, in the neighbourhood of Deinze, a small town between Ghent and Courtrai, relatively large holdings survived into the 14th century,

---

[10] It is possible that some farmers rented or owned other fields outside the domain, but investigation of sample cases has shown that this was a marginal phenomenon and statistically insignificant.

[11] For more details on the origins of this marked tendency towards smaller farms in the sandy terrains of the Flemish interior, see: A.E. Verhulst, *Histoire du paysage rural en Flandre de l'époque romaine au XVIIIe siècle* (Brussels: 1966), pp. 98–140.

but the typical farm consisted of from 1.5 to 3.75 hectares. Taking into account their technical capabilities[12] and the socio-demographic structure of the period,[13] this seems to have been the optimal farm size. On the other hand the tendency towards progressively smaller parcels, noticeable from the 15th century on, cannot be entirely explained by demographic factors. On the contrary, the Flemish population seems to have stagnated during the 15th century,[14] and probably even declined towards the end of the century.[15]

Paradoxically, the annual averages of the total surface of land farmed out by the domanial estate show a substantial rise in the course of the

---

[12] B.H. Slicher van Bath, *De agrarische geschiedenis van West-Europa, 500–1850* (Utrecht–Antwerp: 1960), pp. 196–208. Also 'The Rise of Intensive Husbandry in the Low Countries', *Britain and the Netherlands. Papers delivered to the Oxford–Netherlands Historical Conference of 1959* (London: 1960), pp. 130–53.

[13] E. Sabbe, 'Grondbezit en landbouw: economische en sociale toestanden in de Kasselrij Kortrijk op het einde van de XIVe eeuw', in: *Handelingen van de Koninklijke Geschied-Oudheidkundige Kring van Kortrijk*, Nieuwe Reeks, XV (1936), pp. 394–458.

[14] The general tendency of grain prices to rise and the marked intensity and greater frequency of cyclical crises in Flanders during the 14th century (A.E. Verhulst, 'Bronnen en problemen betreffende de Vlaamse landbouw in de late Middeleeuwen, XIIIe–XVe eeuw', in: *Ceres en Clio, Zeven variaties op het thema landbouwgeschiedenis* (Wageningen: 1964), pp. 218–33) imply pronounced demographic pressure at that time; nevertheless this proves at the same time that tension persisted throughout the entire century, in other words that demographic resilience (either through surviving the crises or by rapid demographic recovery after each crisis) was great. This resilience necessarily had an economic basis. The reverse was the case following the great political crisis of 1379 to 1390: there is a certain degree of recovery but the demographic vigour seems to have definitively abated. Grain prices in Flanders tended to stagnate over the whole 15th century, even declining in the second third of the century. In general such cyclical crises are manifestly less frequent, shorter, and less severe (Verhulst, note 11, p. 231). This dual phenomenon can only be explained by a decrease in demographic pressure, that is to say a tendency for the population to stagnate or even to decline. Naturally, it is always possible, even probable, that the phenomenon was more urban than rural, as was the case for Brabant before the last quarter of the 15th century (after which the countryside was more severely affected), but such a situation also had inevitable negative repercussions on agricultural incomes.

It should be noted that Professor Verhulst interprets the above information differently: he considers it more likely that the population declined in the 14th century and increased during the 15th. If this interpretation is understood as implying a *chronic decline* during the 14th century (in particular at the end of the century) and an *increase in the rural population* during the 15th century, the two interpretations are not mutually exclusive.

[15] Professor Verhulst (note 11, p. 224) does not believe that the acute political crisis and the military depredations in the Flemish countryside at the end of the 15th century resulted in any great demographic decline. We hold a different point of view (Van der Wee, *The Growth of the Antwerp Market...* II, pp. 89–93). See also: C.D.P., 'Etat de la campagne dans notre province au temps de Charles le Téméraire et de Maximilien', in: *Annales de la Société d'Emulation de Bruges* (1844). Also: J.H. Munro, 'Bruges and the Abortive Staple in English Cloth: an Incident in the Shift of Commerce from Bruges to Antwerp in the late Fifteenth Century', in: *Revue Belge de Philologie et d'Histoire* XLIV (1966), 4, pp. 1147–8.

15th century in comparison with the average for 1329 to 1399: 34% for the average between 1400 and 1449, and 57% for the period from 1450 to 1499. The number of farm leases also rose, going from some 50 per year between 1329 and 1449 to as many as 93 yearly between 1450 and 1499. This dual phenomenon can be explained only by the agricultural depression, already apparent in the 14th century and, despite a definite recovery after 1390, again worsening in the second third of the 15th century.[16] The increase in the areas leased out did not in fact involve bringing new portions of the estate under cultivation, but represented the reconversion of the estate's inheritable ground rents and feudal levies into leasehold farms. In general this situation only arose when, upon the decease of the incumbent, the estate's receiver could find nobody willing to take over the encumbered land. It is obvious that stagnating or falling agricultural prices and ground rents were responsible for the reluctance of many 15th century peasants to take over lands encumbered with a hereditary quit rent. The receiver had no other option but to grant leaseholds on those farms. For the count, this practice had, even at the time the first such leases were granted, the disadvantage of following unfavourable trends in prices and rents far more closely, though in more favourable circumstances it could work to the count's advantage, at the same time helping to modernize the institutional structure of the estates.

The phenomenon of reconversion into leasehold farms did not, however, resolve all the problems. Nor does it entirely explain the tendency to subdivide cultivated land into progressively smaller parcels, until typical farm size was no longer of the order of 1.5 to 3.75 hectares, but was firmly established within the three central categories ranging from 0.15 to 3.75 hectares.

We would normally expect demographic stagnation or decline to encourage the concentration of land under cultivation. If this did not occur, other factors must have been at work: either agricultural families split up or urban families, severely affected by the crisis in the textile industry, emigrated to the countryside. This multiplication of the farms was feasible thanks to the fact that rural industry was on the rise, providing a supplementary source of income, and to technical progress that rendered such small farms more than was needed to support a family. It was also

---

[16] A study by H. Neveux, 'Dîmes et production céréalière. L'exemple du Cambrésis (fin XIVᵉ–début XVIIᵉ siècle)', in: *Annales E.S.C.* (1973), 2, pp. 512-8, confirms our interpretation of the Flemish economic cycles, which were directly linked to those of the Cambrésis: agricultural yields in the Cambrésis clearly tended to decline from 1370–80 to 1460–9. The opposition between the recovery observed after 1470 in the Cambrésis and our hypothesis of Flemish stagnation lasting until 1495 can be explained by the catastrophic nature we have attributed to the Flemish political crisis at the close of the century. We wish to extend our sincere thanks to Mr Neveux for having made his text available to us before its publication in the *Annales*.

encouraged by the rise of an urban middle class that tended to boost the demand for animal husbandry, thus increasing the amount of fertilizer available and extracting better yields from smaller fields.[17]

It is of course probable that all these factors operated simultaneously: there are traces of most of them. Which were dominant? It is extremely difficult to determine this since only limited quantitative data are available. Nevertheless, despite the fact that the minimum area of a typical farm declined, the total amount of grain produced by the peasants on the estate seems gradually to have risen (see Figure 4.3). It is thus entirely possible and even probable that there was an increase in land productivity.

The trend towards smaller holdings continued during the 16th century. At the same time the total surface of land leased out yearly was no longer increasing, and thus reconversion no longer played a significant role. The demographic factor on the other hand came into full play. The population increase during the first decades of the 16th century exerted a tangible influence on the continuing tendency towards smaller farms, but its impact was probably not decisive. In fact, from the second half of the 16th century onwards the population again stagnated, declining dramatically during the final third of the century,[18] whereas the trend towards smaller farms continued unabated. Beginning in the period from 1500-49 the relative share of the two categories from 0.15 to 0.75 hectares and from 0.75 to 1.5 hectares, even considered separately, was greater than that of the group from 1.5 to 3.75 hectares. By the end of the period from 1550 to 1604 the two categories grouping farms of from 0.15 to 1.5 hectares had become clearly predominant, in other words the area of the typical farm had again shrunk considerably, though demographic factors cannot be considered decisive in this.

Consequently, other variables also need to be taken into consideration for the 16th century: these were above all the generalized use of technical innovations in Flemish agriculture, particularly noticeable during the first half of the 16th century; and to an even greater extent the expansion of rural industry, becoming extremely marked with the expansion of the linen industry in the second third of the 16th century.[19]

---

[17] P. Lindemans, *Geschiedenis van de landbouw in België* I (Antwerp: 1952), pp. 49–94; A.E. Verhulst, 'Het probleem van de verdwijning van de braak in de Vlaamse landbouw, XIIIe–XVIIe eeuw', in: *Natuurwetenschappelijk Tijdschrift* 38 (1956), pp. 213–9.

[18] See, among others: K. Maddens, 'De krisis op het einde van de XVIe eeuw in de kasselrij Ieper', in: *Revue Belge de Philologie et d'Histoire* 39 (1961), pp. 356–90; Van der Wee, *The Growth of the Antwerp Market* II, pp. 186–91; E. Sabbe, *De Belgische vlasnijverheid* I. *De Zuidnederlandsche vlasnijverheid tot het verdrag van Utrecht (1713)*, pp. 175 ff.

[19] H. Van der Wee, 'Conjunctuur en Economische Groei in de Zuidelijke Nederlanden tijdens de 14e, 15e en 16e eeuw', in: *Mededelingen van de Koninklijke Vlaamse Academie voor Wetenschappen, Letteren en Schone Kunsten van België. Klasse der Letteren* 27 (1965), (Brussels: 1965), pp. 11–3.

Agricultural Trends and the Relationship between the Landlords and Tenants

Figure 4.3 gives an overview of the evolution in variable income from the estate of Deinze-Tronchiennes over several centuries. The relative share of the various groups in comparison to the total variable income can be followed on a yearly basis for the period from 1363 to 1604: it was derived principally from farming out meadows, arable land, tolls and mills.

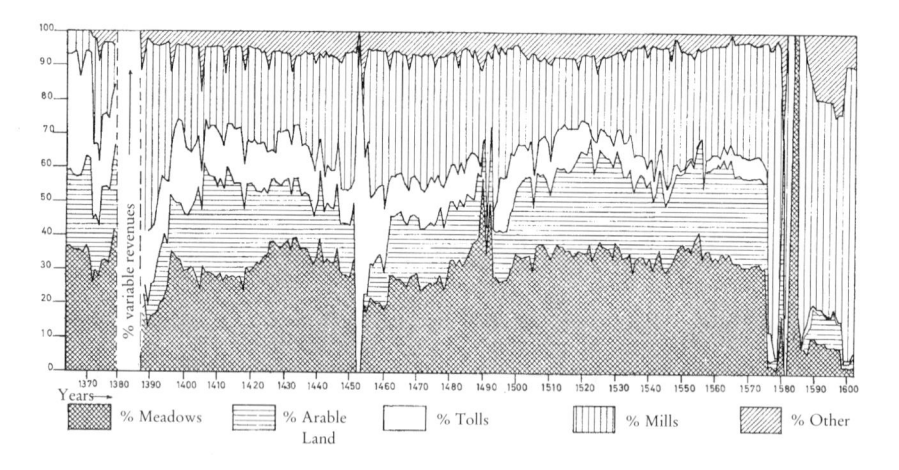

Figure 4.3: *Variable revenues of the domain of Deinze-Tronchiennes: relative distribution of the various categories (1363–1604).*

The progressive decline in the relative contribution of tolls is rather surprising. The considerable expansion of European trade in the 16th century would thus seem to have had no appreciable effect on traffic in that region. On the contrary, there is a clear relative decline in the tolls collected during this period. Nevertheless, Flanders participated actively in the European vitality of the time: its wool and linen industries were flourishing and Deinze, located on the Courtrai–Ghent road, was well-situated geographically.

It should be noted, however, that tolls had little impact on the route between the great urban centres of Flanders and Brabant, affecting mainly the secondary traffic of regional importance. Even in this more limited context the relative decline in the revenues derived from the toll is highly significant. It confirms the stagnation of the Flemish economy in the course of the 15th century and its progressive weakening in comparison with the economies of Brabant and Liège during the following century.[21] Antwerp, Brussels and Liège had doubtless already become the most dynamic growth centres. Flanders had become an industrial satellite of Brabant, its economy based primarily on rural industry.[22] The Flemish urban economy seems to have lost its former vigour in numerous places; towns like Deinze had fallen asleep and returned to their former agricultural and industrial autarky.

Farm rents for meadows, arable land and mills thus took on greater significance. But within this context we discover a surprising tendency towards the simultaneous reduction in the proportion of revenues derived from meadows and arable land beginning in the second third of the 15th century. The decline in the relative contribution of arable land is easily explained by the agricultural depression and by the decline of the traditional urban cloth trade, though on the other hand one would tend to expect a corresponding rise in the relative contribution of meadows. However, the growth of animal husbandry, seemingly significant in the 1420s, either did not continue into the second third of the century or did not entail a corresponding growth of pasturage.

What then did this relative decline in revenues derived from meadows and arable land imply? The domanial mills appreciably increased their relative share in the total. Since the mills always took a fixed percentage of the grain the peasants were obliged to have it ground there, and since these receipts in kind were always sold on the market, it implies that the peasants brought more grain to the domanial mills and, moreover, that the volume of these receipts *in natura* grew out of all proportion to the decline in grain prices.

The above observation is an excellent illustration of the domanial policy of the count. The decline of farm rents[23] increased the amount of grain at the disposal of the peasants (formerly obliged to sell more of their

---

[20] Van der Wee, *The Growth of the Antwerp Market* II, pp. 185–90 and 224–55; E. Coornaert, *La draperie-sayetterie d'Hondschoote (XIVe–XVIIIe siècle)* (Paris: 1931).

[21] H. van der Wee, *Löhne und wirtschaftliches Wachstum. Eine historische Analyse*, Kölner Vorträge zur Sozial- und Wirtschaftsgeschichte 6 (Cologne: 1969), p. 18.

[22] For a more balanced point of view, especially for Bruges: W. Brulez, 'Brugge en Antwerpen in de 15e en 16e eeuw: een tegenstelling?', in: *Tijdschrift voor Geschiedenis* 83 (1970), pp. 15–36.

[23] On the problem of commuting feudal rents to leasehold farms: G. Fourquin, *Histoire économique de l'Occident médiévale* (Paris: 1968), pp. 217–9, 332–45.

crop to pay their rents and tithes). The social stratification of the estate – made up primarily of small holdings – implied that the larger amounts of available grain were not sold on the market to purchase manufactured goods but consumed on the spot. In that case the peasants had to make use of the domanial mill. In this manner the lord recouped any losses from declining farm rents.

Where the domanial and seigneurial structures were still intact the great landowners could thus still use their other domanial or seigneurial rights to recover losses suffered through the diminishing farm rents paid by their tenants. We all know how the feudal lords of Central and Eastern Europe used this option to their own advantage.[24] It is interesting, however, that even in 15th century Flanders the balance of power between the owners and the users of land was still such that the former could exact their seigneurial or domanial rights to compensate for revenue losses due to cyclical economic trends.

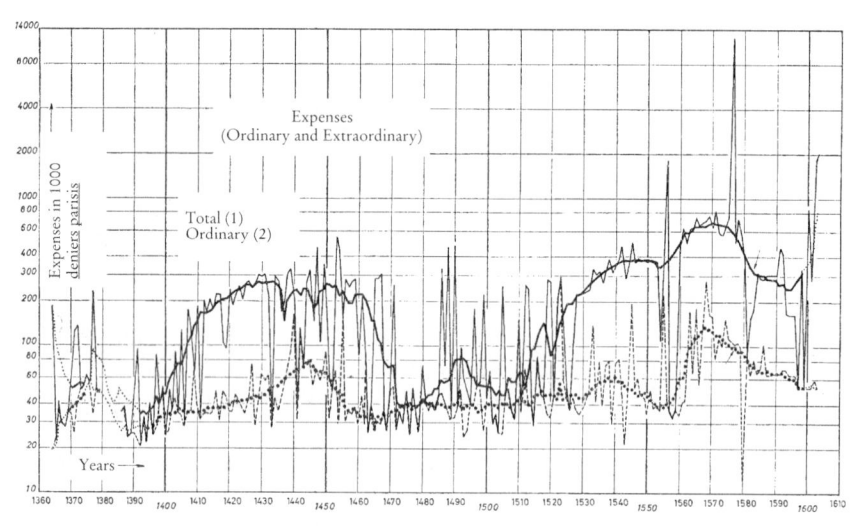

Figure 4.4: *Expenditures on the domain of Deinze-Tronchiennes, 1363–1604 (total/ordinary)*.

Starting at the end of the 15th century, but especially at the beginning of the 16th century, this trend in the relative evolution of the various categories of revenue reversed itself. Under the influence of demographic recovery and rising grain prices, farm rents rose. Arable land was

---

[24] F. Lütge, *Geschichte der deutschen Agrarverfassung vom frühen Mittelalter bis zum 19. Jahrhundert* (Stuttgart: 1963), pp. 100–34; W. Abel, *Geschichte des deutschen Landwirtschaft vom frühen Mittelalter bis zum 19. Jahrhundert* (Stuttgart: 1962), pp. 145–8.

especially sensitive to this. It is very suggestive that until the 1520s revenues derived from rents of mills suffered: the amount of grain available declined since the small farmers, who had higher rents to pay, sold part of their available grain.

This trend again reversed itself in the second quarter of the 16th century: even though the population was still growing the amount of surplus grain began rising once more, without, however, entailing a lasting drop in the relative revenues derived from meadows and arable land. The growing surplus was thus probably the result of technical progress and of the expansion of rural industry, compensating for the rise in farm rents. It should also be kept in mind that the size of the average farm on the estate was smaller than it had been in the 15th century. The rising grain surplus would tend to support the hypothesis that peasant income in Flanders began to increase again in the second quarter of the 16th century.[25]

Domanial Income and Public Finances

The domanial accounts provide us with information about far more than the agriculture of Flanders. They offer suggestive information on the financial methods and policies of the dukes of Burgundy and of the Habsburgs during the 15th and 16th centuries.

Figure 4.4 gives us this macro-economic picture: it juxtaposes the ordinary expenses of the receiver for the estate of Deinze-Tronchiennes with his global expenses for the period 1363-1604. The extraordinary expenses, added to the ordinary expenses to obtain global figures, consist chiefly of the prince's levies, often payable in advance by the domanial receiver to the general receiver of Finances.

The comparison in Figure 4.4 allows us to formulate one immediate conclusion. The reigns of John the Fearless (1404-19), of Philip the Good (1418-65), of Charles V (1515-55) and of Philip II (1555-98) show a systematic integration of the estates into the financial policy of the government. John the Fearless and Philip the Good exploited their domains to the utmost. This integration consisted essentially of regular levies advanced on domanial revenues, that is to say the receivers of the ducal estates had to advance substantial sums to the prince out of their own pockets. In effect they acted as his money-lenders, making short-term loans at no interest. The salaries the prince paid the receivers for their work, under strict supervision of the general receiver, and the honours of their office served in lieu of interest. The method was extremely subtle and

---

[25] H. Van der Wee, 'Das Phänomen des Wachstums und der Stagnation im Lichte des Antwerpenes und südniederländischen Wirtschaft des 16. Jahrhunderts', in: *Vierteljahrschrift für Sozial- und Wirtschaftsgeschichte* 2 (1967), pp. 209-13.

astute. During a period of increasing administrative centralization, the Burgundian state made full use of the heightened respect and honour acquired by their officials in order to demand financial favours from them, in addition to administrative zeal and political loyalty. It is thus by no means surprising that public finances remained quite sound under John the Fearless and especially under Philip the Good. Philip's reign was, moreover, characterized by a clear reduction of monetary debasements after 1430, by a marked decline in short-term borrowing – also reflected in falling interest rates[26] – and by the establishment of treasury reserves.[27]

Philip the Good's successors did not pursue this prudent policy. Charles the Bold and Maximilian of Austria appreciably reduced the advances of the receivers and turned systematically to the money market of Bruges, where bankers regularly made them substantial short-term loans, often at exorbitant interest rates.[28] There is consequently nothing astonishing in the deteriorating financial situation of these two princes, culminating in a flood of monetary devaluations during the reign of Maximilian (1478–89).

The domanial policies of Philip the Good and those of Charles V show clear resemblances. The latter reintroduced the use of systematic advances to integrate the estates more thoroughly into the financial policy of the government, thus deriving maximum yields from them. There was, however, one significant difference. Under Philip the Good assignations were less regular. In addition they were always linked to the real capacity of each estate. Under Charles V, on the other hand, such prudence no longer prevailed. After 1530 the levies were dictated solely by the insatiable needs of the Public Treasury, an inevitable consequence of the policies of Charles V. By that time, moreover, the Emperor had already begun relying more heavily on the Antwerp money market.[29] By combining his Antwerp loans with the levies on his domanial receivers, in addition of course to fiscal measures[30] and shipments from Spain,[31] the Emperor could hold out. Indeed the interest rates paid on the Antwerp money

---

[26] Van der Wee, *The Growth of the Antwerp Market* I, p. 526.

[27] P. Kauch, 'Le trésor de l'Epargne, création de Philippe le Bon', in: *Revue Belge de Philologie et d'Histoire* IX (1932), pp. 703–14.

[28] J. Bartier, *Charles le Téméraire* (Brussels: 1944), pp. 245 ff.; Van der Wee, *The Growth of the Antwerp Market* I, p. 526; II, pp. 86–7.

[29] F. Braudel, 'Les emprunts de Charles Quint sur la place d'Anvers', in: *Charles Quint et son temps* (Paris: 1959), pp. 191–201.

[30] J. Craeybeckx, 'Aperçu sur l'histoire des impôts en Flandre et en Brabant au cours du XVIe siècle', in: *Revue du Nord* 29 (1947), pp. 87–108.

[31] R. Carande, 'Das Westindische Gold und die Kreditpolitik Karls V', in: *Spanische Forschungen des Görresgesellschaft* I, 10 (Münster, Westphalia: 1955), pp. 1–22.

market continued to decline until the mid-16th century.[32] The limits of this financial expansion were reached after 1550. From then on catastrophe became inevitable, resulting in bankruptcy in 1557. The domanial accounts also bear witness to this: they offer proof that these resources, too, had been totally depleted.

Philip II continued to pursue the domanial policies of his father, but the effects of the war and the devastation of the countryside reduced the value of the estates to the Public Treasury. Domanial revenues were permanently marginalized. This was a definitive decline, reflecting 15th and 16th century changes in political structure.

---

[32] Van der Wee, *The Growth of the Antwerp Market* I, p. 526.

III

TRADE

5

Trade in the Southern Netherlands, 1493–1587

The Southern Netherlands and the prince-bishopric of Liège experienced a sharp rise in economic activity during the 16th century, which maintained its basic dynamism until the Peace of Munster (Westphalia) in 1648. The dynamism of both regions was a motive force in the new acceleration of commercial capitalism, an acceleration clearly perceptible throughout Europe following the set-backs of the 14th and 15th centuries. This fundamental movement towards growth and leadership was temporarily eclipsed by significant cyclical fluctuations in the economy: brief, though dramatic, economic recessions recurred on a fairly regular basis for such diverse reasons as famine, epidemics, war and pillaging, commercial embargoes or political intervention. Apart from these short-term ups and downs there were also longer waves of expansion and contraction spanning several decades, wherein structural factors, as well as fortuitous circumstances, played a part. The three periods of vigorous and accelerated economic growth, namely from 1493 to 1520, from 1535 to 1565, and from 1588 to 1621, were repeatedly interrupted by periods of stagnation or even decline. Each of these decades – long rising or falling cyclical movements – was governed, if not exclusively, at least predominantly by one factor in particular: at times exogenous, circumstantial factors weighed heavily, while at others endogenous structural changes predominated. The object of the first part of this chapter is to analyse these variations.

Internal Factors in the First Phase of Growth in the Southern Netherlands, 1493–1520

The political chaos ensuing in the Southern Netherlands after the death of Charles the Bold (1477) did immense damage. The situation became yet more precarious during the Flemish Revolt (1483–92) and during the wars with France and its allies (1488–93). Demographic development, having never fully recovered from the catastrophic effects of the famine

88   THE LOW COUNTRIES IN THE EARLY MODERN WORLD

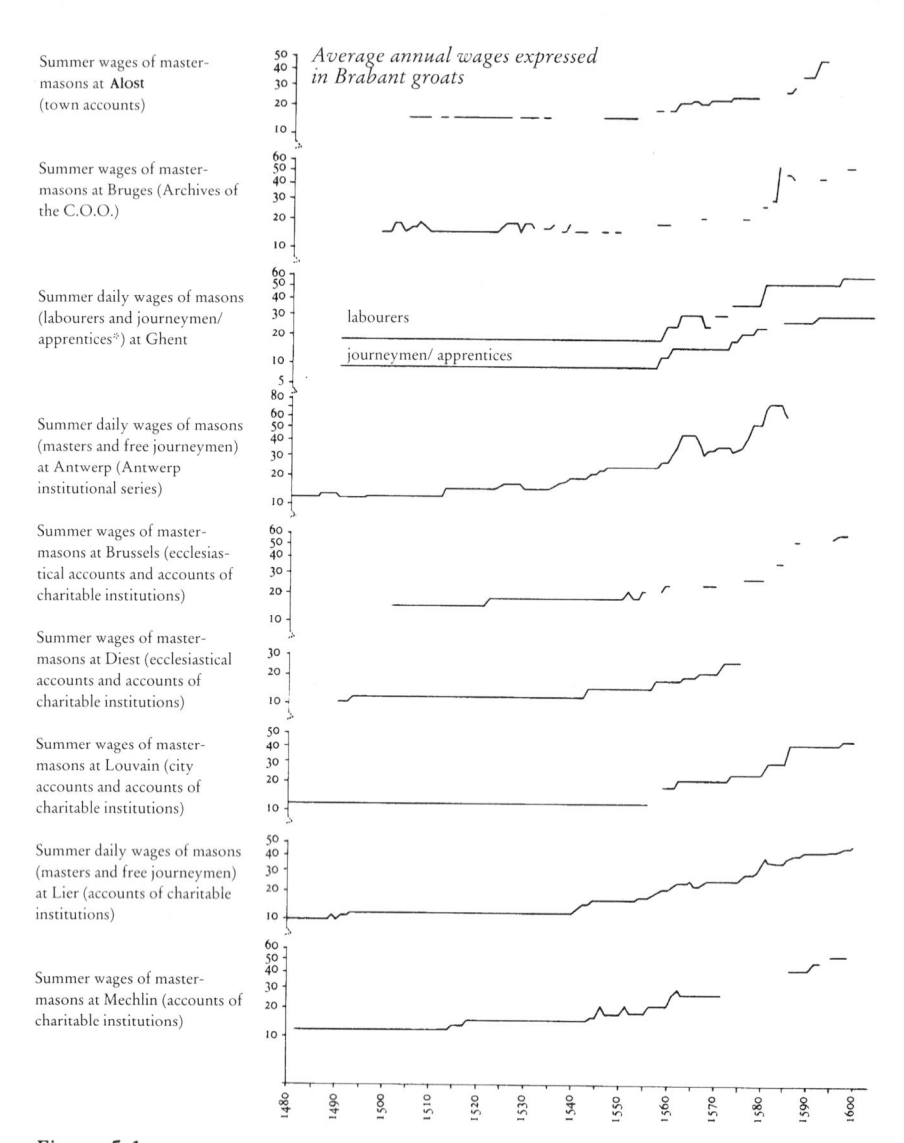

Summer wages of master-masons at **Alost** (town accounts)

Summer wages of master-masons at Bruges (Archives of the C.O.O.)

Average annual wages expressed in Brabant groats

Summer daily wages of masons (labourers and journeymen/apprentices*) at Ghent

labourers

journeymen/ apprentices

Summer daily wages of masons (masters and free journeymen) at Antwerp (Antwerp institutional series)

Summer wages of master-masons at Brussels (ecclesiastical accounts and accounts of charitable institutions)

Summer wages of master-masons at Diest (ecclesiastical accounts and accounts of charitable institutions)

Summer wages of master-masons at Louvain (city accounts and accounts of charitable institutions)

Summer daily wages of masons (masters and free journeymen) at Lier (accounts of charitable institutions)

Summer wages of master-masons at Mechlin (accounts of charitable institutions)

Figure 5.1:
Alost
Source: B. Goffin and E. Scholliers, 'Prijzen en lonen te Aalst (16de eeuw)', in: *Dokumenten voor de geschiedenis van prijzen en lonen in Vlaanderen en Brabant*, III: *XVIe-XIXe eeuw*, C. Verlinden (ed.) (Bruges: 1972), pp. 199–200.
Bruges
Source: E. Scholliers 'Lonen te Brugge en in het Brugse Vrije (XVe–XVIIe eeuw)', in: *Dokumenten voor de geschiedenis van prijzen en lonen in Vlaanderen en Brabant*, II *XIVe–XIXe eeuw*, C. Verlinden (ed.) (Bruges: 1965), pp. 105–10.

Ghent
Source: E. Scholliers, 'De lagere klassen. Een kwantitatieve benadering van levensstandaard en levenswijze', in: *Antwerpen in de XVIde eeuw* (Antwerp: 1975), p. 165. Table 2.
Antwerp
Source: H. Van der Wee, *The Growth of the Antwerp Market and the European Economy (fourteenth–sixteenth centuries)*, I (The Hague: 1963), pp. 459–62.
Brussels
Source: H. Coeckelberghs, 'Lonen en levensstandaard te Brussel in de 16e eeuw', in: *Bijdragen tot de Geschiedenis* 58, 3–4 (1975), p. 172, Table 1.
Diest
Source: M. Van der Eycken, *Stadseconomie en conjunctuur te Diest (1490–1580)* (M.A. thesis, K.U. Leuven) (Louvain, 1973), pp. 219–21, Appendix 18.
Louvain
Source: R. Van Uytven, *Stadsfinanciën en stadsekonomie te Leuven van de XIIde tot het einde der XVIde eeuw* (Brussels: 1961), pp. 577–8.
Lier
Source: H. Van der Wee, *The Growth* ... I (The Hague: 1963), pp. 465–8.
Mechlin
Source: M. Van de Mosselaer, *De levensstandard van de arbeiders in de XVIe eeuw. Een lonenstudie voor Mechelen* (M.A. thesis, K.U. Leuven) (Louvain: 1968), pp. 88–91, Table XV.

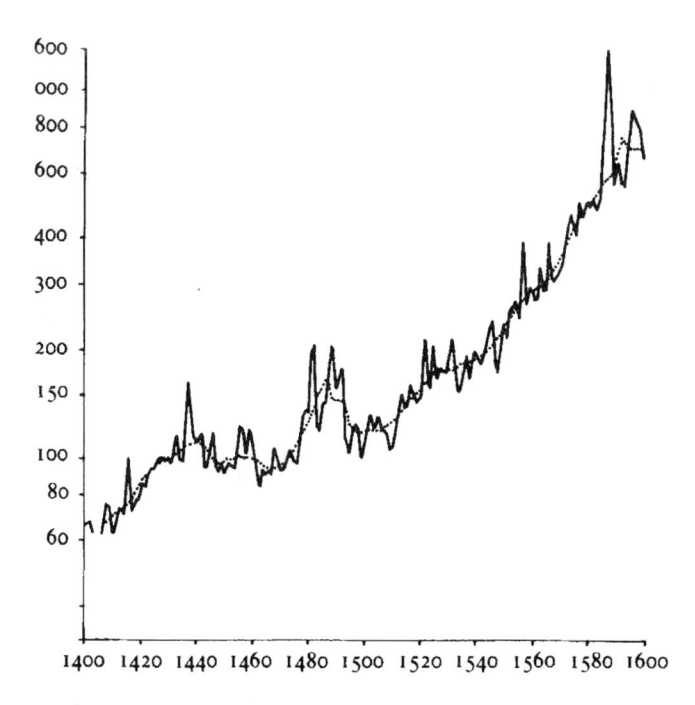

Figure 5.2: *Nominal price index for a 'basket' of consumer goods at Antwerp (1400–1600): annual indices and moving inter-quarterly median per 13 years.*
Note: the reader who wishes to compare the price curve shown here with the wage table in Figure 5.1 must take into account the difference in scale.
Source: H. Van der Wee, 'Prices and Wages as Development Variables: A Comparison between England and the Southern Netherlands, 1400–1700' in: *Acta Historiae Neerlandicae* 10 (1978), p. 75.

of 1437–39, again collapsed. For many years the armies rendered the countryside unsafe, plundering farms and destroying the fields in Brabant as well as in Flanders. Grain exports from the regions of the Somme and the Seine were regularly the object of royal embargo. Between 1480 and 1493 grain prices reached unparalleled heights. This was not only due to the recurring food shortages, but was aggravated by Maximilian of Austria's reckless debasement policy. In both town and countryside real income decreased alarmingly: high food prices, acute unemployment and stagnating nominal wages affected the skilled craftsmen as well as the unskilled labourers (see Figures 5.1 and 5.2). Merchants, with the exception of grain speculators, were confronted by slack trading activity and diminishing profits. Persons of private means waited in vain for their interest payments, already substantially eroded by inflation.

The internal and external political stability during the three decades following the Peace of Senlis (23 May 1493), together with the monetary reorganization of the 1490s, brought a climate of security and renewed optimism to the Southern Netherlands. The promising economic developments of this period were closely related to the dynamics of internal growth, based on demographic recovery, reconstruction of the country and a general resumption of agrarian, industrial, and commercial activity. It was essentially a rapid and vigorous catching-up. Reserves of people and resources that had been untapped or underutilized during the gradual restructuring of the industrial economy in the Southern Netherlands and the political crises of the preceding decades could now be actively integrated into the economy once more. The immediate increase in income that ensued stimulated the birth rate while abating the high mortality rates prevalent in recent years.

The earlier demographic losses were now recouped, making possible new combinations of labour and resources, and hence further growth. Population growth and increased real income were also reflected in more intense trade on the domestic markets. Demand for agrarian and craft products encouraged the division of labour in agriculture and industry, rendering them at the same time more dependent on the market. Reconstruction, necessitating substantial importation of building materials from near and far, also served to intensify commercial activity. There are two conclusive indications of more extensive local and regional trade: first, the general and usually vigorous rise in the revenues derived from tolls exacted on the interregional transport of goods; and second, the more extensive use of credit in retail business that became prominent on the markets of the Southern Netherlands at the beginning of the 16th century.

Naturally commercial development was by no means equally favourable everywhere. In the Hageland and in Haspengouw, for example, where the decay of traditional urban cloth production was not compensated by appropriate adaptation of industrial organization, structural factors cast a pall over the recovery of the domestic market.[1] Both regions lacked rural industry as well, and consequently rural income profited only marginally from rising wages.

External Factors in the First Phase of Growth in the Southern Netherlands, 1483–1520

The commercial economy of the Southern Netherlands was not exclusively dominated by the domestic market's movements to catch up. It was also strongly influenced by external factors, renewing its contacts with European commercial capitalism. After these relations had been resumed, the economy of the Southern Netherlands took advantage of the new external circumstances to take the lead in the accelerating world trade of the early 16th century. Antwerp was at the forefront of this development and became the dominant transit market for all of Europe. Bruges on the other hand saw its relative and perhaps also its absolute share in world trade shrink. These changes in the commercial situation of Bruges and Antwerp also had an impact upon the development of their respective outports and their trading partners. They even influenced the economic balance of power between Flanders and Brabant. Contemporaries viewed these changes as the direct result of the Flemish Revolt. Circumstantial factors often exercise too great an influence on the opinions of contemporaries. This was the case here, too. While one cannot deny the influence of the Flemish Revolt, still the emphasis must lie primarily upon those deeper structural factors that had long been favouring the rise of Antwerp.

The maritime growth of Europe in the 14th and 15th centuries had made Bruges the most important meeting-place for the merchants of the Mediterranean region and the Hanseatics.[2] This state of affairs had also, if indirectly, benefited Antwerp, already a promising commercial centre thanks to its cycles of four trade fairs per year: two in Antwerp itself, two nearby in Bergen-op-Zoom. When in 1356 Flanders annexed Antwerp, it was obvious that one of the goals was to establish Bruges's control over the Brabant fairs, extensively patronized by merchants from Holland, Zeeland and England, in other words by merchants who were only indirectly and marginally involved in world trade at Bruges, where they functioned more as outsiders. After this annexation the foreign merchants of Bruges took an increasing interest in the economic activities

---

[1] R. Van Uyten 'Sociaal-economische evoluties in de Nederlanden voór de Revoluties (veertiende-zestiende eeuw)' in: *Bijdragen en Mededelingen betreffende de Geschiedenis der Nederlanden*, 87 (1972) pp. 60–93.

[2] In the later Middle Ages, Bruges was transformed from a national to an international market: see W. Brulez, 'Brugge en Antwerpen in de 15de en 16de eeuw: een tegenstelling?' in: *Tijdschrift voor Geschiedenis*, 83 (1970) pp. 15–37.

of Antwerp. The result of these new contacts was extremely favourable to the Brabant fairs: their trade volume increased substantially and their international relations were extended to a larger geographical area. One important result was to strengthen the position of Holland and Zeeland in the world trade of the Netherlands, at the expense of the Hanse. Even when Antwerp was finally returned to the duchy of Brabant in 1405, Bruges retained, for all practical purposes and for a considerable time, a dominant commercial influence over the Brabant fairs. However, the foundations for the latter's autonomous development had already been laid and grew steadily stronger. This was chiefly thanks to the continued maritime expansion of Holland and to the resumption of transcontinental European traffic in the course of the 15th century.

During the 15th century Holland and Zeeland had been very active in the herring fishery and export, in the transport, processing, and export of salt, in the brewing and export of beer, in the carrying of grain from Northern France and the Baltic region, in the export of cloth from Holland, in the Rhenish trade, and in ship building. The Brabant fairs were the focal point for all these varied activities. For their part the English were attracted to the free Brabant fairs because, while they were prevented by embargoes (1340, 1434, 1489, 1501) from continuing to use Flanders as a staple market, they still wished to market their textiles in the vicinity of Bruges, both for processing and to take advantage of the contacts provided by the international clientèle of Bruges.[3] English interest was further aroused when resumption of transcontinental traffic brought the Central European market into renewed contact with Italy and the Netherlands. The merchants of Cologne played a prominent part therein: to avoid the numerous Rhine tolls between Cologne and Dordrecht they further developed the direct overland routes between Cologne and the Southern Netherlands. The Brabant fairs became the terminus of this crucial trade route.

Southern Germans appeared in increasing numbers at Antwerp and Bergen-op-Zoom from the second half of the 15th century onwards. They exported cloth from their own region, namely from Swabia and from Upper Franconia ('Fustian' industry). They also increasingly controlled the export of copper and silver to the North and South, since they had been the chief financial backers behind the introduction of the new '*Saigerung*' technology in Central and Southern European mining. Silver was in particular demand in the Netherlands owing to the official overvaluation decreed by Charles the Bold in 1467, and also because of the relative abundance of gold imported from West Africa by

---

[3] The market towns of Brabant did not have to worry about the local textile industry, since they no longer had one.

the Portuguese.[4] This Portuguese trade with West Africa also made the import of Central European copper and Nuremberg copperware to the Brabant fairs exceedingly profitable. Production from Mechlin, Aachen and other nearby centres could no longer keep pace with the demand, particularly after the destruction of Dinant by Charles the Bold, and thus new markets were opened for the Nuremberg copper industry.

In response to the technical difficulties posed by overland transport, transcontinental trade had early been organized via intermediary towns and fixed cycles of annual fairs. When transcontinental trade began to flourish anew in the course of the 15th century the same pattern of organization was retained. Consequently, the network of European fairs was considerably extended. In Central Europe the Leipzig, and especially the Frankfurt, *Messen* were crucial, in Eastern Europe the annual fairs of Posen and Cracow, in the Northern Netherlands those of Deventer, in Switzerland the fairs of Geneva, in France those of Châlon-sur-Saône and soon afterwards Lyons, while on the Iberian peninsula there were the Castilian fairs.

In the Southern Netherlands the Brabant fairs fitted admirably into this pattern of organization. They had by then freed themselves entirely from the tutelage of Bruges, and by the end of the 15th century they had become one of the main links in the European chain, thanks largely to the ascendancy of the Rhineland and Southern Germany. Nor was it mere chance that rental prices for commercial buildings in Antwerp began to rise precipitately in the 1490s. The urban and central governments, moreover, pursued a resolute policy of supporting Antwerp's world trade. In 1491 the city of Antwerp purchased the alum staple. On February 24, 1496 Philip the Fair and Henry VII concluded the *Magnus Intercursus*, paving the way for further expansion of English cloth exports via the Brabant fairs. English exports increased significantly: on average during the period from 1485 to 1491 some 50,878 pieces of English cloth were exported from London, from 1501 to 1507 this average rose to 81,835 pieces, most of which were sold via Bergen-op-Zoom or, more often, via Antwerp.

The second driving force behind the rapid growth of the Brabant fairs beginning in the late 15th century, aside from the revival of transcontinental trade, was the new maritime expansion. Here it was the Portuguese who had taken the initiative. Their preference for the Brabant fairs represented a clear break with the past. During the gradual development of a direct sea route to the Far East in the course of the 15th century, the Portuguese had always chosen the international market of Bruges as the

---

[4] F. Braudel, *La Méditerranée et le monde méditerranéen à l'époque de Philippe II*, 2nd edition, 2 vols (Paris: 1966), I, 427–32; English translation *The Mediterranean and the Mediterranean World in the Age of Philip II*, 2 vols. (London: 1972–73).

strategic base for their factors in Northern Europe. The merchants of Bruges for their part had actively participated in the growing colonial trade of their Portuguese colleagues: among other ventures they had purchased an interest in the sugar plantations of Madeira and in the trade with Guinea in West Africa. Moreover, they controlled the calamine production of Limburg, which provided one of the basic raw materials used in processing Central European copper. This time-honoured relationship notwithstanding, the Portuguese king awarded the staple monopoly for the sale of Portuguese spices north of the Alps and Pyrenees to Antwerp in 1501. In 1508 the *Feitoria de Flandes*, a subsidiary of the *Casa da India*, was also transferred to Antwerp.

Why this sudden change of policy? The Portuguese saw two principal commercial advantages to an establishment at Antwerp, both related to the presence of merchants from Cologne and Southern Germany at the Brabant fairs. In the first place they sought new markets for their spices both in the hinterland of Central Europe, still served by the Southern Germans through the intermediary of the Venetians, and in Germany itself, where the merchants of Cologne distributed spices purchased from the Venetians on the markets of the Netherlands. The merchants of Southern Germany and Cologne thus served the Portuguese as valuable pawns in their rivalry with Venice, and as the intermediary link necessary for the procurement of a huge new market. However, they were much more than that. Between them the two groups controlled the traffic in copper and silver from Central and Southern Europe. The Portuguese purchased vast quantities of both for their trade with West Africa and the Far East (see Figure 5.3).

Contacts and cooperation between the Portuguese and the German merchants consequently held great promise. Each party had both purchasing and sales interests at stake. While the Portuguese dominated the great maritime routes, the Southern Germans were the promoters of transcontinental trade in Central Europe. The two new trade routes met at Antwerp where the establishment of a virtual monopoly on the trade in Portuguese spices gave the starting signal for an acceleration in their activities. The first shipload of Portuguese spices docked at Antwerp in 1501. The Southern Germans, led by the Fuggers and the Welsers, undertook the distribution via Antwerp of Portuguese spices throughout Central Europe. The mercantile houses of Cologne also participated actively in this trade. In 1507 the 'Grosse Ravensburger Handelsgesellschaft' of Southern Germany decided to centralize their spice purchases at Antwerp. In addition to the numerous German merchants, many of the great Italian mercantile houses, such as the Gualterotti, the Frescobaldi and the Affaitadi, took an interest in the spice trade at Antwerp. Local merchants who had previously specialized in the copper and calamine trade, among

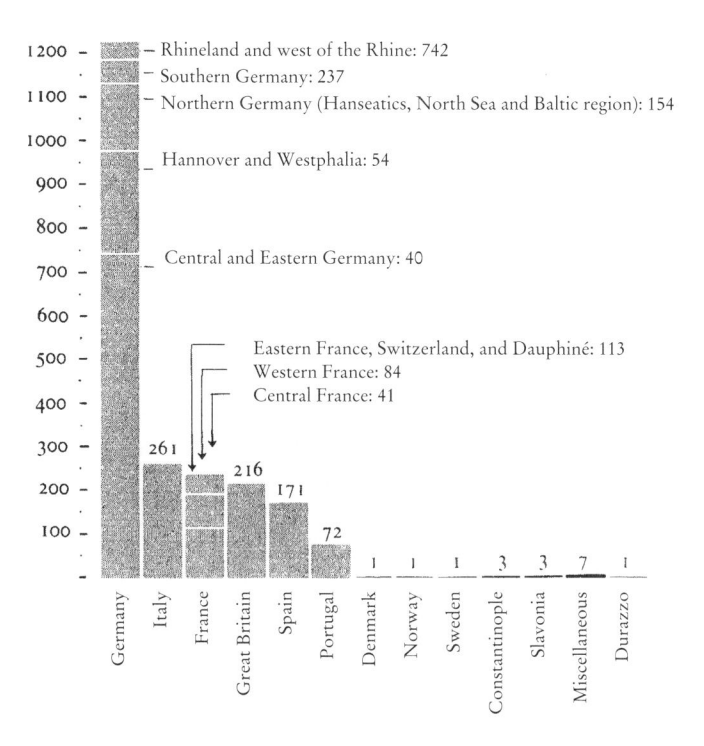

```
1200 -    ▨ — Rhineland and west of the Rhine: 742
          ▨ — Southern Germany: 237
1100 -    ▨ — Northern Germany (Hanseatics, North Sea and Baltic region): 154
1000 -
          ▨ _ Hannover and Westphalia: 54
 900 -
 800 -
          ▨   Central and Eastern Germany: 40
 700 -
 600 -
              ┌─ Eastern France, Switzerland, and Dauphiné: 113
 500 -        ├─ Western France: 84
              └─ Central France: 41
 400 -
 300 -   261 ↓↓↓
              216
 200 -            171
 100 -                 72
                           1   1   1   3   3   7   1
```

Figure 5.3: *Number of foreign merchants at Antwerp, either present or maintaining trade relations with the city, 1488–1513.*

Source: R. Doehaerd, *Etudes Anversoises. Documents sur le commerce international à Anvers, 1488–1514* (Paris: 1963), pp. 31–6 and 85–115.

them Van Rechtergem, Schetz, Pryunen and Vleminx, extended their mercantile activities to include spices. Other Antwerp firms devoted themselves to the sugar trade with Madeira, the Canary Islands and the Azores. The Portuguese or Spanish usually acted as intermediaries in this trade. Occasionally, however, there were cases of direct exploitation: in 1515, for example, Jacob Groenenborg established his own great sugar plantations on Palma, one of the Canary Islands, linking them to his substantial refinery operations.

Thanks to the *Intercursus Malus* of 1506, the English Merchant Adventurers were able further to improve their trading status at the Brabant fairs: the accounts of the Fuggers regarding the Hungarian copper trade show that large quantities of English cloth were purchased at Antwerp and further exported from Antwerp to Lyons and Marseille in 1508; thus regions located further within the French interior now joined the Northern

French grain-exporting regions and the Western French wine- and salt-producing regions as Antwerp's trading partners. Finally, the Hanseatics, and to an even greater extent the Dutch, took an active part in expanding the long-distance trade of which Antwerp was the hub.

Antwerp's transformation into a centre of international transit trade naturally stimulated its internal urban activity. Vigorous growth occurred in building and in the service sectors related to the port and to trade. Rising wages demonstrate that employment levels were sustained, notwithstanding the rapid population growth.[5] The positive effects of this growth were experienced outside the city as well, in Bergen-op-Zoom (its partner in the trade fairs), at the ports on Walcheren (the entrepôt for overseas transports), at Bruges (the traditional trade centre), in 's Hertogenbosch (the town of access to the Northern Netherlands), in West Brabant and the Campine (its neighbouring source of supply and recruitment).

Was Antwerp's transit trade so great as to constitute the crucial variable in explaining the global expansion of the Southern Netherlands from the end of the 15th through the 16th century? To give an unconditionally positive answer to this question would be to distort reality.

Antwerp's importance as a centre for long-distance transit trade was naturally very real, in the first place owing to the direct and positive effects it had on economic activity both within the city and outside its walls, but still more through the psychological stimulus it generated, creating a dynamic and optimistic climate in the region. Still, this influence was chiefly limited to the Brabant fairs and to the satellite towns mentioned above. Most of the other centres and regions of the Southern Netherlands were scarcely affected. It should also be noted that the expansion of the transit trade as such remained quite limited: aside from commercial and financial services, only the processing of English cloth and spices at Antwerp and the copper working at Antwerp and Mechlin were of any real significance. Even the monopoly on Portuguses spices did not fully live up to expectation. First of all, the Portuguese never succeeded in wholly eliminating their rivals from Venice and Alexandria. Moreover, with regard to their own contribution, only a part of the total quantity of spices imported to Lisbon was actually marketed at Antwerp itself. Large quantities were exported directly from Lisbon to the rest of Europe, mostly with but not infrequently without Antwerp's commercial intercession.

Thus, while the contribution of colonial trade, and of the Antwerp transit trade, to the first phase in the economic expansion of the Southern Netherlands cannot be ignored, it should be viewed in perspective.[6]

---

[5] H. Van der Wee, *The Growth of the Antwerp Market and the European Economy* I (Paris–The Hague: 1963), appendices 27–33; graphs 33–40.

[6] Brulez, 'Brugge en Antwerpen...', pp. 26–7.

On the other hand the role of the Antwerp market was not limited exclusively to international transit trade. During the same period Antwerp also strengthened its position as a centre for the long-distance traffic and trade that supplied the Netherlands. As the internal economy strove vigorously to regain lost ground it exerted a dynamic influence on intra- and interregional trade in the area. This new commercial vitality in the Netherlands was of particular benefit to Antwerp and its satellites. The reasons for this are clear: the successful expansion of transit traffic brought about improvements in the infrastructure, and this modern infrastructure could be used to the advantage of Antwerp's own import and export trade to and from the Netherlands, substantially reducing transaction costs. Salt and French wines were offloaded at the ports on Walcheren for consumption in the Netherlands, supplies of herring from Holland and Zeeland and of Dutch and Flemish dairy products reached the Brabant fairs for similar purposes, wheat was imported from Northern France, rye from the Baltic region, and building materials from the Walloon provinces, from the Rhineland, from the Scheldt region, and from Northern Europe: these are just a few examples of the stimulating influence the rapid expansion of the internal economy exerted on the long-distance trade of Antwerp and its satellite towns. The expanding domestic economy stimulated still other markets of the Southern Netherlands. For example, the trade in cattle from Denmark, Schleswig, Holstein, Frisia, Groningen, Drenthe and Overijssel soared during this period, and the various cattle markets of the Southern Netherlands profited thereby. The Walloon provinces' exports to Brabant via the markets of Liège also rose appreciably.

Unfortunately, the relative role that each of these variables played in the first phase of economic growth in the Southern Netherlands between 1493 and 1520 cannot be statistically determined. For this there is insufficient data. Two general hypotheses can, however, be formulated. First, the great importance of the domestic economy to the growth of the Southern Netherlands during the 16th century must receive primary emphasis. Second, economic growth in quantitative terms, impressive between 1493 and 1520, was essentially a recovery to former prosperity, after the disastrous years of high taxation, hyperinflation and wars during the last quarter of the 15th century.

In contrast, the influence exerted upon the global economy of the Southern Netherlands around 1500 by the spectacular expansion of Antwerp's long-distance transit trade, though quantitatively rather limited, was nevertheless of inestimable value from a qualitative point of view. The rise of Antwerp's international market did not merely bring it up to the level of rival Bruges, but actually opened new horizons to the economic development of the Southern Netherlands as a whole. Real organizational progress was achieved. Antwerp's transit market, therefore, was not only the focal point of European innovations in maritime and transcontinental trade, but at the same time this market became the most dynamic base of operations for the revitalization of the Southern Netherlands' own long-distance trade which, thanks to the recovery of the domestic economy, had enormous potential for growth. Antwerp's expansion at the beginning of the 16th century indeed laid the groundwork for the rise of an important market for imports of raw materials and for exports of manufacturers from the Southern Netherlands.

The Delaying Effects of the Franco-Habsburg and German Wars, 1521–39

The Franco-Habsburg war (1521–29) precipitated a serious crisis in the Southern Netherlands, with repercussions lasting for many years after the cessation of hostilities. Antwerp's trade was the first, and perhaps the most badly, affected. The threat of piracy paralysed maritime traffic: ships from Portugal, Spain and Italy avoided the dangerous route to the north, and even the Scottish and English merchants ran considerable risks crossing the North Sea. The unrest in Denmark during the early 1520s put a stop to the grain export from the Baltic region and impeded the import of Hungarian copper via Gdansk and Stettin. Shipments of salt, wine and grain from France also ground to a halt. The German *Bauernkrieg* (1524–26) disrupted transcontinental traffic with Central Europe.[7] The gravity of the situation was reflected in declining toll revenues. The crisis in long-distance trade also had immediate effects on all revenues, and not only on the government's. Merchants, and indeed everyone directly involved in international trade, were the first whose incomes suffered. Afterwards came the entrepreneurs and workers in those industrial sectors that processed imported raw materials or who specialized in finishing foreign goods like English cloth. Finally, the local export industries were cut off from their markets.

The effect of the crisis on food supplies was even more dramatic. Grain prices reached record levels as the chaos of the 1520s rendered grain transports impossible and famine threatened. The vast majority of the population devoted its income almost exclusively to procuring foodstuffs. Nothing was left for manufactured products and local market activity declined. Consequently the fall in real income was accompanied by growing unemployment. Great misery dominated these years of crisis, particularly in those regions and towns that had not profited from Antwerp's first boom and where nominal wages had stagnated at the earlier,

---

[7] In the German hinterlands the crisis was limited to the 1520s. After that, there was an upsurge of the economy connected with the second cycle of Antwerp's expansion.

lower, levels. Moreover, fiscal pressure was further increased to finance the war effort. Tensions rose and serious bread riots broke out in many places (see Figure 5.4).

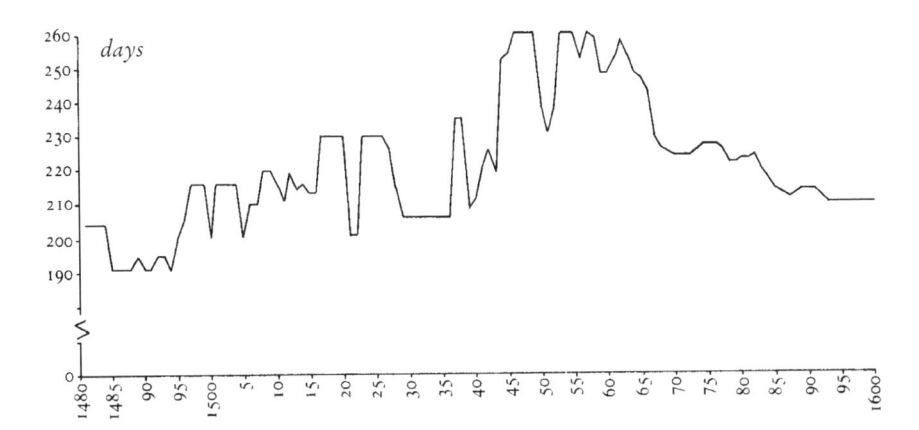

Figure 5.4: *Employment index for the construction industry in the towns of West Brabant, 1481–1600.*

Source: H. Van der Wee, *The Growth of the Antwerp Market and the European Economy (Fourteenth–Sixteenth Centuries)* (Paris–The Hague: 1963), I, appendix 48, pp. 541–4.

The 'Ladies' Peace of Cambrai' (1529) did not bring about the immediate recovery of the domestic and international markets. Grain prices fell little if at all, an indication that a relative shortage of grain persisted. There were several reasons for this. For example, imports of grain from Northern France, one of the traditional suppliers, never really resumed. Was export no longer possible because the population of France itself had so sharply increased, or had the repeated embargoes during the Franco-Habsburg wars made the risks of this trade too great? It is difficult to determine. At the same time the resumption of grain imports from the Baltic region was hindered by the tensions between Holland and the Hanseatics in the 1530s and the beginning of the 1540s.

Aside from external supply problems, the Southern Netherlands were also confronted with substantial losses of arable land. The flood *Sint-Felix quade saterdach* ('Evil' Saturday, Feast of Saint Felix) of 5 November 1530 did enormous damage to the polder regions of Flanders, Zeeland-Flanders, Antwerp, Zeeland, Brabant and South Holland. On 2 November 1532 a second storm tide drowned thousands more hectares under seawater. On this occasion North Holland, Utrecht and Frisia were also affected. Real earned income continued to stagnate in the towns and villages during these years as well, and this had a negative impact on the evolution of the domestic market as a whole. The situation did not significantly improve until the beginning of the 1540s. Only then did employment opportunities increase, chiefly thanks to important structural changes in the domestic and international markets, with wages rising more quickly than food prices in several places.

Antwerp's transit trade never returned to prewar levels. Political and economic developments regularly led to tensions on the European continent during the second third of the 16th century. As a result traditional international trade routes were displaced, often unfavourably for Antwerp's transit trade. For example, during François I's fourth war (1542–44), Maarten van Rossum led his plundering army through the countryside right up to the gates of Antwerp. In the 1550s the French and Spanish armies operated in the region of Saint-Quentin, Calais and Gravelines. Even when the actual warfare was far removed from the Southern Netherlands, the transcontinental links to Antwerp could still be broken, as they were, for example, during the Wars of Religion in Germany during the 1540s and 1550s, and when the Turkish advance reached the walls of Vienna.

The weakening of Antwerp's transit trade was not only due to problems of transport but also to supply factors. Central European copper and silver production for example also suffered from the wars. Moreover, at about the same time the first gold and silver shipments from the New World arrived at Seville. The Portuguese began to purchase the silver needed for their spice trade in Spain, rather than on the Antwerp transit market. They also began to show less interest in copper. Copperware had originally been traded as a luxury product on the coasts of West Africa. In all probability this market had gradually reached its saturation point and the terms of trade grew less advantageous to the Portuguese. Meanwhile, the European spice trade was undergoing substantial changes. The alliance between François I and the Turkish Sultan Suleiman I (1535) reopened the French ports of Marseille and Lyons to the direct import of spices from the Levant. Portugal responded with an intensive marketing campaign of its own: Western France via Bayonne, the Mediterranean region via Marseille, and Southern and Central Germany by way of Italy.

The comeback of the Levantine distributors of Oriental spices was a severe blow to Antwerp's transit function. Venice was the greatest gainer by this: during the second third of the 16th century Venice again became by far the most important European staple market for spices, both those from the Levant and those from Lisbon. The office of the Portuguese crown at Antwerp was closed in 1548. Antwerp did not lose everything, however: it continued to serve the whole of Northwestern Europe and parts of Central Europe as a transit market for Portuguese spices. Even around the middle of the century the annual volume of spices traded remained impressive, and the number of Portuguese ships at the ports on Walcheren was still considerable.[8] However, the dynamism of the beginning of the 16th century had been broken.

Nor was the monetary policy pursued during the 1520s and 1530s such as to stimulate Antwerp's international trade. The official rates (in money of account) of the coins in circulation were lowered in March 1527 and in May of 1539, creating a climate of uncertainty, particularly among foreign merchants. It was decreed in 1539 that all commercial transactions must be paid for two-thirds in gold currency, and one-third in silver. This measure caused an acute shortage of liquid assets on the Antwerp money market and severely hampered international trade.

Thus the European wars of the 1520s and the ensuing political and monetary developments of the 1530s undoubtedly exerted a pronounced negative influence upon trade in the Southern Netherlands. Antwerp's transit trade was most seriously disrupted by these events. It also felt the negative impact of the structural changes taking place in the spice sector due to the commercial revival of Venice. Spices and metals which had formerly, during the first phase of the expansion in Antwerp's international trade, formed the pillars of the transit trade, lost the dynamics to which they owed their original growth. The second phase of Antwerp's expansion therefore would no longer be determined to the same extent by the transit trade.

Export Industry and the Second Growth Phase in the Southern Netherlands, 1536–66

The second third of the 16th century was subject to new waves of war and violence, and Europe once more experienced a period of political uncertainty. Paradoxically enough, Antwerp's long-distance trade reached a second flowering during these troubled times. The political conflicts, this time either very localized in nature, or taking place far from the borders of the Netherlands, formed no impediment to expansion. For one thing, long-distance trade was less dependent on the transit trade, which had proved so vulnerable to external influences during the preceding period. It was oriented more towards the import of bulk goods, like foodstuffs and raw materials, and on the import and export of finished products.

The English cloth trade was the only one of the three traditional pillars of Antwerp's transit trade of the beginning of the 16th century to experience substantial growth as well.[9] The monetary policy of the English

---

[8] W. Brulez, 'Le commerce international des Pays-Bas au XVIe siècle: essai d'appreciation quantitative', in: *Belgisch Tijdschrift voor Filologie en Geschiedenis*, 46, 4 (1968), 1205–21.

[9] F.J. Fisher, 'Commercial trends and policy in sixteenth-century England', in: *Economic History Review*, 10 (1940), 95–117.

kings temporarily stimulated the export of cloth from England: the devaluation of the English pound sterling in 1526, and even more the 'great debasements' unleashed by Henry VIII in 1542, helped to bring the volume of London exports to a level of more than 135,000 pieces of cloth in 1554 even after the revaluations of 1551. This ample supply met with an increasing demand, thanks primarily to the thriving Baltic trade and to the reopening of markets in the Levant through the intermediary of the Venetians. A third, and no less important, factor in the success of English export policies was the organizational talent of the Merchant Adventurers, the guild organization of the London cloth merchants. Their monopoly on exports from London to the continent, within the framework of the English Exchange at Antwerp, proved an invaluable strategy in the uncertain political climate of the second third of the 16th century. It provided a flexible means of attuning supply and demand and, no less important, made it possible to sustain favourable sales prices.

Antwerp continued to function as an important port of transit for certain other products, though none of a volume comparable to that of English cloth. Coarse salt, for example, was imported from the Iberian peninsula, refined in Zeeland and Zeeland-Flanders, and later marketed, via Antwerp, in Germany and the Baltic region. This was also the case for French wines, exotic fruits, dyes, oil, and so on. In these affairs Antwerp usually acted exclusively as a *Dispositionsplatz*: though the transactions were concluded at Antwerp, the goods were not materially present there. This new commercial development was closely related to the tendency, emerging in the mercantile circles of Antwerp, to greater reliance on temporary, specialized companies for long-distance trade with Northern and Southern Europe.

At the same time, the export industries of the Southern Netherlands supplanted transit activity as the dynamic element in the new expansion of Antwerp's long-distance trade. This was no chance event but the result of a long, often difficult, process of structural change in the industry generating new combinations of raw materials, labour and capital within the specific framework of a heavily urbanized region.

The crisis that erupted in the traditional textile industry of the Netherlands at the beginning of the 14th century, and especially during the 15th century, had indeed precipitated profound changes in the production structure. New industries arose in the towns during the 15th–16th centuries, based on highly skilled labour and on the creative efforts of entrepreneurs. Specialization raised the quality of luxury products from the Southern Netherlands to a remarkable extent, and a greater variety of types extended their range. Meanwhile, a rural industry had matured in the villages where a high degree of specialization made it possible to mass-produced articles of satisfactory quality very cheaply. During the 15th century these new sectors had found an adequate market within the

Burgundian Netherlands themselves. Declining grain prices, together with stable wages, rents and salaries, had raised real income to a fairly high level in the towns. By the second third of the 16th century, however, the domestic market for these specialized products had grown too constricted. New markets were sought beyond the borders. Antwerp's international market was the obvious distribution centre for the growing production of the local rural and urban industry.

Two other fortuitous circumstances contributed to the success of Southern Netherlands industry abroad. The first involved the political instability of Italy during the first half of the 16th century and its attendant economic collapse. Italy had always been the undisrupted distributor of luxury products from the Middle East: the transit market in all these goods for the whole of Europe. Later, it had gradually built up an urban luxury industry of its own, replacing imports, and soon becoming an export sector itself. However, political chaos and numerous military interventions devastated both the Italian export industry involving luxury goods and the Italian East–West transit trade in such products.

The resulting relative scarcity of Italian and Levantine products on the European markets facilitated the export of products made in the Southern Netherlands. At the same time the demand for luxury products rose in most countries, all involved in one way or another in the expansion of the European economy during the first half of the 16th century. The Iberian peninsula in particular accumulated vast wealth derived from the Portuguese trade with West Africa and the Far East, and from the influx of American gold and silver into Spain: the infrastructure of Iberian industry, less advanced and too limited in scope and scale, was incapable of meeting the rising demand for luxury products.

The great landowners of Northeastern Europe also made fortunes, thanks to the expansion of the grain trade in the Baltic region. The merchants of the Hanseatic towns derived handsome profits from the commercial and financial services they furnished. In France and Germany the economic recovery, observable since the second half of the 15th century, clearly continued its upward trend during the 16th century. For these lands as well, the upturn in the cyclic movement of the economy brought growing prosperity, although its effects were usually limited to a relatively small segment of society. The demand of these groups for specialized and luxury products rose sharply, and there was a ready market for articles manufactured in the Netherlands, the more so since they were spared – at least temporarily – from Italian competition.

The export industries in the towns of the Southern Netherlands embraced a number of sectors. The most important and varied industry was certainly the manufacture of textiles. The so-called 'light drapery' was the most successful: the production of wools, serges, fustians (a sort of bombazine), and baize rose, particularly in the urban centres of Picardy, Hainault and Flanders. Its principal raw material was Spanish merino wool that was imported exclusively via the staple market at Bruges.[10] Flanders already had an established reputation in the fashion field. Brabant now gradually took over this lead. With export in view this sector now expanded to include a whole series of activities, such as processing furs and leather, shoemaking, the manufacture of hats, stockings and gloves, embroidery and lacemaking, and especially garments. In addition, the processing industry, concentrated especially in Antwerp and Mechlin, specialized in the dyeing and finishing of both domestic and imported cloth, the latter chiefly of English origin. Contemporary business correspondence reveals that the fabrics finished in Brabant were prized above all for the quality of their colours.

The towns were the centres of more than just the full range of the garment industry. The arts and crafts were also flourishing. They presupposed a concentration of highly skilled workers and produced articles of great added value. Painting and sculpture, bell foundry and organ manufacture, furniture and cabinet making, carved altar-pieces, silver- and goldsmithery, the arms industry and cannon foundries, were the most outstanding examples. Thanks to those structural adaptations, already perceptible in the preceding century, the towns of the Southern Netherlands established a world-wide reputation in many of these sectors during the 16th century. The tapestry industry, established in that region since the end of the 14th century, occupied a very particular niche. During the 15th and especially the 16th century, the tapestry industry spread to a number of towns in the Southern Netherlands, first to the old centres like Lille, Bruges, Ghent and Tournai, and later to Antwerp, Brussels, Mechlin and Louvain as well. Finally, tapestry weaving found its way to smaller centres like Edingen, Oudenaarde, Alost, Herentals, Saint-Truiden, Diest, Tienen, and other towns. At one time some 20,000 workers were employed in the tapestry industry. The Southern Netherlands were by far the greatest producers of tapestries in the entire world. Sales continued to be organized in part at Bruges, though here, too, Antwerp gradually began to take the lead and between 1550 and 1554 it built a spacious new *tapissierspand*.

Import substitution also played an important role in the further expansion of the arts and crafts industry. Italian immigrants to the Southern Netherlands, especially to Bruges, had alrady introduced specialized craftsmanship in the course of the 15th century. During the 16th century the industry of the Netherlands was to an even greater extent devoted to the reproduction of imported goods and itself began to export those products

---

[10] Brulez, 'Le commerce international...', p. 1206.

which had formerly been imported, primarily from Italy and from the Levant via Italy. The rising European demand for luxury products and the incapacitation of Italy, the traditional supplier, were the external causes – as explained above – of the success of this export industry from the Southern Netherlands.

The most notable example of the import substitution movement was the silk industry: the spinning, weaving, throwing and dying of silk took place chiefly in Antwerp ateliers that brought a high-quality product to market. The success of silk was partially due to fashion trends as well: silk fabrics were 'in' during the 16th century. Or was it the other way round: was the rapidly growing silk industry itself the basis of the new fashion image? Around 1550 some 4 million guilders' worth of silk – raw materials and fabrics – were imported into the Netherlands from Italy and the Levant.[11] It was the largest category in the Netherlands' imports from those lands.

In addition to silk processing, a whole series of new industries emerged, producing goods that could compete with imported wares. There were ateliers, for example, in Antwerp and the surrounding area for the production of glass, mirrors, and Venetian crystal; for tooling leather and painting fabrics; for the production of majolica, and so on. The printing of books occupied a very special place. Books for religious, scientific and administrative use, but also manuals used in bookkeeping and commerce, and for technical instruction, were printed in quantities exceptionally large for the time. They were distributed in the Netherlands, England, France and Germany, still more on the Iberian peninsula and from there in the New World (see Figure 5.5).

In the villages, and indeed in the rural districts as a whole, the export industry was generally limited to the mass-production of textile and metal bulk goods. This production was efficiently organized through the intermediary of urban merchant-entrepreneurs. Scale enlargement and a far-reaching division of labour could be freely achieved in the absence of limitations imposed by guild regulations. Wages were relatively low: there were no organizations, such as existed in the towns, for the protection of the workers, and their earnings from textile or metalwork were considered a supplement to their rural income. In West Flanders it was chiefly wool that was processed. Hondschoote serges, usually woven from coarse Scottish, Northern German, or Provençal wool, were dyed and finished at Antwerp. Their light weight and softness to the touch, as well as their bright colours, made them very popular in Italian circles, and also in the Levant, where they arrived via Ancona and Venice. Demand also grew abroad for the more traditional high-quality fabrics, like those

---
[11] Ibid., p. 1206.

produced in Bergues Saint-Winoc, Armentières, Nieuwkerke, Dranouter, Hauboudin, Eeke, and so on. In Brabant there was an increase in the production of Duffel serges, of grey cloth and mixed cloth from the neighbourhood of Weert, Maaseik, Hoorn and Maastricht. Large quantities of these fabrics were sold on the Antwerp export market.

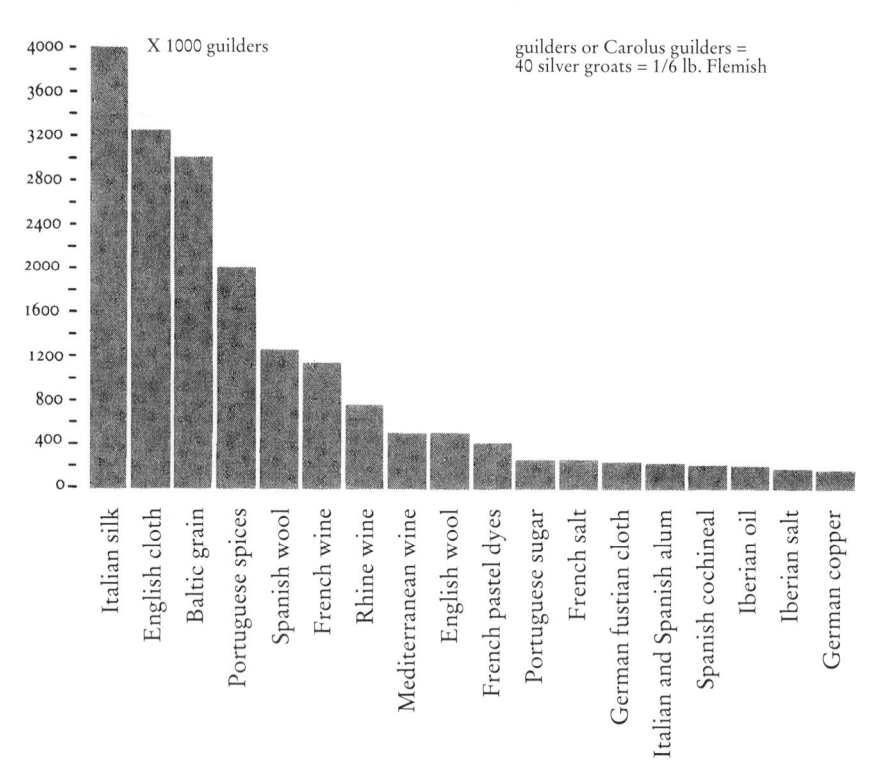

Figure 5.5: *Estimate of the principal imports and their monetary value in the Netherlands around 1560.*

Source: W. Brulez, 'Le commerce international des Pays-Bas au XVIe siècle: essai d'appréciation quantitative', in: *Revue belge de philologie et d'histoire* XLVI, 4 (1968), pp. 1207–8; and W. Brulez, 'De handel', in: *Antwerpen in de XVIde eeuw*, (Antwerp: 1975), pp. 123–4.

During the second third of the 16th century linen surged to the fore in Flanders. The Waasland and the Land of Termonde, the Vier Ambachten, Hulst and Axel, all in East Flanders became important centres for the cultivation and processing of flax. The flax was spun and woven into linen to the west and south, and the finished linen was collected at the local markets of Ghent, Eeklo, Alost, Edingen, and Courtrai among others and then shipped on to Lille, or more often to Antwerp, for export. In Brabant, Turnhout produced ticking and Herentals linen. These centres both worked for the export market at Antwerp. In the rural Walloon provinces the primary industry was the manufacture of nails. A portion of the nail production was exported via the Sambre and Meuse to Holland and Zeeland, primarily for use in the booming shipyards there. Another portion was marketed in Flanders and Brabant, chiefly for local use, but also for export.

A certain degree of specialization in sectors demanding high skills gradually developed in the rural industries as well. The most striking example of this evolution is the production of the *verdures*, simple tapestries, a cruder and cheaper version of the world-famous wall-hangings made in the great centres. *Verdures* were produced in the rural districts between Oudenaarde and Brussels, and sold for export. Lower production costs were unquestionably the motive for the merchant-entrepreneurs' displacement of the industry from the larger to the smaller towns, and from the towns to the countryside. This pattern seems to have been repeated in other sectors of the arts and crafts field, not always with the same success.

The expansion of the export industry in the Southern Netherlands during the second third of the 16th century presupposed extensive importation of raw materials and unfinished products.[12] It also exerted a powerful influence on employment. Both the open and the hidden unemployment in town and countryside were gradually absorbed. The mounting pressure on the labour market was expressed by a rise in nominal, and in some centres even in real, wages.[13] This development was naturally most noticeable in Antwerp, despite its rapid population growth to about 100,000 inhabitants in the 1560s. For instance, the nominal pay of a carpenter around 1555 was almost double that at the beginning of the century. Ten years later it had risen by another 80 to 90%. The rise in wages was particularly sharp after around 1537, and this was the case for both skilled and unskilled workers. Though the increase was less spectacular in the other centres outside Antwerp, nevertheless between 1540 and 1565 wages rose everywhere. Higher incomes in trade and industry for both skilled craftsmen and salaried employees were common and stimulated demand on the domestic market.

The consumption of imported foodstuffs, such as Dutch dairy products, beef cattle from Frisia, Denmark and Northern Germany, and grain from the Baltic region, also rose. Coal was increasingly imported from the prince-bishopric of Liège to provide fuel for the West Brabant towns. The upward cyclical trend also exerted a positive influence on the construction

---

[12] Brulez, *De handel. Antwerpen in de XVIde eeuw* (Antwerp: 1975), pp. 109–42.
[13] Van der Wee, *Growth of the Antwerp Market* I, appendix 48; III, graph 20.

industry, as can be seen from the volume of the trade in building materials, among others: lime from Tournai and Dordrecht, bricks from the Rupel region, roofing slates and freestone from the Walloon provinces, and timber from the Rhineland and Scandinavia.

The domestic market was thus an important component in the second phase of expansion in Southern Netherlands trade between 1536 and 1566. Nevertheless, it should be stressed that the real vitality lay in the export industry, which grew rapidly in both town and countryside during that same period. It should also be emphasized that the infrastructure of Antwerp's port and world trade made possible the distribution of the products of this export industry over a huge market area with minimal transaction costs.

Broadening the Base of Antwerp's World Trade

Thus the Southern Netherlands exported their specialities chiefly in two directions: to Northeastern and to Southern Europe. The expansion towards the Northeast led to the opening of new maritime routes in the Baltic region and to the establishment of new markets, like the port of Narva, which became the official staple market for all Russian goods in 1559. Since the return trade involved bulk goods, it necessitated in the first place a significant expansion of the merchant fleet. In the Netherlands it was primarily shippers from North Holland and from West Frisia who were active along this route, dominating it entirely after the Peace Treaty of Spires in 1544. The shippers from North Holland and West Frisia worked chiefly for shipowners from Amsterdam, though Amsterdam was not their only staple. They often went further afield westward, mainly in the direction of the Southern Netherlands. The Hanseatic shippers and merchants also substantially extended their trading activities, principally with England and with the Netherlands. They decided in 1553 to transfer the Hanse office from Bruges to Antwerp, where the cornerstone for an ambitious, modern Hanse house was laid in 1564.

Some merchants from the Southern Netherlands, who had specialized in the Baltic trade, founded important Baltic companies, like that of Narva and that of Sweden. They imported grain and raw materials from the Baltic region to the Southern Netherlands and, beginning in the 1530s and 1540s, they arranged to transport their grain and raw materials even further, to Italy and Spain via Antwerp. The importation of Baltic grain rose sharply during the second third of the 16th century: at that time it even displaced the traditional grain producers of the Hageland and Haspengouw on the marketplaces of Western Brabant. This development was partially responsible for the economic recession experienced in these two regions during the period.

Southern Europe was the second great market on which the expansion of the new export industry of the Southern Netherlands in the second third of the 16th century was based. Overland transport, together with maritime traffic, continued to play an important role in that region. Maritime traffic was dominated by Antwerp's and Bruges' trade with Spain and Portugal. Shippers from the Southern Netherlands appeared regularly on the Basque and Iberian coasts. Merchants from Bruges and Antwerp were very active in Burgos and at the Castilian fairs, in Lisbon and in Seville. Moreover, they were increasingly involved in trade with the Atlantic sugar islands (the Canaries, Madeira and Saô Tomé). Certain of them even trafficked directly with the New World. This period marked the greatest expansion of trade with the South, and history was made by such renowned trading houses as Della Faille and Harman Janssone. Nor was interest in this trade unilateral: around 1550 there were no fewer than 450 Spanish and Portuguese merchants commercially active at Antwerp.

Northern Italy and the Levant were the principal destinations of overland traffic. Of the two major routes to Northern Italy, one passed through France and Switzerland, and the other followed the Rhine through Germany and the Brenner Pass to Venice and Ancona. Significant organizational progress was made in transcontinental transport during this period of expansion. The Hessians traversed all of Germany with their Hessian waggons. The end of their route lay in Antwerp, where the *Hessenhuis* was constructed for them in 1563–64. There were also prominent Italian firms specializing in long-distance trade overland: to this end they created a network of stage halts embracing the entire European continent. Because of this, Central Germany and Central France were also included in the revival of European overland trade. According to Coornaert there were at least 150 French merchants at Antwerp during the second third of the 16th century.

Later, during the Wars of Religion, overland traffic through France from the Netherlands declined, and trade relations between the two were severely curtailed. In Germany on the other hand the political and economic climate had grown much more favourable during the second half of the 16th century: the traffic from the Netherlands to Italy and from the Netherlands to Germany itself made this a flourishing time. All kinds of textiles from the Southern Netherlands (chiefly serges from Hondschoote, but also many other light fabrics) met with a ready market in the Levant, in Italy and in Germany. The artistic specialities of the Southern Netherlands also found their way into Northern and Western Germany. The Hessians and the Cologne merchants from Antwerp and Cologne sent quantities of goods on overland from the Northern German ports of Lübeck, Hamburg, Bremen, Emden, and so on to markets further inland in Germany.

The growth of the domestic and export markets exerted a powerful influence on the further structural development in the organization of trade in the Southern Netherlands. Since the depression of the 14th and 15th centuries the companies formed by the great Italian families had come to dominate long-distance trade in Bruges and, from the end of the 15th century, in Antwerp too. Southern German firms joined them at the beginning of the 16th century, particularly in Antwerp. However, the passive trade on which they were based required a costly infrastructure which proved impossible to finance efficiently in the face of the simultaneous blossoming of both overland and maritime traffic. The great Italian and Southern German companies therefore began about the middle of the century to concentrate more and more on transactions of a purely financial nature, so that a top-heavy infrastructure became superfluous; in order to manage their affairs successfully they needed only to maintain a presence at the great money markets.

At the same time numerous new trading outposts were created along the new sea routes, along the European coasts and further inland on the Continent. Active trading regained its importance. In Northwestern Europe this was often still within the framework of the existing guild organizations, like that of the Hanseatics or the Merchant Adventurers. Occasionally the greater mercantile houses participated, but the new active trade was soon opened to numerous other shippers, from Holland and Zeeland for example, and to less wealthy merchants, such as those from Cologne or from the Brabant towns. Active trading was also better equipped to operate more efficiently: new commercial methods were introduced, and the implementation of existing methods became more widespread. The bill of exchange, for example, came into more general use in Northwestern Europe during the second third of the 16th century. Furthermore, overland transport made significant organizational progress and great changes, largely inspired by the Dutch, took place in shipbuilding. Maritime insurance was adjusted to the wider range of commercial activity and now offered more effective high-risk coverage. The postal service was also more efficiently organized. Moreover, the invention of the printing press made it possible to publish printed price lists, so that the situation on a given market became swiftly known to interested parties in other places.

Participation and commission selling were the two most important technical innovations in the field of commerce. Participation involved shares in a company established on a temporary basis, for a single, specific commercial voyage, and afterwards dissolved. This enabled merchants with modest capital at their disposal to participate in the rapidly blossoming world trade and to share in the handsome profits associated with it. Just how popular this arrangement was with the lesser and mid-level merchants, particularly for trade with the Baltic and the South, is clearly demonstrated by 16th century commercial documents from Antwerp.[14] Commission selling was another extremely popular arrangement. A merchant could now transfer goods or orders to a colleague abroad, who purchased or sold goods on his behalf, naturally against payment of a stipulated commission. Thus the merchant was himself no longer obliged to travel with his merchandise. Nor was there any longer a need to maintain an expensive network of agencies in the various ports and market towns of Europe. The institution of commission selling, the circulation of newsletters with current price lists, and the rapid delivery of correspondence, contributed to more efficient buying and selling on several different markets, increasing the productivity of both the labour and the capital invested in trade.

The renewal of commercial structures described above amounted to a real broadening of the long-distance trade base. It was implemented, particularly in Antwerp, from the second third of the 16th century onwards and was an important factor in the second phase of economic expansion in the Southern Netherlands, taking place during the same period. Enlarged participation in Antwerp's long-distance trade exerted a decisive influence on the dynamics of trade between the Southern Netherlands and Northern and Southern Europe and, based on the success of the export industries, transformed the active trade of the Netherlands into the driving force behind new economic creativity.

The Economic Resilience of the Southern Netherlands, 1566–87

During its second expansion phase (1536–66), long-distance trade in the Southern Netherlands proved remarkably dynamic in surmounting the external difficulties that gave rise to a whole series of severe political and economic crises in the 1550s, including the terrible famine of 1556–57, which took a dreadful toll among the working classes. The general rise in wages during the following years demonstrates how rapidly and vigorously the economy recovered throughout the region. The outbreak of the Revolt of the Netherlands against Spain in 1568, however, led to a fundamental change. Not that this was experienced as immediate economic ruin: the resilience of the export industries and of long-distance trade was too great for that. But the political and military events that accompanied the Revolt during its first decades gradually led to chaos and to the complete disruption of economic activity in the Southern Netherlands.

The Revolt was no less destructive for the economic structures themselves. At first, the emigration of merchants from the Southern Netherlands probably stimulated the trade of the Southern Netherlands in Europe

---

[14] Brulez, *De handel. Antwerpen...*, passim.

and beyond, for the diaspora strengthened the international infrastructure upon which such trade was based. This effect was, however, strictly transitory. As highly skilled craftsmen also began to emigrate in large numbers from the Southern Netherlands, and the violence of war further depopulated the countryside, as the domestic market shrank due to rising prices and the burdens imposed by the war effort, the fuel that had fed the expansion of long-distance trade disappeared. Although the availability of the best commercial and financial services at Antwerp did stimulate the development of the *Dispositionsgeschäfte*, this was nevertheless only the prelude to a long-term decline that had become irreversible, notwithstanding the economic revival of the beginning of the 17th century.

The trade conflict that erupted between the Regent Margaret of Parma and the English Merchant Adventurers (1563–64), coinciding with the outbreak of the Danish–Polish–Swedish war (1563–70) was the first serious crisis that threatened the expansive economic movement of the second third of the 16th century. It led to a decision by Elizabeth I and her merchants to withdraw the staple for English cloth from Antwerp and move it to Emden. However, the experiment at Emden proved unsatisfactory. In July 1567 an agreement was reached with Hamburg, but here, too, English cloth exports encountered considerable difficulties in the succeeding decades, chiefly for monetary and structural reasons. However, fate had finally turned against the Southern Netherlands.

The withdrawal of the English staple was a measure that had far-reaching economic consequences. The transit trade in English textiles had made an extremely valuable contribution to the revival of long-distance trade in the Southern Netherlands during the 16th century. Moreover, a large portion of the imported cloth was finished locally, leading to the remarkable expansion of Brabant's processing industry. Finally, the contacts between the two lands had facilitated the introduction of specialized industrial and craft products from the Southern Netherlands to the English luxury markets. Thus the withdrawal of the English staple meant a great deal more than the loss of the last important pillar of Antwerp's transit traffic. It represented a severe blow to the processing industry, as well as to the luxury sector, leading to considerable loss of employment. In the long term the English decision appreciably impoverished the economy of the Southern Netherlands.

The trade crisis with England, the political uncertainty in the Baltic region, and the harsh winter of 1565–66 combined to spread a climate of panic over the country. Fears of a shortage of foodstuffs caused grain prices to rise out of all proportion. Unemployment, high grain prices, and an indefinable feeling that the years of prosperity were over, led to rising discontent and unrest. The new doctrine of the Calvinist preachers was greeted with enthusiasm, and the spirit of rebellion spread through a broadening spectrum of society. The tension finally exploded in the iconoclast movement: beginning on 10 August 1566, it swept over the whole of the Netherlands like a violent storm. Philip II reacted to the social and religious disturbances with a series of tough measures. In August of 1567 he sent the duke of Alva to the Netherlands at the head of an impressive army. Military action was followed by a reign of terror and increased fiscal pressure. The Sea Beggars reacted to this with piratical raids in the English Channel (1569-70).

The gravity of the economic crisis just before and at the beginning of the Revolt was most clearly reflected in the evolution of wages. From 1565 on, nominal wages in the majority of towns and villages in Brabant and Flanders gradually declined to a lower level. Such an automatic and generalized decline had hitherto been an exceedingly rare phenomenon in the history of the Southern Netherlands and was clearly indicative of the dramatic nature of the crisis. It was evidently not only domestic and transit trade that was affected; the crisis also hit the export industries hard. All sectors were confronted with grave unemployment problems, experienced not temporarily, but continuously, and hence extremely depressing (see Figure 5.1).

There was clear improvement in the employment situation and in commercial activities beginning in 1570. Maritime traffic from and to the delta of the Scheldt resumed, industrial activity rose again, and wages began to recover. However, the recovery was short-lived. The surprise attack on Brill and the capture of Flushing in April 1572 blocked the Scheldt off entirely. All of Zeeland and Holland gradually passed under control of the rebels, seriously impeding Antwerp's maritime trade with both Northern and Southern Europe. Because at the moment military operations were largely limited to the Northern Netherlands, industrial activity remained for a time relatively unaffected in the towns and villages of the South. The merchants were, however, obliged to seek new outlets for maritime traffic, resorting to the ports at Nieuwpoort, Dunkirk and Calais, and even to those of Rouen, Saint-Malo and Nantes. Furthermore, several successful attempts were made to re-establish Antwerp's trade with England. Antwerp's trade with the Baltic region followed much the same pattern, and to a certain extent so did trade with Holland and Zeeland, albeit through a system of intermediaries and convoys.

In 1576 the tide turned again. The sudden death of governor general Requesens resulted in great confusion. Military operations were for many years now concentrated in the Southern Netherlands. The first peak was reached when mutinous soldiers unleashed the 'Spanish Fury' upon the city of Antwerp on 4 November 1576; the last when Alexander Farnese captured Antwerp from the rebels on 15 August 1585. Between those two dates came a decade during which war, destruction, pillaging, famine, misery and death reigned over the whole of the Southern Netherlands. The countryside was the hardest hit: rural industry virtually died out. For a while it was safer in the towns, but there, too, the export industry suffered from a shortage of raw materials, from the disruption of trade, and from the departure of many skilled workers.

Paradoxically enough, Antwerp initially weathered the storm reasonably well. When in 1577 the town aligned itself with the rebels, it received within its walls an extra contingent of specialized workers who had fled from other places in the Southern Netherlands. Moreover, by joining the Revolt Antwerp's foreign maritime contacts again improved. As a result, the years around 1580 were fairly prosperous. The town fostered hope for peace and, in addition to new initiatives relative to the Portuguese spice trade, Antwerp's long-distance trade with the South revived: direct voyages to Venice and Naples were once more undertaken. In 1580 a merchants' guild was established for trade with Africa and another for trade with England. In 1582 there was even a guild founded for trade with Turkey.

When Farnese's strategy cut off all maritime contact with Antwerp, a darker day dawned for the city. Nor did the crisis end with the city's surrender in 1585, but only after the terrible famine of 1586–87. The city's population had by that time shrunk from a maximum of nearly 100,000 in the 1560s to around 42,000.

Farnese's reconquest of Antwerp sealed the fate of the Scheldt, closing it for a period lasting more than two centuries. Thus it was a crucial and dramatic event in the commercial history of the Southern Netherlands, and of Antwerp in particular. The reconquest, however, implied more than maritime isolation. It represented also the starting point of a revival in both domestic and foreign trade. It also created the conditions for reshaping long distance trade from the Southern Netherlands, a trade with even wider geographical horizons than before, and one wherein the *Dispositionsgeschäfte* played an increasingly central role.

6

Economic Activity and International Trade in the Southern Netherlands, 1538–44

The collection of transcripts of letters sent from Antwerp between 1538 and 1544 by the Flemish brokerage firm Pieter Van der Molen brothers to correspondents in Italy[1] was examined so thoroughly and admirably by Florence Edler[2] in the 1930s that there is no good reason to undertake a similar examination. The aim of the present contribution is merely to add two more price categories to those already established for East Indian pepper and Hondschoote serges, published by Florence Edler on the basis of the surviving Van der Molen letters,[3] i.e. the price list for *Oltrafini* cloth from Armentières and Italian organzine raw silk, which also feature in the same source and, to the best of my knowledge, have not been published by Florence Edler. This contribution will also compare the development of the four price categories and the results of the historical studies which, since the 1930s, have increased our knowledge of economic activity in Europe in general, and in Antwerp in particular.

On behalf of their Italian customers, who gave instructions by correspondence, the Van der Molen brothers bought on commission mainly English, Flemish and Dutch woollen cloth, Flemish and Brabantine tapestry and Flemish, Brabantine and Dutch linen; they also undertook the sending of these goods to Italy, mostly overland.[4] On behalf of the same Italian

---

[1] The notebook is located in the Antwerp City Archives, *Insolvente boedelkamer*, collection no. 2030.

[2] F. Edler, 'The Van der Molen Commission Merchants of Antwerp: Trade with Italy, 1538–44', in: *Mediaeval and Historical Essays in Honor of James Westfall Thompson* (Chicago: 1937), pp. 78–145.

[3] F. Edler, 'Le Commerce d'exportation des sayes d'Hondschoote vers l'Italie d'après la correspondance d'une firme anversoise entre 1538 et 1544', in: *Revue du Nord* XXII (1936), pp. 249–66; F. Edler, 'Winchcombe Kerseys in Antwerp, 1538–1544', in: *The Economic History Review*, 7 (1936), pp. 57–62; F. Edler, 'The Market for Spices in Antwerp, 1538–1544', in: *Revue Belge de Philologie et d'Histoire* 17 (1938), pp. 212–21.

[4] In this connection see also W. Brulez, 'L'exportation des Pays-Bas vers l'Italie par voie de terre au milieu du XVIe siècle', in: *Annales E.S.C.*, 14 (1959), pp. 461–91.

customers, again giving instructions by correspondence, the Van der Molens sold on commission in Antwerp and at the fairs in Bergen-op-Zoom Genoese velvet, Venetian silk satin, Turkish camlets and mohair fabrics and also spices, medicinal herbs and precious stones, which were all sent from Italy to the Netherlands. Most of this merchandise was bought or sold in Antwerp or Bergen-op-Zoom.[5] There were, however, important exceptions, for example, coloured light woollen cloths from Hondschoote – particularly popular with the Italian upper classes – were always bought in Hondschoote by the Van der Molen brothers' local representative and paid for immediately in hard cash. Some English cloth was purchased in England with the help of a local correspondent. This was sometimes the case for other items too, such as Dutch linen or Flemish-Brabantine tapestry, although this was more the exception than the rule.

The prices of the various goods on the Antwerp market and in Hondschoote reflect the usual interplay of supply and demand. However, the specific factors affecting prices may be divided into two main categories: first, fortuitous events between 1538 and 1544 which would have a direct and marked effect on prices; second, the undercurrent of cyclical and structural changes beginning even before 1538.

The first category includes social and political events such as wars and revolts or strikes which proved a considerable hindrance to international trade in Antwerp during the period and which, naturally, are emphasized and dealt with in detail in the Van der Molen letters. The restrictions on trade as a whole were monetary and political. On 8 May 1539, by imperial ordinance, the authorities lowered by approximately 5% the rates for gold coin in terms of silver double groats or stivers (*stuivers*); they were lowered by about a further 5% on 1 July 1539.[6] This brought the rates for gold coin in terms of silver stivers to their 1527 value, which in turn meant a return to the official 1521 rates. The gradual rise of the rates for gold coin on the market was a sign that the market value of gold in relation to silver exceeded the official ratio, and also that the consequent official undervaluing of gold was being eroded continuously by market forces.

For a short time the two 1539 monetary ordinances attempting to counter the rise of the gold rates on the market caused general confusion and uncertainty: the sudden official undervaluation of gold resulting from the reimposed low official rates led to hoarding or, even more frequently,

---

[5] F. Edler, 'De deelname van vreemde kooplieden aan de Bergsche jaarmarkten van 1538 tot 1544', in: *Sinte Geertruydtsbronne* (1936), pp. 1–36.

[6] F. Edler, 'The Effects of the Financial Measures of Charles V on the Commerce of Antwerp, 1539–1542', in: *Revue Belge de Philologie et d'Histoire*, 16 (1937), pp. 665–73.

to the export of gold, in particular to France, thereby creating a critical shortage of coins of large denominations for financing international trade. When the emissary of the Portuguese king was forced by these circumstances to borrow a substantial sum of money, the shortage of cash on the Antwerp money market became even more acute, so that interest rates after December 1539 rose to between 24% and 30% per year. International trade in Antwerp was thus deeply affected by the currency measures of 1539. The prices of Hondschoote woollen serges,[7] *Oltrafini* woollen cloth from Armentières[8] and Italian organzine raw silk all fell[9] rapidly, while pepper prices for the same period also stagnated.

The second significant monetary measure was the imperial ordinance of 10 December 1541.[10] It stipulated that all bills of exchange were to be paid for in hard cash, two-thirds in gold coins and one-third in silver at the official rates. On the Antwerp international market much trading was already being done using bills of exchange: if an Antwerp merchant, for example, needed cash on the Antwerp market to finance his purchasing on behalf of an Italian colleague, he would draw a bill of exchange on his Italian colleague and sell it for cash to a banker in Antwerp, who would immediately mail the document to a fellow banker in Italy: after the latter had received the bill, he would present it to the aforementioned Italian merchant for payment in cash. The December 1541 ordinance hindered these payment practices. Furthermore, most of the gold coins on the list were circulating on the market at a premium and would not have been used for cash payments, had the official rates applied. Similar problems arose if an Antwerp banker accepted for payment in cash a bill of exchange payable on a specific date or at a particular Antwerp fair and wished to redeem it by issuing a new bill drawn on a fellow banker in a foreign country: this form of credit was no longer possible, since all bills of exchange payable in Antwerp had to be redeemed in hard cash. The fall in prices of woollen serges, *Oltrafini* cloth, and organzine raw silk at the beginning of 1542 as a result of Charles V's exchange

---

[7] Further details on the Hondschoote serges in E. Coornaert, *Un centre industriel d'autrefois, la draperie-sayetterie d'Hondschoote* (Paris: 1930).

[8] For the *Oltrafini* cloth from Armentières see E. Coornaert, *Les Français et le commerce international à Anvers* I (Paris: 1961), pp. 171–3: II, p. 115.

[9] J. Denucé, *Koopmansleerboeken van de XVIe en XVIIe eeuwen in handschrift* (Brussels: 1941), pp. 67–8, 180–1; W. Brulez, *De Firma Della Faille en de internationale handel van Vlaamse Firma's in de 16e eeuw* (Brussels: 1959), pp. 279–306; A.K.L. Thijs, *De zijdenijverheid te Antwerpen in de zeventiende eeuw*, (Brussels: 1969), pp. 1–11.

[10] Edler, 'The Effects of the Financial Measures...', pp. 665–75.

ordinances demonstrates that the Antwerp international market was affected considerably by the measure.

Charles V's war against the French and Danish kings and the duke of Cleves, Jülich and Gelderland, which broke out in July 1542 and cut the main road between Antwerp and Cologne for a year, also brought about a fall in the prices of serges, *Oltrafini* and Portuguese pepper and a rise in the price of organzine raw silk. Sales of Portuguese spices, English, Flemish and Brabantine textiles to Southern Europe were greatly impeded by the war, so that stocks built up, thereby putting downward pressure on prices in Antwerp. On the other hand inadequate deliveries of Italian organzine raw silk led at the same time to a shortage of silk yarn, a raw material that was essential to the Flemish-Brabantine silk weavers, and to an increase in price.

The Antwerp spice market had not only to contend with all kinds of official measures and political upheavals, but also to struggle against rumours and internal difficulties. The premature arrival of the Portuguese spice fleet on the isle of Walcheren in 1542 – it arrived in October instead of December – meant an unexpected surplus of goods, which the spice-monopoly merchants could only start selling off slowly after December, aided by rumours that the Portuguese had been forced to abandon the fortress of Diu on the pepper route and of an uprising in India. In 1540 and 1541 spice prices were adversely affected by the arrival of spice ships in Marseilles after the conclusion of an alliance between Suleiman the Magnificent and François I: they were constantly affected by the unpredictable relations between Venice and the Ottoman Empire during the same period. The spread of epidemics among the West Flemish rural population sometimes affected the prices of Hondschoote serges. Prices also tended to rise during the harvest months in Hondschoote because the indigent weavers and fullers could earn more money during this period as seasonal agricultural workers.[11]

As well as considering those events affecting the Antwerp international market, it is important also to examine the structural changes reflected in the price evidence. An initial series of structural changes is related to the rapid expansion of Antwerp's money and capital market and the concomitant increase in the complexity of financial practices. Antwerp had become the hub of financial innovations which Italy in particular, but also the Hanseatic League and England, had introduced in the late Middle Ages; Italy's main contribution was the introduction and enhancement of the system of bills of exchange and the expansion of deposit banking; the Hanseatic League and England had introduced the use of transferable letters obligatory by adding the clause 'payable to X or to the bearer of this letter'.

---

[11] For further details on these events see the previous contributions by Edler.

Antwerp's innovations included the extension of the system of transferability of letters obligatory and bills of exchange to a system of negotiability, and subsequently the introduction of modern discount banking and the setting up of the modern Exchange. Indeed Antwerp, in its own creative way, achieved a fusion of the Italian and Northern European systems which constitutes the foundation of today's finance and banking.[12]

However, innovations of such scope took time. The Antwerp money and capital market did not always enjoy sustained growth during the 1520s and 1530s: the new financial practices sometimes worked against the old ones or the new ones against each other. This gave rise to serious tensions and to a level of speculation, abuses, and corruption that forced the government to take action. It is against this background that we should consider the various measures introduced by Charles V after 1537 concerning money, payments, and credit, aimed particularly at the Antwerp money and capital market.[13] The first ordinances were too vague and therefore not very effective: they tended to increase tensions rather than abate them and had serious consequences for international trade in the Netherlands. Gradually the official measures took clearer shape towards securing monetary stability, improving the payment system, and better organizing the Exchange's activities. As a result of these government ordinances a specific and coherent system of financial practices emerged which brought about lower transaction costs, and thus generated a downward price trend. There are good reasons for believing that this contributed to the downward trend of prices in the years 1538–44.

A second series of structural changes which would have a significant influence on the downward trend of prices between 1538 and 1544 arose from the stagnation of the Antwerp transit trade from the 1530s onwards and from the manner in which the government took action to combat this stagnation.[14] The main factor contributing to the rapid economic recovery in the Netherlands at the end of the 15th century and the beginning of the 16th century had been the powerful expansion of the Antwerp international transit trade as a result of rapidly increasing exports of English cloth, South German fustians (a mixed fabric of cotton and flax yarn), Central European copper and silver and Portuguese colonial products.[15] This thriving Antwerp transit trade was, however, very

---

[12] See below, chapter 8.

[13] See also O. de Smedt, 'De keizerlijke verordeningen van 1537 en 1539 op de obligaties en wisselbrieven', in: *Nederlandsche Historiebladen* III, 1 (January 1940), pp. 15–35.

[14] For these two movements of expansion in Antwerp's economy see H. van der Wee, *The Growth of the Antwerp Market and the European Economy (Fourteenth–Sixteenth Centuries)* II (Paris–The Hague: 1963), pp. 124–36, 166–207.

[15] J.A. Van Houtte, 'La genèse du grand marché international à Anvers à la fin du moyen-âge', in: *Revue Belge de Philologie et d'Histoire* 19 (1940), pp. 87–126.

vulnerable and unstable. The panic caused by the Valois–Habsburg wars of the 1520s, for example, shook the Antwerp transit market very seriously; soon afterwards the gradual revival of the Venetian spice trade, using the traditional Red Sea and Mediterranean route, was threatening the Antwerp monopoly for the European distribution of so-called Portuguese spices, which arrived at Lisbon from overseas and were then sent on to Antwerp; another factor disturbing the Antwerp transit trade was perhaps the drastic lowering of the official rates for large gold and silver coins, a policy originally implemented in 1527 by Charles V: it was clearly a disincentive to foreign merchants to purchase goods at the Brabant fairs and to pay cash with the officially undervalued larger gold and silver coins they had brought with them when travelling to the Netherlands. This monetary policy, which was pursued until the 1550s, was probably also responsible for the downward pressure on Antwerp prices between 1538 and 1544.

There was a sharp contrast between the stagnation and even decline of the Antwerp transit trade from the 1520s onwards and the gradual expansion of the new Flemish and Brabantine export industries. During the Burgundian era many cities in the Netherlands had experienced an impressive restructuring of these industries, whose main sectors included the industrial arts, fashion and ready-made clothes, luxury goods and other forms of specialized merchandise such as paintings, altar screens, musical instruments, illuminated manuscripts, brass, bells and silk fabrics.[16] In the countryside the production of high-quality standardized woollen and linen fabrics, characterized by a systematic division of labour, also expanded considerably. The increasing supply of quality goods from urban and rural industries kept pace with European demand, growing as a result of the economic boom in the late 15th and early 16th centuries which had increased incomes in Spain, France, Italy and Central and Eastern Europe, thereby creating extra demand for goods which were not available locally. Urban and rural industries in the Netherlands, therefore, expanded their markets to the whole of Europe, adding a new dynamism to the Antwerp market, threatened at that time by stagnation in its transit trade. Antwerp now became first and foremost a world-famous export centre for specialized merchandise and luxury goods produced in the Netherlands. This export success in turn constituted an important stimulus for growth in several towns and rural areas of the Netherlands: export-led growth, therefore, was no longer restricted to Antwerp and Bergen-op-Zoom, as had been the case at the beginning of the 16th century, but now embraced a much wider area.

---

[16] This point is dealt with in detail in H. Van der Wee, 'Structural Changes and Specialisation in the Industry of the Southern Netherlands, 1100–1600', in: *The Economic History Review, Second Series* XXVIII (May 1975), pp. 203–21.

To what extent is this second set of structural changes actually reflected in the prices recorded in the Van der Molen letters? The falling prices of Hondschoote serges and grey cloth from Weert between 1538 and 1544 are unexpected in the context of the increasingly successful exports of woollen fabrics from the rural industries in the Netherlands, from which one might anticipate a rising price trend. A possible explanation might be that an increase in scale, due to the expansion of home and export demand, led to an increase in physical productivity of labour in the rural industry, an increase which kept prices down notwithstanding an upward trend in demand for serges and grey cloth. On the other hand the supply of labour in the countryside, because of hidden unemployment, remained large, preventing production costs from rising, even when demand was increasing.

For the traditional *Oltrafini* cloths from Armentières price cuts were the essential weapon in the struggle to retain markets, but were used less successfully than in the case of the Hondschoote and Weert fabrics. Production at Armentières was at its height about 1540, after which there was a gradual decline, notwithstanding falling prices between 1538 and 1545. Why was there such a decline when the rural character of the industry also gave the *Oltrafini* cloth a cost and price advantage? Competition from England is a possible explanation for the paradox. England was still a big producer of high-quality traditional woollen cloth, as was Armentières, but England had the advantage of being the main European producer of top-quality wool, a factor which favoured the English textile industry. Furthermore, during the 1540s England was experiencing Henry VIIIs 'great debasement' policy, which briefly favoured the export of English traditional cloth.

A study of price movements after 1550 reveals a very different picture. The prices of Hondschoote serges[17] and of the grey cloth from Weert[18] rose, while those of *Oltrafini* from Armentières fell even further. As far as the Hondschoote and Weert fabrics are concerned the rising demand this time no longer seemed to be accompanied by cost-reducing supply factors or, if the latter were still present, the influence of demand became predominant. Hondschoote serges became increasingly popular in Italian court circles, in papal Rome and even in the Ottoman Empire. Fashion rather than price, therefore, seems to have become a crucial variable in the explanation of the export success of the Hondschoote serges. A similar explanation can be suggested for the cheap grey cloth from Weert and the surrounding area, but this time domestic demand, and not export demand, was the decisive factor. On the contrary, falling export and

---

[17] V. Vazquez de Prada, *Lettres marchandes d'Anvers* I (Paris: 1960), p. 257.
[18] Van der Wee, *The Growth of the Antwerp Market*... I, p. 272.

domestic demand for *Oltrafini* cloth from Armentières – because heavy high-quality cloth went out of fashion – was a crucial price variable, having the opposite effect where the prices of Hondschoote and Weert fabrics were concerned.

Between 1538 and 1545 price trends in Antwerp for Italian organzine raw silk, an important raw material for the silk industries in the Netherlands, were also linked to demand. Following the closure of the Rhine route in the latter half of 1542, for example, Antwerp silk prices rose sharply, while there was still a big demand for raw silk in the Netherlands, when supplies were cut. After the reopening of the Rhine route, prices of organzine raw silk started declining, as supplies were returning to their normal level again and stocks were being replenished.[19] In the longer term, the price trend of organzine raw silk in Antwerp rose. This rise was similar to the long-term trend of the Hondschoote serges and linked to shifts in fashion and demand. The use of silk in clothing, which was traditionally confined to royalty, the aristocracy and the Church, now also became very popular among the well-to-do urban middle classes. To meet the requirements of this rising fashion, there was a considerable move towards import substitution in silk throwing and silk weaving in the Netherlands, leading to an increase in the demand for raw silk at the Antwerp markets and, therefore, an increase in prices.

A third structural change which characterized the Antwerp international market around the middle of the 16th century arose from broader participation in foreign trade, as the practice of commission and the system of temporary partnership, based on participation by a larger number of small- and medium-sized merchant firms in limited commercial projects, became more widespread.[20] The fall in transaction costs which ensued from the simplifying and competition-stimulating effects of commission trade may also have affected the general price trend. Price trends do not contradict this hypothesis, with the exception of those for pepper, which were affected by the monopolistic character of the spice trade in contrast to the more competitive system of the trade in textiles. The Van der Molen letters, which are rich in evidence of an emerging commission trade in Antwerp in the 1530s and 1540s, confirm the importance of this form of structural change.

Conclusion

The analysis of the movement of market prices as revealed in commercial

---

[19] Silk weaving had already become popular in Bruges in the 15th century. After 1496 the Bruges silk weavers had their own guild. In Antwerp at the beginning of the 16th century there were already silk weavers. In 1533 there was even a municipal ordinance relating to the Antwerp satin weavers (Thijs, *De zijdenijverheid te Antwerpen*..., pp. 61–3).

[20] Van der Wee, *The Growth of the Antwerp Market*... II, pp. 191, 325–6.

ECONOMIC ACTIVITY AND INTERNATIONAL TRADE

letters from Antwerp during a short period around the middle of the 16th century was a hazardous enterprise. However, it was worth undertaking, as market prices reflect the daily conditions of supply and demand as well as underlying structural changes in the economy. The comparison of the Van der Molen price data with information from other sources and the formulation of some hypotheses about structural changes in the Netherlands allow a few tentative explanations that may help the student of 16th-century economic history.

Table 6.1: *Prices of some important goods from Dutch–Italian foreign trade on the Antwerp international market, in pounds, shillings and pence (Flemish money of account).*

Date	Flemish Oltrafini cloth (Armentières)	Organzine raw silk (per pound) Cash	Credit
1538			
11/5			31 S. à 31 S. 6 D.
22/6		29 S.	32 S.
13/7			32 S.
24/8			32 S.
14/9			33 S. à 34 S.
5/10			34 S.
16/11			34 S.
14/12			34 S.
1539			
22/1			34 S.
1/2			34 S.
1/3	6 £ 12 S.		34 S.
29/3			33 S.
26/4			32 S. 6 D.
8/5	6 £ 6 S.		
24/5			31 S.
11/6	6 £ 4 S.		
21/6		28 S.	31 S.
17/8	5 £ 17 S.		30 S.
13/9	5 £ 10 S.		32 S.
12/10	5 £ 6 S.		31 S. 6 D.
9/11			31 S.

Date	Flemish Oltrafini cloth (Armentières)	Organzine raw silk (per pound) Cash	Credit
1540			
4/1		28 S.	
1/2		27 S. 6 D	
29/2			30 S. 6 D.
30/5	5 £ 14 S.		
27/6		25 S.	28 S. 6 D.
25/7	5 £ 12 S.	25 S.	28 S. à 29 S.
22/8		25 S.	27 S.
19/9		25 S.	
14/11			28 S. à 28 S. 6 D.
12/12			28 S. 6 D.
1541			
9/1	5 £ 14 S.		29 S. 6 D. à 30 S.
1/5	5 £ 14 S.		29 S. à 30 S.
29/5	5 £ 12 S.		29 S. 6 D.
13/11	5 £ 12 S.	25 S.	
11/12			29 S.
1542			
8/1			28 S. 6 D.
4/2	5 £ 14 S.		
5/2			29 S.
12/3		25 S. 6 D.	29 S.
16/4		24 S. 1½ D. (1)	29 S. à 29 S. 6 D.
14/5		24 S. 4 D. (2)	29 S.
9/7			28 S. 6 D.
29/10			30 S. à 31 S.
23/12			30 S.
1543			
19/4		27 S.	30 S. à 31 S.
13/10	4 £ 14 S. à 4 £ 15 S.		
1544			
17/5		5 £ 16 S.	
4/10			30 S.

(1) "a contanti 15 bis 20 Percent manco".
(2) "a danari 12, 14, 16 Percent manco".

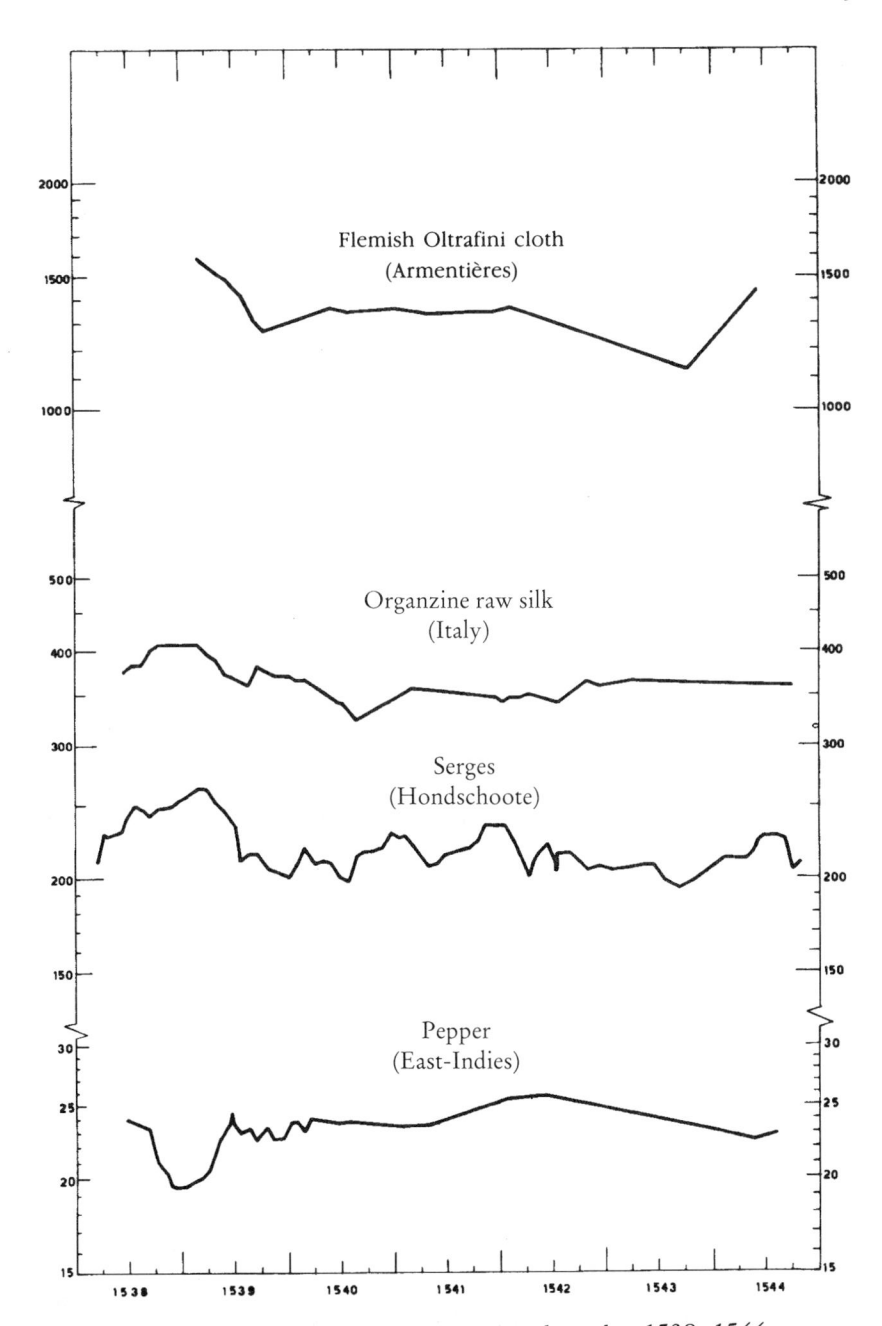

ECONOMIC ACTIVITY AND INTERNATIONAL TRADE 125

Figure 6.1: *Prices on the Antwerp international market 1538–1544.
(Flemish money of account: semi-logarithmic scale).*

7

Trade Relations between Antwerp and the Northern Netherlands, 14th to 16th Century

The expanding maritime development of the 14th century embraced the German, Scandinavian and Baltic worlds, together with the more southerly provinces of Holland, Zeeland and Frisia. One of the factors favourably influencing the economic growth of these regions was their contact with those towns of the Southern Netherlands that had arisen in the 11th–12th centuries and already numbered among the most dynamic centres of the European economy. The strong ties between the Northern and Southern Netherlands facilitated the North's gradual absorption of the modern forms of economic development and organization that had already reached the Southern Netherlands from Italy. Contact between the German Hanse and centres such as Bruges and London, however, remained much more superficial. The Hanseatic towns, with their conservative mentality, tended to form small, isolated centres with a closed, corporative structure abroad.[1] For this reason they slowly lost ground, from a technical and dynamic point of view, to the Northern Netherlands.

Commercially, the latter were perceived in the Southern Netherlands chiefly as trading in salt and herring, in dairy products and hop beer, wine and grain. All these trades were entirely independent of the urban textile industry, they did not threaten the textile towns of the South and consequently could continue their development without hindrance to the economic growth of the South.

Northern German and Dutch Hop Beer (14th–15th Centuries)

From the second half of the 14th century onwards, hop beer became the export product *par excellence* of Northern Germany, and even more so of Holland. The principal production centres were Haarlem,[2] Bremen and

---
[1] M.M. Postan, 'The Trade of Medieval Europe: the North', *The Cambridge Economic History of Europe* II (Cambridge: 1952), pp. 223–32.
[2] J. Van Loenen, *De Haarlemse brouwindustrie vóór 1600* (Amsterdam: 1950).

Hamburg[3], in 1374 already the site of some 450 independent breweries.[4] Flanders and Brabant were their chief customers, to the detriment of their own domestic brewers. For example, the share of domestic beer in urban consumption at Lier had fallen by around 1408–9 to approximately 25% of the town's total consumption. The other three-quarters of Lier's beer consumption consisted of beer imported from the North, almost exclusively from Haarlem, which accounted for 97% of the total import, with Hamburg supplying the rest.[5] From the 14th century onwards the accounts of tolls collected at Antwerp bear witness to the volume of these imports, shipped via Antwerp and a dense network of riverways, deep into the hinterland of Brabant.[6] The imports reached Flanders by way of the port of Sluis, and here, too, the volume rose steeply. By the end of the 14th century even collecting and trading in empty barrels had become extensive enough to prompt a request for a monopoly: Coppin Vigerszone, employee of the chancellor of Burgundy, was granted this monopoly for Flanders in August 1398 by the duke.[7]

What was the secret of the immense success of the North European and Dutch beers? The first and direct cause lay in improved brewing techniques. Whereas in the Southern Netherlands brewing was still done in the traditional manner using grout,[8] in the North, and perhaps for the first time, brewing had been profoundly changed by the addition of hops in beer processing.[9] Hop beer was already being brewed at Dordrecht in 1322, in 1326 at Delft, and in 1327 at Haarlem.[10] Hop beer not only meant better quality, it also kept longer than *gruutebier*, an extremely valuable asset for an export product. It was to remain an important export for both Holland and Northern Germany throughout the whole of the 15th century. From the second quarter of the 15th century on, however, sales of imported hop beer fell in Brabant[11] in favour of domestic beer, now

---

[3] A. Schulte, 'Vom Grutbiere. Eine Studie zur Wirtschafts- und Verfassungsgeschichte', in: *Annalen des Historischen Vereins für den Niederrhein* 85 (1908), pp. 118–46.

[4] E. Daenell, *Die Blütezeit der deutschen Hanse. Hansische Geschichte von der zweiten Hälfte des XIV. bis zum letzten Viertel des XV. Jahrhunderts* I (Leipzig: 1905–6), p. 267.

[5] Brussels, General Archives, Rekenkamer, 5179.

[6] R. Doehaerd, *Comptes du tonlieu d'Anvers, 1365–1404* (Brussels: 1947).

[7] Lille, Archives Départementales du Nord (hereafter ADN), B 1598, f. 101: ordinance of August 1398. Figure taken from a list of ducal ordinances from the archives of Lille, compiled by Prof. Dr J.A. Van Houtte and obligingly placed at our disposal, for which our sincere thanks.

[8] A mixture of bilberries and a variety of herbs: G. Doorman, *De middeleeuwse brouwerij en de gruit* (The Hague: 1955).

[9] H. Van der Wee in: *Atti del X Congresso Internazionale dei Scienze Storiche* (Rome: 1955), p. 404.

[10] Schulte, *Vom Grutbiere*, p. 140.

[11] Van Loenen, *De Haarlemse brouwindustrie*, p. 55.

also brewed by the new method with hops.[12] At that time Delft, and especially Gouda, introduced their famed, inexpensive *koytebier*, compensating to some extent for the drop in Haarlem's export.[13] In 1474 imports of Dutch *koytebier* still accounted for around 25% of total beer consumption at Lier.[14]

Nevertheless, it would be inaccurate to attribute the success of Northern German, and especially of Dutch, beer exclusively to the use of hops. It should also be viewed in the broader context of the 14th-century economy. Economically, the 14th century was characterized by two important phenomena: the agrarian depression and the expansion of maritime traffic through the establishment of a direct sea link between Italy and the Netherlands, coupled with the rise of the Hanseatics. Falling grain prices, a result of the declining population,[15] were the first manifestation of the agrarian depression. Would this not lead to a search for other, industrial uses for grain, specifically in the brewing industry? Did not the great grain-producing regions, such as the East German–Baltic region, see in this new industry an opportunity to obtain relatively better prices for their exports, in comparison with the exports of mere grain and in doing so increase the value of their grain surplus? As early as the 14th-century grain was transported from the Baltic region towards the more southerly of the Hanseatic ports and towards Holland for processing into beer.[16] That their geographical situation facilitated trade relations with other urban consumers is clearly shown by the success of exports to Flanders and Brabant.

In addition to technical innovations and the agrarian depression, the expansion of maritime traffic during the 14th century was another factor favouring the export of hop beer from the North. New generations of merchants, first the Hanseatics, and later merchants from England and Holland as well, were all active in the maritime zones and engaged in this trade. The Hanseatics established themselves at Bruges,[17] while the other two opted for a new base of operations: the burgeoning annual fairs of Antwerp and Bergen-op-Zoom. This was a wager with the future, and one they were destined to win.

---

[12] H. Van der Wee, *The Growth of the Antwerp Market and the European Economy (Fourteenth–Sixteenth Centuries)* I (Paris–The Hague: 1963), pp. 228–9; II, pp. 31, 54.

[13] Van Loenen, *De Haarlemse brouwindustrie*, pp. 61–2.

[14] Lier, City Archives, *Rekenwezen*, 49.

[15] Postan, *The Trade of Medieval Europe: the North*, pp. 205 ff.

[16] W.S. Unger, *De levensmiddelenvoorziening der Hollandsche steen in de middeleeuwen* (Amsterdam: 1916), pp. 1–53. And especially M. Malowist, 'Les produits des pays de la Baltique dans le commerce international au XVIe siècle' in: *Revue du Nord* XLII (1960), pp. 179–82, and M.P. Lesnikov, 'Beiträge zur Baltisch–Niederländischen Handelsgeschichte am Ausgang des 14. und zu Beginn des 15. Jahrhunderts', in: *Wissenschftliche Zeitschrift der Karl-Marx-Universität* VII (Leipzig: 1957–58), pp. 613–26.

[17] Postan, 'The Trade of Medieval Europe: the North', pp. 218 ff.

The Growth of the Herring Industry and the Riddle of Salt from Zeeland and Zeeland–Flanders (14th–15th centuries)

Doorman has suggested, based on existing tradition, that Willem Beukels invented a method of gutting herring at Biervliet around 1320, turning that small town into an important centre for the herring and salt industries.[18] Sources from Brabant, however, clearly confirm the extremely weak position of Flanders and Zeeland in the barrelled herring trade prior to 1400, and bear witness to the unquestioned supremacy of barrelled and gutted herring from the region of Schonen on the Brabant markets.[19]

Already in 1293 and 1321 herring from Schonen was referred to as *tonharing* (barrel herring),[20] as opposed to the Flemish *korfharing* (basket herring), a term which seems to have designated chiefly buckling or smoked herring.[21] Moreover the oldest *Pfundzoll* registers, from 1368 and later, no longer speak of barrels, but express their estimate of the entire herring production of Schonen in terms of the number of *caques*.[22] This suggests either that barrels and *caques* are synonymous, implying that gutting herring (by removing the gills and some of the viscera from the fish through the throat) had been current practice at Schonen for a long while; or that the two terms are not equivalent and the term *caques* reflects a later introduction of gutting in Schonen, although it was already practised by the early 14th century, since gutted herring is mentioned there as early as 1332.

That in the same year Flemish shippers delivered gutted herring to the French Court[23] is not in itself adequate proof that gutting was practised in Flanders at that time. Merchants from Flanders, as well as from England, Zeeland and Holland, regularly attended the annual fairs held at Schonen to purchase herring.[24] Presumably they brought gutted herring from Schonen as well as Flemish buckling south with them. Perhaps they did attempt to imitate the gutting method used in Schonen for processing herring, though at least initially their efforts met with little success, since 14th century sources reveal a systematic preference on the part of Netherlands abbeys and hospitals or almshouses for gutted herring from Schonen.

---

[18] G. Doorman, 'Het haringkaken en Willem Beukels', in: *Tijdschrift voor Geschiedenis* 69 (1956), pp. 371–86. Also 'Nogmaals: de middeleeuwse haringvisserij', in: *Bijdragen voor de Geschiedenis der Nederlanden* XIV (1959), pp. 104–15.

[19] Van der Wee, *The Growth of the Antwerp Market* I, p. 277, n.1.

[20] G. Doorman, 'De haringvisserij in de middeleeuwen', in: *Bijdragen voor de Geschiedenis der Nederlanden* XIX (1965), p. 167.

[21] *Ibid.*, pp. 163–6.

[22] A.E. Christensen, 'La foire de Scanie', in: *Recueils de la Société Jean Bodin, V: La Foire* (Brussels: 1953), pp. 253–4.

[23] Doorman, 'De haringvisserij', p. 168.

[24] Christensen, 'La foire de Scanie', pp. 250 ff.

The Hanse's formal exclusion of the English in 1368, and shortly afterwards of merchants from Flanders, Zeeland and Holland, from the annual fairs of Schonen,[25] perhaps provided the stimulus for a more serious investigation of the possibility of adopting the Schonen method of gutting herring. The sources appear to confirm that Biervliet and Hugevliet became prominent at about that time.[26] Still, gutted herring from the Netherlands established itself in markets in those regions only with difficulty: around 1400 the Brabant abbeys and charitable institutions still purchased gutted herring mainly from Schonen, and only when circumstances made this difficult or impossible did these institutions purchase barrelled herring from the Netherlands. There was, however, an undeniable rise in the sale of the latter after 1400, and in the second third of the 15th century the supremacy of Schonen gutted herring was finally broken by the competition from Flanders, Holland and Brabant.[27] The herring processors of Antwerp, Mechlin, and 's Hertogenbosch, for example, acquired great fame even abroad, both to the East and to the West. Cologne,[28] Rouen and Dieppe[29] became important staple markets for gutted herring from the Netherlands. Together with buckling, traditionally produced mainly in Flanders, it was one of the two pillars of a booming herring industry that continued to prosper throughout the entire 16th century. Along with the herring fishery, based primarily in Zeeland and Holland, fish processing was a crucial sector of economic activity in all the above mentioned territories.[30]

The triumph of barrelled herring from the Netherlands over the gutted herring from Schonen coincided chronologically with a sharp shift in the

---

[25] *Ibid.*, p. 250.

[26] At the end of the 14th century the Flemish were forbidden, *ten versoeke vanden copman vander deutschen Hense* (at the request of the leader of the German Hanse), to gut fish at sea. This ban was lifted as early as 1399 for Biervliet and Hugevliet, but only in 1408 for the other coastal towns as well (Doorman, 'De haringvisserij', p. 171).

For more on this problem see also R. Degrijse, 'Schonense en Vlaamse kaakharing in de 14e eeuw', in: *Bijdragen voor de Geschiedenis der Nederlanden* XII, 157, pp. 100–7. And, by the same author, 'Het begin van het haringkaken te Biervliet (ca. 1400)', in: *Handelingen van het Genootschap voor Geschiedenis* XCV (1958), pp. 72–81.

[27] Van der Wee, *The Growth of the Antwerp Market* I pp. 277–8.

[28] B. Kuske, 'Der Kölner Fischhandel vom 14.–17. Jahrhundert', in: *Westdeutsche Zeitschrift für Geschichte und Kunst* (1905), pp. 261 ff.

[29] M. Mollat, *Le commerce maritime normand au XVe siècle et dans la première moitié du XVI siècle* (Paris: 1952), pp. 103, 313–7.

[30] For the crucial importance of the herring fishery in Holland and Zeeland during the 16th century, see among others the correspondence of Stadtholder Hoogstraten and of the Regentess between 1530 and 1550: R. Häpke, *Niederländische Akten und Urkunden zur Geschichte der Hanse und zur deutschen Seegeschichte* (Munich–Leipzig–Lübeck: 1913–23), among others: I, pp. 302 and 391.

salt market from traditional *Zelzout* to French bay salt. This parallel does not seem to be entirely a matter of chance. Throughout the entire 14th century and at the beginning of the 15th century the *Zelzout* unquestionably took first place in the Brabant sources. It was purchased in vast quantities by all sorts of charitable institutions and hospitals for use at table and for preserving meat, butter and other perishable foodstuffs.[31] It was extracted from salt-holding peat (*darinc* or *zelle*), dug from the salt marshes or river banks. The peat was then burnt to ash, rinsed with sea water, and afterwards cooked in pans over peat fires.[32] The great medieval producers of *Zelzout* were: Goes, Zierikzee, Steenbergen, Tolen, Brielle, Reimerswaal, Schiedam, Axel, Biervliet and Hulst. But all these centres were overshadowed by Zevenbergen, which had come to dominate the salt trade to such an extent that the *zoutmudde* of Zevenbergen became the standard salt measure in general use in all the Brabant towns, from Brussels to Louvain, but especially on the staple market at Mechlin in the 14th and 15th centuries.[33]

During the second quarter of the 15th-century French bay salt appeared in increasing quantities on the Brabant markets, and from the second half of the century on it displaced the traditional *Zelzout*.[34] A variety of factors contributed to this shift; some were inextricably linked to the nature of the article itself, whereas others need to be examined in a broader context, as was done in the analysis of the brewing industry.

Zelzout was a high-quality product but, as its production called for both high wages and enormous quantities of fuel, it remained costly. Investigation of the sources has revealed that its price was as much as 50 to 100% higher than that of bay salt.[35] The fact that even transport costs seem not to have raised the price of bay salt significantly brings us back to the influence of maritime expansion[36] and of the improved maritime technology introduced during the 14th century. Together they made possible the relatively inexpensive transport of heavy bulk cargoes such as salt by sea. Bay salt's breakthrough in the North was temporarily checked, however, by the insecurity of the sea routes stemming from the

---

[31] Van der Wee, *The Growth of the Antwerp Market* I, pp. 287–8. For the export of *Zelzout* from Reimerswaal, Tolen, Steenbergen, and Zevenbergen to Antwerp, Diest, Aachen, Cologne, and further around 1400, see the testimony of the Antwerp shipper Danckaert Peterssone and the Diest merchant Bellen van Breeden: Antwerp, City Archives, (hereafter ASA), T. 584, f° 245r° – v°.

[32] A.R. Bridbury, *England and the Salt Trade in the Later Middle Ages* (Oxford: 1955), pp. 10–11: the salt pans were not, however, so small as Bridbury claims.

[33] Van der Wee, *The Growth of the Antwerp Market* I, p. 95.

[34] *Ibid.*, I, pp. 287–8.

[35] *Ibid.*, I, pp. 289–91; Bridbury, *England and the Salt Trade*, p. 94.

[36] Cf. above.

Hundred Years' War (1337–1453):[37] its definitive breakthrough occurred in the second and third quarters of the 15th century.

In addition to the cost factor, there was also the problem of supply. The supply of salt-rich peat was not unlimited. As early as 1356 Brielle took steps to safeguard its peat supplies,[38] and later Steenbergen also regularly sought *darinc* in Saaftinge.[39] Zeeland-Flanders was not confronted with this problem as early as the more northerly centres of Zeeland and Brabant, probably because peat exploitation began later there. Nevertheless, their supplies, too, were eventually depleted, precisely at a time when the demand for salt, stimulated by the expanding herring industry and by growing urban prosperity, was on the rise in the Netherlands.

Moreover, great floods like the Saint Elizabeth's flood of 1421[40] and bursting dikes, often due at least in part to the excavation of peat banks, had catastrophic effects on the production of *Zelzout* at the end of the 14th and the beginning of the 15th centuries. These periodic disasters cleared the way for the importation of French bay salt, and for some of the *Zelzout*-producing centres this meant the end of their prosperity.[41]

The breakthrough of French bay salt on the markets of the Netherlands thus coincided chronologically with the rise of the gutted-herring industry in the Netherlands. The sources reveal that during the first half of the 15th century the price of gutted herring fluctuated more as a function of the price of bay salt than of *Zelzout*.[42] From this we can conclude that the development of the herring-processing industry and that of the bay salt industry were closely interrelated in the Netherlands of the 15th century. This interdependence could go far to explain the decline of Schonen gutted herring. Not that French bay salt was unknown in the Hanseatic territories;

---

[37] Mollat, *Le commerce maritime normand*, pp. 4–62. Bridbury, *England and the Salt Trade*, p. 76.

[38] Bridbury, *ibid.*, p. 31.

[39] *Ibid.*, p. 14; For more on this, see also J. Mertens, 'Biervliet, een laatmiddeleeuws centrum van zoutwinning (eerste helft der XVe eeuw)', in: *Handelingen der Maatschappij voor Geschiedenis en Oudheidkunde te Gent*. Nieuwe Reeks XVII (1963), p. 107. Regarding intensive private exploitation of the peat bogs of the *Ambacht Axel* and of the *Ambacht Hulst* during the second half of the 14th century: E. de Reu, 'Historisch–geografisch onderzoek betreffende de moergronden in de Vier Ambachten tijdens de 12e, 13e en 14e eeuw', in: *Jaarboek van de Oudheidkundige Kring 'De Vier ambachten' van Hulst* (1960–61), pp. 47–8.

[40] For this see especially: M.K.E. Gottschalk, *Historische geografie van Westelijk Zeeuwsch–Vlaanderen* (Assen: 1955).

[41] For information concerning the tragic demographic decline of the Brabant salt-producing town of Steenbergen during the second third of the 15th century: J. Cuvelier, *Les dénombrements de foyers en Brabant (XIVe–XVIe siècle)* I (Brussels: 1912–13), pp. 474–5.

[42] Van der Wee, *The Growth of the Antwerp Market* I, pp. 278–81 and 289–91.

on the contrary its importation had begun early there.[43] But the conservatism of such cities as Lübeck and Lüneburg forbade its use in the Schonen herring industry, and this ban was probably not entirely groundless. The French bay salt imported was unrefined, and consequently its quality probably failed to meet the requirements for Schonen gutted herring.

With this we arrive at the heart of the problem posed by the history of Zeeland salt. How did Zeeland come to switch from production of the famed *Zelzout* to the refining of French, and later of Portuguese–Spanish, sea salt for which it became equally renowned? Too little is yet known to provide a definitive answer to the question, though we can perhaps make some suggestions and propose hypotheses that could open up new avenues of research and lead to new, more definitive, conclusions.

Three areas played major roles during this period of transition: the first area, located in Northern Zeeland and Brabant, lost its pre-eminence on the salt market about the middle of the 15th century, probably because a second area in Zeeland-Flanders, especially the towns Hulst and Axel, introduced new refining techniques; these centres in their turn lost their edge to a third group, the Zeeland islands around Walcheren.

The sharp decline of Steenbergen and Zevenbergen during the second third of the 15th century leads to the conclusion that the centres in Zeeland and Northern Brabant continued to rely on the *Zelzout* industry even after it had lost all economic vitality. Originally the centres in Zeeland-Flanders took their place,[44] presumably refining French bay salt. There are various indications that such towns as Hulst and Axel in Zeeland-Flanders were the promoters of the new methods for refining bay salt (*Baaizout*). The traditional salt measure, the *zoutmudde* of Zevenbergen, was gradually displaced at the Brabant fairs by the *zoutzak* used in Hulst. Was this new measure for a new kind of salt? In an urban ordinance of Hulst of 1399 (*Voorgeboden*), article 52, there is no mention of the refining of French bay salt.[45] In the 1507 regulations, however, article 18 clearly

---

[43] Bridbury, *England and the Salt Trade*, p. 77.

[44] The increasing importance of Axel and Hulst as exporters of salt is evident from Brabant institutional accounts dating from around the turn of the century and from the first half of the 16th century. Their position appeared equally strong in the county of Flanders: in the *Der cooplieden handboucxken*, printed at Ghent around 1545 and reprinted at Antwerp around 1565, the salt measures of Axel and Hulst were assigned very particular and prominent treatment, along with the old Steenbergen–Zevenbergen *zoutmudde* and the rising Arnemuiden *wage* and *honderd* (sacks). In the *Tresoir vande mate, van gewichte...* (ASA, Pk 2645) published at Antwerp in 1590, however, Axel and Hulst are no longer mentioned. See also J. Craeybeckx, *Un grand commerce d'importation: les vins de France aux anciens Pays-Bas (XIIIe–XVIe siècle)* (Paris: 1958), p. 121.

[45] 'Het voorgebodenboeck uit het Hulstersche archief', J. Adriaanse ed., *Jaarboek van de Oudheidkundige Kring 'De Vier Ambachten' van Hulst* (1932), p. 28.

reveals that refining French bay salt had become an essential activity.[46] The loan granted the town by the salters of Hulst in 1496 is a clear indication that the refineries had brought new life and wealth to the salt industry.[47]

Biervliet, a small neighbouring town and a very important centre of salt production, followed a similar evolution. Initially it remained true to the *Zelzout* industry. Biervliet salt is regularly mentioned as an imported article in the London Customs Accounts, chiefly in the form of fine table salt for London's high society.[48] Biervliet, too, seems to have had its share of difficulties. The sources speak of its being *sehr gedhepeuplert ende verarmpt* (very depopulated and impoverished), and Biervliet resorted to emergency measures. In 1438 it obtained from the duke the right to ban all salt-pans from the surrounding villages (especially Moerspeye, Zuiddorpe and Westdorpe) and to forbid the expansion of salt-pans even in such towns as Axel and Hulst.[49] Perhaps this short-sighted policy forced the other centres in Zeeland-Flanders to cast about them for another solution to their problems, namely the refining of French bay salt. From the accounts of rents paid by tax farmers in the year 1478–79 for salt extracted *in nieuwicheden* (by the new method), it can be deduced that production levels were in the neighbourhood of 33,850 *hoed*, compared to 40,000–45,000 *hoed* of *Zelzout* in 1423. Here, too, the refinery industry seems to have expanded to a remarkable degree in under forty years. At the same time the *Zelzout* industry was totally eclipsed, its production shrinking to only 3% of what it had been at the beginning of the 15th century.[50]

Zeeland-Flanders was, however, unable to maintain its leadership in the field of salt refining. In the second third of the 16th century Goes, Zierikzee and Reimerswaal began surging to the fore.[51] Salt refining

---

[46] Hulst, City Archives (hereafter SAH), *Reglement van de zoutnering*, 1507, art. 18: *Item so sal de soutsiedere ghehouden sijn anders gheen sout te siedene dan van grooven soute commende van over see*. See also the new regulations on salt extraction from the year 1526 (we wish to thank Alderman P.J. Brand most sincerely for his friendly assistance with the study of Hulst's archives).

[47] P.J. Brand, 'De stad Hulst in de strijd tussen Aartschertog Maximiliaan van Oostenrijk en de Vlaamse steden', in: *Jaarboek van de Oudheidkundige Kring 'De Vier Ambachten' van Hulst* (1962–63), pp. 52–172: a detailed analysis of the deep crisis that afflicted Hulst and brought its economic life to a dramatic standstill between 1485 and 1492. The contrast between this misery and the financial reserves of the salters, which surfaced during the loan of 1497, is highly suggestive.

[48] Bridbury, *England and the Salt Trade*, pp. 100 and 117.

[49] ADN, B. 1605, f⁰ 210; SAH, 15th century copy (translated from the French) of a ducal salt act, promulgated at St Omer in October 1439 in favour of the aldermen and inhabitants of Axel, Moerspeye and Hulst, referring to the ordinance of 10 March 1437 (1438 new style) and addressed to Biervliet.

[50] Mertens, 'Biervliet, een laatmiddeleeuws centrum van zoutwinning', pp. 107–9.

[51] Van der Wee, *The Growth of the Antwerp Market* I, pp. 96, 288.

became a prominent and largely export-oriented industry in these centres. A memorandum dating from 1603–4 indicates that of a total refinery production of 16,000 Arnemuiden *honderd* (one *honderd* = 100 sacks of roughly 114 litres each),[52] only a quarter was sold for domestic use, including the requirements of the local herring industry; the rest was exported throughout Europe.[53] The coarse salt no longer came from the Bay of Bourgneuf, but from Brouage and Ré in France, and especially from Lisbon and Setubal in Portugal, or from San Lucar de Barrameda and Cadiz or Puerto de Santa Maria in Spain.[54] Whole fleets loaded with salt arrived at the island of Walcheren, and the coarse salt was warehoused in the salt houses of Middelburg and Arnemuiden. It was usually bought up by the various great monopoly-holders and resold to smaller salters.[55]

The decline of the salt industry in Zeeland-Flanders has never been systematically investigated. Did it rely for too long on French bay salt, while the salt producers of Zeeland began to profit from the Spanish–Portuguese imports? Did the more favourable geographical situation of Goes, Zierikzee and Reimerswaal with respect to Middelburg and Arnemuiden play a decisive role? Or was it their closer ties to Holland that favoured the salt refiners of Zeeland? Were they better situated to supply the Dutch fleet with salt for their rising export to the Baltic grain-producing region? These are all questions that can be answered only by further research. It is certain, however, that the Revolt and the closure of the Scheldt represented a death knell for the salt industry in Zeeland-Flanders. It died out entirely then,[56] whereas the salt refineries on the islands of Zeeland made their greatest breakthrough and finally triumphed. The prevalence of the Zeeland *zoutzak* throughout Europe provides a striking illustration.[57] The memoranda of Juan de Gauna, economic

---

[52] *Ibid.*, I, p. 102.

[53] W. Brulez, 'De zoutinvoer in de Nederlanden in de 16e eeuw', in: *Tijdschrift voor Geschiedenis* 68 (1955), pp. 185–6.

[54] *Ibid.*, pp. 181–3; ASA, *Tresory*, 590; H. Lapeyre, *Une famille de marchands: les Ruiz* (Paris: 1955), p. 543; V. Rau, 'A exploraçao e o commercio do sal de Setubal', *Estudo de Historia Economica, T.I.* (Lisbon: 1951).

[55] Cf. the first memorandum of G. Grammaye (A° 1576): Brulez, 'De zoutinvoer in de Nederlanden', pp. 186–8.

For information on the various proposals to establish a government monopoly on salt in the Netherlands: J.A. Goris, *Etude sur les colonies marchandes méridionales (Portugais, Espagnols, Italiens) à Anvers de 1488 à 1567* (Louvain: 1925), pp. 465–77.

[56] SAH, n° 690: in 1575 there were still some thirty salt pans active at Hulst; these, too, ceased to operate a short time later (cf. the petition of the Hulst salters in the year 1580).

[57] *Het tresoir vande mate, van gewichte* (ASA, Pk 2645), printed at Amsterdam in 1590, speaks primarily of *het hondert Zeelants, alomme meest bekent* (this designated the salt measure of Arnemuiden, Goes, Zierikzee, and Middelburg).

For the 17th and 18th centuries, see N.W. Posthumus, *Nederlandsche prijsgeschiedenis. Deel I. Goederenprijzen op de Beurs van Amsterdam, 1585–1914. Wisselkoersen te*

adviser of the archdukes, as well as an anonymous memorandum of 1603–4, also attest to the European supremacy of Zeeland's salt refineries.[58]

The Dutch Butter and Cheese Trade and the Cattle Trade of the Northern Netherlands (15th–16th Centuries)

Until the end of the 15th century the dairy products imported for the Brabant fairs came chiefly from Flanders. Dutch cheese and butter were, however, present at the Antwerp *Sinksenmarkt* and *Bamismarkt*,[59] though they were purchased only exceptionally by the various charitable institutions and hospitals of Brabant and only in limited quantity.[60]

Flemish domination of the Brabant dairy market was first broken by the outbreak of the Flemish Revolt against Maximilian of Austria at the end of the 15th century. War and panic led to an alarming rise in prices,[61] while normal deliveries to the Brabant fairs were compromised by Antwerp's alignment with Maximilian. Did the Dutch dairy producers seize this opportunity to expand their market in Brabant? Presumably they did. At any rate they began increasingly to contest Flemish supremacy, even after peace was restored and Flemish products reappeared on the Brabant markets. From the second decade of the 16th century onwards, butter from Delft and cheese from Holland were the market leaders at the Antwerp fairs and Flemish dairy products receded definitively from the foreground.[62] Only at the end of the 16th century, when the Revolt cut off all dairy supplies from the North, did Flemish butter, produced mainly in the region of Dixmuide, again take the lead on the Brabant markets.

The breakthrough of Dutch dairy products was accompanied in the 16th century by active trading in beef cattle from North to South. The success achieved in the dairy trade had stimulated Northern interest in cattle breeding. Urban prosperity in the South had clearly increased meat consumption. Fattened oxen were imported in quantity from the North (for as far away as Drenthe, Overijssel, Frisia, Groningen, Schleswig and Holstein) by way of 's Hertogenbosch to the great Brabant cattle market at Lier.[63]

The Wine Staples of Dordrecht and Middelburg

The falling population in Europe during the 14th and 15th centuries led to

---

Amsterdam, 1609–1914 (Leyden: 1943), p. LIV, and our comments and rectifications on this topic in Van der Wee, *The Growth of the Antwerp Market* I, p. 96, footnote 126.

[58] Brulez, 'De zoutinvoer in de Nederlanden', pp. 184–6.

[59] P. Lindemans, *Geschiedenis van de landbouw in België* II (Antwerp: 1952), pp. 367 and 374.

[60] Van der Wee, *The Growth of the Antwerp Market* I, pp. 210, 217.

[61] *Ibid.*, I, p. 221.

[62] *Ibid.*, I, pp. 210, 217.

[63] *Ibid.*, II, pp. 115, 301; B.H. Slicher van Bath, *De agrarische geschiedenis van West-Europa (500–1850)* (Utrecht–Antwerp: 1960), p. 313.

a sharp decline in grain prices. As a result interest in the cultivation of grain diminished throughout Western Europe, and more attention was devoted to the systematic expansion of cattle breeding, viticulture and other, similar, specialities.[64] Increasing specialization entailed profound changes in the agrarian structure of Western Europe. This was decidedly to the advantage of those regions optimally situated, geologically and geographically, for a given speciality, such as viticulture in the Rhine and Mosel regions on the one hand and in Burgundy and Poitou on the other. At the same time specialization posed a serious threat to such marginal wine producers as Brabant, who gradually lost ground in the face of such sharp competition.[65]

The Rhine and Mosel regions, with their old trade routes oriented towards Brabant, were the first to profit from the new situation. They exported increasing quantities of Rhine wines to the towns of Brabant: a great deal came down the Rhine via the staple market of Dordrecht, which experienced an increase in its commercial activity during the 14th century due to the transit traffic in wine.[66] Though direct overland transport of wine from the Rhine and Mosel regions to Brabant increased, as is clearly demonstrated by the Lier certificates issued at the beginning of the 15th century to claim exemption from Brabant's land tolls,[67] river traffic and Dordrecht were never abandoned.[68]

---

[64] Slicher van Bath, *De agrarische geschiedenis van West-Europa*, pp. 157–60. W. Abel, *Agrarkrisen und Agrarkonjunktur. Eine Geschichte der Land- und Ernährungswirtschaft Mitteleuropas seit dem hohen Mittelalter* (Hamburg–Berlin: 1966), pp. 72–4.

[65] During the first wave of agricultural depression even the marginal wine-producing regions, like Brabant and the area around Paris, shifted from grain cultivation to viticulture: for example even at the beginning of the 15th century an increase in viticulture is mentioned with regard to the abbey of St-Truiden's possessions situated in Brabant and Limburg: G. Simenon *L'organisation de l'abbaye de Saint-Trond depuis la fin du XIIIe siècle jusqu'au commencement du XVIIIe siècle* (Louvain: 1912), pp. 42–3. Nevertheless, the specialization resulting from the expansion of viticulture tended to profit the more favourably situated wine-producing regions. In the course of the 15th century and at the beginning of the 16th century viticulture in the marginal regions was threatened, and began an irrversible decline: Van der Wee, *The Growth of the Antwerp Market* I, pp. 294–5. R. van Uytven, 'Het verbruik van land- en vreemde wijnen in Brabant gedurende de 16e eeuw', in: *De Brabantse Folklore* 167 (October, 1965), p. 300. G. Simenon, *L'organisation de l'abbaye de Saint-Trond*, p. 43.

For the decline of viticulture in the region of Paris: Y. Bezard, *La vie rurale dans le sud de la région parisienne de 1450 à 1560* (Paris: 1929), p. 152.

[66] W. Jappe Alberts, H.P.H. Janssen, *Welvaart in wording. Sociaal-economische geschiedenis van Nederland van de vroegste tijden tot het einde van de middeleeuwen* (The Hague: 1964), pp. 197–200.

[67] H. Van der Wee, 'Die Wirtschaft der Stadt Lier zum Beginn des 15. Jahrhunderts. Analyse eines Zollbuches und eines Wollinspektionregisters', *Beiträge zur Wirtschafts- und Stadtgeschichte. Festschrift für Hektor Ammann* (Wiesbaden: 1965), pp. 158–9. See also R. Van Uytven, *Stadsfinanciën en stadseconomie te Leuven van de XIIe tot het einde der XVIE eeuw* (Brussels: 1961), pp. 307–9.

[68] Craybeckx, *Un grand commerce d'importation: les vins de France*, pp. 26, 30.

The rising traffic in Rhine wines thus provided a vital stimulus to the intensification of commercial relations between Holland and Brabant during the 14th and 15th centuries: the volume of wine consumption in medieval towns,[69] the gradual decline of Brabant *lantwijn*, the increasing, even predominant, share of Rhine wine in Brabant's wine consumption,[70] and last, but not least, the vitality of the staple market at Dordrecht, were decisive in this evolution.

Once the Hundred Years' War was over, trade again flourished between France, Spain, Portugal and the ports of the North Sea, partly under the influence of Brittany's shipping industry.[71] This trade initially remained concentrated, in so far as the Southern Netherlands were concerned, at the wine staple of Damme and the markets of Bruges, thus substantially reinforcing the established Flemish preference for French wines.[72]

Trade with Southern Europe took on a new and striking significance in the wake of the momentous maritime discoveries in the East and West Indies at the end of the 15th century. The Brabant fairs and the isle of Walcheren now became the permanent bases of most trading operations with Southern Europe, displacing the commercial centre of gravity from Flanders to Brabant and Zeeland. This decisive shift gradually opened up new northern markets for French wines.

In 1523 the wine staple for Zeeland was finally awarded to Middelburg by Emperor Charles V.[73] In so doing he laid the judicial foundations for a flourishing wine market, based largely on the increasing success of French wines in Zeeland, Holland and Brabant. A 1559 edict even confirms Middelburg's right to subject all wines in transit to Antwerp and Brabant to measurement:[74] this conclusively established Brabant's dependence on the staple market of Zeeland.

French wines had long been known in Brabant, with the Burgundian wines better known in the southern part of the duchy,[75] and varieties from Poitou in the north.[76] They did not, however, represent a threat to the pre-eminence of the Rhine wines, which remained the unchallenged market leaders until well into the 16th century. Still, it was through the Middelburg staple market that French wines made their first significant

---

[69] *Ibid.*, pp. 5–14; R. Van Uytven, *Stadsfinanciën en stadseconomie te Leuven*, p. 310. Also, 'Het verbruik van land- en vreemde wijnen', pp. 313–4.
[70] Van der Wee, *The Growth of the Antwerp Market* I, p. 295.
[71] Z.W. Snellner, *Walcheren in de vijftiende eeuw* (Utrecht: 1916), pp. 63–4.
[72] Craeybeckx, *Un grand commerce d'importation: les vins de France*, pp. 135–8.
[73] S.T. Bindoff, *The Scheldt Question to 1839* (London: 1945), pp. 74–81.
[74] *Ibid., passim.*
[75] Van Uytven, 'Het verbruik van land- en vreemde wijnen', pp. 330–1.
[76] Craeybeckx, *Un grand commerce d'importation: les vins de France*, pp. 114–23.

foray into Brabant. In Antwerp, and soon afterwards in surrounding towns like Lier, Herentals and Mechlin, they met with undeniable success, making a real breakthrough and, particularly after 1560, increasingly replacing Rhine wines.[77]

In the more southerly towns of the duchy, like Louvain and Diest, and in Saint-Truiden, the Rhine wines better withstood this onslaught, maintaining a strong presence until the 17th century. They were, however, unable to forestall the gradual infiltration of French wines, under the influence of the Middelburg transit trade.[78]

The Eastern Sea Routes and the Dutch Grain Trade to Southern Europe

The staple markets of Douai and Ghent, together with the transit traffic reaching the towns of the Northern Netherlands by way of Antwerp, had always been vital[79] to the import of grain to the Netherlands from the neighbouring territories of Northern France. In the 15th century and at the beginning of the 16th century grain was also exported on a regular basis from Haspengouw to the Antwerp Market via Louvain.[80] As early as the 14th century there is mention of grain imports from Eastern Germany and the Baltic region:[81] these imports presumably rose both suddenly and sharply in the face of the political crisis under Maximilian of Austria and the alarmingly high prices associated with it.

Although grain prices returned to normal levels after 1492–93, and Dutch–Hanseatic tensions continued to hinder Baltic trade until the Peace of Spires (1544), grain imports from the East were gradually organized, playing even during this period already a vital role in Europe's commercial expansion.[82] The rising population of the Netherlands and the price revolution which soon followed assuredly contributed to this development. The growing specialization of Northern Netherlands' agriculture in cattle breeding and dairy farming, and of Zeeland and the Southern Netherlands in the cultivation of industrial crops, together with expanding industrialization in the towns and countryside, increasingly necessitated a systematic importation of grain. Gradually the Baltic zone began to derive more profit from this new situation than the traditional grain-exporting regions of Northern France. It was a far more dynamic growth sector and, supported by the shipping industry of Zeeland and Holland, it was able to substantially increase its competitiveness during the first half of the 16th century. Grain

---

[77] Van der Wee, *The Growth of the Antwerp Market* I, pp. 294–5.
[78] Van Uytven, 'Het verbruik van land- en vreemde wijnen', p. 336.
[79] Van der Wee, *The Growth of the Antwerp Market* II, pp. 120–1.
[80] Van Uytven, *Stadsfinanciën en stadseconomie te Leuven*, pp. 265–71.
[81] See footnote 16.
[82] A.E. Christensen, *Dutch Trade to the Baltic about 1600* (Copenhagen–The Hague: 1941), pp. 34–8.

exports from the West on the other hand were increasingly threatened by the Valois–Habsburg wars under Emperor Charles V, while the resurgence of the French economy and the growth of the French population provided an easier and more promising market on the domestic front.

The staple market of Ghent fell victim to this gradual shift towards more imports from the East. Nevertheless Amsterdam did not immediately emerge as the dominant West European grain market. Everything points to Antwerp and the isle of Walcheren as the pivotal points of the grain trade in the Netherlands during the first decades of the 16th century. The extent to which these ports, and especially Middelburg, Antwerp and Veere, fought for the grain trade during the whole first half of that 16th century has, indeed, never been sufficiently emphasized, nor has their active intervention in the Baltic region.[83]

By around 1550 the transition was accomplished. French imports were virtually moribund, first as a result of the new war with France, and afterwards due to the grim religious wars there. Grain production in Haspengouw was oriented more and more towards the rising brewing industry of Louvain, Diest and Hoegaarden, and exports to Antwerp declined.[84] Baltic grain imports, on the other hand, stimulated by the Peace of Spires (1544), ultimately came to dominate the Netherlands grain trade entirely, and Amsterdam became the preferred staple market. Roughly a quarter of the grain consumed in the Netherlands was now imported,[85] coming chiefly from the Baltic region and marketed via the Amsterdam grain staple.

The Amsterdam grain trade began at the end of the 16th century to expand its horizons. Aside from the Netherlands, Amsterdam now drew from the Iberian peninsula, the Mediterranean region, and especially Italy in its activities,[86] so that we can speak of a real world trade in grain under the hegemony of Amsterdam. But the primary foundations of this European rise lay in trade within the Netherlands themselves.

There is certainly need for further research: for instance the export of madder from Zeeland to the Netherlands during the 15th and 16th centuries, the import of raw materials for Leyden's cloth industry from

---

[83] Van der Wee, *The Growth of the Antwerp Market* II, pp. 121–2. For other facts on this topic see Christensen, *Dutch Trade to the Baltic*, pp. 37–8. G. Mickwitz, *Aus Revaler Handelsbüchern. Zur Technik des Ostseehandels in der ersten Hälfte des 16. Jahrhunderts* (Helsinki: 1938), pp. 41–2, 68. P. Jeannin, 'Les relations économiques des villes de la Baltique avec Anvers au XVIe siècle', in: *Vierteljahrschrift für Sozial- und Wirtschaftsgeschichte* XLIII (1956), pp. 200–1, 207–8, 334–6.

[84] Van der Wee, *The Growth of the Antwerp Market* II, p. 172.

[85] C. Verlinden, J. Craeybeckx and others (eds), *Dokumenten voor de geschiedenis van prijzen en lonen in Vlaanderen en Brabant (XVe–XVIIIe eeuw)* (Bruges: 1959), p. XVI.

[86] F. Braudel, *La Méditerranée et le monde méditerranéen à l'époque de Philippe II* (Paris: 1949), pp. 494–502. J.H. Kernkamp, *De handel op de vijand, 1572–1609* (Utrecht: 1931–34), 2 vols.

Calais–Bruges and Antwerp, the marketing of cloth from Leyden via Bruges and the Brabant fairs; there were also the links between Haarlem's linen bleacheries and Flanders and Brabant, and many other sectors would bear further investigation. But this short analysis suffices to demonstrate clearly the strong interdependence of the rise of the Northern Netherlands and the economic lead of the Southern Netherlands.

IV

MONEY AND FINANCE

8

Antwerp and the New Financial Methods of the 16th and 17th Centuries[1]

The revitalization of financial methods in the 15th and 16th centuries followed two distinct paths of development: one inspired by Italian procedures and passing from Geneva–Lyons–Genoa to Amsterdam; the other, more independent of Italian influence and more innovative, went from Antwerp to London.

The Traditionalists: Geneva–Lyons–Castile–Genoa–Amsterdam

Sixteenth century economic expansion was originally a product of the extension of continental trade. As far as Western Europe was concerned it began in the South when the fairs of Geneva and Châlon-sur-Saône[2] reached their greatest heights, followed afterwards by the fairs of Lyons, Castile and Piacenza.[3] This renewal, dating from before 1500 and rooted in the rhythm of the medieval fairs, accentuates the continuity of economic evolution over time. Moreover, the Italian merchant-bankers never lost their control over the financial activities of these fairs. Arbitrage on the exchange rates lost little of its influence. Based on the *cambium et recambium* principle and intimately associated with European commerce, the trade in bills of exchange was reanimated by the vigour of the European economy in the 16th century and by the participation of new generations of merchants: the Southern Germans, the Portuguese and the Spanish. Under Italian influence the expansion of public finance was

---

[1] I wish to extend warm thanks to Professors J.A. van Houtte and F. Braudel, to J. Meuvret and P. Jeannin, O. De Smedt and H.L.V. de Groote for their helpful suggestions.

[2] The fairs of Geneva were considerably older, but they assumed a 'European' character only in the 15th century: J.F. Bergier, *Genève et l'économie européene de la Renaissance* (Paris: 1963), pp. 262–70 and 432.

[3] Concerning the fairs of Lyons and Castile: H. Lapeyre, *Une famille de marchands: les Ruis* (Paris: 1955), pp. 283–310 and 439–501. Concerning the Genoa fairs: R. Ehrenberg, *Das Zeitalter der Fugger. Geldkapital und Kreditverkehr im 16. Jahrhundert* II (Jena: 1922), pp. 231–6; D. Gioffre, *Gênes et les foires de change (de Lyon à Besançon)* (Paris: 1960).

also integrated into the traditional structure, especially by way of the *asientos*.

Though the bill of exchange retained its central position, the merchant-bankers nevertheless began progressively to simplify the rather complicated, and consequently often cumbersome, system of exchange credit. Beginning in the 15th century immediate re-exchange (Piccamiglio)[4] appeared, followed by inland bills of exchange and somewhat later by bills of exchange from fair to fair.[5] The latter, though still respecting the exchange form, had become thinly veiled loans at interest.[6] The normal bill of exchange, on the contrary, though retaining its characteristic use as an instrument of credit, began more and more to assert its function as an instrument of international payment. And it was precisely in this field that in Southern Europe technical innovations were most successful.

First of all, the old Italian clearing banks' practice of expressing all operations and keeping all accounts in a single currency[7] was adopted by the Geneva fairs, where the Savoy gold écu was the monetary unit for all payments at the fair.[8] In the 16th century this rationalization was further perfected by substituting for this real currency a pure money of account, that is to say a purely theoretical money, having no link whatsoever with any real metallic coin in circulation at the time, but representing a fixed and immutable weight in gold:[9] this was the gold Lyons mark and the *scudi di marcho* of Piacenza. The fairs of Lyons and Piacenza went further still. The merchant community proceeded to fix the official exchange rate at the date the payments became due. Afterwards payments began, made by means of 'transfers between parties' according to well-defined rules.[10]

The development of the system of the *dépôts de foire en foire* and

---

[4] J. Heers, *Le livre de comptes de Giovanni Piccamiglio, homme d'affaires génois (1456–1459)* (Paris: 1959), pp. 34–5; Lapeyre, *Une famille de marchands: les Ruiz*, pp. 320–5.

[5] For the 15th century: De Roover, *The Rise and Decline of the Medici Bank*, p. 295. For the 16th century: Lapeyre, *Une famille de marchands: les Ruiz*, pp. 313–9 and H. Van der Wee, *The Growth of the Antwerp Market and the European Economy (Fourteenth–Sixteenth Centuries)* II (The Hague: 1963), p. 353.

[6] It was not only the Renaissance that stimulated the search for simpler forms of credit, but also the fact that exchange credit had become more expensive: De Roover, *The Rise and Decline of the Medici Bank*, p. 13.

[7] J. Heers, *L'Occident aux XIVe et XVe siècles. Aspects économiques et sociaux* (Paris: 1963), p. 181.

[8] Bergier, *Genève et l'économie européene de la Renaissance*, p. 272.

[9] According to the terminology and the distinction made by H. Van Werveke in 'Monnaie de compte et monnaie réelle', in: *Revue Belge de Philologie et d'Histoire* XIII (1934) nos 1–2, pp. 123–52.

[10] P. Savonne, *Instruction et manière de tenir livres de raison ou de comptes par parties doubles* (Antwerp: 1567).

of the current accounts system paralleled the abovementioned rationalizations in the South. In the 15th and 16th centuries transfers from one account to the other (*giro di partita*) became: *une pratique très répandue dans tous les milieux sociaux et une véritable routine au mode des affaires du sud*.[11] International finances were in turn integrated into this system by the payment of bills of exchange *in banco*. It is certain that the *virement des parties* (transfer between parties) at Lyons and at Piacenza already included a great many transfers from one account to another.

In 16th-century Castile the money-changers of the Rua virtually monopolized all the payments at the fair, either transferring from one account to the other on their own books or using mutual transfers between themselves and various colleagues: *car ils étaient en compte les uns avec les autres et tous les deux jours ils procédaient aux liquidations*.[12] Castile's more limited number of money-changers, compared to the hordes of merchants at Lyons and Piacenza, represented another large step towards greater rationalization.

Inherent in the generalization of bank transfers in the South was the reappearance of public clearing banks beginning in the second half of the 16th century: Palermo (1552), Gerona (1568), Genoa (1586), Venice (1587), Milan (1597), Rome (1605).[13] The vicissitudes of the period were unquestionably responsible for their success: economic uncertainty, together with the Wars of Religion, made a secure and stable financial base desirable, and public banks could provide it better than the private ones. And who could deny that the cities themselves saw this as a means of safeguarding their own finances should the need arise?

All these efforts to rationalize and protect money transfers and international clearing culminated in the foundation of the Bank of Amsterdam in 1609. This establishment was originally intended to bring order to the monetary chaos caused by the war and posing a threat to the commercial prosperity of Amsterdam. At the same time the city believed that it was likely to prove an extremely useful financial instrument for merchants: it was its brilliant success in this field that enabled the Bank of Amsterdam financially to dominate the European continent during the 17th century.[14] As a public clearing bank the Bank of Amsterdam enjoyed the confidence of the merchants. Following the example of the fairs of Lyons and Piacenza it introduced a stable money of account based upon a fixed

---

[11] Heers, *L'Occident aux XIVe et XVe siècles. Aspects économiques et sociaux*, pp. 180–1; R. de Roover, 'Cambium ad Venetias', in: *Studi in onore di Armando Sapori* II (Milan: 1957), p. 632; A.E. Sayous, 'Les transformations des méthodes commerciales dans l'Italie médiévale', in: *Annales d'Histoire Economique et Sociale* I (1929), 2, p. 170.

[12] Lapeyre, *Une famille de marchands: les Ruiz*, pp. 259–60.

[13] R. de Roover, *L'évolution de la lettre de change, XIVe–XVIIIe siècles* (Paris: 1953), p. 136.

[14] J.G. Van Dillen, *The Bank of Amsterdam (History of the Principal Public Banks)* (The Hague: 1934), pp. 79–84.

amount of silver, i.e. the bankgulden.[15] It imitated the system of multilateral balancing of credits and debits in use at the fairs of Castile and further simplified it by placing all operations in the hands of a single monopoly. This ensured that virtually all international payments were made through the Bank. Finally, it served as a model for the many similar banks afterwards established in the North: Middelburg (1616), Hamburg (1619), Delft (1621) and Rotterdam (1635).[16]

The Bank of Amsterdam, acting as a clearing bank, formed the crest of a centuries-long wave of technico-financial innovation inspired by the Italian merchant-bankers since the 13th century. Numerous commercial and financial transactions spanning the whole of Europe could now be completed in all security. Payments could be assigned through bills of exchange drawn on the Bank of Amsterdam (as previously on the fairs), where multilateral balancing realized a system of international clearing. As a result, in normal times few commercial debts were still paid out in cash.[17] This meant an appreciable acceleration in monetary circulation, as well as a more rational and flexible mechanism for achieving equilibrium in European balances of payment.

Why did Amsterdam adopt and integrate the technical improvements of the South in its system of payment? Why did it not follow in the footsteps of the more progressive city of Antwerp? The problem is all the more enigmatic in that, particularly from 1585–88 onwards, Amsterdam had welcomed substantial numbers of bankers immigrating from Antwerp. Were Antwerp's innovations too recent to have inspired confidence? Did the war psychosis and the ensuing monetary chaos favour a return to the Italian tradition, more secure in its centuries-long experience? Were the financial experiments of Genoa and the fairs of Piacenza responsible? Or did the vitality of Zeeland's and Holland's commerce with Spain and Italy (*Straatvaart*) around 1600 influence this option? Or was it simply the authority of certain personages educated in Italy? The problem has not yet been sufficiently investigated for us to suggest definitive answers. But on 10 May 1606 the aldermen of Amsterdam noted in their resolutions register that the most influential merchants of the city had insisted on several occasions that a bank be established similar to those at Seville

---

[15] The *bankgulden* was originally a real monetary unit, that is, a type B money of account; but under the influence of successive debasements of the real *gulden*, the *bankgulden* (money of account), established to retain its metallic value, differentiated itself from the real, current *gulden*, thus becoming a type A money of account. For more on the distinction between type A and type B moneys of account see note 9.

[16] *Ibid.*, p. 84; De Roover, *L'évolution de la lettre de change*, p. 136.

[17] In the case of a negative balance the merchant-bankers even arranged to issue bills of exchange in which the creditor became the 'giver' and the debtor the 'taker': see Lapeyre, *Une famille de marchands: les Ruiz*, pp. 296–7.

and Venice.[18] In this context it is probable that the 1585 speech of the Venetian senator Tommaso Contarini, advocating the establishment of a public clearing bank at Venice and strongly attacking the Antwerp system of assignments, had tangible repercussions in the North.[19]

A New Perspective in Antwerp–London: the Birth of Negotiability

In the 15th century the Brabant fairs became a busy crossroad for new generations of expansionists in European commerce: English, Dutch and Germans from the Rhine, followed soon afterwards by Southern Germans. Their credit methods had remained primitive, based essentially on letters obligatory made payable to bearer.[20] Naturally, under the decisive influence of Antwerp, where various arithmetic and accounting manuals were published in the course of the 16th century,[21] the Italian methods, particularly the use of the bill of exchange and of double-entry bookkeeping,[22] were more and more frequently adopted by Northern merchants, by that time including the Hanseatics[23] and the French as well. But for them the bill of exchange became primarily and essentially

---

[18] Van Dillen, *The Bank of Amsterdam*, p. 79.

[19] *Ibid.*, p. 80; G. Luzzato, 'Les Banques Publiques de Venise', in: *History of the Principal Public Banks, collected by J.G. Van Dillen* (The Hague: 1934), pp. 39–78.

[20] De Roover, *L'évolution de la lettre de change*, p. 97.

[21] On this subject see especially: R. de Roover, 'Een en ander over Jan Ympyn Christoffels, den schrijver van de eerste Nederlandsche handleiding over het koopmansboekhouden', in: *Tijdschrift voor Gechiedenis* II (1937), pp. 163–78; A.J.E.M. Smeur, *De zestiende-eeuwse Nederlandse rekenboeken* (The Hague: 1960); H.L.V. de Groote, 'Zestiende-eeuwse Antwerpse boekhoudingen en cijfermeesters', in: *Scientiarum Historia* II (1960), 4, pp. 161–72; H.V.L. de Groote, 'Zestiende-eeuwse boekhoudingen en cijfermeesters in betrekking met Antwerpen', in: *Scientiarum Historia* III (1961), 3, pp. 142–56; H.L.V. de Groote, 'Kanttekeningen bij een bibliografie van zestiende-eeuwse rekenboeken. Een aanvulling: François Flory de Lille, arithméticien', in: *Scientiarum Historia* IV (1962), 3, 14p (offprint); H.L.V. de Groote, 'De "Arithmétique" van Mellema', in: *Scientiarum Historia* V (1963), 4, pp. 133–46.
A good example of the influence of Antwerp on this subject: in 1570 the accountant and teacher Hercules de Cordes travelled to Lübeck 'pour y mettre de l'ordre dans la compatabilité d'Herman Boelemann': De Groote, *Zestiende-eeuwse boekhoudingen...* III (1961), no. 3, p. 148.

[22] On this subject see the interesting study published by F. Melis, 'Aspetti della vita economica medievale', in: *Studi nell'archivio Datini di Prato* (Siena: 1962) pp. 339–454.

[23] There is a suggestive text in the alderman's registers of Danzig, cited by M. Neumann, *Geschichte des Wechsels im Hansagebiet bis zum 17. Jahrhundert* (Erlangen: 1863), and amended by Jeannin, to whom I extend sincere thanks. Mattis Zimmermann's answer to Hans von Pelcken: 'dath em dath bewusth dath eth mith den wechselbrieffen manck den koepleuden sunderlinck tho Anthwerpen, dar vele mede umbgangen werth, also gehelden werth szo enem en wechsellbrieff aferanthwerth werth unde he den selfen acceptireth unde underschriffth, szo moeth he ock den selfenn unde bethalen...' (Aldermen's Registers of Danzig, 1556, f. 37).

a means of transferring capital:[24] its role as an instrument of credit was still of secondary importance. Thus during the entire 16th century, or at least during its first three-quarters, the letter obligatory, payable to the bearer, continued to dominate payment of commercial debts on the Antwerp market.[25]

Along with this rather rigid structure of commercial credit went the absence of deposit and clearing banks in the North, and particularly at Antwerp, during the 16th century. This is all the more surprising since banks had flourished at Bruges during the 14th century[26] and since Antwerp and Bergen-op-Zoom themselves had known banks owned by the local money-changers in the course of the 15th century.[27] The decline of deposit and clearing banks in the Netherlands remains a very thorny problem. According to de Roover the responsibility lay with the restrictive, even prohibitive, ordinances of 1433, 1467, 1480, 1488 and especially 1489, supported by the strong centralization policy of the dukes of Burgundy.[28] Certainly, these ordinances were very influential, but we believe that the monetary chaos of the second half of the 14th century and the brutal crisis at the end of the 15th century were also determining factors in their decline[29]: the monetary crisis of 1480–90 ruined and eliminated the last deposit and clearing banks at the fairs of Antwerp and Bergen-op-Zoom. There were probably other causes as well: the activity of the money-changer-bankers of Flanders and Brabant for example was closely linked with the exports of the traditional cloth

---

[24] There is a clear example in a notarized protocol from Antwerp dated 13 April 1558 and drafted for the creation of a commercial company of three Antwerp merchants: 'welcke 200 ₤ sullen die voirs. Sobrecht ende Pauwels voirs. gebruycken op Spaingien in Hontscoten saeyen ende fusteynen te coopen met gereeden ghelde ende in Spaengien mit gereeden ghelde wederom te vercoopen ende het ghelt op wissel wederom over te seynden', (text published by J. Strieder, *Aus Antwerpener Notariatsarchiven* (Wiesbaden: 1962), p. 313, no. 609). See also; G. Mickwitz, *Aus Revaler Handelsbüchern. Zur Technik des Ostseehandels in der erste Hälfte des 16. Jahrhunderts* (Helsingfors: 1938), p. 94; W. Brulez, *De Firma Della Faille en de internationale handel van Vlaamse firma's in de 16^e eeuw* (Brussels: 1959), pp. 398–9. See also the 'Kitson Papers' (Cambridge University Library, *Hengrave Hall*, no. 78, no. 4 and Harman Janssone's journal (*Archives of the Plantijn and Moretus Museum at Antwerp*, no. 681).

[25] O. De Smedt, *De Engelse natie te Antwerpen in de XVIe eeuw, 1486–1582* II (Antwerp: 1954), p. 569. There is also a clear indication of this in the request of various merchant nations to the town of Antwerp signed by the nation of Lucca on 4 July 1565: City Archives of Antwerp; hereafter ASA, Pk 1076. G. de Malynes, *Lex Mercatoria* (London: 1622), pp. 96 and 394, reaffirms in 1622 that letters obligatory payable to bearer were in extremely current use 'beyond the seas.'

[26] R. de Roover, *Money, Banking and Credit in Medieval Bruges* (Cambridge, Mass.: 1948).

[27] Van der Wee, *The Growth of the Antwerp Market* II, pp. 355–7.

[28] De Roover, *Money, Banking and Credit*, pp. 339–41.

[29] Van der Wee, *The Growth of Antwerp* II, pp. 357–8.

industry, and these exports were faced with a growing crisis in the course of the 15th century.

At the beginning of the 16th century a new flowering of Antwerp's international trade suddenly appeared against the backdrop of the still primitive financial methods of Northwestern Europe. It was accompanied by a speculative transfer via Antwerp of Southern German silver in the direction of Lisbon, creating a liquidity problem.[30] The enormous pressures resulting from these confrontations made technico-financial innovation inevitable at Antwerp. Rapid acceleration in monetary circulation was first attained by appreciably extending the use of deferred payment, supported by the generalized use of letters obligatory, the current account, and the tally even in the private sector.[31] Moreover, the deferment of payment increased the opportunity of *rescontre* , as the debtor himself could become, before the due date of his debt, the creditor of his own creditor.[32] Finally there was the transferability of letters obligatory, payable to bearer, enabling them to change hands.[33] But the immediate intensification of this circulation was inhibited by the insufficient guarantees available to creditors, a particularly serious obstacle in a centre of recent expansion where the numerous newcomers were still regarded with suspicion. Herein lay the beginning of Antwerp's long journey towards the negotiability of commercial bills.

An improvement in the legal protection of the bearer was the first step. The clause 'payable to bearer' had made early on its appearance on letters obligatory.[34] Nevertheless during the Middle Ages their simple transfer

---

[30] *Ibid.* II, pp. 124–7.

[31] *Ibid.* II, pp. 331–5.

[32] The *rescontre* had become common practice in 16th century Antwerp. There is a very suggestive text in a 1567 lawsuit: 'Waere betaalt deen helft van dander helft bij den supplicant met tellinge van gelde ende dat resterende vierendeel oyck waere den voers. Quellaers goetgedaen ende by hen onderlinghe gerescontreert op hunne loopende rekeninge ende in hun rekenboecken', (ASA, *Vierschaar*, 1249, f. 165–6). There are also extremely clear examples in the book-keeping of the Van Immerseele firm from the end of the 16th century (ASA, I B, 218). The practice of *rescontre* also enjoyed considerable official support: De Moy noted in his commentaries on the published customary laws of Antwerp: 'By ordonnantie van 29 februari 1599 is gestatueerd dat niemant en soude gehouden syn taenveerden eenighe assignatie, ten waere dat de selve wezen in rescontreiringhe van eene andere assignatie' (ASA, *Vierschaar*, 23, III, f. 580).

[33] The circulation of such letters obligatory was also frequently linked to the practice of *rescontre*: merchants would pass a letter obligatory from hand to hand among themselves until the creditor receiving the letter obligatory in payment was himself the original debtor named in it. Numerous examples of this practice are given in manuals by J. Weddington, V. Mennher, M. Cognet, etc.

[34] M.M. Postan, 'Private Financial Instruments in Mediaeval England', in: *Vierteljahrschrift für Sozial- und Wirtschaftsgeschichte* XXIII (1930), p. 40; N.W. Posthumus, *De geschiedenis van de Leidsche lakenindustrie* I (The Hague: 1908), p. 229; G. Bigwood, *Le régime juridique et économique du commerce et de l'argent dans la Belgique du moyen âge* I (Brussels: 1921), pp. 507–10.

remained limited since in case of non-payment a specific power of attorney had to be obtained from the original creditor in order to take judicial action. For this reason the majority of transfers during the late Middle Ages were accompanied by a formal *cessio*, a wordy formality.[35] An Antwerp *tourbe*[36] of 1507, however, explicitly confirmed the right of the holder of a letter obligatory payable to bearer to undertake legal action against the signatory, without recourse to a power of attorney from the original creditor.[37] Bruges, Dordrecht and Utrecht, among others, followed suit and on 7 March 1537 an imperial ordinance generalized this principle throughout the Netherlands.[38]

The second step concerned the financial protection of the bearer. This step was more delicate. Since the formal *cessio* freed the granting debtor entirely of all obligation towards his original creditor, Antwerp's commercial jurisprudence, in accepting the validity of legal action by every bearer of a letter obligatory, tended, as a matter of fact, to equate the *cessio* with an actual payment. Under these conditions it is immediately clear that better legal protection for the bearer meant that he lost much of his financial security in actually acquitting the ceding creditor of his debt.[39] How did 16th-century Antwerp set about resolving this thorny problem? In the first place through the introduction of the assignation principle, already in current use in the Netherlands during

---

[35] *Ibid.*, I, pp. 513–5; There are various examples of *cessio* in the aldermen's registers and the *certificatieboeken* of Antwerp at the end of the 15th and the beginning of the 16th century, from which those acts concerning international commerce have been published as regests by R. Doehaerd, *Etudes anversoises. Documents sur le commerce international à Anvers, 1488–1514* (Paris: 1963): vol. II, 484, 1002, 2081; vol. III, 3037, 3124, 3126, 3184, 3218, 3417, 3869.

[36] A *tourbe* is the collective testimony of a group of honourable merchants before the magistrate of Antwerp that such and such a practice is in accordance with the customary commercial law of the town.

[37] O. De Smedt, 'De keizerlijke verordeningen van 1537 en 1539 op de obligaties en wisselbrieven. Enige kanttekeningen', in: *Nederlandsche Historiebladen* III (1940), 1, p. 32.

[38] De Roover, *L'évolution de la lettre de change*, pp. 95–6. However, a lively resistance persisted on the part of the jurists of the *Parlement de Malines* (De Smedt, *De Engelse natie...* II, pp. 570–1). At Antwerp on the other hand the *tourbes* of 1557, 1561, 1565 and 1567 (ASA, *Vierschaar*, f. 22 v° – 23, 39 v°, 169–169 v°, 59 v° – 60) and the published customary laws *in antiquis* of 1570 (G. de Longé, *Coutumes du Pays et Duché de Brabant. Quartier d'Anvers. Coutumes de la ville d'Anvers* (Brussels: 1870), p. 596) confirm that judicial protection for the bearer had become a well-established mercantile custom. Such protection was already customary in London and in the Hanseatic area during the 15th century (kindly communicated to me by P. Jeannin).

[39] Due to this loss of financial security on the part of the receiving creditor, acts of *cessio* drawn up between 1491 and 1499 stipulated explicitly that the ceding creditor would repay the debt in the case of non-payment on the part of the scheduled debtor (ASA, *Certificatieboeken*, 2, f. 68 v°, July 8, 1491; ASA, *Schepenbrieven*, 116, f. 121 v°, 15 October 1499).

the Middle Ages, particularly for payments made in cash[40] whereby creditor A requested his debtor B to make the payment to a third party C, himself the creditor of creditor A. This assignment had the substantial advantage of not being viewed judicially as 'payment in full'; consequently, the assignor A was not quit of his indebtedness until after creditor C actually received the sum due in valid metal currency from assigned debtor B and declared himself satisfied.[41]

It is quite remarkable to observe that the brilliant commercial growth of Antwerp during the first decades of the 16th century was accompanied by a correspondingly appreciable increase in the circulation of letters obligatory from hand to hand. Both Van Bombergen in 1532[42] and Thomas Washington in 1537[43] explicitly attested that this circulation had become a customary mode of payment at Antwerp. But the essential characteristic of this new custom should be kept in mind: most of these transfers were in the form of *assignments*. The formula had become so common that Erasmus Schetz wrote on 1 July 1537 to the *grand pensionnaire* of Antwerp at Brussels that he should insist that the government legalize and regulate this mode of payment.[44] An imperial ordinance of 31 October 1541, published at Antwerp on 17 November 1541, probably the result of this lobbying, regulated the problem very concretely:

---

[40] Bigwood, *Le régime juridique et économique du commerce et de l'argent...* I, pp. 526–34; Van der Wee, *The Growth of the Antwerp Market* II, p. 334; cf. the famed text in Lemington's letter to George Cely at the end of the 15th century: 'You shall not fault of your money in the Cold Mart... by such men as I shall have my money of' (quoted by J.M. Holden, *The History of Negotiable Instruments in English Law* (London: 1955), p. 12).

[41] De Roover, *The Rise and Decline of the Medici Bank*, p. 19. The judicial status of this assignation was thus in clear contrast to that of the bank assignation (payment by bank transfer from one account to another): in the case of a bank assignation, the debtor was entirely acquitted of his debt from the moment the creditor's account was duly credited in the banker's books: De Roover, *Lettre de change*, pp. 206–7, 212–3.

[42] W. Brulez, 'Lettres commerciales de Daniël et Antoine van Bombergen à Antonio Grimani (1532–1543)', in: *Bulletin de l'Institut Historique Belge de Rome* XXXI (1958), pp. 183–4.

[43] ASA, Pk 1052, act dated 21 March 1536 ('37): 'hij [T. Washington] myds der afflivicheyt van hueren manne de voirs. [4] obligatien... nyet over getransporteren noch zijn prouffijt daermede gedaen en conste, gelijck andere cooplieden vanden Natien van Engelant gewoenlijck waeren van doene als zij reydsen nae huys.'

[44] Schets wrote to Herbouts: 'dat by edict gestatueert worde... dat alle betaelinge staende up die merckten van Antwerpen ende Bergen te bevelen, begijnnen sullen ter expiracyen vanden vrijheeden der sees weeken vanden merckten, ende dat bynnen den naesten XIIII daegen daerna, alle debiteurs huer crediteurs schuldich zullen zijn, tzij bij assignacye ter zelves crediteurs contentement, oft in prompten gelde te voldoen,' (ASA, Pk 1052, act dated 1 July 1573).

> *Ordonnons que doresenavant tous ceulx qui aueront accepté... quelque lettre de change, seront tenus de payer la somme contenue en ycelle en deniers évaluez... sans que pour lesdits changes ou aultres obligations contractez entre marchans on puist donner en payement aultres obligations par forme d'assignacions, lesquelles le créditeur ne sera tenu dacceptor sil ne veult, et en acceptant lassignacion demeurera neantmoins le premier debteur obligé tant que le marchant sera réalement payé ou effectuellement contente de son due.*[45]

Legalization surely stimulated the use of assignment.[46] Between 1560 and 1569 Jeronimo De Curiel wrote of Antwerp: *je paierai par assignation comme est nostre usance mercantil*.[47] In 1565 the nation of Lucca also attested explicitly to this practice.[48] In 1585 Tomasso Contarini solemnly confirmed before the Venetian senate that most payments at Antwerp were made by transfer of commercial effects in the form of assignments.[49] In a 1606 lawsuit at Antwerp, the defendant explained that the office of *caissier* involved keeping the books and being present at the Exchange to pay and receive cash or assignments.[50]

Finally, the practice of assignment had become so current by the end of the 16th century and the beginning of the 17th century that the city of Antwerp felt obliged to add a new paragraph on the subject to its Customs in the year 1608: if payments were made by the circulation of commercial titles in the form of assignments from hand to hand, *up to four, five, or even more times*, all the successive debtors, who as ceding creditors had assigned their debt on a credit that they were themselves owed, remained linked to the last debtor.[51] The text is explicit and suggests the generalization of the practice during the preceding decades.

Though the assignment principle was already the fundamental basis of the principle of negotiability, guaranteeing the new holder of a title the

---

[45] According to the text published at Antwerp: ASA, Pk 2763, f. 132.

[46] The sentence registers of the town of Antwerp from the last two-thirds of the 16th century also bear irrefutable witness to this.

[47] J.A. Goris, *Etude sur les colonies marchandes méridionales (Portugais, Espagnols, Italiens) à Anvers de 1488 à 1567* (Louvain: 1925), p. 370.

[48] ASA, Pk 1076, Remonstrance of various merchant nations signed by the Nation of Lucca on 4 July 1565.

[49] Van Dillen, *The Bank of Amsterdam*, p. 80.

[50] 'Houdende de balanche, ter borsse heure penninghen ontfanghende ende schulden innende, soo in comptant als bij middele van assignatien, ende doende betaelinghe soo met gelde als met assignatien.' ASA, *Proces Suppl.*, 52, A° 1604–10.

[51] 'Als ijmant bij sijnen schuldenaer op eenen anderen wort bewesen, om bij hem betaelt te worden, ende alsoo van handen tot handen voorts tot vier oft vijff persoenen ende meer, die de bewijsinge al aenveerden, indijen hij bij den lesten niet en wort betaelt, heeft tot sijne voldoeninge verbonden alle degene daerop hij bewezen is.'; G. de Longé, *Coutumes du Pays et Duché de Brabant. Quartier d'Anvers. Coutumes de la ville d'Anvers* IV (Brussels: 1874), p. 380, art. 14.

right to greater recourse than that to which the earlier bearer had been entitled, it remained nevertheless an imperfect basis. Various uncertainties persisted, clouding this greater protection, particularly with regard to proof of 'payment by assignment'. The transfer of a letter obligatory payable to bearer to a third party was not considered *ipso facto* a payment in the form of an assignment. The sentence registers of the 16th century still distinguish clearly between the transfer of a letter obligatory as definitive payment and transfer by assignment.[52] In the first case the payment was *fynalycke ende absoluut*, that is to say that creditor A, by transferring the title, was entirely freed of his indebtedness to his own creditor C. In the second case he was not.

The registers nevertheless confirm that assignment had become the most current method of transferring obligatory letters and that it was the method favoured by contemporary jurisprudence. In case of litigation and in the absence of proof to the contrary, the principle of assignment was *always* accepted by the tribunal, on the simple say-so of the bearer of the obligation. Thus the ceding creditor had to produce proof in order to present his case as one of transfer as 'final and absolute' payment if brought before the court by the bearer for payment in lieu of an insolvent or recalcitrant debtor.[53] Clearly, this climate favoured the use of formal proofs in making transfers as definitive payment: the *tourbes* of 1565 and 1568 and the Customs of Antwerp, confirmed in 1572, show that in such 'transports' it was customary to sign the agreement before the notaries or aldermen, or to compose a private document.

---

[52] Some examples: ASA, *Vierschaar*, 1237, f. 98 v°–100, decision dated 15 January 1542 ('43), f. 21–22, decision dated October 1542; ASA, *Vierschaar*, 1244, f. 73v°–74, decision dated 7 December 1555; ASA, *Vierschaar*, 1249, f. 136 v°–138, decision dated 31 May 1567, f. 140 v°–151, decision dated 30 May 1567, f. 157–8, 23 June 1567; ASA, *Proces Suppl.*, 52, A° 1604–10. It is significant that no such distinction seems to have been made at the beginning of the 16th century: cf. the aforementioned (see note 39) acts of the *certificatieboeken* and the aldermen's registers of the town of Antwerp from the end of the 15th and beginning of the 16th centuries. In the *cessio* of a letter obligatory for £10 18s. 4d. in Flemish groats, for example: 'geloevende wairt dat de voirs. Jacques nyet voldaen en worde... dat hij (= the ceding creditor) alsdan ende in dien gevalle de selve somme terstont opbrengen ende betalen sal, gelijc oft de voirs. bewijsinge nyet geschiet en ware.' (ASA, *Schepenbrieven*, 116, f. 121 v°, 15 October 1499).

[53] The Antwerp published customary laws of 1608 suggest that this was still the state of affairs at the beginning of the 17th century: the law required an 'explicit declaration' on the part of the creditor-beneficiary as proof of 'final and absolute' acquittal where a transfer payment was concerned; De Longé, *Coutumes du Pays et Duché de Brabant* IV, p. 380, art. 15). The customs of the English Nation at Antwerp were the only exception in the 16th century: among them the Merchants Adventurers needed to prove a payment by assignation; otherwise the payment was considered final: De Smedt, *De Engelse natie* II, p. 583. Cf. below.

But, according to the *tourbes*, oral 'transports' before witnesses were also valid.[54]

Although in principle no formal proof was required for assignments, as the most usual method of transfer in mercantile circles, its absence must nevertheless have complicated things considerably. The greater intensity of circulation from hand to hand, attested by all sources,[55] implied the existence of a continuous chain of assignments. The swift growth of Antwerp's commerce in the second third of the 16th century[56] increased anonymity in mercantile circles to such an extent that in the absence of written formalities the assigning creditor was no longer necessarily recognizable after the second assignment. Only the first creditor A was always known, since he was mentioned by name on the document. Hence guarantees for the holder remained substantially inadequate.

Under these conditions it was only to be expected that it would become customary to provide formal proof along with the assignment. A notation in the accounting books or simple notebooks could always serve as proof. John Weddington, in giving examples of assignment and of *rescontre* in his accounting manual, printed at Antwerp in 1560, always added explicitly 'clearly set ouer unto hym.'[57] We have also established that in Antwerp lawsuits the various parties often presented their books as an element of proof.[58] But not all merchants kept books and verification remained a difficult and delicate task.

Gerard de Malynes, an enthusiastic partisan of the continental practice of circulating letters obligatory from hand to hand, suggested in 1622 that the English establish an official registry system to record all transfers, based on those at Rouen and Lisbon.[59] We have not, however, established the existence of any such registry system at Antwerp. On the other hand we have

---

[54] ASA, *Vierschaar*, 69, f. 60 v°–61 (*tourbe* dated 26 June 1568); f. 169–169 v° (*tourbe* dated 2 August 1565). De Longé, *Coutumes du Pays et Duché de Brabant* I, p. 524. It was probably in order to resolve this source of possible confusion that in 1565 the town of Antwerp expressed the intention of requiring everyone to make all 'transports' of personal chattels exceeding the value of £100 Flemish groats before notaries, which provoked the 4 July 1565 reaction of the Nation of Lucca (ASA, Pk 1076), among others.

[55] The sentence registers attest this from the last third of the 16th century onwards: for example ASA, *Vierschaar*, 1249, f. 242–3, decision dating from 16 August 1567. See also the arithmetic and accounting manuals of the period, and article 14 of the Customs of the year 1608 (see note 53 above).

[56] The rise of a new middle class of merchants was responsible for this: Van der Wee, *The Growth of the Antwerp Market* II, pp. 321–3.

[57] *Ibid.* II, pp. 347–8.

[58] 'Ende dattet nae recht notoir waere dat om probatien te doene eenyegelick schuldich ware te doene exhibitien van syne rekenboecken': decision dated 23 June 1567 (ASA, *Vierschaar*, 1249, f. 165–6); See also ASA, *Vierschaar*, 1237, f. 30–30 v°.

[59] De Malynes, *Lex mercatoria*, p. 100.

confirmed the existence of bills of assignment in the sentence books and in litigation dossiers from the second half of the 16th century. One example found, dating from around 1567, involved a partial assignment,[60] though shortly thereafter this separate document began appearing frequently in any assignment of commercial titles.[61] The influence of the Company of Merchants Adventurers was probably important to this development: contrary to Antwerp custom the Merchants Adventurers were required to produce explicit proof of payment in the form of assignment and therefore they normally produced a separate document.[62]

The Genesis of Modern Endorsement

One step from producing an assignment bill to noting that assignment on the title itself was really a very small one. Nevertheless, it was not taken for 16th century letters obligatory.[63] There were a number of reasons for this. The practice of appending a signature at the bottom of the letter obligatory was already extremely current at Antwerp, though it was normally accompanied by the words *als principael* or *als borge*, making it more a formal guarantee.[64] It is certain that the ceding creditor often followed this custom in the transfer of a title from hand to hand, as is clearly proven by a 1574–78 lawsuit.[65] Although the 'reason' for this signature was the same, it did not constitute a modern endorsement as such: the signature did not have the judicial value of a transfer and the Antwerp

---

[60] Litigation between Gillis de Visen and Daniel de Bruyne: decision of 16 August 1567: 'Nyettemin tevreden hem verweerdere te restitueren sekere billiet van assignatie op Anthoni Raedt' (ASA, *Vierschaar*, 1249, f. 266 v⁰–267).

[61] 'Soo de verweerder noch wisselbrief, noch assignatie, noch eenich ander bescheet tot verificatie van dyen en heeft geexhibeert', litigation between Augustyn van Merstraeten and Hans Verleyen, A⁰ 1608–9 (ASA, *Proces suppl.*, 1032).

[62] 'De coopluyden uuyt Ingelant... waeren geaccoustumeert ende gewoonlyck alle obligatien absolutelycken over te settene ende over te nemen, ende zoe wanneer dat zij anders accordeerden, zoe namen zij daeraf contreobligatie oft gelooften van den debiteur goet oft solvent te moeten houdene', Litigation between Joris Nedham and Janne Voye, decision of 24 November 1546 (ASA, *Vierschaar*, 1242, f. 226–7). See also De Smedt, *De Engelse natie* II, pp. 582–3.

[63] Professor J. Meuvret has informed me that in France the endorsement of letters obligatory seems to have preceded the endorsement of bills of exchange in the 17th century.

[64] There are abundant examples, among others: Strieder, *Aus Antwerpener Notariats-archiven...*, p. 304, no. 590 (4 November 1556); (ASA, *Vierschaar* 1237, f. 163 v⁰–164), decision dated 21 March 1542 ('43); (ASA, *Vierschaar*, 1249, f. 150 v⁰–151), decision dated 30 May 1567, and f. 209 v⁰, decision dated 17 June 1567; (ASA, *Proces suppl.*, 922), letter obligatory dated 5 August 1595, etc. Occasionally the signature of the guarantor was noted on the back of the document (ASA, *Not. protoc*, 3133, f. 212).

[65] 'Hebbende de voers. Bento Rodrigues voer het overgeven van der selven obligatien aender voers. De Gauna de voers. obligatie van der producent selver als principael moeten onderteekenen, mits de voers. Gauna den producent soo vele niet en souden hebben betrouwt', Lawsuit brought by Pedro Gomez de Meza against Bento Rodrigues, A⁰ 1574–8 (ASA, *Proces suppl.*, 642).

Custom of 1570 provided that a guarantor *als principael* could be charged with payment and even sued in preference to the principal debtor.[66]

The practice of noting partial payments on the reverse side of the letter obligatory had also become extensive in 16th century Antwerp.[67] Even the terminology of *endossement* had come into current use for this sort of operation.[68] It is possible that this custom, too, constituted a temporary obstacle to the introduction of modern endorsement methods at Antwerp. Nevertheless, we believe that Antwerp's hesitation before taking the last step towards modern endorsement of letters obligatory had other, more general and fundamental, reasons. It is easy to suppose that modern endorsement would penetrate more slowly into a category of commercial paper where the clause 'payable to bearer' had for a long time already provided a convenient means of transfer.[69] Letters obligatory payable to bearer remained very popular indeed in the Northern commercial centres during the 17th century, as demonstrated by the enthusiasm of de Malynes in 1622 for this continental practice, especially typical of Antwerp.[70] They remained particularly popular in those cases where the original debtor was a person enjoying general confidence or a government institution. The *rentmeesterbrieven* of Gaspar Ducci, the letters obligatory of the Estates of Brabant, Flanders and Mechlin and of the Estates General already circulated freely from hand to hand on the Antwerp Exchange in the 16th century. They continued to do so in the 17th century.[71] They were often given as payment of commercial debts or as a guarantee.[72] Predictably, this tendency appeared later in London and paved the way

---

[66] De Longé, *Coutumes du Pays et Duché de Brabant. Quartier d'Anvers* I, p. 598.

[67] Van der Wee, *The Growth of the Antwerp Market* II, pp. 348–9, note 78. There are other examples in the archives of lawsuits, notarial protocols, in the files of the Van Immerseele firm, and in the cashier's journal of Jaspar van Bell: L.P.L. Pirenne–W.J. Forsma, *Koopmansgeest te 's-Hertogenbosch in de vijftiende en zestiende eeuw. Het kasboek van Jaspar van Bell, 1564–1568* (Nijmegen: 1962), pp. 64 (no. 1), 68 (no. 4), 70 (no. 6), 77 (no. 17), 78 (nos 18–20).

[68] 'Want bleke uuyten indossemente vanden selve obligatie' (ASA, *Vierschaar*, 1249, f. 209 v°, decision dated 17 June 1567). 'Obligatien..., ende daerop men gewoone is de betaelinghen te endorsseren, ende als de obligatien te vollen betaelt sijn, de selve inne te trecken' (ASA, *Proces Suppl.*, 87, Reply of Jacop Verreycken, A° 1600).

[69] Cf. below.

[70] De Malynes, *Lex mercatoria*, pp. 96 ff.

[71] Van der Wee, *The Growth of the Antwerp Market* II, p. 355. Nevertheless, the money market of Antwerp held no monopoly on such circulation. On the circulation of *juros de resguando* in Spain under Philip II, for example, see F. Braudel, 'Le pacte de ricorsa au service du roi d'Espagne et de ses prêteurs à la fin du XVIe siècle,' in: *Studi in onore di A. Sapori* II (Milan: 1957), p. 1118.

[72] Strieder, *Aus Antwerpener Notariatsarchiven*, p. 406 (no. 805): 21 July 1588; ASA, *Proces suppl.*, litigation between Philips van Waelput and Master Jaspar Schuermans, 23 April 1608–5 November 1608.

for the circulation of goldsmiths' notes, exchequer bills, and other promissory notes of 17th-century England.[73]

For several years now numerous historians have drawn attention to the existence in Southern Europe of endorsed bills of exchange and cheques dating from well before 1600.[74]

It is thus clear that the transfer of commercial titles to third parties sometimes took place in the mercantile circles of the South in the 14th, 15th and 16th centuries, and that such transfers were not always made by means of a separate document but were already noted directly at the bottom or on the reverse side of the title. Nevertheless, we remain convinced, as is de Roover, that in the global context of Italian commerce and finance this practice remained limited and did not develop into an *institution typique*.[75] In reality, the vast majority of large commercial and financial payments were made in banks, transferring funds from one account to another, with the oral order remaining in current use. Even payments in currency, assigned on the current account of a merchant at his bank, were generally made upon verbal request, and only infrequently upon written request (cheque, *polizze*).[76] Moreover, the account book of Piccamiglio, the accounting of the Medicis, the study of Lapeyre on the fairs of Castile, and the remarks of Contarini at Venice all support the notion that the payment of bills of exchange was normally arranged through the banks as well.[77] Transfer clauses in the text of the bills themselves often arranged payment between drawer and drawee.[78] Payment of the bill to the beneficiary was also frequently arranged at the bank, normally upon the verbal instructions of the beneficiary, occasionally upon receipt of

---

[73] Holden, *The History of Negotiable Instruments*, pp. 66–98.

[74] Teja (1386: Florence–Zara–Venice), Melis (1394 and 1410: Datini archives at Prato), Lapeyre (1430: Rome–Barcelona), De Roover (1430 and 1494: Medici Bank), Heers (1459: Piccamiglio of Genoa), Melis (1519, 1537 and 1547: Florence–Lyons), Lapeyre (1537: Lyons–Seville; 1561: Antwerp–Medina del Campo; from 1574 to 1598: Ruiz archives: Medina del Campo), among others. There is a good overview in De Roover, *Lettre de change*, pp. 100–14 and De Roover, *The Rise and Decline of the Medici Bank*, pp. 137–40. See also Heers, *Le livre de comptes de Giovanni Piccamiglio*, pp. 350–6; H. Lapeyre, 'Las origines del Endoso de letras de cambio en España', in: *Moneda y Credito. Revista de Economia* LII (1955).

[75] De Roover, *The Rise and Decline of the Medici Bank*, p. 140.

[76] *Ibid.*, p. 19 and p. 413, note 75.

[77] *Ibid.*, p. 18; Heers, *Le livre de comptes de Giovanni Piccamiglio*, p. 38; Lapeyre, *Une famille de marchands: les Ruiz*, pp. 259–61; Van Dillen, *The Bank of Amsterdam*, pp. 80–1.

[78] For example: *E ponete a conto nostro* or *et mettez-le à mon compte*: (ASA, IB, 1, Balthasar Andrea file).

written instructions.[79] However, a written order for the payment *in banco* of a mature bill of exchange does not precisely correspond to the principle of negotiability. In the first place it does not involve any real circulation from hand to hand, nor is it an ordinary transfer, subject to successive operations. Finally, the idea of possessing a better title, an essential condition for negotiability, did not apply here since in case of non-payment the banker simply returned the title to his client.

Following the example set by the letter obligatory, the addition of the clause 'or to the bearer of this letter' to bills of exchange became increasingly common in the Netherlands in the course of the 16th century.[80] Thus in principle bills of exchange, too, could circulate from hand to hand as did letters obligatory. The two methods of payment became increasingly similar. In 1537 the Antwerp magistrate wrote to the emperor that an accepted bill of exchange had the same judicial value as a duly signed letter obligatory.[81] A letter from Erasmus Schetz to Herbouts dated July 1537 and an imperial ordinance of October 1541 also equate letters obligatory and bills of exchange with regard to payment by assignation.[82]

As early as 1538 the Van der Molen correspondence alludes to the practice at the Antwerp Exchange of paying bills of exchange that had fallen due with assignations on other bills of exchange that the debtor-merchant himself held as creditor or that he drew on his agents abroad.[83] Around 1540 Van der Molen regularly noted next to his listing of the exchange rates: *como hora li contanti val piu di bona assignacione de lettre di cambio, 2½%*.[84] However, litigation dating from the second third of the 16th century shows that the merchants of Antwerp usually assigned letters obligatory and only rarely bills of exchange. This leads to the conclusion that the 'payable to bearer' clause at that moment was far from common on bills of exchange and that the merchants of the North were still relatively unfamiliar with bills of exchange, which they used chiefly to transfer capital balances.[85]

By the final third of the 16th century the climate had entirely changed.

---

[79] Cf. the Spanish examples from 1537 and 1561 cited by Lapeyre and the 1457 example cited by Heers (Heers, *Le livre de comptes de Giovanni Piccamiglio*, pp. 345–6).

[80] Various examples can be found in: De Smedt, *De Engelse natie* II, p. 569; Holden, *The History of Negotiable Instruments*, p. 39. For the Hanseatics at Antwerp: Strieder, *Aus Antwerpener Notariatsarchiven*, p. 165 (no. 237), pp. 375–7 (no. 714).

[81] ASA, Pk 1052. See also the reply of Mattis Zimmermann to Hans von Pelcken (see note 23 above).

[82] ASA, Pk 1052.

[83] ASA, IB, 2039, f. 132, letter dated 4 January 1540.

[84] ASA, IB 2039, f. 88 v°.

[85] Cf. above.

The use of the bill of exchange was manifestly becoming widespread in Northern commercial circles. The sources are overflowing with testimony. The change in the registers of notarial regulations is truly amazing.[86] That the bill of exchange had become a first-class instrument of credit is demonstrated by a 1588 text as far as the Hanseatic merchants are concerned[87] and by the Van Immerseele correspondence as far as the Flemish are concerned.[88] Tawney and Christensen also provide valuable and persuasive information regarding English and Dutch commercial circles.[89] Finally the Customs of Antwerp unequivocally attest this development: the 1572 version devoted 8 articles to letters obligatory and only 3 to bills of exchange; the 1582 version devoted 10 and 11 articles respectively and the 1608 version devoted 17 articles to documents and letters obligatory and 77 to bills of exchange.[90]

It is probable that Italy's renewed traffic with the Levant, the Northern merchants' penetration of the Mediterranean, and perhaps above all the financial vitality of Genoa and of the Piacenza fairs, served to stimulate the dissemination of Italian financial methods and especially of the bill of exchange. But Antwerp's stimulating influence was unquestionably decisive in the generalization of Italian financial methods in the North beginning with the end of the 16th century. It was at Antwerp after all that the majority of the Northern merchants had met during the first two-thirds of the 16th century and there that they became better versed in the Italian methods. The large number of manuals and technical treatises published at Antwerp in the course of the 16th century and the prominence of Antwerp's commercial schools were also important factors.[91]

It was, moreover, at Antwerp that the circulation of commercial letters obligatory from hand to hand in the form of assignations had become so commonplace, and the guarantees for their transfer so refined, that the generalized endorsement of bills of exchange was a natural consequence. The Antwerp Customs of 1608 forbade bills of exchange being transferred

---

[86] Strieder's publication, *Aus Antwerpener Notariatsarchiven*, provides incontrovertible proof of this.

[87] 'Daer Brentens de comodityet nyet en hadde ihn zu bazahlen, so hatte Hulscher mit einwilligung des Brentens die Summe auf Wechsel auf Frankfurt genommen' (*Ibid.*, p. 406, no. 806: 11 July 1588).

[88] E. Stols, *Zuidnederlandse firma's en de inrichting van hun handel op de Iberische wereld, 1598–1648* II (Ph.D., Louvain University, 1965) (Louvain: 1965), pp. 36–7.

[89] R.H. Tawney, 'The Eastland Trade', in: *The Economic History Review* 2nd Series XII (1959), 2, pp. 280–2; A.E. Christensen, *Dutch Trade to the Baltic about 1600* (Copenhagen–The Hague: 1941), pp. 394–5.

[90] De Longé, *Coutumes du Pays et Duché de Brabant. Quartier d'Anvers* I, pp. 596–8; II, pp. 396–400 and 408–12; IV, pp. 10–43.

[91] Cf. above, note 21.

by means of a formal *cessio*, but they confirmed at the same time the practice of circulating letters obligatory from hand to hand as many as four, five, or even more times.[92] And those Customs explicitly insisted that transfers in the form of assignations were made essentially to protect the beneficiary creditors.[93] To ensure a maximum of financial security in the transfer of bills of exchange the Customs codified the *avallo* system, whereby all successive assigning creditors had to be listed by name on the bill, thus remaining linked to the final debtor.[94]

Antwerp's *avallo* system had some serious drawbacks because it required that all assigning creditors be known in advance. Moreover, it implied that in 1608 modern endorsement was not yet in current use at Antwerp. Nevertheless, the dossiers of commercial firms, dating from the first and second decades of the 17th century and preserved in the town archives, confirm the notion that modern endorsement was introduced around that very time.[95] It is even possible that the actual method of endorsing bills came from Italy, where the practice had been spreading slowly since the end of the 16th century, particularly in Tuscany, though it encountered lively legislative opposition throughout the 17th century.[96] At Antwerp on the other hand the judicial principles of negotiability inherent in modern endorsement were the result of financial–technical evolution in the preceding century, and consequently all the essential judicial foundations of modern endorsement were present from the outset.

The first examples of endorsement found at Antwerp were still imbued with the spirit of assignation, as shown by a sample dated April 20, 1611: *Received by me underwritten by Mr. Robert Rug, who I have assigned to receive it...* (signed by W. Selby).[97] It is thus quite clear that endorsement developed as an improved system of assignation, a system that in the course of the 16th century became typical of Antwerp, where it was granted elaborate legislative protection.

Though in England de Malynes did not yet discuss modern endorsement in his *Lex Mercatoria* of 1622,[98] John Marius's 1651 treatise dealt with it *in extenso*.[99] Still, it is striking that in the examples cited by Marius the older formula 'A or his assigns' still appeared frequently

---

[92] *Ibid*. IV, p. 28, art. 30 and p. 380, art. 14.

[93] 'Mits dat de bewijsinge geene betaelinge en is, maer alleenelyck dient tot versekeringe ende pantschappe' (*Ibid*. IV, p. 378, art. 11).

[94] *Ibid*., IV, pp. 40–1, art. 70–5.

[95] ASA, IB, 1 and 218. Cf. also De Roover, *L'évolution de la lettre de change*, p. 99.

[96] De Roover, *ibid*., pp. 102–3.

[97] Example published by De Roover, *ibid*., p. 155.

[98] Holden, *The History of Negotiable Instruments*, pp. 40–1.

[99] *Ibid*., p. 44.

alongside the formula 'A or order'. This leads one to suppose that in England modern endorsement had direct links to the Antwerp practice of assignation.

The Antwerp Origins of Modern Discounting

Discount, in the modern sense of the word – the assignation of a commercial effect or other financial title to a third party before its due date and for a sum less than the amount nominally due – was not practised before the 16th century. The first example we have discovered of such a practice at Antwerp was for the year 1536: this involved the discounting of a letter obligatory, found among the Kitson Papers.[100] These documents, accounts of the Antwerp fairs, also demonstrate that discount remained a relatively exceptional practice since Kitson's agent kept all the other letters and bills in portfolio until they fell due.

Nevertheless, the specific evolution of financial methods at Antwerp led to the creation of a climate extremely favourable to the development of the principle of modern discount. The growth of the practice of assignation and the circulation of letters obligatory and bills of exchange from hand to hand necessarily led to a more urgent and general need for cash in times of crisis or acute tension. All the more so since 16th century merchants often agreed to much longer terms of payment than had previously been usual, especially for letters obligatory, and to assigning not only papers due, but also letters or bills not yet due.[101]

We also observe the gradual acceptance of the idea of the simple loan at interest, under the influence of the Renaissance, among the Northern merchants and even in official circles during the 16th century. In this context it is interesting to note the imperial ordinance of 1540 officially permitting simple loans at interest; it mentions in passing the appearance of a group of merchant-financiers at Antwerp: *faisant des marchandises d'argent les donnant à gaing et frait*.[102] The *tourbes* of 1559 and 1570 show us how the trade in money had gained ground at Antwerp in the course of the second third of the century, especially in the area of deposits from one fair to the other.[103] But other financing was also available, as shown in detail by the Van der Molen correspondence from 1538 to 1544. These letters specify how the merchant-financiers, having no merchandise to pay for and disposing of cash funds, paid cash for assignations on letters

---

[100] H. Van der Wee, 'Sporen van Disconto te Antwerpen tijdens de XVIe eeuw,' in: *Bijdragen voor de Geschiedenis der Nederlanden* X (1955), pp. 68–70.

[101] Cf. the sentence registers and lawsuit dossiers dating from the second half of the 16th century. See also Brulez, *De Firma Della Faille*, p. 403.

[102] ASA, Pk 2763, f. 173.

[103] ASA, *Vierschaar*, 69, f. 25 v°–26 and f. 71.

obligatory and bills of exchange for a percentage premium when there was tension on the money market.[104]

It is probable that this was not yet a true discount in the modern sense. The financiers only appeared at the Exchange during the days of payment, especially in difficult times. They purchased only mature letters obligatory and bills of exchange, so that their percentage deducted was really only a special discount for cash payment. But it was not far from there to the purchase of commercial effects *not yet due*, particularly in view of the modern commercial climate of Antwerp and the increasing trend towards assigning commercial titles before their due date. Mennher's manual (*Pratique brifue pour cyfrer et tenir liures de comptes*), printed at Antwerp around 1560, already gives several examples of the discounting, in the modern sense, of letters obligatory.[105] Mellema's 1582 *Arithmétique* gives a yet clearer example.[106] An Antwerp magistrate's text, dated 19 March 1560,[107] explains to the Antwerp representatives to the Council of Brabant that the agents of various merchant-financiers had been making cash purchases of letters obligatory and of bills of exchange on that day (19 March) and on the day before. The first payments of the trimestrial fair, discussed in the text, were not normally made until the beginning of May and those bills of exchange from Lyons and Besançon that were payable at that fair had just arrived at Antwerp. It is thus possible, even probable, that in the majority of cases such purchases were not mere promises of purchase on the due date at the following fair but real purchases, that is to say the premium included not only an agio for cash payment, but also interest for prepayment and risks incurred. It was thus already an example of the current use of modern discount. During the years 1563–64 Daniel de Bruyne regularly purchased from third parties letters obligatory that fell due only some six to twelve months later.[108] In the *Della Faille* archives from the end of the 16th century it is apparent that the discounting of letters obligatory was already normal practice.[109] The practice already existed at the end of the 16th century in Hamburg,

---

[104] ASA, IB, 2039, f. 132, letter dated 4 January 1540. We cannot agree with Brulez's critical remarks concerning it (W. Brulez, 'Antwerpens Bloeitijd', in: *Bijdragen voor de Geschiedenis der Nederlanden* XIX (1964), 2, p. 160). The central argument that a merchant wishing to purchase merchandise needed cash is not valid since an established firm could always purchase on credit.

[105] Re-edited by Michel Coignet in 1573 (Antwerp Municipal Library, G. 4815, f. I–IIII). See also Van der Wee, *The Growth of the Antwerp Market* II, p. 350.

[106] De Groote, *De "Arithmétique" van Mellema*, p. 144.

[107] De Smedt, *De Engelse natie* II, p. 573, note 19. We have discussed the precise interpretation of this text at length with De Smedt and De Groote and wish to extend our sincere thanks to them for their very suggestive remarks on the subject.

[108] Van der Wee, *The Growth of the Antwerp Market* II, pp. 350–1.

[109] Brulez, *De Firma Della Faille*, p. 402.

which, particularly during the great waves of emigration, was in direct contact with Antwerp.[110] Nevertheless, discounting bills of exchange is mentioned neither in the *Della Faille* archives nor at Hamburg. It is possible that discount was more readily applied to letters obligatory, since they more frequently involved medium- to long-term commercial credit, in contrast to bills of exchange, which were strictly short-term credit and hence less attractive to discount.[111]

Nevertheless, in 1576 there were regular entries in the accounts of the Fuggers of Augsburg recording the payment of bills of exchange before their due date, minus the interest in view of prepayment.[112] These payments were in all probability made by those who had accepted the bills, that is to say this represented a discount in the older acceptance (*rabats*). However, since the Antwerp Customs of 1570 and 1608 explicitly forbade this practice for bills of exchange[113] but made no mention of the sale of such bills to third parties before their due date, it is possible and even probable that Antwerp merchants began to apply the modern discount system, already in current use for letters obligatory, to bills of exchange in view of the growing success of the bill of exchange in Northern commerce. Moreover, the town ordinances of 1600 demonstrate that the cash purchase of bills of exchange by merchant-bankers at times of *strettezza* was still normal practice on the Antwerp Exchange.[114] The texts do not explicitly distinguish between mature bills and bills not yet due, but from the above it can be deduced that both were purchased in this manner.

De Malynes, in his 1622 analysis of the advantages of continental customs involving the transferability of letters obligatory, gives a very clear example of discount in the modern sense.[115] Marius explains in 1651 that the modern discount of bills of exchange had become current practice in England and also mentions *inland bills* for the first time.[116] Taking into

---

[110] R. Ehrenberg, *Hamburg und England im Zeitalter der Koningin Elisabeth* (Jena: 1896), p. 308.

[111] Brulez, *De Firma Della Faille*, pp. 403–4.

[112] Various examples in: Van der Wee, *The Growth of the Antwerp Market* II, pp. 349–50, note 85.

[113] De Longé, *Coutumes du Pays et Duché de Brabant* IV, p. 26, art. 29.

[114] ASA, Pk 918, f. 135 and 141–141 v°: 'dat sedert eenighe maenden herwaerts [opnieuw] diverse cooplieden hen hebben vervoirdert contante penningen te coopen ende te vercoopen waerdore tusschen contanten ende bewijsingen oft assignatien onderscheet werdde gemaeckt van 1½ jae 2%, niet alleenlijck in de betaelinghen, maer oyck in den prijse van de wisselen, die op ander plaetsen worden getrocken.'

[115] De Malynes, *Lex mercatoria*, p. 99: *Nay more, if he will have readie money for these bills, he may sell them to other merchants that are moneyed men.*

[116] Holden, *The History of Negotiable Instruments*, pp. 43 and 47.

account what we have just stated regarding the Antwerp discounts of the 16th century and the fact that the files of the Van Immerseele firm already mentioned *inland bills* at the beginning of the 17th century,[117] all the elements characteristic of *domestic banking* as practised in the second half of the 17th century by the London goldsmith-bankers, universally recognized as the direct ancestors of the modern discount bankers, were present in the evolving financial techniques at Antwerp.[118]

Conclusion

Let us summarize our conclusions. We do not wish to deny that Antwerp's technico-financial innovations in the 16th century were rooted directly in the refined and traditional methods of the Italians. But it is equally indisputable that these innovations began to grow apart from the parent plant, differentiating themselves clearly from it. They did not come to final fruition, of course, but England in particular reaped the harvest of Antwerp's achievements and refined them into a complete, homogeneous, modern system. The close links of the Company of Merchants Adventurers and the English government with the Antwerp Exchange, persisting at least until the *Court* was transferred to Middelburg in 1582, ensured an effective continuity. That is, the financial creativity of 17th century England was rooted above all in Antwerp's innovations of the preceding century.

---

[117] Stols, *Zuidnederlandse firma's* II, p. 234.
[118] De Smedt, *De Engelse natie* II, p. 574.

9

Monetary Policy in the Duchy of Brabant, Late Middle Ages to Early Modern Times

Carolingian Monetary Reform: the Basis of the Late Medieval Monetary System

In the course of the 8th century the Carolingian rulers embarked on an energetic policy of monetary reform better to meet the needs of the flourishing Carolingian agricultural economy and to provide a uniform measure of value in the face of the prevailing monetary chaos. The first goal of this policy was to restore a royal monopoly on the mintage of coin, which had passed into private hands (those of the so-called *monetarii*, usually gold- or silversmiths) during the Merovingian period: a centralizing policy implemented only slowly and with great difficulty. Monetary unity was the second goal of this reform: specifically, the introduction of an adequate silver-based money of account to be used as legal tender throughout the Frankish realm. The new system was based on three monetary units: the pound or *libra*, the shilling or *solidus*, and the penny or *denarius*, with their relative values established at: 1 pound = 20 shillings = 240 pennies, and 1 shilling = 12 pennies.[1]

Neither the pound nor the shilling actually circulated as real coins in the new Carolingian monetary system. Pounds and shillings existed only on paper, and were used exclusively as theoretical units in accounts, and were thus literally 'monies of account.' The penny (or *denier*) on the other hand did circulate as a coin. It thus had a dual nature: on the one hand the penny (*denier*), as a fraction of the pound and the shilling, acted as

---

[1] M. Bloch, 'Esquisse d'une histoire monétaire de l'Europe', *Cahiers des Annales* IX (Paris: 1954), p. 27; R. Delort, *Le monde de Charlemagne* (Paris: 1986), pp. 132–3; H. Frère, *Le denier carolingien spécialement en Belgique* I (Louvain-la-Neuve: 1977), pp. 83, 89–90; E. Fournial, *Histoire monétaire de l'Occident médiévale*, (Paris: 1970), pp. 28, 54–8.

an accounting unit, useful in computing accounts and calculating transactions, and on the other the penny (*denier*) circulated as a silver coin in daily life. In this sense the pound and the shilling were merely accounting multiples of the penny (*denier*), which was both an accounting unit and a real coin. Thus a payment recorded in the domanial accounts as 1 pound 6 shillings was actually paid with 312 silver pennies or *deniers*, that is 240 pennies for the pound recorded, and six times 12 pennies for the 6 shillings on record.[2]

By the beginning of the 9th century Charlemagne, with his great authority as emperor, had succeeded in introducing the new silver coin and the new money of account throughout his realm. After his death in 814, and during the consequent fragmenting of the Frankish empire, the principles of the new monetary system survived, though the silver penny (*denier*) soon fell victim to the disintegration of political power.[3]

From Coin of the Realm to Regional Money: the Devaluation of the Silver Penny

Usurpation of political power and of the right to mint coins by regional administrators such as counts or dukes, by abbeys or churches and by feudal lords, led to regional and local mintage and to monetary chaos. During the 9th and 10th centuries dozens of monetary systems sprang into existence, based on the Carolingian model. In France and Flanders the penny *Parisis*, the penny *Tournois*, and the penny *Flandriensis* met with

---

[2] E. Aerts, 'Quelques réflexions sur les comptes du duché de brabant au bas moyen âge', in: *Archief- en Bibliotheekwezen in België* LIII (1982), pp. 136–50; H. van Werveke, 'Monnaie de compte et monnaie réelle', in: *Belgisch Tijdschrift voor Filologie en Geschiedenis* XIII (1934), pp. 123–52, republished in *Idem, Miscellanea mediaevalia: Verspreide opstellen over economische en social geschiedenis van de Middeleeuwen* (Ghent: 1968), pp. 133–59; G.M. De Meyer and E.W.F. van den Elzen, 'Van geschenk tot getal: Geschiedenis van een hoofse rekenmunt', in: *Belgisch Tijdschrift voor Filologie en Geschiedenis* LVIII (1980), pp. 317–36; J.W. Marsilje, *Het financiële beleid van Leiden in de laat-Beierse en Bourgondische periode, ca. 1390–1477* (Hilversum: 1985), pp. 148–51; J.-P. Peters, 'Excursus. De mideleeuwse rekenmunt in de Nederlanden. Een status quaestionis', in J. Baerten, *Muntslag en -circulatie in de Nederlanden, Noord en Zuid op de weegschaal. 7de–16de eeuw* (Brussels: 1983), pp. 121–32; P. Spufford, *Monetary Problems and Policies in the Burgundian Netherlands, 1433–1492*, (Leyden: 1970), pp. 13–29; also, *Handbook of Medieval Exchange* (London: 1986), pp. XX–XXVI; H. Van der Wee, *The Growth of the Antwerp Market and the European Economy (Fourteenth–Sixteenth Centuries)* II (Paris–The Hague: 1963), pp. 107–13; R. Van Uytven, *Stadsfinanciën en stadsekonomie te Leuven van de XIIe tot het einde der XVIe eeuw* (Brussels: 1961), pp. 56–73.

[3] J. Baerten, *Muntslag en -circulatie in de Nederlanden. Noord en Zuid op de weegschaal, 7de–16de eeuw* (Brussels: 1983), pp. 8–9.

great success. Later a number of coins, each named for its place of origin, circulated in Brabant as well: the penny *Lovens*, the penny *Brussels*, and so on. The pound *Brussels*, for example, was thus a 'money of account,' deriving its value from the silver content of the only basic coin actually in circulation in Brussels: the penny or *denier Brussels*.[4]

The introduction of a whole series of local or regional basic monetary units in itself created many problems. Even greater confusion was posed by the progressive debasement of the various local or regional silver *deniers* or pennies. While in Charlemagne's time the penny contained approximately 1.71 grams of silver, pennies have been found that date from the beginning of the 12th century and contain only 0.87 grams of silver.[5] The most important cause of this consistent tendency to debase the penny lay with the feudal rulers, who considered mintage a seigneurial right and the ruler's prerogative. Each new mintage offered them an opportunity to impose a tax, the so-called *sleischat* or *droit de seigneuriage*.[6] The potential for taxation was based primarily on the higher value of minted precious metals relative to unminted precious metals. The ruler could pocket the difference, less the production costs of minting, as a source of income. Debasing the silver penny had a second advantage: by lowering the precious metal content of the standard coin through a new issue, the ruler could disburse the new, slightly debased, pennies at the same official rate as the older, somewhat heavier pennies he had abandoned. The rulers often used this kind of monetary manipulation to increase their income quickly and easily in difficult circumstances such as political upheavals and wars.[7]

The Rise of Heavy Silver and Gold Coins

As long as interregional trade was disrupted (mainly from the 9th to the 11th century), the debasement of silver coins had little or no negative effect on commercial activity. However, when around 1100 regional and international trade expanded, the money economy penetrated urban and rural life more deeply. The substantially debased and wildly variable local or regional silver pennies became less and less suitable, either as a general medium of exchange or as a universal measure of value.[8]

---

[4] *Op. cit.*, pp. 14–5.

[5] W.P. Blockmans, 'Le poids des deniers carolingiens', in: *Revue Belge de Numismatique* CXIX (1973), pp. 179–81; Furnial, *Histoire monétaire*, pp. 61–2, 67–8.

[6] R. Van Uytven, 'Munt en muntslag', in H. Baudet and H. van der Meulen (eds), *Kernproblemen der economische geschiedenis*, (Groningen: 1978), pp. 84–9.

[7] J.H. Munro, *Wool, Cloth and Gold: the Struggle for Bullion in Anglo-Burgundian Trade, 1340–1478* (Brussels–Toronto: 1972), pp. 15–22.

[8] E. Aerts, 'Laatmiddeleeuwse Brabantse rekeningen in het historisch onderzoek', in: *Gemeentekrediet van België. Driemaandelijks tijdschrift* XXXVI (1982), pp. 288–9.

The circulation of larger, and particularly of heavier, silver coins must be seen in this context. The demand factor was met by an accommodating supply factor. Thanks to the exploitation of new silver mines in Alsace, Saxony, Transylvania and Bohemia, Europe was in a position to begin producing, from the beginning of the 13th century onwards, a new silver coin, generally known as the 'groat.' This groat eventually took the place of the old silver penny or *denier* as the basic coin used in the monetary system.[9]

In 1266, after a number of Italian cities had begun producing their own *grossi*, Saint Louis followed, minting a French *gros Tournois* with a silver content of approximately 4 grams, whereas the traditional French penny at that time contained only a third of a gram of silver. In England the groat met with success only after 1346, since Henry II Plantagenet (1154–89) had already introduced his own uniform and stable silver coin to 12th-century England: the sterling.[10]

The Netherlands could not lag behind in this development. In 1250 Flanders began to imitate the English silver sterling, which at that time was worth 4 silver pence Flemish. The idea was to use these Flemish sterlings to finance Flemish wool imports from England. Brabant followed suit in 1273, and shortly afterwards, again following the Flemish lead, began minting double Brabant sterlings worth 8 silver pence Flemish. The stimulus for this was the English embargo on wool export to Flanders during the 1270s. The embargo had considerably strengthened Brabant's position in textile production, and consequently as an importer of English wool. Brabant's mintage of sterlings and double sterlings now became so prominent that they were known as *anglici Brabantini*.[11]

Towards the end of the 13th century Flanders and Brabant also began minting a silver groat, with the French *gros Tournois* as their model. The great influence of French monetary policies on Flanders and Brabant during that period originated in the increasing interest of the annual fairs of Champagne as a southerly market for Flemish and Brabantine woollen cloth. Flemish and Brabantine merchants received their payments at these annual fairs in heavy *gros Tournois*, bringing them into circulation in

---

[9] Fournial, *Histoire monétaire*, pp. 78–87; H. Van der Wee, E. Aerts and W. Dupon, *De economische ontwikkeling van Europa. Documenten: Middeleeuwen, 950–1450* (Louvain: 1985), pp. 244–5.

[10] H. Van der Wee and E. Aerts, *De economische ontwikkeling van Europa, 950–1950* (Louvain–Amersfoort: 1982), p. 53.

[11] Baerten, *Muntslag en -circulatie*, pp. 24–5; N.J. Mayhew, 'The Circulation and Imitation of Sterlings in the Low Countries (880–1500),' in Mayhew (ed.), *Coinage in the Low Countries (880–1500)* (Oxford: 1979), pp. 56–7; J.A. Van Houtte, *Economische Geschiedenis van de Lage Landen, 800–1800* (Haarlem: 1979), p. 49.

Flanders and Brabant as a solid and reliable silver currency, encouraging the Flemish count and the duke of Brabant to circulate their own imitations of these French groats at home. In the course of time the silver groats of Flanders and Brabant went their own, separate ways, becoming distinctive Flemish and Brabant groats.[12]

Meanwhile gold coins, with a value yet greater than that of the large silver coins, were again being minted in Europe. Because of their high value and the remarkable stability of their precious metal content, they inspired extraordinary confidence and in so doing met the needs of Europe's increasingly flourishing continental and maritime trade. The crusades, but especially the positive balance of trade with the Middle East and North Africa, where gold was abundant thanks to the mines along the west coast, ensured a steady flow of the yellow metal towards Europe. Around the middle of the 13th century the Italian cities took the lead in gold coinage, minting florins in Florence and ducats in Venice. Under Louis IX, France followed suit in 1266, minting an *écu d'or* or golden crown. England was just ahead of France in minting its own gold coin.[13] In the second quarter of the 14th century Flanders and Brabant began minting their own *guldens* and golden crowns, after 1325 and 1330 respectively.[14]

The silver coins, as the basic coinage, continued to determine the money of account. In time, however, the drastically debased, blackened silver pence survived solely as small change.[15] The heavier silver groats and their multiples and fractions assumed their full function as the link between accounting and real currency: they became the basic coin in the system of money of account: pound Flemish groats, pound Brabant groats, pound Artois groats, etc.

Harmonization with a View to Unification: the Monetary Policies of Flanders and Brabant on the Eve of the Burgundian Union

During the 13th century the French Crown had succeeded in enhancing its monetary prestige. French efforts at centralization, symbolized by the establishment of a royal monopoly of minting and the successful rise of the *gros Tournois*, directly affected those parts of Flanders owing feudal

---

[12] Baerten, *Muntslag en -circulatie*, pp. 28 ff.

[13] Fournial, *Histoire monétaire*, pp. 80–1.

[14] Van Houtte, *Economische geschiedenis*, p. 99; H. Van der Wee and E. Aerts, *Vlaams-Brabantse muntstatistieken. Deel II: de aanmuntingsgegevens van de gouden munten (1330–1506)*, Workshop on Quantitative Economic History, Discussion Paper 81.01 (Louvain: 1985), pp. 2–3.

[15] P. Spufford, 'Dans l'espace bourguignon, 1477. Un tournant monétaire?' in: *Actes du Colloque organisé par l'Institut de Recherche Régionale en Sciences Sociales, Humaines et Economiques de l'Université de Nancy II. 22–24 septembre 1977* (Nancy: 1977), pp. 187–8.

allegiance to France. There were repercussions in imperial Flanders as well, even though the Flemish counts had no feudal obligations to France for those territories.[16]

However, the vigorous economic growth of Flanders in the 12th and 13th centuries created a need for an autonomous monetary system of heavy silver coins. To strengthen their position with respect to the French sovereign, the Flemish counts sought support in other territories. Only Brabant was prepared to join them. In 1299 the Flemish count Robrecht of Bethune and John II of Brabant agreed to become partners in mintage. A new, common, silver coin valued at one half groat and distinct from the French prototype was to be minted. In both principalities only these Flemish and Brabant heavy coins would be tolerated. Finally, measures were taken to provide the mints of both regions with sufficient precious metal.

The agreement appears to have been inadequate. Already in 1300, before the date of initial implementation had elapsed, a new agreement was reached further detailing the monetary union of Flanders and Brabant. It laid the immediate foundations for the joint issue of a full common groat after the French model, but again distinct from it.

The agreements of 1299-1300 between Flanders and Brabant were invalidated *de facto* by the French invasion of Flanders at the beginning of the 14th century. As soon as the pact of Athus-sur-Orge (1305) was signed, however, Flanders resumed minting its own distinctive version of the *gros Tournois*.[17]

The costs of the Franco-Flemish war had caused general monetary confusion in France. This uncertainty led the Flemish count to establish, between 1317 and 1319, an autonomous Flemish money of account based on the silver groat, as minted in Flanders since the pact of Athus-sur-Orge.[18] When in 1337 the imminence of the Hundred Years' War between England and France led the French kings to heavy debasements of the French *gros* to secure the funds necessary to finance the war, it led to a definitive parting of the ways for the French and Flemish monetary systems. The Flemish count of course also regularly changed the intrinsic value of his own silver groats, but autonomously this time; the

---

[16] Fournial, *Histoire monétaire*, pp. 82-3; H. Van Werveke, 'Munt en politiek. De Frans-Vlaamse verhoudingen vóór en na 1300', in: *Bijdragen voor de Geschiedenis der Nederlanden* VIII (1953), pp. 3-9, reprinted in Van Werveke, *Miscellanea mediaevalia*, pp. 211-7.

[17] Baerten, *Muntslag en -circulatie*, pp. 28-30; Van Werveke, 'Munt en politiek', pp. 217-8; C. Wyffels, 'Contribution à l'histoire monétaire de Flandre au XIIIe siècle', in *Belgisch Tijdschrift voor Filologie en Geschiedenis* XLV (1967), pp. 1113-41, reprinted in Wyffels, *Miscellanea Archivistica et Historica*, Extranummer 27 (Brussels: 1987), p. 496.

[18] Van Werveke, 'Munt en politiek', pp. 224-5.

changes no longer corresponded to alterations in the silver content of French groats.[19]

Once again there was a rapprochement between Flanders and Brabant. In 1339 Duke John III of Brabant concluded a treaty with Louis of Crécy, count of Flanders, intended to arrive at the mintage of a common standard silver coin. This was the lion groat on which appeared the names of the mints at Ghent and Louvain and those of both rulers. The lion groat, some 60 million of which were put into circulation, met with immense success and was imitated far and wide, even as far away as Aquitaine and Brittany.[20]

Fourteenth-century Debasements in Flanders and Brabant

However successful the mintage of the Flemish and Brabant lion groat, the monetary policy of Flanders and Brabant was still not entirely in harmony even after 1339. The debasement policy of the French kings exerted a pernicious influence: it undermined the monetary policy of the Flemish count, putting pressure in turn on the duke of Brabant's monetary policy.

This chain reaction was the result of what is known as Gresham's law, the implications of which were sufficiently well understood by late medieval rulers. When for example the ruler of country A minted silver groats, an analogous coinage could be minted in territory B, similar in appearance but containing slightly less silver. Especially when the standard silver coin of land B had a long-standing affinity with the standard coin of country A, the ruler of country B could rely on spreading his new, less valuable, coins across the borders into country A. With the extra profits made possible by reducing the silver content of each coin, ruler B could then offer higher prices to the merchants and exchange agents supplying precious metals to his mint, thus drawing off the good coin of country A to the mint of land B. For the ruler of country A, more and more frequently confronted with a reduction in the supply of his own good coins, there was only one possible means of reversing this trend, namely to reduce the silver content of his own coins, preferably even more than had territory B. During the 14th century Flanders suffered greatly from the successive debasements of the French groat, and was thus repeatedly

---

[19] Van Werveke, 'Currency Manipulation in the Middle Ages: the Case of Louis de Male, Count of Flanders', in: *Transactions of the Royal Historical Society*, 4th Series XXXI (1949), pp. 122-3, reprinted in: Van Werveke, *Miscellanea mediaevalia*, pp. 261-2; J. Ghyssens, 'Le monnayage d'argent en Flandre, Hainaut et Brabant au début de la guerre de Cent Ans', in: *Revue Belge de Numismatique* CXX (1974), pp. 114-24.

[20] Baerten, *Muntslag en -circulatie*, pp. 32-3; J.H. Munro, 'Monnayage, monnaies de compte et mutations monétaires au Brabant à la fin du moyen âge', in J. Day (ed.), *Etudes d'histoire monétaire XIIe-XIXe siècles* (Lille: 1984), p. 277.

obliged to reduce the value of the Flemish groat. Debasement of the Flemish lion groat in turn put pressure on the Brabant lion groat, forcing the duke of Brabant to debase as well. The duke of Brabant went even further in this than did the Flemish count.[21]

Gold coins escaped the debasement fever affecting silver money. The rulers took care not to allow their debasements to disrupt international trade, where payment in gold coin had by then become customary. The social consequences of the disparate policies pursued with respect to gold and silver coins were disastrous for craftsmen and labourers. When the ruler resorted to a reduction in the silver content of the standard coin and imposed the new, weaker coin as the basis for the current monetary system, he also devalued the money of account in which all rents, prices and wages were expressed. On the one hand debasements of the Brabant and Flemish groats in time led to rising market prices for consumer goods. Wages, on the other hand, set at fixed tariffs by urban regulations, remained stable. As a result the purchasing power of wages declined. A general impoverishment of the mass of wage- and piece-workers was inevitable, as were the ensuing social tensions. On the positive side the lower export prices made possible by the debasements stimulated the export of woollen cloth during the third quarter of the 14th century, strengthening the textile industry in Flanders and Brabant.[22]

The Currency War between Flanders and Brabant in the Shadow of the Burgundians (1384–89)

The monetary competition between Brabant and Flanders entered a decisive phase at the end of Louis of Male's and the beginning of Philip the Bold's reign in Flanders. At the end of 1380 and the beginning of

---

[21] While the silver content of the Flemish groat gradually fell from 2.91 grams to 0.97 grams between 1339 and 1383, the silver content of the Brabant groat fell to 0.33 grams during the same period. F. and W.P. Blockmans, 'Devaluation, Coinage and Seignorage under Louis de Nevers and Louis de Male, Counts of Flanders, 1330–84', in: Mayhew (ed.), *Coinage in the Low Countries*, pp. 69, 72–81, in which the international context is stressed, together with attempts to derive income from mintage; J.H. Munro, 'Monetary Contraction and Industrial Change in the Late–Medieval Low Countries, 1335–1500', in: *ibid.*, p. 100; Van Werveke, 'Currency manipulation', pp. 258–62; Van der Wee, *The Growth* I, pp. 125–7; H. Van der Wee and E. Aerts, *Vlaams-Brabantse muntstatistieken 1300–1506. Deel I. De aanmuntingsgegevens van de zilvermunten*, Workshop on Quantitative Economic History, Discussion Paper: 80.02 (Louvain: 1980), pp. 24, 43–4.

[22] Munro, 'Monetary Contraction,' p. 102; Van Werveke, 'Currency Manipulation,' pp. 262–5; also 'De economische en sociale gevolgen van de muntpolitiek der graven van Vlaanderen (1337–1433),' in: *Annales de la Société d'Emulation de Bruges* LXXIV (1931), pp. 1–15, reprinted in: Van Werveke, *Miscellanea mediaevalia*, pp. 243–53; Van der Wee, *The Growth* II, p. 13.

1381, Joan and Wenceslaus of Brabant were already complaining that their mints were virtually idle due to the continual debasement of the Flemish groat.[23]

A new debasement of the Flemish silver groat in 1383 again put pressure on Brabant. Presumably Philip the Bold hoped that this step would weaken Brabant, making it more amenable to negotiation. Philip used this opportunity to assume control of Brabant's monetary policy and to strengthen his authority in the duchy. Philip was able to reach an agreement with Joan of Brabant in 1384, whereby both principalities agreed, with mutual guarantees, to mint the same gold and silver coins for the coming five-year period, sharing in the mint revenues. The common silver groat would even, as a token of the good intentions of both rulers, return to a silver content higher than that of the previous mintage.[24]

Since the 1384 agreement by no means forbade the Burgundian duke Philip the Bold to mint his own coins in addition to the common coinage, the mint at Ghent proceeded to do so. Gradually Philip the Bold put Flemish silver coins into circulation at Ghent containing less silver than the apparently similar, but intrinsically more valuable Flemish–Brabant groats. In this way Philip succeeded in luring considerable amounts of mintable metal or bullion from Brabant to Ghent. When Joan perceived Philip's treachery, she also decided to begin producing her own lighter Brabantine groats, even lighter than the Flemish. As a result, Philip simply closed the mint at Louvain in 1388. Duchess Joan, under obligation to Philip the Bold for his military and financial aid to Brabant in its war against Gelderland, was unable to reverse the trend. When the five-year agreement of 1384 expired, Philip the Bold proposed uniting the mints of both principalities, Flanders and Brabant, under his own control and adopting definitive reforms, and the duchess of Brabant accepted this offer, on condition that the profits be shared.[25]

---

[23] H. Van Werveke, 'De Vlaamse munthervorming van 1389–1390', in: *Nederlandsche Historiebladen* I (1938), p. 338, reprinted in: Van Werweke, *Miscellanea mediaevalia*, p. 270.

[24] *Ibid.*, p. 271; A. De Witte, *Histoire monétaire des comtes de Louvain, ducs de Brabant, et marquis du Saint-Empire Romain* I (Antwerp: 1894), pp. 164–79.

[25] Van Werveke, 'De Vlaamse munthervorming', pp. 271–3; H. Laurent, *La loi de Gresham au moyen âge. Essai sur la circulation monétaire entre la Flandre et le Brabant à la fin du XIVe siècle* (Brussels: 1933), pp. 39–82. This position was somewhat modified and amended by: W.P. Blockmans, 'La participation des sujets flamands à la politique monétaire des ducs de Bourgogne', in: *Revue Belge de Numismatique* CXIX (1973), pp. 104–5; P. Cockshaw, 'A propos de la circulation monétaire entre la Flandre et le Brabant de 1384 à 1390', *Contributions à l'Histoire Economique et Sociale* VI (1970–71), p. 108; also 'The Flemish Monetary Policy of the Dukes of Burgundy of the House of Valois, 1384–1430,' in: Mayhew, *Coinage in the Low Countries*, pp. 167–9; H. Enno van Gelder,

The Monetary Reform of 1389–90 and the Reorganization of the Monetary System up to the Beginning of the 15th Century

Philip the Bold's debasements of the 1380s should not be viewed solely in the context of his relations with Brabant. They were also reactions to debasements in Hainault, Holland and France during the same period. In time, however, the French currency stabilized. The Dutch towns were also able to persuade the regent Albert of Bavaria to refrain from further debasements. Thus there, too, conditions were ripe for monetary reorganization.[26]

The new Flemish groat of 1389–90 recovered part of its earlier silver content: the amount of pure silver in the groat increased from 0.78 grams to 1.02 grams.[27] At the same time Philip the Bold imposed an obligatory exchange rate for those coins permitted to circulate.[28] The Flemish–Brabant groat of the 1384 convention, by treaty the standard coin of the monetary system of Flanders and Brabant, continued to play that role in Brabant even after 1389 under the name 'light Flemish groat'. The new, stronger Flemish groat of 1389–90 on the other hand became the standard coin in the Flemish monetary system, under the name 'heavy Flemish groat', later known simply as the Flemish groat.[29]

In 1399 Brabant, too, adopted the new system: the new, heavy Flemish groat became the standard coin of Brabant's monetary system. The old, light Flemish groat came to be valued against it at the fixed ratio of one heavy Flemish groat to two light Flemish groats. The extent to which Brabant's system was overshadowed by the Flemish monetary system is again apparent.[30]

The socio-economic impact of the monetary reforms of 1389–90 and 1399 was extremely negative. The heavier silver groat accompanying the monetary reform was of greatest benefit to creditors and had disastrous effects on the repayment obligations of the mass of debtors, essentially members of the poorer social strata. The debtors, who had received light

---

'Aantekeningen bij de Vlaamse muntslag 1384–1434', in: *Revue Belge de Numismatique* CVII (1961) pp. 138–41; J.H. Munro, 'Mint Policies, Ratios, and Outputs in the Low Countries and England, 1335–1420: Some Reflections on New Data', in: *The Numismatic Chronicle* CXLI (1981), pp. 80–1 (no. 22), 88.

[26] H. Enno van Gelder, *De Nederlandse munten* (Utrecht–Antwerp: 1968), pp. 35–41; P. Cockshaw, 'A propos de la circulation monétaire', pp. 108–9: J.H. Munro, 'Mint Policies', pp. 80–1 expressed doubt that English debasements exerted any influence.

[27] Van der Wee, *The Growth* I, pp. 125–6; H. Van der Wee and E. Aerts, 'De Vlaams-Brabantse muntgeschiedenis in cijfers: een poging tot homogenisering van de veertiende- en vijftiende-eeuwse gegevens', in: *Revue Belge de Numismatique* CXXV (1979), p. 83.

[28] Van Werveke, 'De Vlaamse munthervorming', pp. 273–4.

[29] Van der Wee, *The Growth* I, pp. 123–4.

[30] *Ibid.*, p. 124.

groats, or had purchased goods against high prices in light groats, were now obliged to repay the same sums in the new heavy groats. This was often a millstone round the neck for the poor. Wage-earners were also badly affected. The stronger employers took advantage of the monetary reform, reducing nominal wages, though the market price of essential goods did not decline to the same extent.

Wage-earners were thus the dupe of virtually every monetary manipulation: debasements were always more rapidly reflected in prices than in wages; a stronger currency on the contrary led immediately to a decline in wages, whereas prices followed the declining trend more slowly and less completely than wages.[31] Nobles, clerics and burghers of private means on the other hand exerted an increasingly powerful influence on the ruler's policies in the regional Estates and the Estates-General. They lobbied more and more strenuously to maintain a good, strong currency. The Burgundian dukes in the end promised to do so, but in the beginning were unable to keep their promise.[32]

Towards Monetary Unity and Stability under Philip the Good (1433–66)

From the second decade of the 15th century onwards the common Flemish groat, used as standard coin in both Brabant and Flanders, was again subject to a series of debasements. The debasements were greatest in Brabant, again generating an independent Brabant monetary system linked with a new series of light Brabant silver groats. Between 1410 and 1430 the Brabant currency lost nearly half of its silver content through successive debasements, in other words the silver content of groats minted during the second and third decades of the 15th century gradually declined to roughly half that of the groat accepted as the standard coin in 1399.[33]

In 1430 Brabant was annexed, following the death of the childless Duke Philip of St-Pol, to the Burgundian realm of Philip the Good. The monetary reforms Philip the Good devised for the whole of his realm in 1433–35 put a final end to the autonomy of Brabant's currency. The new Flemish silver groat of 1433–35 became the standard currency not only for the Flemish monetary system, but also for Brabant's. From that moment onward there was no longer an independent Brabant silver groat, only a Brabant currency associated with the Flemish currency in a fixed ratio of 1:1½. Brabant's money of account thus became a mere satellite of the

---

[31] Van Werveke, 'De Vlaamse munthervorming', pp. 274–6.

[32] W. Prevenier and W.P Blockmans, *De Bourgondische Nederlanden* (Antwerp: 1983), pp. 118–9; P. Spufford, 'Coinage, Taxation and the Estates General of the Burgundian Netherlands', in: *Standen en Landen* XL (1966), pp. 63–88.

[33] Van der Wee, *The Growth* I, pp. 124–7; Van der Wee and Aerts, 'De Vlaams-Brabantse muntgeschiedenis', pp. 83–5.

Flemish money of account, with the value of both based on the silver content of the new, solid Flemish groat, its silver content remaining unchanged for more than 30 years. The 1:1½ ratio between the Flemish and Brabant money of account never did change; the harmony between Flemish and Brabantine monetary systems had been decided once and for all in favour of stronger Flanders.[34]

The new Flemish silver groat also became, after the reform of 1433-35, the standard currency for the other monetary systems of the Netherlands, like those of Namur, Hainault, Holland, Artois and Frisia. In these territories, all of them extremely sensitive to any infringement of their autonomy, the duke nominally permitted the continued existence of the local money of account while firmly attaching them to the Flemish money of account by means of frozen ratios: thus all of them became satellites of the Flemish money of account, their value finally determined by the silver content of a single standard coin, namely the Flemish groat.[35]

The flood of debasements, continuing throughout the 14th century and even into the beginning of Philip the Good's reign, cannot be understood within the sole framework of Flemish–Brabantine relations and Burgundian monetary policy. They must also be seen against the background of the international economy of the period. The silver production of the German and Central European mines began to decline as early as the beginning of the 14th century.[36] At the same time Europe's positive balance of trade with North Africa and the Levant was gradually eroded, leaving a substantial deficit in its place to be settled with silver (as silver was relatively scarce in the Southern and Eastern Mediterranean region). This drain on European silver stocks on the one hand, and the gradual depletion of the European silver stocks on the other, were responsible for an increasing shortage of silver money in the late Middle Ages. The temptation was thus great for the minters to alleviate this problem by minting more coins from the same quantity of silver. A side-effect, however, was that the debased silver coins were less and less functional as instruments of interregional and international trade. This forced the rulers to create multiples of the standard coin. Philip the Good thus brought his famed *Vierlanders*, worth two Flemish groats, into circulation with the monetary reform of 1433–35. At the beginning of the 16th century this double groat or stiver became the standard currency in the new monetary system of the Netherlands based on the guilder (1 guilder = 20 stivers).[37]

---

[34] Van der Wee and Aerts, *Vlaams-Brabantse muntstatistieken*, pp. 4–5.
[35] Van der Wee, *The Growth* II p. 48.
[36] Munro, 'Monetary Contraction', pp. 98–9.
[37] Van der Wee and Aerts, *Vlaams-Brabantse muntstatistieken*, pp. 2–3.

The new monetary policy, in force between 1433 and 1466, had a highly favourable effect on the social and economic climate. The stable, strong currency ensured that all fixed incomes, like wages, annuities and rents, represented a constant weight of silver over a long period. At the same time the stagnation of the European population exerted a downwards pressure on the price of essential foodstuffs. Both factors tended to increase the purchasing power of the income of wage-earners and persons of private means. The rising real income was increasingly devoted to non-essential foodstuffs, to services and industrial products. This in turn had a favourable effect on general economic activity in both towns and countryside.[38]

Philip the Good also put many high-denomination gold coins into circulation. Still, these Burgundian gold coins, despite a policy of systematically overrating their value against silver coins, had difficulty retaining their position in the market. They had trouble competing with the slightly lighter Rhine guilders, the penetration of which was enhanced by the increasing commercial contacts between Germany and the Netherlands. The Rhine guilders became very common and popular in the Burgundian Netherlands. In time the Rhine guilders even became the prototype for the creation of a new series of Burgundian gold coins, like the *Sint-Andriesgulden* and later the Habsburg *Carolus gulden*.

The Reversal of Monetary Policy during the Last Third of the 15th century

Philip's son, Charles the Bold, pursued a monetary policy that deviated drastically from his father's. From 1466–67 onwards it was no longer gold coins, but silver coins that were systematically overvalued by ducal ordinance. In contrast to Philip the Good, who by overvaluing gold succeeded diplomatically in luring the lighter gold coins from the surrounding countries such as Gelderland and the Rhine region into the Netherlands, Charles the Bold was more a 'warrior with his hands full of silver'. By overvaluing silver the silver production of Central Europe, once more on the rise, could be attracted to the Brabant fairs of Antwerp and Bergen-op-Zoom. Moreover, this development was closely linked to the revival of transcontinental trade via Germany, to which the Brabant fairs were finely attuned. The strong ties between the Brabant fairs and those of Germany clearly favoured Brabant's silver mintage, which surpassed that of Flanders from the last quarter of the 15th century onwards.

After 1496 the mint at Antwerp also surpassed the Flemish mint in the emission of gold coins. The latter development was associated with the

---

[38] R. Van Uytven, 'Sociaal-economische evoluties in de Nederlanden vóór de Revoluties (veertiende-zestiende eeuw)', in *Bijdragen en Mededelingen betreffende de Geschiedenis der Nederlanden* LXXXVII (1972), pp. 60–93.
[39] Baerten, *Muntslag en -circulatie*, p. 56; Van der Wee, *The Growth* II, p. 53.

establishment of the Crown monopoly on Portuguese spices at Antwerp: the Portuguese, controlling as they did the occidental supply of African gold and bringing vast quantities of this gold to Antwerp, because there it was – despite the policy of overvaluing silver – of relatively greater final value than in Southern Europe.[40]

The expansion of the domestic market brought on by rising real wage income ceased abruptly in the last quarter of the 15th century with the threat of war and the debasement fever of that period. As a result prices for many essential products soared. The standard of living for the average Brabanter was dealt a severe blow, while the more well-to-do were forced to economize in their purchases of non-essential foodstuffs and manufactured goods, leading to all the unfortunate consequences for economic activity associated with such a development. Maximilian's wars with France, as well as the civil war fought in Flanders and Brabant, had particularly disastrous effects, at times paralysing social and economic life entirely.[41]

Charles the Bold and Maximilian of Austria financed their military activities chiefly with income derived from their mints. While the duke's mint revenue generally amounted to less than 3% of the value of the precious metals supplied to the mints, under Maximilian this amount rose to 12%. Where Philip the Good's average annual profit from mints in the Netherlands was of the order of 3,000 pounds *Parisis* between 1433 and 1466, in several years Maximilian of Austria derived an income of more than 60,000 pounds *Parisis* from the mints. These revenues were indeed essential for Maximilian, since his normal sources of revenue suffered so greatly from the Revolt of the Netherlands against his authority.[42]

The successful revaluation of 1489 shows that Maximilian, despite all his difficulties, was able to recover from his reputation as a despoiler of the coinage. The official rates for all coins in Flemish money of account were reduced to 33% of their former value, in other words the accounting value of the Flemish silver groat was strengthened and drastically revalued.[43]

---

[40] E. Aerts and E. Van Cauwenberghe, 'Die Grafschaft Flandern und die sogenannte spätmittelalterliche Depression', in: F. Seibt and W. Eberhard (eds), *Europa 1400. Die Krise des Spätmittelalters* (Stuttgart: 1984), pp. 106–7; Baerten, *Muntslag en -circulatie*, pp. 60–1; Van Uytven, 'Sociaal-economische evoluties', pp. 61–5; Van der Wee, *The Growth* II, pp. 124–30.

[41] R. Van Uytven, 'Politiek en economie: de crisis der late XVe eeuw in de Nederlanden', in: *Belgisch Tijdschrift voor Filologie en Geschiedenis* LIII (1975), pp. 1095–1149.

[42] Spufford, 'Coinage', pp. 82–3; J.A. Van Houtte and R. Van Uytven, 'Financiën', in: *Algemene Geschiedenis der Nederlanden* IV (Haarlem: 1980), pp. 118–9.

[43] E. Van Cauwenberghe, *Het vorstelijk domein en de overheidsfinanciën in de Nederlanden, 15de en 16de eeuw. Een kwantitatieve analyse van Vlaamse en Brabantse domeinrekeningen* (Brussels: 1982), p.337. From 1496 onwards a more stable monetary

Monetary Policy between Tradition and Renewal: Attempts to Establish Bimetallic Monetary Standards

Under Maximilian of Austria a first attempt was made to break with the monometallic silver standard of the Middle Ages and to replace it with a bimetallic system. In 1487 Maximilian issued gold and silver reals with official exchange rates established according to a fixed ratio between them. He thus strove to integrate the increasing circulation of gold coins into the monetary system under more stable conditions. In the course of the 15th century the proportion of gold coins relative to the money in circulation had already risen considerably in Brabant and the surrounding area. As a result of increasing imports from West Africa via Portugal, and later of imports from the New World, the yellow metal played for a time at the beginning of the 16th century a leading role in the circulation of large-denomination coins.[44]

Although Maximilian failed to integrate gold into the monetary circuit on a stable basis, the idea of a bimetallic standard again emerged under the Habsburg emperor Charles V. Charles had a heavy gold *Carolus gulden* minted in 1526, with the official exchange rate fixed at 20 silver stivers or double groats, that is to say 40 Flemish silver groats. This assigned both the guilder and the stiver functions as units in a new monetary system with the following relative values: 1 guilder = 20 stivers = 40 Flemish groats. Emperor Charles hoped to link gold and silver to each other in a fixed ratio through this money of account, based on two real supports (a gold guilder and a silver stiver).[45]

However, it soon became apparent that the officially fixed gold/silver ratio could not stand in the face of economic reality. From the third quarter of the 16th century onwards a veritable flood of silver began to flow into Europe from the mines of Zacatecas in Mexico and Potosí in Peru. This flood led to a rise in the free market price of gold relative to that of silver. This was also the case in Brabant and the Netherlands where the market exchange rate for the gold *Carolus gulden* gradually rose against the silver stiver. Since the Habsburg government was unwilling to alter the official exchange rate of 20 stivers to the gulden, the *Carolus gulden* as a real gold coin became undervalued and disappeared from circulation. Once out of

---

policy was resumed: Baerten, *Muntslag en -circulatie*, pp. 73–5; H. Enno van Gelder, 'De muntpolitiek van Filips de Schone, 1482–1496', in: *Jaarboek van het Koninklijke Genootschap voor Munt- en Penningkunde* XXXIII–XXXIV (1946–47), pp. 122–31.

[44] Van der Wee, 'Monetary, Credit and Bankings Systems', in: *The Cambridge Economic History of Europe* V (Cambridge: 1977), pp. 289–300.

[45] G. Pusch, *Staatliche Münz- und Geldpolitik in den Niederlanden unter den Burgundischen und Habsburgischen Herrschern, besonders unter Kaiser Karl V* (Munich: 1932), p. 68.

circulation the guilders remained in use solely as an accounting unit: the guilders became an accounting and calculating multiple of 20 silver stivers: the value of the new system of monetary units (1 guilder = 20 stivers) was thus once more entirely determined by the silver content of the stiver. Since the silver stiver and its multiples continued to form the basic currency, the silver standard remained characteristic for the monetary system of Brabant and the surrounding area until the end of the Ancien Régime.[46]

---

[46] H. Van der Wee, 'Geld-, krediet- en bankwezen in de Zuidelijke Nederlanden', in: *Algemene Geschiedenis der Nederlanden* VI (Haarlem: 1979), p. 98.

10

Credit in Brabant, Late Middle Ages to Early Modern Times

Innovations in the Credit System

The rise of the towns during the late Middle Ages vigorously stimulated the development of money and credit. Through the markets, industrial and commercial expansion in town and countryside increased the need for payment in money, the need often surpassing the amount of metal money available. The shortage of liquid assets increased the importance of moneylending, which might be seen as the exchange of merchandise physically present for merchandise yet to arrive.[1] Moreover, the great variety of coins in circulation encouraged the appearence of specialists in the exchange of currency. The public confidence they had gained through their handling of monetary and financial matters made it appropriate for them to introduce a variety of credit and banking facilities.[2]

Between the 13th century and the beginning of the 17th century various forms of credit were granted, on a short-term, medium-term or long-term basis, by individuals, private institutions or government institutions, not only in a local economic context but also in a regional and international economic one. Credit was needed not only for purposes of consumption, but also for production. Finally, credit was granted not only to individuals of every sort, but also to governments: first to the municipalities, but later increasingly to the modern territorial states.[3]

The transition to the Early Modern period did not involve a clear break with the Middle Ages in the credit field: the emphasis lay rather on

---

[1] H. Van der Wee, 'Monetary, Credit and Banking Systems', in: *The Cambridge Economic History of Europe* V (Cambridge: 1977), pp. 290–392.

[2] E. Vercouteren, 'De geldwisselaars in Brabant (1430–1506): een bijdrage tot de economische geschiedenis van de Zuidelijke Nederlanden', *Bijdragen en Mededelingen betreffende de Geschiedenis der Nederlanden* C (1985), pp. 3–25.

[3] A. de Maddalena and H. Kellenbenz (eds), *La republica internazionale del denara tra XV e XVII secolo* (Bologna: 1986).

continuity. Any financial differences between the late Middle Ages and the Early Modern period were more quantitative than qualitative, though it was precisely the quantitative intensification of credit activities that gradually opened the way for qualitative, that is, more fundamental and innovative progress.[4]

Brabant, as the most economically progressive region of Northern Europe during the late Middle Ages and the beginning of the Early Modern period, is the ideal frame of reference for an explanation of the nature and development of credit during this time.[5]

From Usury to 'Socially Responsible' Consumer Credit

The use of consumer credit in the local economy of Brabant increased enormously during the late Middle Ages and the beginning of the Early Modern period. Although not always uniform, consumer credit was linked to well-defined forms of credit and to specific lenders.[6]

Consumer loans at interest generally involved a pawn. The initiative always lay with the person in need of a loan: craftsmen, labourers, widows, invalids, the ill and others in need of money received loans upon depositing a pawn, whether in the form of household equipment, tools, clothing, or (in the case of the wealthier) of jewellery, merchandise, or such works of art as manuscripts and tapestries.[7] Usually such pawns could be redeemed, and their sale at public auction prevented, only by repaying the full sum of the loan, plus the accrued interest, within one year.[8]

However strictly the Church's teachings on usury forbade demanding interest for a loan, the economic need for consumer credit increased so greatly in late medieval towns that from the 13th century on the Church

---

[4] Van der Wee, 'Monetary', pp. 290-392.

[5] H. Van der Wee, 'Industrial Dynamics and the Process of Urbanization and De-Urbanization in the Low Countries from the Late Middle Ages to the Eighteenth Century. A Synthesis', in: Van der Wee (ed.), *The Rise and Decline of Urban Industries in Italy and the Low Countries during the late Middle Ages and the Early Modern Times* (Louvain: 1988).

[6] G. Bigwood, *Le régime juridique et économique du commerce de l'argent dans la Belgique du Moyen Age* I (Brussels: 1921), p. 392; R. De Roover, *Money, Banking and Credit in Mediaeval Bruges, Italian Merchant-Bankers, Lombards and Money-Changers. A Study in the Origins of Banking* (Cambridge, Mass.: 1948) pp. 106, 141; J. Stengers, *Les Juifs dans les Pays-Bas au moyen âge* (Brussels: 1949), pp. 40-5.

[7] Bigwood, *Le régime juridique*, I, pp. 476-86, 496-525.

[8] De Roover, *Money*, pp. 123-4; J. Somers, 'Het laatmiddeleeuws pandbedrijf in de Nederlanden,' in: *Handelingen der Koninklijke Zuidnederlandse Maatschappij voor Taal- en Letterkunde en Geschiedenis* XXXVI (1982), p. 176.

tolerated the practice *de facto*, usually in the hands of non-natives.[9] Merchants from Asti and Chieri in Lombardy and merchants from Cahors in Southwestern France soon organized secured loans at interest on a large scale throughout Europe.[10] These regional names soon came to denote the practitioners. 'Lombard' or *cahorsijn* meant the keeper of a pawnbrokerage and, in the language of the time, a usurer.[11] Jews were also involved in pawnbrokerage; they were the oldest pawnbrokers in Brabant.[12]

The first Jews came from the Rhineland, settling in a number of towns along the route from Cologne to Bruges from 1200. Their presence in Brabant remained limited, however, and was of short duration. The secured loans held by Jews were, moreover, modest: they involved small sums of money, usually lent for a relatively short period and chiefly to a poorer public.[13]

Partly due to their greed during hard times, which struck hardest precisely at the lower income groups, the Jews acquired an unsavoury reputation. From time to time these hostile popular feelings degenerated into true programs against the Jews like those of 1349–50. Furthermore in 1370, according to the chronicles, all the Jews in Brussels and Louvain were actually burned alive on the pretext of an accusation of sacrilege. After this series of violent actions the Jews were replaced more and more on Brabant's money market by the less frequently targeted Lombards.[14] The latter were not unknown in the region; their presence in Waasten and Zoutleeuw was mentioned as early as the mid-13th century, and by the beginning of the 14th century Lombards were present in some forty localities within the duchy of Brabant.[15] Whereas the Jewish pawnbrokers of Tienen loaned money in 1303 at an interest rate of

---

[9] P. Soetaert, *De Bergen van Barmhartigheid in de Spaanse, de Oostenrijkse en de Franse Nederlanden (1618–1795)* (Brussels: 1986), p. 66.

[10] Somers, 'Het laatmiddeleeuws pandbedrijf', p. 170; P. Wolff, 'Le problème des Cahorsins', in: *Annales du Midi* LXII (1950), pp. 229–38.

[11] De Roover, *Money*, p. 99; J. Maréchal, *Bijdrage tot de geschiedenis van het bankwezen te Brugge*, (Bruges: 1955), pp. 12–3; Somers, 'Het laatmiddeleeuws pandbedrijf', pp. 169–70; C. Tihon, 'Aperçus sur l'établissement des Lombards dans les Pays-Bas aux XIIIe et XIVe siècles', in: Tihon, *Recueil d'articles* (Brussels: 1972), pp. 250–2.

[12] Stengers, *Les Juifs*, pp. 11–29; J. Tollebeek, 'De joden in de Zuidelijke Nederlanden tijdens de late Middeleeuwen. Kritisch-bibliografisch overzicht (1949–1983)', in: *Bijdragen tot de Geschiedenis* LXVI (1983), pp. 13–34.

[13] Soetaert, *De Bergen van Barmhartigheid*, p. 55.

[14] Stengers, *Les juifs*, pp. 21–7.

[15] P. Morel. *Les Lombards dans la Frandre française et le Hainaut* (Lille: 1908), p. 104; Soetaert, *De Bergen van Barmhartigheid*, p. 56; F. Vercauteren, 'Document pour servir à l'histoire des financiers Lombards en Belgique (1309)' in: *Bulletin de l'Institut Historique Belge de Rome* (1950–51), pp. 43–67, reprinted in Vercauteren, *Etudes d'histoire médiévale* (Brussels: 1978), pp. 419–44.

12 pennies per pound per month, or 60% per year, by 1306 the interest rate of the Lombards of Antwerp had risen to 65% per year for borrowers from outside Antwerp.[16]

The government tolerated the Lombard pawnbrokerages on condition that they did not exceed a given interest rate, that they paid an annual licensing fee (*censive*), and that they were willing to grant short-term credit to the government.[17] Such conditional tolerance was by no means incompatible with the rulers' various attempts to abolish the pawnshops, on the contrary! When in 1307 Duke John II of Brabant had Pope Clement V release him from all his obligations to the Lombards, the idea was assuredly not to combat usurious practices, but rather to gain ready access to extra credit. Nor did he banish the Lombards from his duchy, but exerted pressure on them until they were prepared to grant new loans.[18] Even when the Burgundian ruler Philip the Good closed all the pawnshops both in and outside Brabant in 1451, 1457 and 1462, it was more a question of making a favourable impression on the Estates to gain their approval of the aids he requested than any desire on his part wholly to eliminate the Lombards.[19] At any rate the Lombards were repeatedly approached for loans during Philip's reign, with an eye to the future collection of licensing fees. Charles the Bold also revoked all existing licences in 1473, only to reopen the pawnshops in the same year for a period of ten years upon payment of higher licensing fees. The 45 pawnbrokerages in the Burgundian Netherlands were now in total responsible for the payment of an annual sum of 9,600 pounds Artois (valued at 40 Flemish groats each). The individual share of Brabant's pawnshops in the collective payment is known only for Louvain and for Brussels: at Louvain and Brussels the licensing fees were, respectively, some 50% and 66% higher than earlier.[20] Moreoever, in the same year the Lombards paid an extra, once-only, subsidy of 60,000 pounds *à cause de certaine composicion*. In 1476 they loaned the duke another 16,800 pounds to finance what was destined to become his last campaign.[21]

---

[16] P. Soetaert, 'Consumptief krediet te Antwerpen (14de–18de eeuw)', in: *Driemaandelijks Tijdschrift van het Gemeentekrediet van België* XXXI (1977), p. 257; also *De Bergen van Barmhartigheid*, p. 55; P. de Ridder, 'Een paleografische en diplomatische studie van de oorkonden verleend door hertog Jan II van Brabant (1294–1312) aan Antwerpen (6 december 1306) en Zoutleeuw (7 mei 1307)', in: *Bijdragen tot de Geschiedenis* LVI (1973), p. 153.

[17] Somers, 'Het laatmiddeleeuws pandbedrijf', p. 172.

[18] Tihon, 'Aperçus', p. 261.

[19] Bigwood, *Le régime juridique* I, pp. 585–6; II, pp. 40–41.

[20] J. Somers, *Bijdrage tot de geschiedenis van de lombarden in Brabant tijdens de late middeleeuwen (1406–1511)*, (M.A. thesis, History Department, K.U. Leuven) (Louvain: 1980) p. 74.

[21] Somers, 'Het laatmiddeleeuws pandbedrijf', p. 187.

The resilience of the Lombards before 1500 was not due solely to their financial links to the government, but also in part to more general economic factors.[22] During the reign of Philip the Good the traditional textile industry of Brabant was in rapid decline. The miserable economic situation to which a large portion of the urban population was reduced strongly favoured the rise of consumer credit. In 1432 pawnbrokerages were again active at Lier and at Nivelles, in 1433 at Vilvoorde, in 1444 at Herentals, and in 1451 at Zoutleeuw. This brought Brabant to its peak of eleven ducal pawnshops, a number which remained stable until almost the end of the 15th century.[23] At the same time the pawn trade became more concentrated: the owners of the head offices (Brussels, Antwerp, 's-Hertogenbosch and Louvain) were often the owners or co-owners of smaller neighbouring pawnshops as well. At the end of the 15th century a rapid decline set in for Brabant's pawnbroking business. From eleven in 1490, the number of pawnshops in Brabant sank to five in 1510. This swift decline was dictated by several causes. In the first place the working capital of the pawnshops was drained by the repeated and forced loans of large sums to Maximilian of Austria who, after the death of his wife Mary of Burgundy in 1482, pursued a rash policy of war. The ducal revaluation policy of 1489–90 also dealt them a severe blow, since the Lombards had to pay their licensing fees in heavy silver coin.[24]

Finally, around 1500 there was a rapid rise in other forms of consumer credit. Deferred payment became extremely common. In Brabant's retail trade both the practice of buying on the tally and the use of current accounts became widespread. Both formulas gave retailers and craftsmen the opportunity to apply forms of bilateral settlement: only after the passage of some time did the parties make their settlement, with only the balance being paid in cash. Written letters obligatory or debentures were increasingly used in private transactions. These documents increasingly included the clause: 'payable to bearer', thus becoming transferable.[25]

The tally, the current account and the letter obligatory provided flexible methods for individuals to bridge temporary income crises in the rising prosperity of the 16th century. In the second half of the century, when the price revolution and the wars of religion severely affected the income of the lower social classes in Brabant and the local crises became both

---

[22] Soetaert, *De Bergen van Barmhartigheid*, p. 63; H. Van der Wee, *The Growth of the Antwerp Market and the European Economy (Fourteenth-Sixteenth Centuries)* II (Paris–The Hague: 1963), pp. 67–73.

[23] H. Van der Wee, 'Structural Changes and Specialization in the Industry of the Southern Netherlands, 1100–1600', in: *The Economic History Review*, 2nd Series, XXVIII (1975), pp. 203–21; Somers, *Bijdrage*, pp. 54–5, 156.

[24] Somers, 'Het laatmiddeleeuws pandbedrijf', pp. 189–92.

[25] Van der Wee, 'Monetary', pp. 300–3.

sharper and more frequent, these new forms of consumer credit no longer sufficed to alleviate rising poverty and misery. Moneylenders and pawnshops again multiplied after 1550, albeit in a different moral climate under the influence of the Reformation and Counter-Reformation. Speculating on the misery of the population was now more strongly condemned by public opinion. A growing conviction that poverty was rather sharpened than alleviated by granting consumer credit through private or clandestine pawnbrokers led to the notion that the pernicious practice of usury could best be combated by government-organized pawn credit.[26]

Meanwhile the government strove to exert all possible pressure on the Lombards to lower their interest rates. From a maximum of 65% per annum in the 15th century, the maximum interest rate allowed by the government was reduced to 32½% halfway through the 16th century, and to 21⅓% in 1600. In 1618 Wenzel Cobergher, with the support of Archduke Albert and Archduchess Isabella, was able to found a public pawnshop at Brussels: the *Mont de Piété* of Brussels. This example was followed in 1620 at Antwerp and at Mechlin, and shortly afterwards throughout the Southern Netherlands outside Brabant. With their interest rate of roughly 15% these urban, public pawnshops better complied with the new norms for meeting popular needs.[27]

As these *Monts de Piété* operated successfully in the towns, the practice became more difficult for the licensed private pawnbrokers. And in the second half of the 17th century there is scant mention of private pawnshops or moneylenders. Only at Louvain did a private moneylender, who was integrated into Coberghe's 'national' network of public pawnshops only in the course of the 18th century, continue to operate. Secret pawnbrokerage never disappeared entirely, but diminished considerably: where it did continue to exist, it was kept within bounds by the threat of legal confiscation of goods or by the possibility of demanding the return of the pledge without restitution of the sum loaned.[28]

The Annuity as a Form of Long-term Credit

The credit forms so far described were used in the private sector not only to obtain short-term consumer credit, but sometimes also to obtain short- or even long-term investment credit.[29] The sale of life or perpetual annuities on the other hand was typically used in the late Middle Ages and at the beginning of Early Modern Times to obtain long-term credit. Moreover, it was usually organized to procure investment credit. This

---

[26] Soetaert, *De Bergen van Barmhartigheid*, p. 84.
[27] *Ibid.*, pp. 86, 89–104, 190–1, 197.
[28] *Ibid.*, pp. 111–6.
[29] Van der Wee, 'Monetary', pp. 303–6.

expansion was primarily the result of fundamental changes in the judicial status of medieval dues and rents. From the feudal system of dues based on real property arose the idea of the hereditary leasehold (*bail à rente*) and the sale of annuities (*constitution de rente*). Both cases involved periodic and perpetual payment of annuities, in money or in kind: in the first case the leaseholder received, in exchange for periodic payments of rent, real property from the property owners, in the second case the seller of the annuity received in exchange for the periodic payment of rents a certain capital sum from the purchaser of the annuity, a given real property originally always being the security for the payment of the annuity. Such annuities could be perpetual or on a life basis, the latter being linked to the life of one, two or even three annuitants.[30]

The sale of perpetual or life annuities in exchange for a capital sum implied *de facto* a long-term credit operation. If the return of the real property pledged as security increased, a new sale of annuities secured by the extra return, i.e. a new long-term credit operation, could be organized. Under the influence of the papal bulls *Regimini* of 1426 and 1455, as well as the royal ordinance of Emperor Charles V in 1520, the sale of annuities became a fully fledged instrument of credit. In Brabant annuities became both transferable and redeemable. Redemption of annuities could take place only at the request of the seller of annuities: only he could decide on the redemption and on the time limits for redemption. Should the annuitant himself be short of money, then he could not unilaterally demand the return of his capital: at most he could sell his annuity to a third party, in other words titles to annuities were transferable. In Brabant the transfer of annuity titles was not subject to complicated civil procedures in the 16th century: at Antwerp, especially, it was extremely common.[31]

Annuity sales allowed long- or mid-term investments in the basic sectors of the local Brabant economy. Improvement and renovation of agricultural land was largely financed by means of annuities. The same means were used to obtain credit for building in the towns, as in 16th-century Antwerp: craftsmen or small-scale entrepreneurs purchased subdivided land as a leasehold, laid the foundations for a number of houses and sold annuities pledged on the future rents from these houses: they then used the capital sum received in exchange for the annuities to finance further construction. In this way long-term investment credit became available to small urban enterprises and to small independent farms. This trend was reinforced by the declining interest rates for annuities, which went down from

---

[30] H. Soly, *Urbanisme en kapitalisme te Antwerpen in de 16de eeuw. De stedebouwkundige en industriële ondernemingen van Gilbert van Schoonbeke* (Brussels: 1977), p. 55.

[31] Van der Wee, 'Monetary', pp. 305–6.

10–12% in the 15th century to 5–7% in the 16th century. The penetration of the smaller production units of the local economy by long-term annuity credit unquestionably lent extra impetus to 16th-century economic expansion in Brabant.[32]

Clearing and Deposit Banking in Brabant: Fiction or Waning Reality?

During the transition from the late Middle Ages to Early Modern Times significant innovations in financial methods gradually took place in the international economy. The role played by Brabant, and by Antwerp in particular, in this progress cannot be overemphasized: via Antwerp the Italian achievements in financial techniques of the late Middle Ages penetrated more deeply into Northern and Northwestern Europe; moreover, from the 16th century onwards Antwerp's own innovations made their mark, opening a direct route to the world of modern discount banks and issuing houses.[33] To assess this importance, late medieval money changing has to be examined first.

The great variety of coins within and outside the region made resort to moneychangers indispensable in every medieval town of any significance. The orginal function of the moneychangers was thus purely monetary in nature: manually exchanging coins and supplying bullion to the ducal mint. Alongside these monetary functions some moneychangers also played a role in financial transactions, acting for example as intermediaries in the sale of annuities. The town moneychanger, who differed in judicial status from the commercial moneychangers, owed his lasting importance in the urban life of late medieval Brabant and Flanders precisely to these financial functions.[34]

Since the moneychangers possessed secure chests to protect their own monetary reserves, in time they also began to hold other people's money for safe-keeping. On this basis they developed a fully fledged deposit banking business after the Italian model: merchants, individuals, and even institutions, entrusted the moneychanger-bankers with payments and collections to be made in their name, the transfer of debts to the account of the creditor, or the transfer of credits to their own account.[35]

The moneychanger–bankers knew from experience that the deposits

---

[32] *Ibid.*, 322–3.

[33] H. Van der Wee, 'Anvers et les innovations de la technique financière aux XVIe et XVIIe siècles', in: *Annales E.S.C.* XXII (1967), p. 1067.

[34] Vercouteren, 'De geldwisselaars', pp. 8–9.

[35] A. Aerts, 'Middeleeuwse bankgeschiedenis volgens Professor Raymond de Roover', in: *Bijdragen tot de Geschiedenis* LXIII (1980), pp. 57–8.

would never all be demanded back at once. Therefore, they used a portion of them for investments on their own account: commercial transactions in wines and cloth were candidates for this; they sometimes invested in tax farms for the collection of urban or ducal tax revenues; occasionally cash credit or long-term loans were extended to account holders or other clients. In this fashion the Bruges moneychangers Colaert van Marcke and Willem Ruweel organized true transfer and deposit banking during the second half of the 14th century.[36]

It remains to be seen, however, if these moneychanger–bankers were really so numerous during the 14th and 15th centuries as the great specialist in the financial history of Bruges, de Roover, would have us believe.[37] In the Netherlands there are not many traces of deposit and transfer banks outside Bruges. Where there are traces, the system seems to have been relatively primitive: Berthelmeeus Alfer, moneychanger-banker at Louvain (Brabant) at the beginning of the 15th century, noted in his journal that transfers could be made only in the presence of the depositor in person, and upon presentation of an official debenture by the creditor. Sometimes there was no mention whatsoever of transfer banking even in circles where it might be expected: Jacob van den Bloke, moneychanger–banker for the Cologne merchants at Antwerp (Brabant) around the same period, still consistently paid out the sums owed by the Cologne merchants to their London trading partners in hard cash at the Brabant fairs.[38]

Towards the end of the 15th century the situation in any case deteriorated dramatically: private moneychanging and the deposit and transfer banking associated with it virtually disappeared in both Flanders and Brabant. The reasons for the decline of private moneychanging and associated banking activities in the course of the 15th century are far from clear. De Roover stresses the intervention of the Burgundian government, and more specifically its centralization policy, as the determining factor. He even goes so far as to speak of a frankly hostile attitude towards moneychangers and their banking activities on the part of the dukes. This simplistic view has since been questioned.[39]

Strongly influenced by the developments at Louvain, Van Uytven is of the opinion that the insistence on the Burgundian centralization polity is not entirely satisfactory. While in 1367 Louvain still had 13 moneychangers, by 1374 their number had declined to 6, by 1377 to 4,

---

[36] De Roover, *Money*, pp. 204, 293, 310.
[37] Aerts, 'Middeleeuwse bankgeschiedenis', p. 63.
[38] Vercouteren, 'De geldwisselaars', pp. 11–2.
[39] De Roover, *Money*, pp. 183, 195, 340; J.G. Dillen, 'Bankiers te Brugge', in: *Tijdschrift voor Geschiedenis* LXVI (1953), p. 239; J.H. Munro, *Wool, Cloth and Gold. The Struggle for Bullion in Anglo-Burgundian Trade 1340–1478* (Brussels–Toronto: 1972), pp. 20–1.

and by 1388 to 3; this dramatic decline took place before the Burgundian centralization policy took concrete form, i.e. before the 15th century.[40]

The Louvain case proves clearly that a general economic factor, i.e. the decline of the traditional cloth industry producing for export – a decline already begun in the course of the 14th century – was mainly responsible for the decay of moneychanging in the Brabant textile towns. Moneychanging in Antwerp and Bergen-op-Zoom, however, did not decline at that moment: they were not cloth-producing towns but mainly commercial centres whose fairs participated actively in the new expansion of Europe's long-distance trade.[41]

In attempts to explain the decline of private moneychanging and associated banking activities monetary policy cannot be excluded as a factor either. From 1389 onwards the Burgundian dukes pursued a vigorous policy of monetary stability. This led, beginning in 1433, to a successful policy of monetary unification, embracing virtually the whole of the Netherlands. Monetary chaos was diminished for decades, moneychanging declined, the commissions paid for changing money dwindled, and profitable currency speculation and manipulation became exceptional. Things went badly for moneychangers. Normally they would have been able to compensate for their losses in the field of monetary services with the profits from expanding financial services as bankers. This, however, occurred only to a limited extent: the general decline of the traditional textile industry not only threatened the monetary functions of the moneychangers, but also weighed heavily on their functions as cashiers and bankers: the export crisis cost the moneychangers the greater portion of their mercantile and entrepreneurial clientèle.[42]

After 1470 the dukes again abandoned their policy of monetary stability. There was a short-lived revival of moneychanging. The multiple and significant currency debasements led the moneychangers to indulge in culling (*bicqueteren*), that is separating the good, heavy coins from the lighter ones. Since the moneychangers then exported the heavy coins to foreign mints, bringing into domestic circulation the lighter coins or *haagmunten* they received in exchange, they tended to undermine ducal monetary policy. The dukes wished to keep bullion within their own borders so as to increase their mintage and the profits they derived from it. A December 1489 ordinance accordingly strengthened ducal control over the moneychangers, and even forbade the associated banking activities.[43]

---

[40] R. Van Uytven, *Stadsfinanciëen en stadsekonomie te Leuven van de XIIe tot het einde der XVe eeuw* (Brussels: 1961), p. 456.

[41] Vercouteren, 'De geldwisselaars', p. 15.

[42] H. Van der Wee, 'Geld-, krediet- en bankwezen in de Zuidelijke Nederlanden', in: *Algemene Geschiedenis der Nederlanden* VI (Haarlem: 1979), p. 104.

[43] Van der Wee, *The Growth* II, p. 358.

There were other motives behind the 1489 measure as well: occasionally during the difficult and chaotic 1480s moneychanger–bankers absconded with the cashbox, which naturally did nothing to enhance their reputation. The urban administration of Antwerp repeatedly felt obliged to warn foreign merchants of the risks associated with depositing money with private *bancquiers*.[44]

If deposit and transfer banks had virtually disappeared from the Brabant textile towns in the course of the 15th century, they also disappeared from the Brabant fairs of Antwerp and Bergen-op-Zoom towards the end of the century. The remarkable ease with which the Burgundian rulers here eliminated the banking activities associated with moneychanging is to a certain extent illustrative of their rather marginal role at these fairs at that moment. Only moneychangers in the narrow, literal sense of the word remained active at the 16th century fairs of Brabant. These *taflettiers* looked askance at any form of transfer banking. During the vigorous expansion of world trade at the beginning of the 16th century this proved a gap in the market. It was precisely this gap that would eventually set in motion a whole new process of development in financial methods on the Antwerp money market, namely the transition to the negotiability of commercial paper.[45]

Antwerp's Contribution to the Development of Endorsement and Modern Discount Banking

Letters obligatory to bearer were not only common in the local economy, but beginning in the late Middle Ages they were also widely used in international commercial circles. English Merchants Adventurers, Hansards, Rhenish and Dutch merchants all frequently made payments with letters obligatory made out to bearer and used the Brabant fairs as quarterly terms of expiry. Until 1500 there were, however, both judicial and financial obstacles impeding transferability on a large scale: letters obligatory usually remained in the possession of the creditor until their expiry date. This substantially inhibited the development of a more flexible commercial credit system.[46]

Antwerp, ever dynamic, was the first to attempt to overcome these judicial and financial barriers. As early as 1507 every holder of a letter obligatory with the clause 'to bearer' was allowed immediately and independently to initiate a suit against recalcitrant debtors. Formerly,

---

[44] Van der Wee, 'Geld', p. 104.

[45] Aerts, 'Middeleeuwse bankgeschiedenis', pp. 60–1.

[46] H. Van der Wee, 'Antwerpens bijdrage tot de ontwikkeling van de moderne banktechniek', in: Van der Wee, *Historische aspecten van de economische groei. Tien studies over de economische ontwikkeling van West-Europa en van de Nederlanden in het bijzonder (12e–19e eeuw)* (Antwerp–Utrecht: 1972), p. 152.

prosecution had been legally possible only after the formal transfer or *cessio* of the title.[47]

This equivalence of formal and informal transfers of letters obligatory did, however, involve a significant financial disadvantage for the new bearer. Since informal transfer was regarded as a formal *cessio*, the transferring creditor was entirely free of all obligation. Consequently the new bearer could no longer make demands on the transferring creditor should the new debtor default. The application of the principle of assignment to the transfer of letters obligatory resolved this troublesome new financial uncertainty. Even after the transfer of a letter obligatory the transferring debtor was still held responsible, by means of assignment, until the debt was fully repaid to the satisfaction of the last receiving creditor.[48]

The success of this Antwerp financial innovation provided an irresistible example to the other towns. Royal ordinances of 1537 and 1541 declared that all transfers of letters obligatory made out to bearer in the Netherlands were judged to have taken place by means of assignment.[49] Under pressure of the vigorous expansion of trade in the 16th century payment by transfer of letters obligatory made out to bearer, by means of assignment, grew into *la usanza entre mercadores* at Antwerp. Commercial titles often passed through five, ten, up to a hundred different hands before payment was finally made in cash. In principle the more hand-to-hand circulation took place through assignment, the greater the financial certainty became for the last creditor. Transferability thus evolved into fully fledged negotiability.[50]

Until now the circulation of commercial paper from hand to hand had been limited chiefly to letters obligatory made out to bearer: these were usually medium- to long-term, encouraging circulation before the expiry date. Bills of exchange on the other hand were usually short-term and therefore tended to remain in the hands of the creditor until their due date. During the second half of the 16th century, however, this changed at Antwerp.[51]

One of the most remarkable phenomena of the 16th century was the increasing popularity of the bill of exchange in wholesale trade throughout Northwestern Europe. English, Hanseatic, Dutch and Brabantine merchants made increasing use of bills of exchange with the clause 'to bearer' to build up their international trade. Bills of exchange now became, in addition

---

[47] Van der Wee, 'Anvers', pp. 1074–5.
[48] Van der Wee, *The Growth* II, pp. 343–4.
[49] Van der Wee, 'Geld', pp. 102–3.
[50] H. Van der Wee, 'Opkomst van een wereldstad: handel en nijverheid te Antwerpen van de veertiende tot de achttiende eeuw', in: *Academia Analecta* (Brussels: 1990).
[51] Van der Wee, 'Antwerpens bijdrage', pp. 159–61.

to their function as an instrument of exchange, also the instruments of credit *par excellence*. This shifted the core of progress in financial methods slowly but surely towards the modernization of exchange credit. The transfer of bills made out to bearer as assignments now became common as well. Originally this took the form of an informal circulation from hand to hand on the Antwerp Exchange on the due date of the bills: these bills often continued to circulate until the creditor finally received a bill which he had himself signed as a debtor. Later on, the bills were transferred before they were due.

Gradually the need arose for greater formality in these transfers, and for the greater financial security provided by the assignment principle. The endorsement of bills, occurring sporadically at Antwerp from 1571 onwards, came into general use at the beginning of the 17th century. The legalization of the *avallo* system in 1608 represented the first great leap forwards in this development. To ensure a maximum of financial surety to the negotiability of bills of exchange, the written customary law (*costuymen*) of Antwerp obliged all assigning creditors to be listed by name on the bill of exchange and thus held responsible for the eventual repayment of the debt. The *avallo* system was, however, too cumbersome. For that reason it was soon replaced by simple endorsement. This provided a firm formal footing for the negotiability of bills and a tremendous stimulous to the circulation of short-term commercial paper.[52]

Meanwhile, Antwerp had also laid the foundations for the development of the modern discount. By this we mean the surrender of commercial titles to a third party before their due date and for a sum lower than the nominal value of the titles in question. The first traces of such a discount at Antwerp are to be found in the Kitson papers and concern the sale at the Brabant fairs in the 1530s of letters obligatory by the representative of the English merchant Thomas Kitson. Gradually money-changers *faisant des marchandises d'argent les donnant à gaing et frait*, began purchasing for cash mature but temporarily frozen commercial papers for a commission on the Antwerp Exchange in times of financial crisis. This was no longer far from the decisive step of systematically purchasing commercial titles before their due date outside moments of financial crisis. Even before the end of the 16th century the systematic discounting of long-term letters obligatory made out to bearer but not

---

[52] J. Schneider and O. Schwarzer, 'International Rates of Exchange: Structures and Trends of Payment Mechanisms in Europe, 17th to 19th Century', in W.F. Fischer, R.M. McInnis and J. Schneider (eds), *The Emergence of a World Economy 1500–1914* (Bamberg: 1986), p. 150.

yet due had become widely accepted. By around 1600 the discounting of short-term bills not yet due had also become commonplace.[53]

The fatal aftermath of the crisis with which Antwerp was then confronted prevented the Antwerp money market from further developing a modern system of issuing houses and discount banking based on these innovations. Ultimately, it was Amsterdam, and especially London, that did so.[54]

Growing Government Credit and the Importance of Antwerp's Money Market

From the 13th century onwards the financial needs of Brabant's towns and rulers rose steeply. Government credit thus took concrete form in Brabant as well.[55] The government began to make continual use of all sorts of credit to cover the deficits resulting from their manifest lack of budgetary foresight and their inadequate planning.

Originally the forms of government credit in Brabant were relatively primitive. Money was sometimes obtained by purchasing merchandise on credit for immediate resale on a cash basis. Occasionally minor officials and others, whether domanial stewards, judicial officers or Lombards, were obliged to provide advances on their obligations. Occasionally public offices like that of master of the mint, tax farmer or treasurer were awarded on favourable terms in exchange for loans.[56]

As the money market of Bruges grew more sharply defined under the influence of the Italian *banchieri* in the course of the 14th century, the dukes of Brabant and of Burgundy, along with some Brabant towns, began to increase their borrowing from the bankers of Bruges, at interest rates as high as 50% or more *per annum*: the interest rate was clearly dependent not only on the current situation of the money market itself, but also on that of the borrowers in question. To obtain long-term credit the rulers and towns of Brabant frequently sold annuities, or *seigneuries* or even certain feudal rights, reserving the right to redeem them later.[57]

Charles the Bold's disastrous policies and the chaos resulting from the

---

[53] Van der Wee, 'Geld', pp. 104–6.

[54] Van der Wee, 'Monetary', pp. 335–54.

[55] W.P. Blockmans, 'Le crédit public dans les Pays-Bas méridionaux au bas moyen âge', in: H. Dubois (ed.), *Local and International Credit in the Middle Ages and the 16th Century* (Bern: 1986), pp. 1–7.

[56] E. Aerts, 'De inhoud der rekeningen van de Brabantse algemeen-ontvangerij (1430–1440). Moeilijkheden en mogelijkheden voor het historisch onderzoek', in: *Bijdragen tot de Geschiedenis* LXI (1978), pp. 72 ff.

[57] Blockmans, 'Le crédit', pp. 1–2; also 'Finances publiques et inégalité dans les Pays-Bas aux XIVe–XVIe siècles', in: *Genèse de l'état moderne. Prélèvement et redistribution* (Paris: 1987), p. 85.

Flemish Revolt at the end of the 15th century ultimately crushed the vigour of Bruges's money market, even as a source of credit for the government. At the end of the 15th century, however, Antwerp was not immediately able to fill the vacuum.[58] In 1517 Charles V began to take out short-term government loans on the Antwerp money market. This was the signal for a rapid growth in Habsburg demand for government credit, a demand that substantially stimulated activity on the Antwerp money and capital market in the following decades. Antwerp, partly because of this, evolved into the financial metropolis of the West.[59] The financial crisis of 1557, provoked by the Habsburg moratorium on payments in that year, seriously affected the resilience of Antwerp's money and capital markets in the area of international government credit. A number of the great South German bankers active at Antwerp went bankrupt. Antwerp's role in financing Habsburg and French world policy visibly declined in favour of Seville and the Genoese financial fairs of Piacenza.[60]

The money and capital markets of Antwerp recovered to a certain extent during the Revolt of the Netherlands against Spain. Although panic over the war, the drain of capital abroad, and the second Spanish moratorium of 1575 repeatedly disrupted the money and capital markets, financial transactions involved in the payment of armies and the reconquest were invariably accompanied by new flurries of intensive financial activity. Antwerp's abiding influence as a *Dispositionsplatz* and the development of *asiento* contracts, whereby merchant-bankers provided money on easy terms to the Spanish government in the Netherlands for military purposes, ensured that the Antwerp money market still occupied a strategic position in the financial activities of the European world even after 1585.[61]

After the Treaty of Munster in Westphalia (1648) these favourable circumstances disappeared. Antwerp's money and capital markets were soon reduced to mere satellites of Amsterdam's.[62]

---

[58] Van der Wee, 'Geld', p. 106.

[59] H. Van der Wee, 'Die Niederlande 1350–1650', in: W. Fischer (ed.), *Handbuch der europäischen Wirtschafts- und Sozialgeschichte*, vol. III: *Europäische Wirtschafts- und Socialgeschichte von ausgehenden Mittelalter bis zur Mitte des 17. Jahrhunderts* (Stuttgart: 1986), p. 602.

[60] Van der Wee, *The Growth* II, pp. 363–4.

[61] Van der Wee, 'Geld', p. 108.

[62] Van der Wee, 'Monetary', pp. 335–6, 348–9.

V

INDUSTRY

11

Structural Changes and Specialization in Southern Netherlands Industry, 1100–1600[1]

The long-run analysis of industrial developments in the Southern Netherlands which is exemplified in this article is based on two premises. The first, of an epistemological nature, involves the acceptance of a synchronic and diachronic coherence of economic reality in the late Middle Ages and Early Modern period, which means that it is possible to distinguish an explicable structure in the industrial development of the Low Countries.[2] In order, however, to make such a deep analysis it is necessary to use a certain degree of abstraction or generalization. However, this article is based as far as possible on induction from historical data, even though it is only possible to present a limited amount of empirical information. The second premise is concerned more with economic theory and can best be expressed as follows: when economic activity expands in a spectacular way – as in periods of quantitative growth within a given economic structure – questions of demand exert a strategic role in the historical process. On the other hand, during periods of basic structural change – as in periods of qualitative growth with fundamental changes of the macro-economic production function – supply factors are more dominant. Consequently, since this article is especially concerned with structural changes in an industrial sector, it will probably show a certain degree of bias in favour of questions of supply, although questions of demand will not of course be ignored.

---

[1] The original version of this text was presented as the Tawney Memorial Lecture at the 1974 Conference of the Economic History Society in Bristol. I should like here to thank all those who contributed to the discussion and so to the improvement of the manuscript. I should also like to thank particularly Mrs Kristien De Blonde-Cottenier, for her help in the preparatory research, Prof. J.H. Munro, for his generous communication of so far unpublished information, and Mrs Patricia Van Caenegem-Carson, for her help in translation.

[2] For a more extensive discussion see H. Van der Wee, 'Perspektiven und Grenzen wirtschaftshistorischer Betrachtungsweise: methodologische Bemerkungen', in: *Vierteljahrschrift für Sozial- und Wirtschaftsgeschichte*, 62 (1975), pp. 1–18.

The Instability of Medieval Urban Textile Trade

Towns and cloth manufacturing obviously existed in Western Europe before the 11th century. What was new was that the growth of numerous towns depended on the development of a textile industry systematically aiming at division of labour, standardization, and export.[3] The emergence of such urban manufacturing centres was unique to Western Europe and had important long-term social and economic consequences. Technical progress, especially the change from the old vertical looms to the narrow horizontal pedal looms and the subsequent invention of the wide horizontal pedal loom in the 11th century,[4] was certainly essential for the expansion of the West European textile industry. Nevertheless, this factor was not decisive in the particularly *urban* character of the textile industry which became obvious in the first phase of expansion, from the 11th to the 13th century. Other factors of production, especially labour and technical–commercial progress, were more responsible for the urban form of the industrial growth of the 11th, 12th, and 13th centuries. These could be combined much more effectively in the developing towns than in any setting available in the earlier, more primitive, agricultural economy. The concentration of the work force in the towns made the division of labour (among other things: parting, picking, greasing, combing, carding, spinning, twining, spooling, shearing, weaving, burling, dressing, dry-shearing, dyeing, finishing) much more possible. It also allowed further specialization within a single manufacturing process. The dyers, for example, subdivided themselves into groups each of which concentrated on a particular colour.[5]

Commercial capital was an even more decisive factor of production: by its means the textile industry could be integrated in the technical–commercial progress of the expanding towns. With the help of financial capital, concentrated in the hands of urban merchant-entrepreneurs, local raw materials could be supplemented or replaced by the importation of cheaper or better wool from distant areas. Considerable additional supplies of wool came especially from the Cistercian and Premonstratensian abbeys and other domains in England and Scotland. The concentration of income and wealth also allowed important investments in warehouses and stocks,

---

[3] F. Braudel, *Civilisation matérielle et capitalisme (XVe–XVIIIe siècle)*: Tome I (Paris: 1967), pp. 391–404.

[4] E. Endrei, 'Changements dans la productivité de l'industrie au Moyen-âge', *Seconda Settimana di Studio, Prato 1970: Produzione, commercio e consumo dei panni di lana, XII–XVII secolo*, polycopied text.

[5] G. de Poerck, *La draperie médiévale en Flandre et en Artois. I. La technique* (Bruges: 1951). Espinas mentions 30 to 32 different processes in the cloth towns of Artois and West Flanders; see G. Espinas, *La draperie dans la Flandre française au Moyen-Age* (Paris: 1923), II, p. 311.

in fairs and sale-rooms, in harbours and ships, in organized land and sea transport, and in the control of production and in trade regulations. More efficient trade connections were set up with more distant parts of the world, which led not only to new areas of demand but also to new sources of raw and subsidiary materials. By these means medieval cloth towns won important gains in physical and economic productivity in comparison with the traditional production pattern in the domains. Nevertheless, the towns did not manage to obtain, on this basis, a lasting industrial monopoly or even a lasting industrial advantage for themselves. There were several reasons for this. Excessive division of labour in the textile sector, except where dyeing was concerned, had depressed the workers' standing to the semi- or unskilled category. Hence, as soon as urban growth led to diseconomies of scale (because of too rapid population expansion or of overmultiplication of institutional structures), there was a great temptation to introduce textile production in younger centres or rural areas, where wages were lower because of the lower standard of living and the absence or slow development of guild organization.

Neither did the concentration of financial capital in the hands of merchant-entrepreneurs ensure that textile production would remain in the original cloth towns. Increasing activity by merchants in outlying regions, with an eye on sales, extended the areas from which they drew their supplies. The expansion of a relationship between one particular merchant and one particular industrial town, into a network of commercial connections between him and a whole group of textile centres in his own region, was, moreover, a logical commercial development. If commercial expansion was set going by the comparative advantages of exchanging two products between two areas, the merchants' export profits would be gradually diminished given an immobile or nearly immobile technological structure; export profits came, in fact, from the relative scarcity of the product in the importing area – a scarcity which was of course removed by just this increased importation. Further commercial growth could then be achieved only if the exchange was broadened from two to a greater number of products.[6] Although such diversification was originally obtained inside one and the same industrial town, it was undoubtedly more sensible to organize it regionally than locally, in order to retain the scale effects. The mobility of commercial capital, through the intervention of the *active* merchant, helped this transition.

If this proposed pattern is applied to the economy of Western Europe in the 11th to the 13th centuries, the following characteristics can be stressed. First, towns producing textiles for export sprang up all over Western Europe especially in the Ile-de-France, Flanders, Picardy, Artois,

---

[6] J. Hicks, *A Theory of Economic History* (Oxford: 1969), pp. 45–6.

Brabant, Hainault, Liège, Normandy, Champagne, England, Languedoc, Catalonia and Northern Italy.[7] Second, this urban textile industry was very unstable, and subject to constant geographical movements. This was logical: as European trade increased in success and intensity, as the industrial lead of some centres became available to a wider range of consumers and their comparative advantages became more obvious, textile centres in less favoured regions could no longer maintain their export positions. Thus, in these areas the industrial activity of the cloth towns gradually stagnated.[8] Luckily in some of these areas, like Languedoc, Catalonia, and above all in England, a rural textile industry gradually developed out of this urban decline. (This will be considered below.) The towns in and round Flanders, on the other hand, thanks to a polarization effect in the building up of their institutions and infrastructure, managed to develop into leading areas of *urban* textile industry directed towards export.

The further expansion of urban industry in the region of Hainault, Flanders and Brabant in the 12th and 13th centuries was ensured by an obvious diversification of products in each centre. Thus we find mention in most cloth towns during this period, of the production of a whole range of high-quality 'oiled' cloth, cheaper 'unoiled' cloth, and a series of mixed cloth sorts.[9] In the same area, at this time, traces can already be found of a certain *interurban* specialization, which gave the process of diversification a regional dimension. But such intraregional specialization must also be seen in the context of the geographical instability of the urban textile industry within the region itself. Indeed, even if Flanders, Hainault and Brabant had become the leading industrial areas of Europe, industrial activity within them was, geographically speaking, unstable. Export seemed initially most successful in towns nearest to the Ile-de-France and the fairs of Champagne, such as Saint-Omer and Arras in Artois, but the centre of gravity soon moved to towns further east: in the 12th century, Cambrai, Lille, Douai, Tournai and Valenciennes were already important as export centres, quickly followed by Ghent, Bruges and Ypres, which were joined by Dixmuide and Bergues Saint-Winoc from the wool-producing Flemish

---

[7] R.S. Lopez, *Naissance de l'Europe, Ve–XIVe siècle* (Paris: 1962), p. 288.

[8] For Catalonia–Aragon see C. Carrere, 'La draperie en Catalogne et en Aragon au 15e siècle' (Prato: 1970), polycopied text; for Languedoc see P. Wolff, 'Esquisse d'une histoire de la draperie en Languedoc du 12e au 17e siècle' (Prato: 1970), polycopied text; and for England see H. Van Werveke, 'Introduction historique' in: De Poerck, *La draperie médiévale* pp. 13–4.

[9] J.H. Munro, 'The Transformation of the Flemish Woollen Industries, ca. 1250–ca. 1400: The Response to Changing Factor Costs and Market Demand', *Workshop on Quantitative Economic History* (University of Leuven, paper 7103, 1971).

coastal plain.[10] In the 13th century the ascendancy of the three great Flemish cloth towns was obvious, but by the end of the century, and especially early in the next, the cloth towns of Brabant (Mechlin, Brussels and Louvain) triumphantly appeared on the European export scene with cheaper cloth.[11] Of course the older, more westerly centres did not decline at once, but stayed in the running in particular with their large range of better products, so that diversification of production took place on a local and on an intraregional level[12] (see Figure 11.1).

The ability of the urban textile industry in Flanders and Brabant to expand was not exhausted by this process. The shift to lower wage zones and the possibility of further intraregional diversification were not confined to a few large cloth towns, but became, in the 14th and 15th centuries, more general. In Flanders and Brabant the traditional textile export industry was gradually introduced in the smaller towns of Brabant, such as Herentals, Lier, Diest, Tienen, Vilvoorde, Aarschot and Zoutleeuw, which developed into successful cloth centres working for the European export market.[13] In Flanders a group of small towns in the south of the county (e.g. Oudenaarde, Termonde, Alost, Grammont, Ninove and Deinze) advanced towards introducing the traditional cloth industry, in the shadow of Ghent. Round the river Lys, and more influenced by Bruges–Ypres, a similar group of small centres with a dynamic export policy also emerged: they included especially Wervik, Courtrai, Comines, Langemark, Menen, Roulers, Poperinghe and Warneton.[14] Moreover, the towns of the Lys area did not confine themselves to imitating the textiles produced by the larger centres at a lower cost of production, but in addition launched the 'new drapery': although this aimed at imitating traditional textiles, it was characterized by a deliberate simplification of production, so that the advantage of low production costs was magnified (see Figures 11.2 and 11.3).

---

[10] H. Van Werveke, 'Introduction historique', in De Poerck, *op. cit.* pp. 10–1; G. Espinas and H. Pirenne, *Recueil de documents relatifs à l'histoire de l'industrie en Flandre. Première partie: des origines à l'époque bourguignonne* (Brussels: 4 vols, 1906–24); for Dixmuide and Bergues Saint-Winoc, see A.E. Verhulst, 'La laine indigène dans les Anciens Pay-Bas entre le XIIe et le XVIIe siècle', in: *Revue Historique*, XCVI (1972), p. 291.

[11] R.H. Bautier, 'La place de la draperie brabançonne et plus particulièrement bruxelloise dans l'industrie textile du Moyen Age', *In Memoriam P. Bonenfant* (Brussels: 1966), pp. 31–63; G.A. Derville, 'Les draperies flamandes et artésiennes vers 1250–1350', in: *Revue du Nord*, LIV (1972), pp. 353–70.

[12] Bautier, 'Le place de la draperie', pp. 36, 42, 45.

[13] R. Van Uytven, *Stadsfinanciën en stadseconomie te Leuven van de XIIe tot het einde der XVIe eeuw* (Brussels: 1961), pp. 358–9.

[14] Verhulst, 'La laine indigène', pp. 282, 294.

Figure 11.1: *West–East displacement of most important textile centres between 12th and early 14th centuries*

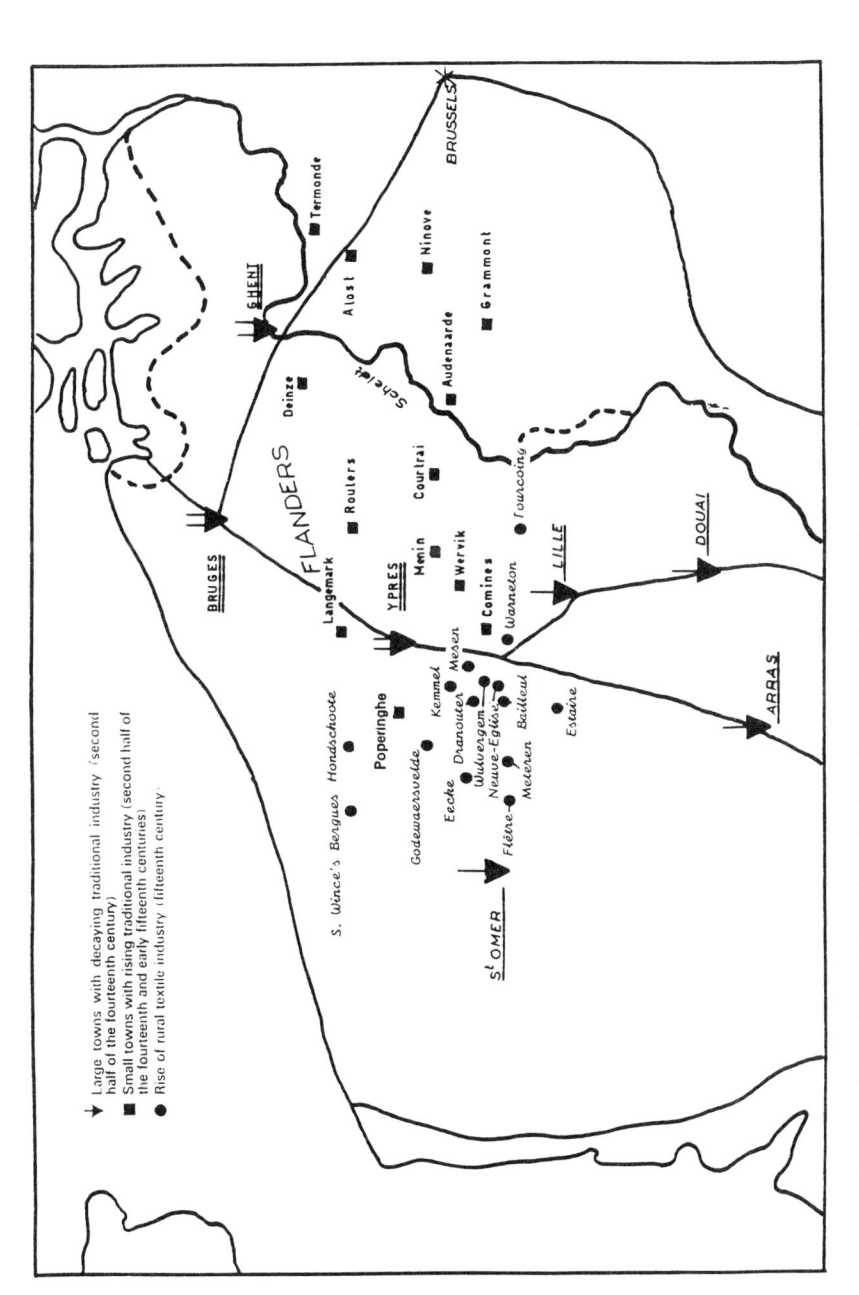

Figure 11.2: Decline of traditional and rise of new leading textile centres in Flanders and Northern France (14th–15th centuries)

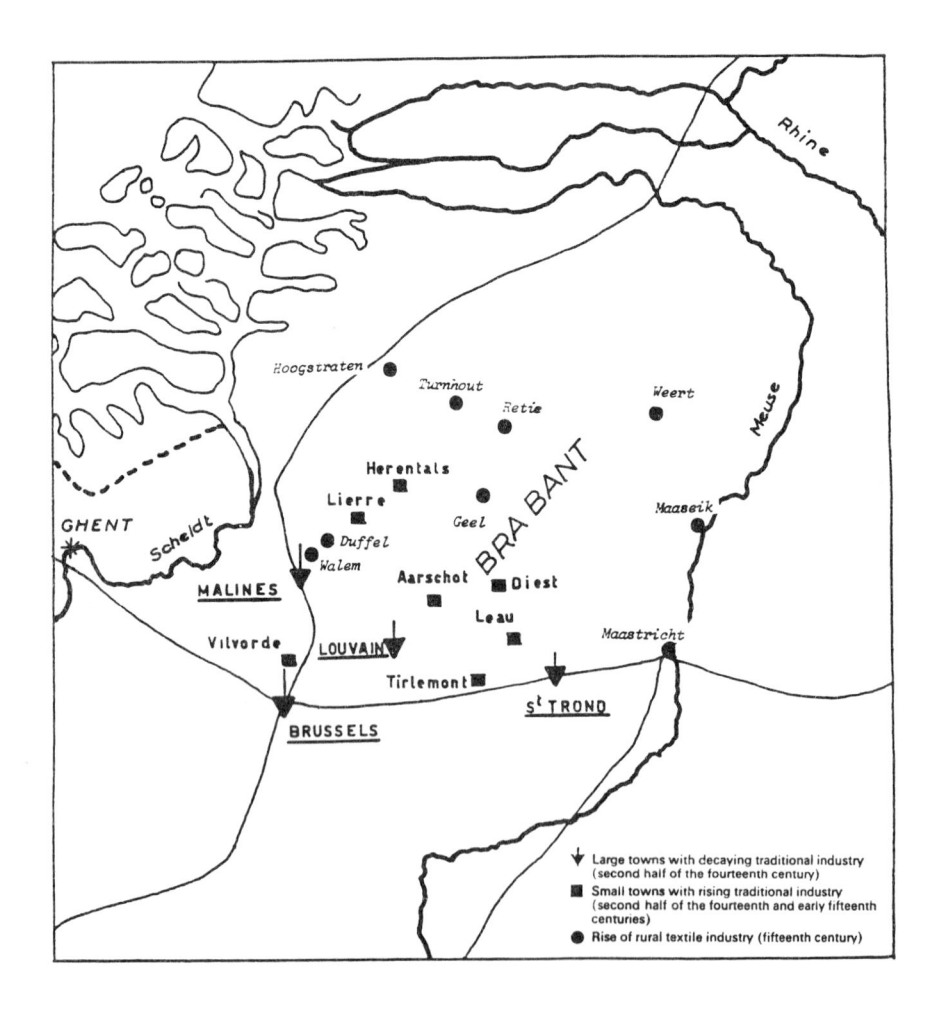

Figure 11.3: *Decline of traditional and rise of new leading textile centres in Brabant (14th–15th centuries)*

The Response of Supply within the Framework of the Traditional Production Pattern

While expansion in Europe continued, the possible losses of the old centres could be made good by diversification of production both inside and outside those centres; and unemployment could be absorbed by migration to newly developing towns within the region. Moreover diversification was an appropriate response to the growing shortage of native raw material and to the increasing importation of foreign – especially Scottish and English – wool,[15] which were initially caused by the general growth in cloth production in the Low Countries and by the growth of population which necessitated land reclamation at the expense of grassland.

The fate of the traditional industry, however, changed radically during the 14th century when, in Europe, a long term phase of stagnation and depression took place. This was engendered by the pressure of numbers on the land, followed by a fall in population, political chaos, and a contraction of transcontinental transport.[16] In relation to the development of supply in the Southern Netherlands, there was now a clear weakening in European export demand. Stresses in the export industry therefore were unavoidable and traditional production was severely threatened in many centres. The immediate question was how the cloth towns of the Southern Netherlands should react to this threat. Initially, most towns confined their efforts within the traditional structures of production – in other words, within the limits of the old or new drapery itself and within the limits of the old production function. The guilds of the large towns (for example, Brussels and Ypres) organized warlike expeditions to destroy looms in the rural areas round the towns.[17] Such intimidation, however, could not continue and was, in any case, useless against the competition of the smaller cloth towns which possessed charters of freedom. Legal steps were sometimes taken against imitation, as in the case of Ypres against Poperinghe,[18] but they were agonizingly

---

[15] R. Van Uytven, 'Hierlandsche wol en lakens in Brabantse documenten (XIII–XVIe eeuw)', *Bijdragen tot de Geschiedenis LIII*, 1–2 (1970), pp. 14–5; Verhulst, 'La laine indigène', pp. 296–7.

[16] H. Van der Wee, *Historische Aspecten van de economische groei. Tien studies over de economische ontwikkeling van West-Europa en van de Nederlanden in het bijzonder (12e–19e eeuw)* (Antwerp–Utrecht: 1972), pp. 10–20.

[17] See *inter alia* the privileges of Ghent (1302), Bruges (1322) and Ypres (1322) concerning their exclusive rights to cloth-making as against the surrounding countryside; H. Van Werveke, 'Economische Geschiedenis' in: *Geschiedenis van Vlaanderen* (Brussels: 1938), II, pp. 232–3; see also Ghent's reactions to Termonde, Brussels to Merchtem, Saint-Omer to Arques; see G. Des Marez, *L'organisation du travail à Bruxelles au XVe siècle* (Brussels: 1904), p. 482.

[18] N. De Pauw, *Ypre jeghen Poperinghe* (Ghent: 1899).

expensive and prolonged, and in any case did not produce the desired result. The cloth towns, in conjunction with the duke or count, also dealt firmly with foreign competition by protectionism. In Flanders, for example, the importation of English cloth was forbidden between 1340 and 1489–1501, although numerous exceptions were made.[19] Sometimes, as in 1428, 1434 and 1464, the importation of English cloth was forbidden in the whole of Burgundian Netherlands.[20] Although such resistance had some effect on the home market, it certainly did not solve the export problem and, moreover, it tended to impede the supply of English raw materials in the most unfortunate manner.

Technological progress might have provided a way out. But employers were organized in guilds imbued with the spirit of group solidarity. Technological improvements, which could give an inventive employer an advantage over the group were, therefore, systematically repulsed. Guild solidarity was, however, supported by agreements between employers to reduce labour costs by reducing the real wages of the mass of dependent textile workers. Such savings could very easily be made because the clothiers' corporation played a role in urban government which enabled it to fix wage rates. The slow adaptations of day and piece wages to the rise in the cost of living, brought about *inter alia* by the frequent debasements of the currency, ensured the desired effect in an unobtrusive way during the 13th and 14th centuries.[21]

The gradual depression of workers' living standards, often encouraged by growing unemployment, affected the dependent textile workers and even became a decisive factor in the creation of the craft guilds. There is evidence for such organizations in Saint-Omer and Arras (Artois) before 1280[22] and shortly afterwards craft guilds also appeared in the towns of Flanders and Brabant. Initially, they were clandestine, militant organizations which provoked chronic social disturbances and were, therefore, vigorously opposed by the patrician urban administration.[23] But social agitation reached a first successful climax with lasting results at the beginning of the 14th century. The Mattins of Bruges in 1302 started

---

[19] W. Brulez, 'Engels Laken in Vlaanderen in de 14e–15e eeuw', in: *Handelingen van het Genootschap 'Société d'Emulation' te Brugge* CVIII (1971), pp. 5–25.

[20] J.H. Munro, *Wool, Cloth and Gold. The Struggle for Bullion in Anglo-Burgundian Trade, 1340–1478* (Brussels–Toronto: 1973), Chapters IV, V, VI.

[21] H. Van Werveke, 'De economische en sociale gevolgen van de muntpolitiek der graven van Vlaanderen (1337–1433)', in: Miscellanea Mediaevalia (Ghent: 1968), pp. 243–54; *ibid.*, 'Currency Manipulation in the Middle Ages: the Case of Louis of Male, Count of Flanders', pp. 255–67.

[22] G. Fourquin, *Histoire économique de l'Occident Médiéval* (Paris: 1969), p. 249.

[23] For interurban agreements in Flanders and Brabant of 1242, 1249, 1274 and 1277 as well as common suppression of the fullers' revolts etc. see H. Van der Wee, 'Het Sociaaleconomisch leven te Lier in de Middeleeuwen', in: *'t Land van Ryen* (1952), pp. 2–3, 13.

a wave of unrest which spread through many textile towns in Flanders and Brabant and took on the character of a genuine democratic revolution. Similar social revolts continued to occur throughout the 14th century, especially in its third quarter, and fairly often gave the textile workers temporary control over the town.[24] The final result was the success of corporatism. The craft guilds, which had been at first so vigorously kept down, were gradually accepted as locally recognized organizations and fully absorbed into the mechanisms of urban government. This sociopolitical development, which began with the revolt of 1302–6, had been mainly completed in the larger towns by the end of the 14th century and in the smaller ones somewhat later.[25] The effect of the success of corporatism on the textile industry in the 14th and 15th centuries was obviously disastrous. Corporate control of the urban government or political participation in it immediately provided higher wages in the towns, but at the same time pushed up wage costs and in so doing posed a disastrous threat to the traditional urban export industry. Even when massive unemployment was the result, wages did not fall, because of the inertia of corporate interests.

In addition to their attempts to reduce real wages, employers also attempted to find a solution for growing market difficulties by regulations concerning the product itself. From the first half of the 14th century onwards the older towns of Flanders and Brabant gradually gave up many types of product, developed for export in the phase of expansion. They concentrated more and more, and often exclusively, on expensive cloth from the finest wool.[26] For this they depended chiefly on English varieties such as March, Cotswold and Lindsey. It is remarkable how strict the guild regulations in the big cloth towns became on this point between 1300 and 1400, as Munro has shown for Flanders and Brabant. The smaller towns soon followed their example: the move towards dearer products became general in Flanders, even in the 'new drapery' centres of the Lys area. And the same development was exemplified in the younger and smaller cloth towns of Brabant.[27]

The tendency to concentrate the export production of the traditional

---

[24] R. Van Uytven, 'Plutokratie in de oude demokratieën der Nederlanden', in: *Handelingen van de Zuidnederlandse Maatschappij voor Taal- en Letterkunde en Geschiedenis* XVI (1962), pp. 373–409.

[25] See the study by F. Favresse, *L'avènement du régime démocratique à Bruxelles pendant le Moyen-Age, 1306–1423* (Brussels: 1932), especially for Brussels.

[26] J.H. Munro, *The Transformation of the Flemish Woollen Industries* (Leuven: 1971), pp. 2–5; H. Van der Wee, 'Die Wirtschaft der Stadt Lier zu Beginn des 15. Jahrhunderts', in: *Beiträge zur Wirtschafts- und Stadtgeschichte. Festschrift für H. Amann* (Wiesbaden: 1965), p. 146.

[27] Verhulst, 'La laine indigène', pp. 296–7; Munro, *Wool, Cloth and Gold*, pp. 2–3.

industry on the best cloth was logical in the circumstances. In the first place it fitted in with the growing success of corporatism which aimed at consumer protection and control of all producers. Second, the move towards higher quality was an economically valid attempt to avoid the threat to the export industry. The most expensive types of cloth needed particularly skillful spinning, weaving and finishing, and suitable workers for this were available nearly exclusively in Flanders and Brabant. As a result, concentrating on the production of the best cloth meant that these two regions could make effective use of the prime skills of local manpower – which could therefore be paid high wages.

Moreover, since more expensive sorts of wool were used in these luxury goods, the high cost of wages per unit was relatively reduced. This shift in relative factor prices had a remarkable effect on entrepreneurial attitudes. And the systematic refusal, during this period, of every technological invention which might have increased *physical* productivity, indicates that the *economic* productivity was a more important variable in the explanation of contemporary supply changes. It is, indeed, remarkable that the fulling mills which had been introduced in several towns in Brabant and Flanders in the 12th and 13th century, were no longer used in the 14th when fulling was again exclusively carried out with the feet in the centres of the old and the new drapery.[28] During the same period even the spinning-wheel could not replace the spindle in these centres[29] – the quality of the spinning process being more decisive than its physical efficiency.

Obviously, questions of demand also played an important role in the move towards more expensive products. The European depression which became general during the 14th century affected export demand. Population decline generally affected the lower more than the higher income groups, while the inheritance effect brought a more highly skewed distribution of wealth and income.[30] In such circumstances the demand for cheaper goods for export was particularly constrained and, as a result, commercial economies of scale could no longer be so easily realized for the long-distance trade in cheaper fabrics. The situation was aggravated by the fact that at the same time Italy, England, Normandy, Languedoc, Catalonia and Southern Germany were extending the production of their own cheap textiles.[31] On the other hand, the export demand for the

---

[28] R. Van Uytven, 'The Fulling Mill: Dynamic of the Revolution of Industrial Attitudes', in: *Acta Historia Neerlandica* V (Leyden: 1971), pp. 1–14.

[29] Endrei, 'Changements dans la productivité'.

[30] Munro, *Wool, Cloth and Gold*, p. 3; D. Herlihy, *Medieval and Renaissance Pistoia* (New Haven: 1967), pp. 180–212.

[31] In Languedoc and Catalonia, cheap rural production was chiefly concerned, see note 7; for Italy, see especially R.H. Bautier, 'Les Foires de Champagne' in: *Recueils de la Société*

most expensive luxury fabrics from Flanders and Brabant was not so price-elastic. This cloth had a special image and was used chiefly by the rich; increases in price or changes in income of the potential buyers had therefore less effect on the export demand.

However economically defensible such a change to expensive cloth was, it nevertheless made the traditional cloth trade of Flanders and Brabant extremely vulnerable, since technical requirements and strict regulations meant that it was increasingly dependent on the best quality English wool. The demand for English wool of these towns therefore became entirely price-inelastic – and the English kings immediately took advantage of this in their financial difficulties in the Hundred Years' War. Munro has shown how from 1336 onwards taxes on wool were raised, how in 1340 the Bullion Acts forced merchants to pay two marks silver to the Tower Mint on every sack of wool exported, and how after 1340 an export tax was imposed on wool. Moreover, wool exports were concentrated from 1363 onwards in the Staple of Calais, strengthening the monopoly of the more important merchants and enabling higher costs to be more easily passed on to the buyers.

Of all the Bullion Acts the Calais Staple Partition and the Bullion Ordinance of 1429 were particular hindrances to wool exports, because of the several Anglo-Burgundian conflicts and the drastic limitation of buying on credit which resulted. But the last sharp decline in wool exports, which followed the events of 1429, only completed a process which was already underway.[32]

Indeed, increases in export taxes were already having a considerable negative effect on wool exports in the 14th century: even before the end of the century the taxes on wool exports had risen to 30 to 35% *ad valorem* for residents and even higher for non-residents, while the exports of English cloth were taxed at only 1 to 3%.[33] Moreover, the comparative advantage in price of English cloth over cloth from the Southern Netherlands went hand in hand with the localization of the English cloth industry, which after the decline of urban production had taken refuge in rural areas. Rural wages were low because they formed only a subsidiary source of income and because corporatism was weak. In addition, as Carus-Wilson has shown, the fulling mill and spinning-wheel had been

---

Jean Bodin, vol. V: La Foire (Brussels, 1953), pp. 97–147: the stress here lies on the strong development of Italian cloth trade (especially in Florence and Milan) during the 13th and 14th centuries; this first brought about import substitution for Flemish–Brabant cloth, based on the direct importation of English wool, and gradually developed into an export industry in the Mediterranean area at the expense of the cloth industry of Flanders and Brabant.

[32] For extensive information on this subject see Munro, *Wool, Cloth and Gold, passim*.

[33] *Ibid.* p. 6; E.M. Carus-Wilson and O. Coleman, *England's Export Trade, 1275–1547* (Oxford: 1963), pp. 194–5.

successfully introduced in English rural industry in the 13th century, with the result that increases in physical productivity had pushed costs down.[34]

The combination of all these factors undoubtedly explains the growing success of English cloth exports and from the mid-14th century onwards the simultaneous fall in wool exports.[35] The falling trend in the price of English cloth and the coincident increase in price of cloth from Flanders and Brabant during the 14th and 15th centuries illustrate this development very clearly.[36] We are therefore driven to conclude that the Calais Staple Partition and Bullion Ordinance of 1429 and the Anglo-Burgundian war which followed marked the fatal moment in the long drawn-out decline of the *urban* cloth industry in Flanders and Brabant.[37]

The Slow Development of a New Production Function

The economy of Brabant and Flanders needed a basic reconstruction in order to escape the threat of complete industrial decline. This was not an easy task, but the industrial advantages which the Southern Netherlands had built up in the preceding period of expansion provided the necessary maturity and vitality. The renewal was twofold: a first series of adaptations took place within the framework of the old export industry, and concentrated on reintroducing the diversification of cloth production mainly in the smaller towns and in the rural areas; while a second series of adaptations, mainly in the large towns, aimed at introducing highly specialized luxury fabrics outside the framework of the traditional cloth trade, intended less for export and more for the home market.

The first series of changes affected the centres which had given up the production of luxury cloth from English wool and replaced it by a series of cheaper, although still valuable, sorts of cloth made from Scottish or native wool, but increasingly with Spanish material. In the 14th century, Spanish sheep had been successfully crossed with North African Merinids

---

[34] E.M. Carus-Wilson, 'An Industrial Revolution of the Thirteenth Century' in E.M. Carus-Wilson (ed.), *Essays in Economic History*, I (1954), pp. 45–60.

[35] Carus-Wilson and Coleman, *ibid.*, pp. 122–3, 138–9.

[36] I am indebted to Prof. J.H. Munro for this valuable information.

[37] There is no doubt that certain circumstances such as the Flemish Revolt of 1379–85 brought about an increase in the difficulties surrounding the export of English wool to Flanders. See a recent interesting study by W. Prevenier, 'Les perturbations dans les relations commerciales anglo-flamandes entre 1389 et 1407. Causes de désaccord et raisons d'une réconciliation?' in: *Mélanges Edouard Perroy: Publications de la Sorbonne, Série Etudes, Vol. 5* (Paris: 1973), pp. 478–97.

and produced merino sheep which gradually improved the quality of Spanish wool and thus promised (in the 15th, 16th and 17th centuries) great benefits to the Spanish mesta and *transhumance*.[38] The special quality of this Spanish merino wool was attractive to the Flemish industry because a traditional type of cloth could be made from it which was easily distinguishable from its English competitors. Munro in a recent article has pointed out that as early as the second quarter of the 15th century, during the great textile crisis in the Southern Netherlands, several centres changed over to the use of Spanish and other non-English sorts of wool.[39] And at about the same time Castilian and Basque merchants opened sales agencies in Bruges. In the event it was particularly the rural and small-town 'new drapery' in Flanders which decided on such adaptation: Poperinghe originally set the pattern, and during the second half of the 15th century was selling its Spanish wool textiles quite well in the Hanse area. Other small towns and villages in Flanders, such as Termonde, Ninove, Comines, Estaire, Warneton, Bailleul, Tourcoing, Neuve-Eglise, Eeke, Flètre, Armentières and Dranouter adopted similar new types of cloth and achieved some export successes in North and Central Germany. Even the great cloth towns in Flanders and Brabant and the smaller towns of Brabant were persuaded to develop their own 'new drapery', although in the event this did not come to much.[40]

The trend in Brabant was towards the production of cheaper quality cloth from *native* Campine wool, prepared in the countryside: Retie, Duffel, Hoogstraten, Geel and Walem and increasingly the rural centres in the northeast of the duchy (in the neighbourhood of Weert, Maaseik, Hoorn and Maastricht), well known for the *graulaken*, became relatively important in the export field.[41]

Finally the new 'light drapery' from cheap, native unoiled wool spread throughout town and country, but its significance was still rather limited during the 15th century.

However important the adaptations within the traditional cloth industry may have been, they were not at the heart of the structural changes in the economy of the Southern Netherlands. Broadly speaking, exports of this line of products remained marginal during the 15th century. This could

---

[38] J. Heers, *L'occident aux XIVe et XVe siècles. Aspects économiques et sociaux* (Paris: 1963), pp. 118–9.

[39] J.H. Munro, 'The Coming of Spanish Wools to the Low Countries' (manuscript kindly put at the author's disposal).

[40] *Ibid.*

[41] H. Van der Wee, *The Growth of the Antwerp Market and the European Economy. (Fourteenth–Sixteenth Centuries)* II (Paris–The Hague: 1963), pp. 8–10, 42, 59, 99; G. Daems, *De Lakenindustrie in de stad Mechelen, 1480–1580* (unpublished M.A. thesis, University of Leuven) (Louvain: 1974), pp. 122–6.

not be otherwise while the general European export demand remained low and there was strong competition from cheap English and local cloth. The drastic fall in population in the small textile towns in Brabant during the last two-thirds of the 15th century offers an impressive illustration of the weakness of export demand at that moment and of the decay of the urban old and new cloth trade.[42] Structural reforms could be effective only when they took place outside the traditional export industry: this happened through the development of an *urban* luxury industry, dependent on highly skilled labour, on artisan creativity, and on fashionable refinements in the beginning essentially intended for home consumption.

Such a choice was certainly not haphazard. In the first place, certain supply factors were responsible. The towns of the Southern Netherlands could rely on an old industrial tradition, which had led to the creation of a strong technical infrastructure. Moreover, the education which was penetrating into the artisan sphere, thanks to the strength of the craft guilds, strengthened the human capital factor to a remarkable degree. Technical monopolies could be obtained by the further refinement of skills, which allowed high wages without damaging the competitive position. At the same time the income structure and the cultural climate in the towns ensured that fashion and the spread of luxury became factors in industrial development.

The changeover to urban industry demanding highly skilled labour was not accompanied by a substantial increase in *physical* productivity, although this was achieved in some sectors. The advance in *economic* productivity was more critical: by using better-qualified workers and by increased artisan creativity, substantial improvements in quality and value of goods produced per working hour input were realized. What was involved was more the *deepening* than the *widening* of human capital. Looked at from the point of view of the very long-term growth of the economy of the Southern Netherlands, the effect was very positive, and amounted to a turning-point in their economic history, typified by an important shift in the production function which stressed the input of labour, as against capital and raw materials. The Flemish and Brabant Primitives were undoubtedly the most illustrious exponents of the urban industrial renewal. Other sectors were probably not so famous but involved more employment opportunities. Examples are: sculpture, marvellously represented in Flemish and Brabant high Gothic; wood carving, which was at its best in the Antwerp and Mechlin altar screens; furniture making; chest making; the industrial production of textile tools; tapestry weaving; leather work; embroidery; miniature painting; music; enamel and jewellery; metal work; copper and bronze; the arms industry;

---

[42] Van der Wee, *The Growth of the Antwerp Market* I, pp. 547–8, app. 49/2, 3.

and, last but not least, fashion – which, in the form of furs, hats, gloves and the confection industry, reached such a degree of development that the foundation was laid for the triumph of Brabant fashions throughout Northwestern Europe in the 16th century.[43]

Industrial renewal was in general easier in the larger than in the smaller towns. The latter, as has been emphasized, often continued with the traditional cloth making or had adapted themselves by changes which, because aimed at export, did not bring about lasting improvement. The large towns, on the other hand, had long collected many commercial, administrative, religious and political functions within their walls, which meant that the seeds of the luxury trades on a local or regional scale were already developing early, beside the traditional export industry. The large towns also had advantages when the industrial revival was institutionalized by the triumph of corporatism: the old guild organizations there could more easily be divided into a whole series of specialized craft guilds which could exert a stricter control over the workers' specific skill and over the quality of the goods produced. The large towns were therefore most successful in building up a luxury industry based on the high qualifications of their workers.[44]

The revival was based not only on factors of supply. Changes in demand, quantitative as well as qualitative, also played a decisive role. In an atmosphere of European malaise there was not much to expect from export demand. Domestic demand, on the other hand, was characterized by a powerful increase in the Southern Netherlands. This was caused by a further flowering of the maritime economy, at the precise moment when the continental economy was weakening. I have attempted to explain this contrast in an earlier study on European trade.[45] The quantitative expansion of home consumption and the reorientation of demand in the maritime areas of the Burgundian Netherlands were based primarily on a growing income elasticity of demand in the middle income groups. The levelling of urban incomes was an important factor in this. The stabilization of the money of account – begun with the revaluation of the silver groat of Flanders and Brabant in 1389–90 and completed in the Burgundian currency reform of 1433–35 under Philip the Good – initiated

---

[43] For the development of fashion and confection see K. Slootmans, 'Huiden en pelzen of de jaarmarkten van Bergen-op-Zoom', in: *Land van mijn Hart* (Tilburg: 1952), pp. 100–8. For more general examples see R. Van Uytven, 'La Flandre et le Brabant, "Terres de promission" sous les ducs de Bourgogne', in: *Revue du Nord*, XLIII (1961), pp. 297–9.

[44] This explains the demographically favourable development in comparison with the smaller cloth towns, in spite of the fact that in the big towns the decline of cloth industry was already complete.

[45] H. Van der Wee, 'Un modèle dynamique de croissance interséculaire du commerce mondial', *Annales E.S.C.* XXV (1970), pp. 100–28.

a healthy monetary climate. In such conditions the egalitarian influence of corporatism could have a greater effect.[46] Moreover, the grain markets of the Netherlands were not uninfluenced by the falling price trend, which had been noticeable in the rest of Europe since the 14th century.[47] With enough work opportunities provided by industrial revival and a flourishing maritime trade, the members of the craft guilds saw their real wages progressing towards an age of gold. Even the wages of the urban lower income groups rose above the necessary minimum;[48] new consumption patterns developed which, in their turn, encouraged the expansion of the local and specialized craft guilds.

Internal demand was also favourably influenced by the expansion and high living standards of the upper middle classes in the towns. This was particularly significant for the artistic and specialized luxury crafts. Special circumstances favoured such a development in the Southern Netherlands from the 14th century onwards. The strengthening of central authority, culminating in the unified Burgundian state, created many new administrative jobs. The brilliant Burgundian court in Mechlin and Brussels, the growth of the university of Louvain, the important flowering of the Brabant fairs, the increasing presence in Bruges of foreign merchants – all increased the number of rich people with sophisticated tastes. Finally, there were the merchants and entrepreneurs of the traditional export industry, the 'new men' of the previous centuries. Many had retired from business because of difficulties in the export field or increasing competition from foreign merchants. They had invested their fortunes in houses, land, or urban annuities and had married into the landed aristocracy. As men of independent means (*ledichgangers*) they also profited from the stability of the currency and the fall in the cost of living. Finally, completely absorbed into urban politics, they had both the time and the interest in luxury and comfort to establish a thriving market for high-quality goods and services.

The brilliant Burgundian prosperity contained nevertheless a tragic paradox. It was confined especially to the larger towns, which had made the necessary structural changes most successfully; and within their walls it applied chiefly to upper and middle classes. The increased prosperity was achieved at the expense of poverty and misery among the rural population, hit hard by the fall in agricultural prices. It was also achieved through the disappearance or emigration of large numbers of low-paid workers from the traditional export industry of towns, both large and small, where

---

[46] P. Spufford, *Monetary Problems and Policies in the Burgundian Netherlands, 1433-1496* (Leiden: 1970), pp. 5-12.
[47] W. Abel, *Agrarkrisen und Agrarkonjunktur* (Hamburg, Berlin: 1966), pp. 65-70.
[48] Van der Wee, *The Growth of the Antwerp Market* III, graph 39.

demographic losses could only partly be made good by the industrial adaptation process. Rural poverty was undoubtedly important in the gradual development of rural industries during the 14th and 15th centuries.[49] The traditional wool processing, and linen weaving especially, moved from town to country. An additional income was attractive to agricultural workers; low rural wages and lower rural taxes appealed to the employers, especially as the work demanded no particular qualifications. Technically, it was therefore easy to move such production from town to country as soon as the urban decay became obvious enough to overcome the hostility of the craft guilds.

Certain other supply factors were also significant. The density of towns in the Netherlands favoured commercial contact between town and countryside. The lead in intensive farming ensured high-quality flax in East Flanders and Zeeland-Flanders, while wool production in the Campine and French Flanders, which rose thanks to falling grain prices,[50] provided the raw materials necessary respectively for the cloth industry round Weert and for the serge industry in Flanders. Finally, the importation of Spanish wool via Bruges was on the increase.[51]

It is remarkable that linen weaving and light drapery had a slow start in the countryside during the 15th century. The old and new draperies grew more easily in the countryside during that time. In other words, the new rural industry in Flanders and Brabant began its history, thanks to the taking over of old urban production. Only on the foundations of this infrastructure were the rural linen industry and the rural 'light drapery' able to build their 16th century expansion.

Export and the Widening of Human Capital

The transition to a new industrial structure in the Burgundian Netherlands in the 14th and 15th centuries was chiefly the result of the interaction of supply and domestic demand. Supply, in the context of a progressive infrastructure, was probably the most important factor. Obviously, export demand had not been entirely absent, as we have seen, but in those industrial sectors where the renewal was based on greater skill and on highly qualified labour, the influence of export demand was rather limited and marginal.

With the discovery of new sea routes and the far-reaching development of maritime and transcontinental trade during the 16th century, the moment had come for the new industrial structure to be absorbed

---

[49] E. Coornaert, 'Draperies rurales, draperies urbaines', in: *Revue Belge de Philologie et d'Histoire*, XXVIII (1950), pp. 59–86.
[50] Verhulst, 'La laine indigène', pp. 304–13.
[51] Cf. above.

systematically into European commercial expansion. The phase of qualitative growth, or deepening of human capital, was past, and quantitative growth – the widening of human capital – would take its place. The first step towards this was the increase in money incomes throughout Europe and, as a result, a growing demand for non-essential consumer goods. This also occurred in areas with a more primitive industrial structure, where elasticity of supply of such goods was much more limited than in the advanced regions.

The 16th century was marked by a strong expansion of intra-European trade and as well as the income elasticity, the price elasticity of export demand had risen noticeably. Hence, progressive areas which could offer better-quality products for relatively low prices naturally diverted the demand for specialized goods from more primitive areas. The Southern Netherlands, which for dynastic, commercial or historical reasons had contacts with many countries, profited from this enormously: what was produced for internal consumption during the Burgundian period gradually conquered European markets. Thus the fashion, luxury and artistic products of the Southern Netherlands developed into an important and diversified export industry. This was often at the expense of similar urban industries in more primitive areas such as the Baltic lands, Poland and Hungary.[52] The transformation of the urban luxury trade in the Netherlands into a vital export industry had valuable side-effects. It allowed important economies of scale, which meant, even within the luxury sector, some division of labour and as a result further refinements of skill: there are many well-known examples of this in connection with painting, tapestry weaving and embroidery. Moreover, greater skill allowed the introduction of specialities from Italy; for example at about this time, mirror making, crystal, glass and majolica work were well under way in the Netherlands.[53] The spinning, weaving and dyeing of silk in Bruges and more especially in Antwerp increased spectacularly in the 16th century; initially successful as an import substitute it gradually developed into an export industry in its own right.[54]

The second important support of the industrial growth of the Southern

---

[52] M. Malowist, 'L'évolution industrielle en Pologne du XIVe au XVIIe siècle', in: M. Malowist, *Croissance et régression en Europe, XIV–XVIIe siècles* (Paris: 1972), pp. 191–215; S.P. Pach, 'Favourable and Unfavourable Conditions for Capitalist Growth: The Shifts of International Trade Routes in the 15th to 17th Centuries', in: F.C. Lane (ed.), *Fourth International Congress of Economic History, Bloomington 1968* (Paris–The Hague: 1973), pp. 62–8.

[53] J.A. Goris, *Etude sur les colonies marchandes méridonales (portugais, espagnols et italiens) à Anvers de 1488 à 1567* (Louvain: 1925), pp. 429–42.

[54] A. Thijs, 'De Zijdenijverheid te Antwerpen in de zeventiende eeuw', in: *Tijdschrift voor Geschiedenis*, LXXIX (1966), pp. 386–406.

Netherlands in the 16th century was the inclusion of rural industry in European commercial expansion. I have already referred to the importance of the supply factor in the emergence of rural industry in the 14th and 15th centuries. However important this remained, the new orientation of export demand, concerned with lighter fabrics, was undoubtedly the most decisive stimulus for the strong expansion of rural industry in the 16th century. As far as linen was concerned this meant especially export to Spain *en route* for the New World.[55] The woollens of the rural 'new drapery' maintained their position reasonably well: Armentières with its *oltrafini* and Neuve-Eglise, for example, achieved good export results.[56] In addition, the production of cheaper and mixed sorts of cloth, especially in North Brabant round Weert[57] and in French Flanders, was quite successful.[58] However, the development of the 'light drapery', or serge industry round Hondschoote for export to the Mediterranean area was the most spectacular of all.[59]

In the 16th century export demand for lighter materials led to a new lease of life for serge manufacture in the old textile towns of Arras, Douai, Saint-Omer and Lille.[60] 'Light drapery' also spread in diverse forms to Tournai and Valenciennes.[61] Even Bruges, Ypres and Ghent tried at that time to introduce it again. Such developments indicate a new increase in capitalistic tendencies and a new rise of a proletariat in the towns of Flanders and Hainault. It was the first sign of changes in the production structure of the Flemish textile industry which were fully realized only in the 17th century.[62] We cannot pursue this theme, however, in the context of this article.

There is no doubt that the urban art, luxury and fashion trades, as well as rural industry, absorbed much open and hidden unemployment in the second third of the 16th century. Moreover, economies of scale and technological progress (exemplified in the powerful expansion of the printing industry in the Low Countries) ensured significant gains in *physical* productivity. However, the increase of *economic* productivity,

---

[55] E. Sabbe, *De Belgische vlasnijverheid. T.I.: De Zuidnederlandsche vlasnijverheid tot het verdrag van Utrecht, 1713* (Bruges: 1943), pp. 175–286.

[56] Munro, 'The Coming of Spanish Wools', p. 212, n. I.

[57] Van der Wee, *The Growth of the Antwerp Market* II, p. 137.

[58] H.E. de Sagher, *et al.*, *Recueil de documents relatifs a l'histoire de l'industrie drapière en Flandre. Deuxieme Partie: le Sud-Ouest de la Flandre depuis l'époque bourguignonne* (Brussels 1951–61, 2 vols); J. De Mey, 'De mislukte aanpassing van de nieuwe draperie, de saainijverheid en de lichte draperie te Ieper', in: *Tijdschrift voor Geschiedenis* LXXXIII (1970), pp. 222–35.

[59] E. Coornaert, *La Draperie-sayetterie d'Hondschoote* (Paris: 1930).

[60] Coornaert, 'Draperies rurales, draperies urbaines', *passim*.

[61] Verhulst, 'La laine indigène', p. 297.

[62] *Ibid.*, p. 295; Munro, 'The Coming of Spanish Wools'.

by further refinements of skill and especially by the increase in the skilled group of urban workers, was probably much more important. A rise of wages – greater than of prices – meant a favourable development of real income.[63]

Because so much hidden and open unemployment was absorbed, industrial expansion meant some increase in *per capita* income in spite of the simultaneous growth in population;[64] this is in vivid contrast with most other parts of Europe, where real wages went down disastrously during the 16th-century Price Revolution.[65] This outstanding achievement in terms of income development in the Netherlands is perhaps the main reason for the Emperor Charles V's reputation in popular tradition.[66]

The Eighty Years' War, partly caused by the economic emancipation of the preceding century, meant serious dislocation in the industrial development of the Southern Netherlands. In the first place the military operations had a harsh, direct effect, on rural industry. Towns more easily escaped the effects of military depredation, since the conquests were limited to an occasional, if furious, outburst by the troops. But the war had a second and much more tragic effect: it was one of the main causes of the massive emigration of tens of thousands of specially skilled workers who, for religious, psychological, or economic reasons, left the region to spread their industrial know-how over the whole of Europe.[67] However, the threat to the export industry and the emigration resulting from it had also deeper causes. The growth of national states during the 16th century leading to the triumph of state mercantilism in the 17th, undoubtedly strengthened the desire for economic independence in Europe. Import substitution for all goods, but especially for luxury articles, was one *leitmotif* in the economic policy of all European governments at the same time. The expansion of an administrative class and of a bourgeoisie of independent means in European political centres in the 17th century provided growing markets for local luxury industries. This was the death warrant for the specialized luxury industries of the Southern Netherlands.

---

[63] Van der Wee, *The Growth of the Antwerp Market* III, Graph 39.

[64] *Ibid.* I, app. 48.

[65] E.H. Phelps Brown and S.V. Hopkins, 'Wage-rates and Prices: Evidence for Population Pressure in the Sixteenth Century', in: *Economica* XXIV (1957), pp. 289–306; also 'Builders' Wage Rates, Prices and Population: Some Further Evidence', *ibid.* XXVI (1959), pp. 18–38.

[66] J. Craeybeckx, 'Aperçu sur l'histoire des impôts en Flandre et en Brabant au cours du XVIe siècle', in: *Revue du Nord*, XXIX (1947), pp. 87–108.

[67] W. Brulez, 'De diaspora der Antwerpse kooplui op het einde van de 16e eeuw', in: *Bijdragen voor de Geschiedenis der Nederlanden*, XV (1960), pp. 279–306.

12

Prices and Wages as Development Variables: A Comparison between England and the Southern Netherlands, 1400–1700[*]

The study of prices and wages has become of the highest importance in Belgium since the Second World War, due among other things to the stimulus of Verlinden and his collaborators. The great amount of information on prices, wages and rents that has been collected and published provides a basis for the study of the relationship between prices and the quantity of money available, to determine whether 'quantitative theory' is applicable to the history of prices in the Southern Netherlands during the Ancien Régime. Prices, wages and rents have also been even more useful in the study of social and economic conditions, making possible an answer to the following questions: Which factors governed the long-term movement of prices or the short-run price cycle? What was the latter's influence on rural incomes, on the incomes of commercial speculators and of urban wage-earners? Which variables governed the movement of house rents and land leases?

Belgian price historians have paid less attention to the problem of economic development. This is understandable. Modern development theories primarily rely on volume statistics of production, consumption, savings, investment, employment, population, etc., and few representative and dependable volume statistics are available for the Ancien Régime. On the other hand, price and wage statistics are copious for the latter period and can also be approached more critically and with greater precision. It may be considered therefore whether prices and wages cannot be used in the study of economic development, as a substitute for the missing

---

[*] This article is a translation of 'Prijzen en lonen als ontwikkelingsvariabelen. Een vergelijkend onderzoek tussen Engeland en de Zuidelijke Nederlanden, 1400–1700' in *Album offert à Charles Verlinden à l'occasion de ses trente ans de professorat* (Ghent: 1975) pp. 413–35. The price and wage series on which this article is based have been published in *Album Verlinden*, pp. 436–47. The author would like to thank Mr M. Grow and Mrs M. Pappas for their assistance and, particularly, Professors J.H. Munro, S. Eddie and C. Harley of the University of Toronto for their most useful comments.

volume statistics and as the basic information for the elaboration of explicative working hypotheses. The present study is an attempt to determine whether an interregional comparison of prices and wages in Brabant and Southern England for the period 1400–1700 can, by reflecting the evolution of real wages, suggest certain development variables in the preindustrial economy.

The period 1400–1700 was chosen for the following reasons: during the 15th and 16th centuries Southern England and Brabant had narrow commercial ties but different economic infrastructures, clearly less primitive in Brabant than in England. During the 17th century both regions continued to develop within the framework of a preindustrial economy, but the common factors weakened; moreover, Brabant stagnated and showed signs of regression in some sectors while England gradually evolved into a leading European economy. An investigation of the causes or mechanisms of these movements within a homogeneous technological structure could shed light on the conditions necessary for the transformation from a preindustrial to an industrial society.

Statistical Information: Heuristic and Methodological Remarks

Four studies by Phelps Brown and Hopkins published in *Economica* from 1955 to 1959 were taken as a point of departure for a comparative analysis.[1] Phelps Brown and Hopkins examined the development of prices of consumption goods in comparison with the evolution of wages in the building sector for the period 1264–1954 in Southern England, and tested their results against analogous information from France, Alsace, Munster (Westphalia), Augsburg, Vienna and Valencia. Our aim is to compare the information from Southern England with price and wage material from Brabant between 1400 and 1700.

To preserve the homogeneity of our comparative study, the method Phelps Brown and Hopkins created with the economic historians of the London School of Economics is taken as a guide. The authors used six subgroups of essential consumer goods to make up their annual price index. The choice of the essential consumer goods inside each subgroup and the probable amount of each product used per adult male person per year were based on historical budget information. The total annual cost

---

[1] E.H. Phelps Brown and S.V. Hopkins, 'Seven Centuries of Building Wages', in: *Economica*, N.S. XXII, 87 (London: August 1955), pp. 195–206; see also other articles in: *Economica*: 'Seven Centuries of the Prices of Consumables compared with Builders' Wage-Rates', XXIII, 92 (November 1956), pp. 296–314; 'Wage-rates and Prices: Evidence for Population Pressure in the Sixteenth Century', XXIV, 96 (November 1957), pp. 289–306; 'Builders' Wage-Rates, Prices and Population: some Further Evidence', XXVI, 101 (February 1959), pp. 18–38.

per subgroup was reduced each time to one index figure with the average of the stable years 1451–75 as a base period. The six partial index figures thus arrived at were combined to form one average annual global index figure, with the help of a weighting coefficient which referred to budgets of the period studied. Lord Beveridge's price lists provided the English price series between 1400 and 1700, together with as yet unpublished information from the Beveridge archives. Thorold Rogers's publications provided series of wages. Two annual budget tables and one weighting table were used for the choice of products and the weighting coefficient, as can be seen in Table 12.1.

Table 12.1: *Annual budgetary basket of essential consumer goods for an adult male, Southern England, 1200–1700.*

	1275	1500	Weighting coefficient per subgroup to calculate the annual index
1. Meal products	1¼ bushels wheat 1 bushel rye ½ bushel barley ⅔ bushel peas	1¼ bushels wheat 1 bushel rye ½ bushel barley ⅔ bushel peas	20%
2. Meat and fish	½ pig ½ sheep 40 herrings	1½ sheep 15 white herrings 25 red herrings	25%
3. Butter and cheese	10 lbs butter 10 lbs cheese	nil	12½%
4. Drink	4½ bushels malt	4½ bushels malt	22½%
5. Heating and lighting	nil	4½ bushels charcoal 2¾ lbs candles ½ pint oil	8½%
6. Textiles	3¼ yds canvas	⅔ yd canvas ½ yd shirting ⅓ yd woollen cloth	12½%

In their 1959 publication Phelps Brown and Hopkins indicated that meal products had received too low a weight in the weighting coefficients for the essential foodstuffs while drink, meat and fish had received too high a figure. Mutual changes of these coefficients for meal products and drink would have little effect on the result because both groups are based on grain prices. The observation is chiefly relevant in the case of meat and fish consumption for the period after 1700, but our study does not extend beyond that date. Moreover, budget information for the Southern Netherlands for the period 1400–1800 indicates a high meat and fish consumption.[2] We have, therefore, retained the Phelps Brown and Hopkins calculations.

On the basis of the daily summer money wage of a master-mason in Southern England, an annual money wage index figure based on the average money wage during the period 1451–75 was calculated. The annual global price index figure for basic maintenance was then put beside the annual money wage index figure, producing an annual index series which expressed the real wage income of an English master-mason in terms of a basket of essential consumer goods as described above.

For the statistics concerning prices and wages in Brabant and Antwerp published and still unpublished information from our study of Antwerp,[3] supplemented by figures published by E. Scholliers and J. Craeybeckx in the series edited by C. Verlinden and his collaborators, has been used.[4] Just as in the work of Phelps Brown and Hopkins, a budgetary basket of essential consumer goods was composed, but the availability of price series had to be taken into account for determining the articles selection. Because the budgetary difference between the Southern English tables of 1275 and 1500 was so slight, only one annual budgetary basket was composed for Brabant (Table 12.2).

There was little sense in arranging the calculations concerning the annual price index figures in Antwerp and Brabant in two stages, as Phelps Brown and Hopkins did, because the number of selected consumer goods available per subgroup was so small. Prices from Antwerp and Brabant were therefore only weighted once, by multiplying the price of each relevant product by the amount given in the annual budget. The average of the

---

[2] H. Van der Wee, 'Voeding en dieet in het *Ancien Régime*', in: *Spiegel Historiael* I (Bussum: 1966), pp. 94–101.

[3] H. Van der Wee, *The Growth of the Antwerp Market and the European Economy (Fourteenth–Sixteenth Centuries)* I (Paris–The Hague: 1963), pp. 173–8 (rye in Antwerp), pp. 189–93 (barley in Antwerp), pp. 210–6 (butter in Brussels), pp. 217–24 (cheese in Antwerp), pp. 225–7 (salt beef in Mechlin), pp. 249–53 (tallow candles in West Brabant), pp. 254–6 (charcoal in Antwerp), pp. 269–72 (Weerts' grey cloth in Antwerp), pp. 273–6 (sail cloth in Mechlin), pp. 277–86 (dried herring in Mechlin), pp. 336–49 and pp. 457–63 (summer daily wage of master mason in Antwerp). This information was supplemented with non-published figures from the same sources. For grain and cloth prices in the 17th century, non-published accounts from charitable and ecclesiastical institutions in Brussels and Antwerp and the official urban list of grain prices in Brussels, were used.

[4] Ch. Verlinden, J. Craeybeckx, E. Scholliers and others, *Dokumenten voor de geschiedenis van prijzen en lonen in Vlaanderen en Brabant (XVe–XVIIIe eeuw)*, (Bruges: 1959–73) 4 vols, I, pp. 501–3 (barley in Brussels); II (19), pp. 692–712 (meat in Antwerp), pp. 726–37 (herring in Antwerp), pp. 712–21 (butter in Antwerp), pp. 723–5 (cheese in Antwerp), pp. 843–5 (flax in Antwerp), pp. 977–1056 (wages in Antwerp), pp. 92–135 and pp. 360–461 (wages in Bruges and Ghent for comparison).

stable years 1451–75 again served as a base period. The calculation of the annual money wage index figures was based on the daily summer wage of a master-mason in Antwerp and used the same 1451–75 base period. The two index series were compared in the same way as those for Southern England. Both the annual money wage index series (Figure 12.2) and the annual price index series (Figure 12.1) and their mutual comparison were expressed in graphs in a semi-logarithmic scale. Moreover, the price trend was calculated by interquartile moving averages over thirteen years, which are also expressed on the graphs.

Table 12.2: *Annual budgetary basket of essential consumer goods for an adult male, Brabant, 1400–1700.*

Essential consumer goods	Annual budget per person	Daily budget per person
1. Meal products	rye: 126 litres	0.345 litres
2. Drink	barley: 162 litres	0.444 litres
3. Meat and fish	beef: 23.5 kg (salted)	0.065 kg
	herrings: 40	0.11
4. Butter and cheese	butter: 4.8 kg	0.013 kg
	cheese: 4.7 kg	0.013 kg
5. Heating and lighting	charcoal: 162 litres	0.444 litres
	tallow candles: 1⅓ kg	0.004 kg
6. Textiles	woollens from Weert, etc. 1.125 metres	0.003 metres
	linen: 1.80 metres [5]	0.005 metres

Complete price series existed for most of the consumer goods selected. The occasional gaps were filled by indirect information. Such interpolations have been given in brackets in the published series. For budget groups one and two, the principal ingredients of the end products such as bread and beer were included rather than the end products themselves. In periods of falling price trends and of wage inertia, such calculations based on ingredients distort the increase in purchasing power in an upward direction, while in periods of rising prices and slower wage increases they overaccentuate the decrease of purchasing power. On the other hand,

---

[5] Because there was no continuous series for linen, it was replaced by coarse linen sail cloth. Because this has about half the value, the annual amount of 1.80 m. linen was replaced by 3.60 m. sail cloth.

228   THE LOW COUNTRIES IN THE EARLY MODERN WORLD

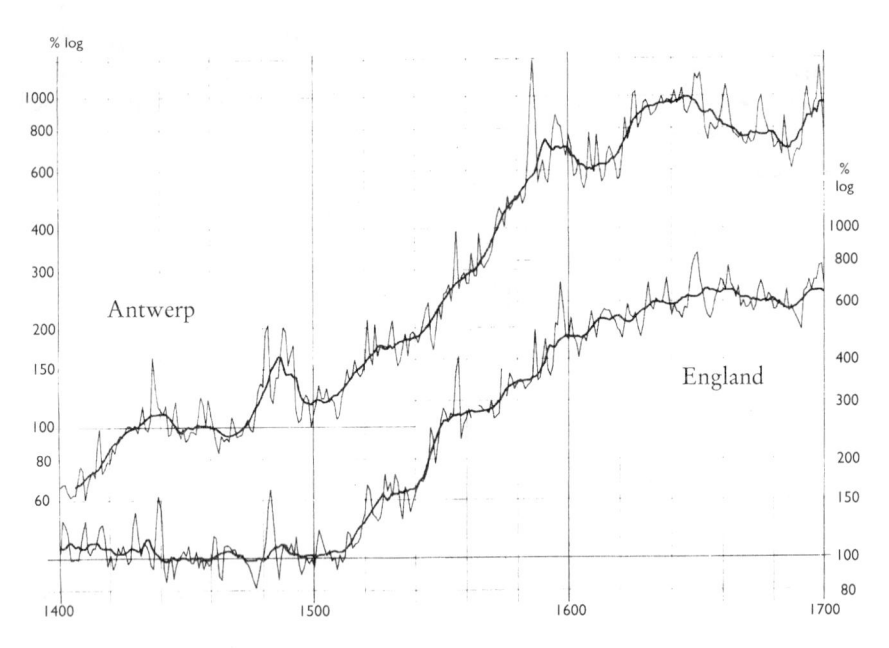

Figure 12.1: *Weighted nominal price index of a packet of essential consumer goods in West Brabant and Southern England, 1400–1700: annual indexes and moving interquartile medians per 13 years (semi-logarithmic scale).*

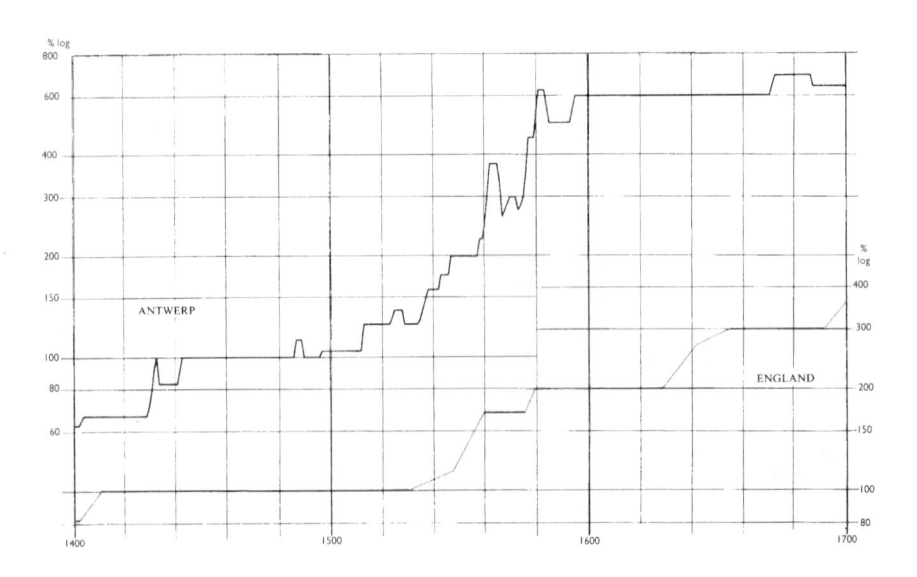

Figure 12.2: *Nominal daily wage index of a master-mason in Antwerp and Southern England, 1400–1700 (semi-logarithmic scale).*

the wage index series does not take employment into account. This is unfortunate, because employment was not static throughout and because there were differences in the situation in Brabant and Southern England. An employment index for Brabant in the building sector is available,[6] but for England there is no such information. To retain a homogeneous study the Brabant information was not included in the calculations, but was used for the interpretation of the figures. In any event, the differences are not, globally speaking, large enough to distort the main conclusions.

The choice of the price and wage information from Antwerp–Brabant and in particular the selection of building wages must also be justified. In the first place the price series from Antwerp and Brabant are the most complete and homogeneous available for the period in Brabant. They are also representative of the western urban region of the duchy, a region which from about 1400 showed a marked tendency towards market unity. On the other hand, Antwerp building money wages represent more exclusively the wage sector of the town itself. They reflect, for the 15th and 16th centuries, the economic rise of the trading metropolis of Brabant, and, because of the building multiplier in Antwerp, they even tend to exaggerate it too much. The relationship was reversed in the following century of commercial decline. Various sectors, such as printing, weaving, etc., defended themselves much better in Antwerp than the building sector, and therefore enjoyed a more favourable money wage development – in other words, the figures for building wages in Antwerp in the 17th century tend to understate global money wage development.

Comparisons between money wages in Antwerp and the other towns of Brabant tend to favour Antwerp as far as rate is concerned, but certain costs, like house rents, were markedly higher there too. Antwerp did not always have the highest rate of increase; Brussels' linen weavers' money wages, for example, as well as rural money wages around Lier and even some building money wages outside Antwerp, rose more quickly between 1480 and 1650 then did masons' money wages in Antwerp. Generally, therefore, information about money wages in Antwerp was sufficiently representative for all Western Brabant.

Finally, on a separate graph, the trend of rye prices in Antwerp is compared with the price of building materials and building money wages, with the price of textiles and textile money wages, and with rents and rural money wages (Figure 12.4). For the method of calculation, see our study of Antwerp.[7]

---

[6] Van der Wee, *Growth of the Antwerp Market* I, appendix 48, pp. 539–44.
[7] This graph is no. 53 in Van der Wee, *Growth of the Antwerp Market*.

Analysis of the Statistical Results

The curves for the 15th, 16th and early 17th centuries are analysed together, because they can be treated as a single cycle of intersecular development. The comparison of the trend of the nominal prices for a basket of essential consumer goods in Southern England and in Brabant between 1400 and 1650 (Figure 12.1) reveals – in spite of a fundamental analogy in their intersecular movement – substantial mutual differences, especially in connection with the interdecennial situation. In contrast to Brabant the trend in Southern England is very continuous and clear: slowly falling prices moving into stagnation from 1400 to 1510; regularly rising prices between 1510 and 1610 (except the noticeable quickening during the Great Debasement period in the 1540s and early 1550s) and a weakening of price rises between 1610 and 1650. When the English price series are divided between groups of goods, the general picture of the different price categories remains the same, although prices for essential foods fall more quickly between 1400 and 1510 than prices of non-essential agricultural produce and industrial goods; on the other hand essential food prices rose during the following Price Revolution more quickly than the two other groups of goods.[8] Finally, English daily money wages rose at the beginning of the 15th century and remained at a high level in spite of the falling and stagnant price trend until 1510 (Figure 12.2). In other words, the purchasing power of wages increased and retained its position well in relation to a basket of essential consumer goods in England throughout the 15th century (Figure 12.3). During the 16th century, on the other hand, the situation was reversed: English daily money wages failed to keep up with price rises and did so only with a marked difference in timing (Figure 12.2) so that the purchasing power of wages collapsed in an alarming manner, until by the first quarter of the 17th century it had fallen to less than 40% of its 15th century level (Figure 12.3).

The evolution of population in England coincided closely with this price-wage movement. Demographic stagnation followed the sharp fall in population caused by the Black Death of the mid-14th century, while a slow recovery took place in the second half of the 15th century; the recovery widened into a strong growth in population during the 16th century with saturation about 1600.[9] A Malthusian macro-interpretation is obvious: a relative abundance of land and a relative scarcity of labour

---

[8] F. Simiand, *Recherches anciennes et nouvelles sur le mouvement des prix du XVe au XIXe siècle* (Paris: 1932); I. Hammarström, 'The Price Revolution of the Sixteenth Century: some Swedish Evidence', in: P.H. Ramsey (ed.), *The Price Revolution in Sixteenth Century England* (London: 1971), pp. 63–5.

[9] M. Reinhard, A. Armengaud and J. Dupaquier, *Histoire générale de la population mondiale* (Paris: 1968), pp. 98, 100–1, 118.

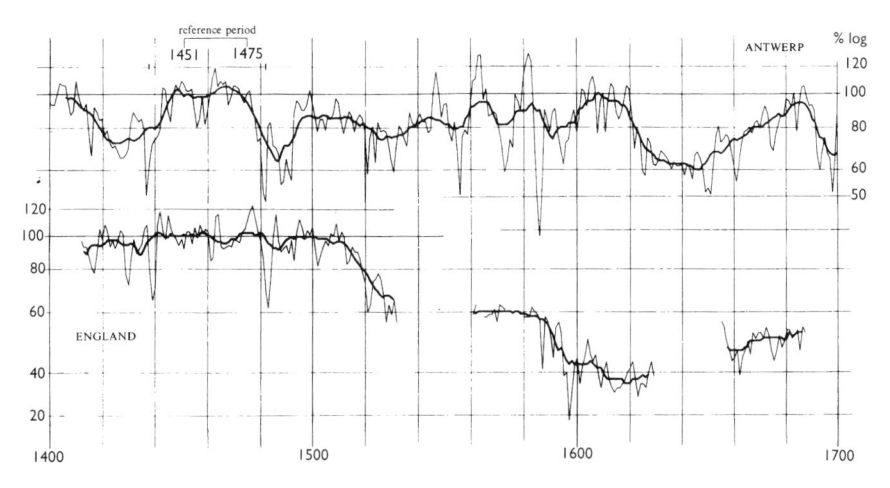

Figure 12.3: *Index of the purchasing power of the annual wage of a master-mason expressed in a packet of essential consumer goods in West Brabant and Southern England 1400–1700: annual indexes and moving interquartile medians per 13 years (semi-logarithmic scale).*

explain the development of prices, money wages and purchasing power during the 15th century, while the relative abundance of labour and consequent increasing scarcity of land can be seen as decisive factors in the development of the following period. The *strategic variable* was, therefore, population, and quantity of money, debasements, investment, etc. were only secondary factors.[10]

The trend in Brabant of prices, money wages and purchasing power was obviously less continuous. Population development remained an important variable in explaining price, money wage, and purchasing power movements in the long term, but other variables were also active both in deciding the secular movement and in the interdecennial cycles. Moreover, it is useful to include the graphs of nominal prices (Figures 12.2 and 12.3) and those transposed into precious metals equivalents (Figure 12.4) in the Brabant analysis. In Figure 12.1 the 15th century trend can be seen as a hesitating preamble to the price rises of the 16th, although declines after 1438 and 1495 are undeniable. In Figure 12.4 the trend in silver equivalent prices can be seen to rise in the 15th century until the crisis of 1437–38; thereafter the drop is more obvious than in the graphs of nominal prices.

---

[10] See in this connection M.J. Elsas, *Umriss einer Geschichte der Preise und Löhne in Deutschland vom ausgehenden Mittalalter bis zum Beginn des neunzehnten Jahrhunderts* (Leyden: 1936–49); M. Postan, 'The Trade of Medieval Europe: the North', in: M. Postan and E.E. Rich (eds), *The Cambridge Economic History of Europe* II (Cambridge, 1952), pp. 119–256; W. Abel, *Agrarkrisen und Agrarkonjunktur* (Hamburg: 1966).

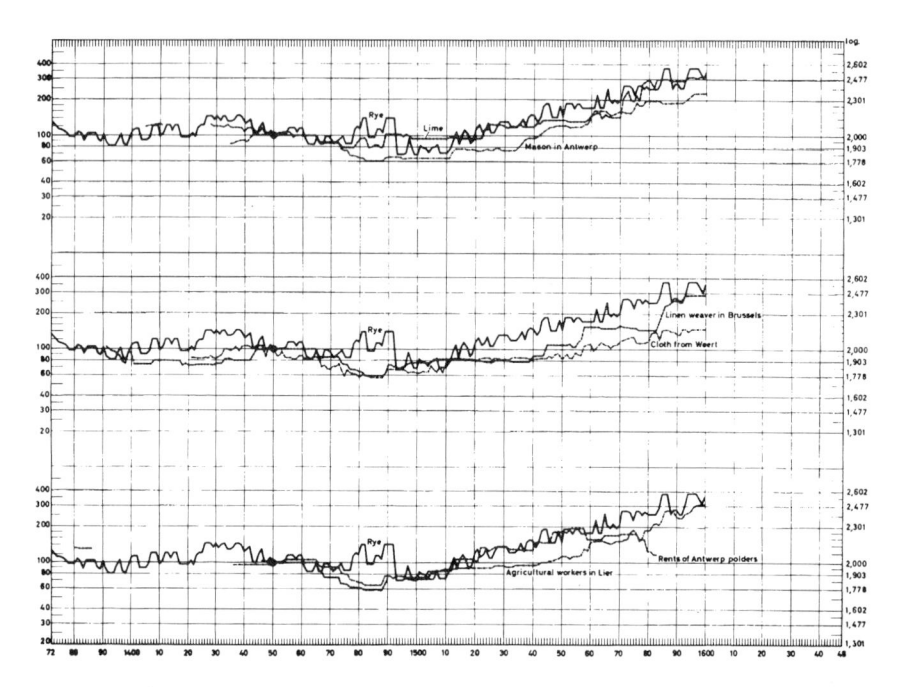

Figure 12.4: *Trends in rye, lime, textile prices and agricultural rents in West Brabant, masons' daily wages in Antwerp, linen weavers' piece wages in Brussels, and rural piece wages from around Lier, 1372–1600 (silver equivalents, transposed logarithmically) (calculation of the trend by Meuvret's option method on moving 13 yearly averages).*

The demographic factor cannot be ignored for Brabant. Probably influenced by still flourishing industry and trade in the larger and smaller towns of the duchy, the population of Brabant increased in the late 14th–early 15th centuries, but it stagnated after the famine of 1437–38, and diminished quite impressively during the last third of the 15th century.[11] The increase in nominal and real prices until 1437–38 (Figures 12.1 and 12.4) and the fall in purchasing power of wage-earners' incomes during the first quarter of the 15th century (Figure 12.3) agrees with this. The price stagnation after 1437–38 and price declines after 1495 (Figures 12.1 and 12.4), as well as favourable purchasing power between 1440 and 1480 (Figure 12.3), can also be generally reconciled with a demographic interpretation. But the sharp rises of nominal and real prices at the beginning of the 15th century and during the 1480s were also closely

---

[11] J. Cuvelier, *Les dénombrements de foyers en Brabant (XIVe–XVIe siècles)* (Brussels: 1912). For statistical adaptation see H. Van der Wee, *Growth of the Antwerp Market* I, appendix 49, pp. 545–8.

connected with money policies and their psychological implications: in other words, with the debasements of the Brabant groat from 1.02 to 0.54 g. fine silver between 1400 and 1435 and with the heavy debasements under Maximilian of Austria when the Brabant groat fell from 0.35 to 0.16 g. fine silver between 1480 and 1489.[12]

The demographic interpretation, however, does not explain the sharp rise in money wages during the first third of the 15th century, a period of marked population growth (Figure 12.2). This deviation must be considered in the special context of the economy of the Low Countries in comparison with the rest of Europe north of the Alps. While the 14th and 15th centuries saw demographic stagnation and economic malaise throughout Europe, urban Brabant, although not immune, had sufficient power to resist.

Although the price trend was clearly influenced by the unfavourable European situation, it nevertheless showed a tendency to rise. In addition, a more dynamic development of money wages took place, although still not sufficient to maintain the purchasing power of workmen's money wages at a high level throughout the whole century. From this point of view, an institutional factor seems in Brabant to be the strategic independent variable, while the population factor is reduced to the position of a secondary explaining variable (see below).

During the 16th century Brabant's exceptional economic position became still more pronounced. To be sure, the important population increase until the Revolt ran parallel, as in the rest of Europe, with the rise in prices and in land rents during the second and third quarter of the 16th century. Moreover, Brabant prices for essential foodstuffs also increased faster than those for non-essential foodstuffs and industrial goods (Figures 12.1 and 12.4). Nevertheless, population cannot be considered the determining variable in explaining the sharp increase of nominal wages and the gradual improvement of purchasing power of the wage-earner's income during the same period (Figures 12.2 and 12.3).

During the early Revolt, it is even more difficult to use the population variable as the decisive explicatory factor. Although the population increase obviously diminished and soon turned into a drastic decrease depressing demand, prices still rose considerably. The demographic decrease had a braking effect on prices only near the end of the century, especially during the reconquest of the Southern Netherlands by Farnese and during the Twelve Year Truce (1609–21), but the Price Revolution continued unabated when war began again in 1621.[13]

---

[12] *Ibid.*, pp. 127–8.
[13] There was even a slow demographic improvement after the brutal decrease of the 1570s and 1580s caused by the war, plundering of the country areas, emigration and the great famine

After the Eighty Years' War and the English Civil War, the relationship between population, economy and price–wage movements, as far as those factors can be compared in Southern England and Brabant, reversed itself. In England, where the population rose until the second half of the 17th century and did not fall seriously afterwards,[14] prices started to stagnate, money wage rises occurred, and the purchasing power of the working man's income began to improve. In Brabant, on the other hand, population, even when regaining its losses, stagnated again after the 1660s, while prices, except during the war years around 1700, tended to fall, with money wages holding their own, i.e., with a favourable effect on the purchasing power of the wage-earners. As far as the 17th century is concerned, the Malthusian interpretation, which stresses population as the strategic variable, can thus be better applied to the development of Brabant than to the English situation. Brabant seemed to be integrated into the less developed European agricultural economy, while England moved forward to develop a modern economy.

From Economic Interpretation to Working Hypothesis

To transform the conclusions reached above into a unifying working hypothesis, the dual economic structure of preindustrial Europe must be accepted as a basic assumption: certain regions, like Northern Italy and Flanders–Brabant, already then possessed a very modern money economy in contrast with most other European areas which still had a primitive agrarian economy. The degree of urbanization can be taken as the main criterion of distinction between the regions. In Flanders–Brabant, for example, urban population already comprised 35 to 40% of the total in the 15th and 16th centuries, while in less developed areas the urban sector fluctuated around 5% and only reached 10% very rarely. The less developed areas were, moreover, dominated by autarkic agriculture and only gradually experienced the expansion of urban money and credit in contrast to more modern zones, where agriculture was closely connected with the urban money economies both geographically and sectorially.

Fifteenth and 16th century trends of prices and real wages suggest that Southern England was obviously still one of the less developed regions. Such a conclusion coincides with those of Phelps Brown and Hopkins, who showed clear analogies between Southern England and France, Alsace,

---

of 1586–7; but this was initially on a lower level than before the Revolt and only gathered momentum during the second quarter of the century; P. Klep, 'Urbanization in a Pre-industrial Economy. The Case of Brabant, 1374–1930', in: *Belgisch tijdschrift voor nieuwste geschiedenis* VII (1976), pp. 1–2, 153–68.

[14] Reinhard, Armengaud and Dupaquier, *Histoire générale*, pp. 169–70.

Northwestern Germany, Austria and Spain.[15] The English 15th- and 16th-century experience can therefore be considered as typical for less developed European economies, dominated by primitive agriculture. Brabant, on the other hand, can be considered a European centre of more highly developed, already largely urban, money economies.

As indicated above, the population factor, with its own internal dynamics, serves as the *strategic* variable in explaining the intersecular development of the primitive European economy. Because of the demographic relapse of the 14th and 15th centuries (itself a complex result of the tendency towards relative overpopulation during preceding centuries), subsequent increasing labour productivity led both to higher or stable wages for labourers and to falling prices for essential foodstuffs, so that real *per capita* incomes (employment prospects considered as remaining constant), increased substantially in the urban and rural wage sector. In the towns, favourable wage development was vigorously supported by increased corporatism and the expansion of craft guilds.

On the other hand, the new relationship between population and acreage (i.e., the changed land–labour ratio) and the rise in marginal labour productivity which resulted from it, did not automatically lead to a speedy recovery of agricultural incomes for various reasons. Falling productivity of cultivated land caused by the catastrophic character of the depopulation, offset the rising labour productivity in the agricultural sector. For big landowners, higher wages also meant higher costs for the domains they themselves exploited while cheaper land lease implied that they received lower incomes from their tenants. For independent farmers, falling agricultural prices meant a lower monetary return from their own acres. Another reason for the decline in income of the landowners and independent farmers was rigidity: productivity gains which might have occurred from a shift to lands of better quality or from a consolidation of parcels into larger units failed to materialize, due to the built-in rigidity and immobilism which characterized primitive, self-sufficient agriculture.

The falling prices for agricultural produce meant as we have seen substantial market losses for landowners. Since social relations in the agricultural economy still depended to some extent on seigneurial relationships even when land was leased to tenants, allowing the landowners to retain some authority over the farmers and tenants, the former tried to compensate for the threat to their profits by making new claims on the latter. In other words, while the increase in marginal labour productivity meant, in principle, higher incomes for farmers and tenants, there were nevertheless attempts by the landlords to skim off some of that income

---

[15] Phelps Brown and Hopkins, 'Wage-Rates and Prices', pp. 291–9; also 'Builders' wage-rates', pp. 18–29.

by introducing new feudal duties or imposing new feudal charges. When the landlords succeeded, which they often did, the richer groups (which as landowners should have suffered most from falling rents) were not the worst off and were not forced to use their savings for consumption but instead could maintain their established habits of saving. On balance the new transfers of income meant a continuing impoverishment of the mass of farmers and tenants whose loss of income was not compensated by an increased inflow of money from the rich landowners into the urban and rural wage sector and then back to the agricultural producers. Although the favourable development of urban and rural wages included the possibility of creating potential inflow of money into the urban economy, both income sectors were in fact too narrow in the less developed areas of Europe to allow a sufficiently dynamic demand effect.

Finally, the political factor must not be forgotten. Europe's demographic decline in the 14th and 15th centuries, by drastically reducing fiscal income, severely threatened the maintenance of the administrative structure of the state. Many European rulers sought recourse in war believing that territorial expansion would help compensate for the loss in revenues. The net result was usually disastrous: conflicts dragged on for years and were accompanied by the endless plundering of the countryside, higher taxes, increasing misery for the peasantry, and growing rural depopulation. Many peasant revolts were provoked by fiscal regulations imposed by the rulers during war or as a result of the landlords' abuses of power described above.

The population factor and the other variables connected with it were strong enough to ensure an extended stagnation of European development in the 14th and 15th centuries; therefore the normal internal dynamic for re-establishing income equilibrium through a better land–labour ratio could not easily work. In England, moreover, particular factors in the economic structure meant that efforts to cope with the threat to farmers' and landowners' incomes took a specific direction. The slower decline in wool and meat prices in comparison with grain prices prompted landowners to enclose their land and turn it into pastures to breed more sheep. The unemployment and loss in income that resulted for the rural population was compensated, to some extent, by the creation of an English cloth industry based on rural labour. The growth of the cloth industry in the countryside was therefore an important factor in the revival of English agriculture beginning in the second half of the 15th century.

Stagnation in the rest of Europe seemed to end at about the same moment: the gap between the relative factor prices seemed to have assumed such proportions that the obstacles started to yield to the forces of adjustment. The rising marginal labour productivity also led to higher incomes of farmers and tenants, creating a stimulus to demographic revival, which initially meant increasing returns in European agricultural produce. Agricultural renewal, strengthened by special exogenous commercial factors, led to the powerful expansion of the 16th century. Unavoidably, this cumulative development eventually passed its peak; in the course of the 16th century the threat of relative overpopulation again appeared in many parts of Western Europe, with relative factor proportions evolving towards relative land shortage and an excess of labour. Land rents rose while marginal labour productivity gradually edged toward zero as a result of relative overpopulation.

The effect on wage incomes in the more primitive economies was particularly negative. The corporate structure in the towns was not yet strong enough to push wages above prices. There was a painful fall in the purchasing power of *per capita* wage income. On the other hand, the outflow of money that financed the urban purchases of the more expensive foodstuffs only partially returned to the towns in the form of purchases of urban manufactured goods and services by the rural population. In the less developed parts of Europe, considerable delays occurred owing to traditions of autarky and hoarding among rural people. In addition, the great landowners tended to display an increasing marginal propensity to save and/or orientate their consumption towards the importation of luxury articles from the more highly developed areas of Europe and towards the importation of exotic products. In Eastern and Central Europe these circumstances led to an obvious weakening of the urban economy in the course of the 16th century.[16]

In the agricultural sector of the primitive economies the purchasing power of money wages slipped speedily back for the same reasons. On the contrary, independent farmers and to a greater extent, landowners had sufficient reserves to sell at the best moment, and profited from the increase in land rents; tenants were also favoured by quickly rising prices for foodstuffs, in so far as these benefits were not reduced by higher leases or taxes paid to the owners. Generally it can be stated that the profit from rising land rents led to a greater concentration of incomes when the agricultural economy was more primitive as in Eastern and Central Europe. Alternatively, the more modernized the agriculture as in Western Europe, the wider the benefits of a higher land rent were spread over the rural population. In England, where traditional rural industry was essentially aimed at export, falling wage costs were an extra impetus to export, so that merchant-entrepreneurs felt no need to adapt their production and accordingly made few creative changes in rural industry.

The region of Flanders and Brabant, as a nucleus of economic growth in Northwestern Europe, developed differently. The strategic variable in

---

[16] Communicated to me by Professor Z.P. Pach for which I thank him very much.

this case was less the population than an institutional factor generating a more dynamic macro-behaviour in economic affairs. The more progressive institutional environment indeed created a most powerful stimulus for creative change and structural progress in response to the threat that future income levels would not meet expectations based on past favourable results.

The continuing importance of urban trade and industry in Brabant throughout the 14th and early 15th centuries ensured permanent possibilities for emigration from the country; it was an additional element in weakening the landlords' authority over the farmers, who were not exposed to the pressure of new feudal taxes or duties, and also helped perpetuate a very intense movement of money between agriculture, industry and the tertiary sector. Because of these special circumstances surrounding agricultural incomes, the population in Brabant grew until 1437–38 and even maintained a high level during the second third of the 15th century. Acreage therefore remained relatively scarce and there was plenty of labour in contrast with the situation in the less developed parts of Europe, where the relative factor prices were evolving in the opposite direction.

The wage-earners of Brabant should, in such circumstances, have been victimized by their great numbers. Workers' real income should normally, under the influence of the factor prices, have evolved negatively; and indeed, for precisely this reason the curve of the purchasing power of the workers' *per capita* income in Brabant in the 15th century (Figure 12.1) shows a greater nervousness than in England. But on the whole, the impression concerning the real wage situation in Brabant is quite favourable throughout the 15th century; in spite of the unfavourable land–labour ratio, real incomes of wage-earners in Brabant reached a high level.[17]

The crucial impact of the institutional factor must, therefore, be stressed. The broad artisanal sector, particularly in the towns of Brabant, felt itself threatened as far as future income was concerned. Because of the happy income experience before, the artisans fell back on the now strongly rooted corporatism in Brabant in order to insist successfully on higher wages. At the same time, the Brabant towns began to build up a new industrial structure principally aimed at a diversification of production, at the improvement of skills, at an increase in the economic productivity of labour and resources (which meant more value for the same physical

---

[17] Some would explain this particular situation by an exogenous circumstance: the decline in foodstuff prices in Europe undoubtedly also slowed down prices in the Low Countries and, by so doing, indirectly pushed up real wage incomes in Brabant. On the other hand, such a positive influence could be counteracted by the negative effect of low world prices for industrial products on artisans' incomes in the Brabant towns as far as their products were sold on the markets.

use of labour and raw materials), and at a reorientation from external to internal markets. This institutional factor was particularly important during the 15th century in saving real wage incomes in advanced areas such as Brabant, carrying the whole economy forward in its wake.

Agriculture in Brabant developed in a similar way. Because of a continuing high population density, land remained relatively scarce and labour relatively plentiful, once again in contrast with the rest of Europe. Agricultural prices in Brabant were not proof against the fall or stagnation of European prices and reflected them even if incompletely and with important gaps. Excessive splitting up of acreage and the pressure of slackening food prices, in time, had serious consequences for rural incomes, which could not be compensated by the continuous flow of money between town and country. On the other hand, in more advanced agricultural areas like Brabant, the authority of the landlords was no longer strong enough to recuperate losses in income at the expense of dependent farmers, thus leaving some incentive for initiative in the small peasantry. In these circumstances the institutional factor also became crucial in the agricultural sector: the threat to the farmers' income generated a powerful creative impulse towards technical innovation by intensifying farming and introducing rural industry. The renewal was slow because the rural sector was more rigid than the urban and because taxation and war had considerable influence in the last third of the 15th century. But it was clearly present during the whole century.

Sixteenth century development in urban and rural Brabant followed the same pattern of the previous century, yet it was much more intense. The marked increase of population accentuated still more the shortage of land and the relative abundance of labour. The threat to real wage incomes was again very strong, but in contrast to trends in less developed parts of Europe, this threat was overcome by very substantial nominal wage increases. The successful action by urban wage-earners showed group consciousness, but was also helped by the powerful guild structure and favoured by the growing export demand. It meant that the modern character of the economic structure and of the institutional environment was most responsible for the successful artisan. The time-lag of world prices for industrial products behind grain price increases certainly affected prices in Brabant and therefore became a new threat to wage evolution there. But in an ambitious economy such as that of Brabant this new difficulty only acted as a stimulus for creative innovation, for a further astonishing development of physical and economic productivity in the newly developed artisanal sectors. The continuing flowering of specialized urban industry throughout the critical years of the Revolt is a striking proof of this.

The situation in agriculture was the same. The rising trend in the economic rent on land favoured a large section of the rural population because the extensive parcelling of land in developed areas like Brabant implied a widespread fragmentation of private property resulting in a distribution of the increasing returns on land over a very large number of small independent farmers. Important flows in money between town and country also continued. On the other hand, the threat to the farmers' income, because of the danger of diminishing returns when private exploitation became too small, was compensated by the introduction of new techniques of intensive husbandry, by the quick growth of rural industry, and by important wage increases, similar to those in the towns and in spite of the relative abundance of labour in the countryside. This creativity helped the rural sector, similar to the urban sector in Brabant, to withstand the storms of the Price Revolution and the Revolt.

From 1600 onwards the situation was entirely different. Brabant had deteriorated into one of the less developed areas, while England began to assume a more advanced position. Population gradually became the strategic variable in Brabant: the drastic reductions in population caused by the first years of war and emigration resulted in relatively too much land and too few workers. The result was a rise in the real *per capita* wage income from 1587 onwards. The vigorous demographic revival during and after the Twelve Years' Truce resulted in a spectacular fall of the real *per capita* wage income during the second quarter of the 17th century. Demographic stagnation and even decline from the 1660s onwards reversed the trend until the new exceptional conditions of war at the end of the century disturbed the process once again.

The Eighty Years' War was clearly an important factor in the structural decline of the economy in Brabant: it gradually stifled the possibility of further creativity, particularly in the countryside but also in the towns. Yet it would be a mistake to identify the war as the sole explanatory variable in the economic decay of Brabant. In the first place the Revolt was itself the result of the economic, social, intellectual and religious emancipation of the inhabitants of the Low Countries during the preceding decades; moreover, a second factor was the growing mercantile policy of the European nation states, who considered import substitution a necessary condition for national economic progress and therefore stimulated the production of luxury or semi-luxury goods within their own borders. Finally, within the artisanal structure of existing specialized industries, the potential for further technical innovation and diversification was bound to become increasingly limited. Hence the much higher wages in Brabant in comparison with the rest of Europe gradually failed to be justified by continuing industrial progress and turned into a cost disadvantage for the region.

In England, on the other hand, falling real wage rates in the 16th century had long helped the export of traditional textiles. At the beginning of the

17th century, however, the wage cost factor as a result of relative abundance of labour could no longer be exploited, the subsistence level being reached. Gradually the institutional factor emerged and became the most important. First, the threat of industrial decline provided the stimulus necessary for a structural renewal of export industry. Helped by emigrants from the Southern Netherlands and the commercial–maritime expansion of the 17th century, England developed an industrial growth dynamic, which allowed her to combine a high level of population, in other words a relative labour surplus, with a growth in the purchasing power of wage-earners' incomes (Figure 12.3). Meanwhile it may not be forgotten that 17th century commercial–maritime expansion was nourished largely by the surplus values that originated in industry. The very low 16th-century wage level opened wide prospects of extra profits for those entrepreneurs who succeeded in developing and launching new products. Even when nominal and real wages rose, this favourable situation continued because the new products still contained a vast potential for increasing returns. This was the beginning of England's move into a modern economy.

Conclusion

Our proposed working hypothesis is an abstract framework derived from the historical facts. Yet the synthesis might be somewhat too general for adequate empirical testing. Carving out several subhypotheses and testing them in turn seems to be the most promising avenue. This however is clearly beyond the scope of the present study. Our main purpose was to demonstrate that descriptive statistics derived from price and wage series are useful building blocks for a tentative theory.

VI

SOCIAL HISTORY

13

Typology of Crises and Structural Changes in the Netherlands, 15th to 16th Century[1]

The study of crises in Western Europe before the Industrial Revolution can be substantially furthered through the use of quantitative data. Labrousse has been the leading innovator in this domain, working within the broad framework of 18th-century France.[2] Notably, he has been able to shed light on crises of 'the older type' characterized, in contrast to the crises of the end of the 19th century or those of the 20th century, by a negative correlation between price movements on the grain markets and those in other sectors of the economy.

The goal of the present article is to extend this sort of study by applying it to the 15th and 16th centuries. This will lead to a typological study sensitive to the finer nuances. In its course we must not lose sight of the commercial and industrial precocity of that part of Western Europe made up of the old Netherlands. Further, the statistical treatment of the data brings to light a clear division into three periods: the Burgundian era,[3] the period of Antwerp's great expansion,[4] and finally the time of the Revolt against Spain.[5] The political and economic circumstances successively dominating each of these phases differ significantly: within

---

[1] We wish to extend warm thanks to Professors F. Braudel, J. Meuvret and J.A. Van Houtte for their helpful critical remarks.

[2] E. Labrousse, *Esquisse du mouvement des prix et des revenus en France au XVIIIe siècle* (Paris: 1933); and *La crise de l'économie française à la fin de l'Ancien Régime et au début de la Révolution* (Paris: 1944). We have adopted Labrousse's terminology in order to simplify our explanation. But we wish to warn the reader that the crises of the 15th and 16th centuries are more frequent and fortuitous, but non-continuous, ups and downs than mathematically regular or circularly determined cycles.

[3] We have examined all the major famines between 1403 and 1486. We have not included the 1489 famine because it was entirely dominated by the monetary panic of the day.

[4] All the famines between 1495 and 1564.

[5] All the famines between 1565 and 1599.

a framework of fundamental unity these pronounced and characteristic differences emerge distinctly.

Some Preliminary Remarks on Statistics[6]

Historians of the crises of the Ancien Régime have hitherto studied each crisis separately, that is to say in their specific (even anecdotal) manifestations. In order to find more universal characteristics and to reach more general conclusions – at least within the limits stated above – we have attempted to reduce the quantitative evolution of the crises in the Netherlands during the 15th and 16th centuries to a single, typical evolution.

Both qualitative and quantitative data make it immediately apparent that in the 15th and 16th centuries, just as in the two preceding centuries, famine was the motive force of crisis. This served as our point of departure and immediately led us to adopt the harvest year (from 1 August to 31 July) as the chronological unit for our whole series.

Moreover, the experience of contemporaries remains an important criterion in the statistical treatment. That is why we have retained the nominal monetary value of wages and prices in our calculations, that is to say we have not converted them to their equivalents in gold or silver.[7] For the same reason the cyclical evolution has been presented in percentages, the annual figures being calculated against the medians of prices over the preceding five years.[8] This method gives us a good picture of the brutal and violent reality of the crises, as experienced by people at the time.

Taking famine as the decisive element in the crisis, it is not difficult to determine, from a chronological point of view, the most dramatic year and, indeed, the entire framework of each crisis. For the whole series of prices and wages the year of maximal rise in grain prices and the surrounding years have been taken as the chronological framework. We have thus been able to calculate an unweighted arithmetical mean of the cyclical movements of each series of prices for various products or revenues during a specific period.[9] Naturally, the choice of statistical data

---

[6] For a more detailed analysis we refer to the methodological chapters of our study, *The Growth of the Antwerp Market and the European Economy (Fourteenth-Sixteenth Centuries)* I (Paris–The Hague: 1963).

[7] See also R. Baehrel, *Une croissance: la Basse-Provence rurale (fin du XVIe siècle–1789)* (Paris: 1961), pp. 2–20.

[8] See also J. Meuvret, 'Les crises de subsistences et la démographie de la France d'Ancien Régime', in: *Population*, 4 (1946), pp. 643–99.

[9] For more information on this subject see the methodological remarks of A.D. Gayer, W.W. Rostow, A.J. Schwartz, *The Growth and Fluctuation of the British Economy, 1790–1850. An Historical, Statistical and Theoretical Study of Britain's Economic Development* (Oxford: 1953), pp. 531 ff.

remains relatively limited. Only information on prices and wages is relatively abundant. These are always the prices found on the markets of the urban zone of Western Brabant (Antwerp, Brussels, Mechlin, Lier). The data on wages come from the same region. A certain number of reliable statistics were also available, if more sporadically, concerning commerce and production, as well as financial series. We have of course based our study only on those series sufficiently continuous to be trustworthy and capable of fairly representing the development of the markets.

The Burgundian Period (15th century): Misery or Prosperity?

The extreme violence of the cyclical amplitude of grain prices, in comparison with other series of prices, wages and revenues, clearly reveals the crucial importance of grain prices in Brabant's crises. Hence it is essential to examine this sector first. A first question: do the cyclical oscillations lead to displacement of the demand for certain varieties of grain or not? A comparison between the graphs for wheat, rye, barley and oats can shed some light on this point. Rye was unquestionably the leading product during the whole of the 15th and 16th centuries, the intensity of its cyclical variation being always the greatest (see Figure 13.1). Thus the reinforcement of this intensity as we descend from a richer to a poorer grain does not precisely follow the order observed by Labrousse for 18th century France from wheat to rye and from rye to barley.[10] Moreover, the very low cyclical intensity of oat prices leads to the conclusion that demand for this product in the Netherlands remained relatively stable even during periods of famine. Finally, during the Burgundian period the cyclical intensity of barley prices in the Netherlands was much greater than that of wheat prices. Thus wheat seems to have been consumed only within limited circles whose consumption of superior grains appears to have remained unaffected even by the famines. For the rest, the masses, traditionally consumers of rye, seem to have had recourse to a significant increase in their barley consumption, thus more than compensating for the breweries' decreasing demand for barley.[11]

The question arises whether shifts in agricultural production, influenced by changing grain prices, are not reflected in the grain price graphs. The data on harvests, like the extremely valuable information that Ruwet was able to glean for the 18th century from documents on

---

[10] Labrousse, *Esquisse du mouvement des prix...* I, p. 188.

[11] The budgetary information at our disposal for the 16th century fully confirms the decline in beer production. Moreover, during the famine years the urban authorities took numerous measures to limit the use of grain in the breweries.

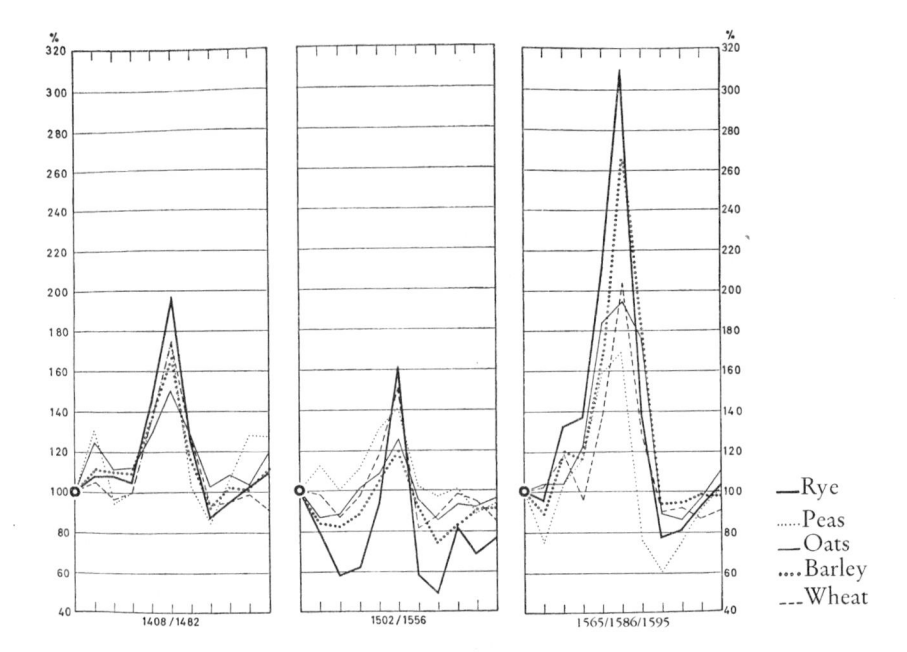

Figure 13.1: *Cyclical evolution of grain prices in Brabant during the three successive phases (15th–16th centuries).*

the collection of tithes,[12] is unfortunately not available for the period we wish to examine.

An analysis of the price of dairy products allows us to draw important conclusions regarding the prosperity of Flanders and Brabant in the 15th century (Figure 13.2). During that century only the price of cheese appears to have been sensitive to the increasing demand for grain in times of crisis:[13] this leads to the conclusion that cheese was the only dairy product

---

[12] J. Ruwet, 'Prix, production et bénéfices agricoles. Le pays de Liège au XVIIIe siècle', in: *Cahiers d'histoire des prix, publiés par le Centre Interuniversitaire pour l'Histoire des Prix et Salaires en Belgique* II (1957), pp. 69–109; Ruwet was also able to compile a table of grain production in the 15th and 16th centuries based on ecclesiastical tithes.

[13] This cyclical variation in demand, very pronounced for cheese in the 15th century, had its roots in the specific organization of the food sector of the time which was based essentially on bread. Substitutes giving equal or superior calorie content for the same money were not yet on the market (B. Slicher van Bath, *De agrarische geschiedenis van West-Europa (500–1850)* (Utrecht–Antwerp: 1960), p. 93; E. Scholliers, 'De levensstandaard der arbeiders op het einde der XVIe eeuw te Antwerpen', in: *Tijdschrift voor Geschiedenis* LXVIII (1955), p. 169; J. Craeybeckx, 'Brood en levensstandaard. Kritische nota betreffende de prijs van het brood te Antwerpen en te Brussel in de XVIIe en XVIIIe eeuw', in: *Cahiers d'histoire des prix, publiés par le Centre Interuniversitaire pour l'Histoire des Prix et Salaires en Belgique* III (1958), p. 134). During a period when income was still very modest, the demand for foodstuffs became concentrated entirely on grains in famine years.

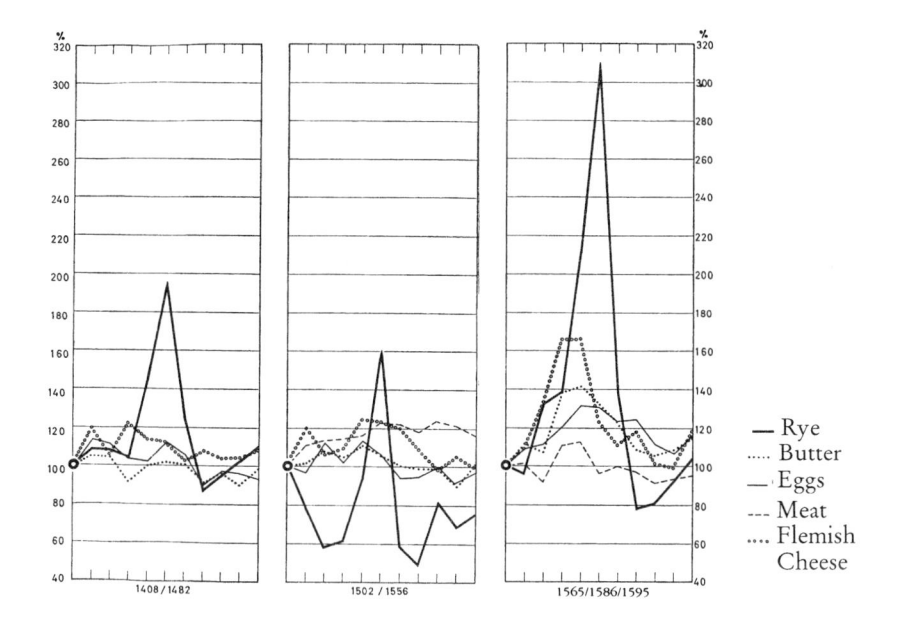

Figure 13.2: *Cyclical evolution of meat and dairy prices in Brabant during the three successive phases (15th–16th centuries).*

fully integrated into the day-to-day consumption pattern of the masses in the 15th century. Butter on the other hand appears to have been out of reach of all but the limited group of the privileged: cyclical variation in the demand for it was extremely limited.[14] This was *a fortiori* the case for luxury articles like Rhine wine and spices. In the 15th century the price fluctuations of these two articles were determined almost exclusively by purely commercial factors. Evidently the economic emancipation of the urban lower middle class under the influence of the changing price–wage ratio in the Burgundian Netherlands emerged only very slowly, delayed by the late decline of the traditional industries.

The prices of herring and of salt from the French salt pans were, like the price of Rhine wine and spices, scarcely affected by regional famines. This was equally true of the English cloth exports that reached the Continent by way of the Brabant fairs (Figure 13.3). Consequently, Brabant's international commerce appears to have been reduced to transport and transit, or to those consumer products reaching only a very limited group within the population of Brabant. Immune to the effects of regional famines, it was

---

[14] For the importance of the price of butter as a gauge of prosperity, see M.M. Postan, 'Trade and Industry in the Middle Ages', in: Cambridge Economic History of Europe II (Cambridge: 1952), pp. 209–10.

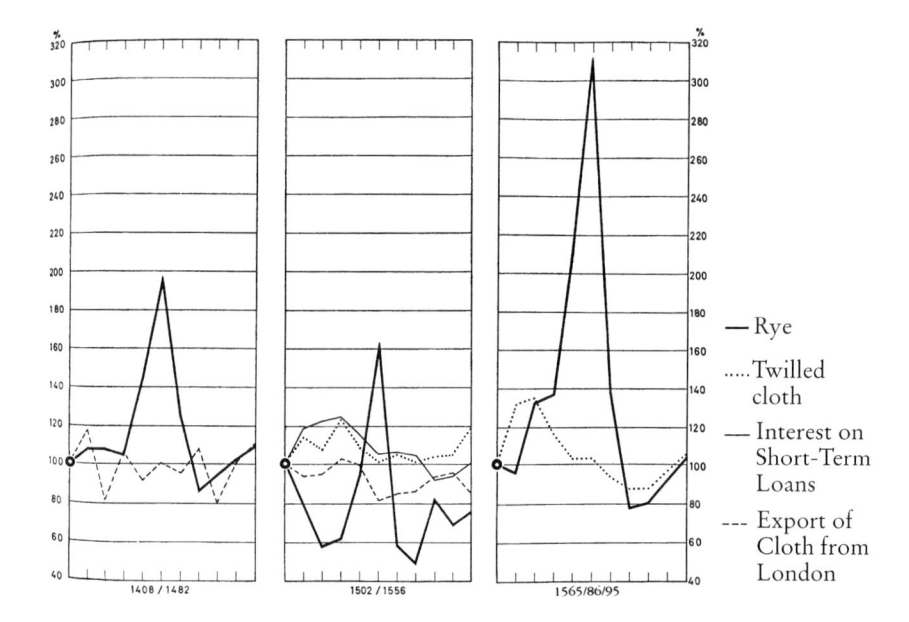

Figure 13.3: *Cyclical evolution of the transit trade, industrial production, and the money market in Flanders and Brabant during the three successive phases (15th–16th centuries).*

susceptible above all to purely commercial influences, chiefly those of supply. For example herring prices were influenced by fluctuations in the supply and price of French salt.

On the other hand, prices of industrial goods produced and consumed in the region were very sensitive to famine crises during the 15th century, an era darkened by the spread of decay in the export industries (Figure 13.4). The famine effectively paralysed the construction industry.[15] The price of charcoal was also seriously affected. Even the Weert textile industry, producing cheap woollen cloth mainly for consumption in the Netherlands, suffered the consequences. Within the context of a decaying export centre,

---

[15] Investments in the construction industry were curtailed not only in the private sector but also in the public sector during famine crises. It is also obvious that declining consumption had a disastrous effect on the incomes both of the municipalities and of the central government, since funding was derived largely from customs and excise taxes. Thus the 1437 crisis put enormous pressure on the resources of Philip the Good (J. Bartier, in *Algemene Geschiedenis der Nederlanden* III (1951), p 267). The same was true of the crisis of 1482. An ordinance of the town of Antwerp dated 24 November 1482 says on this subject: *overmids den costelycken dieren tyde jegenwoirdich loopende van alle goeden ende sunderlinge van vitaelgien... dwelck oic komt in groeten achterdeele ende scade vanden assyzen ende ander incomen der stad* (Antwerp City Archives, Pk 913, f. 72).

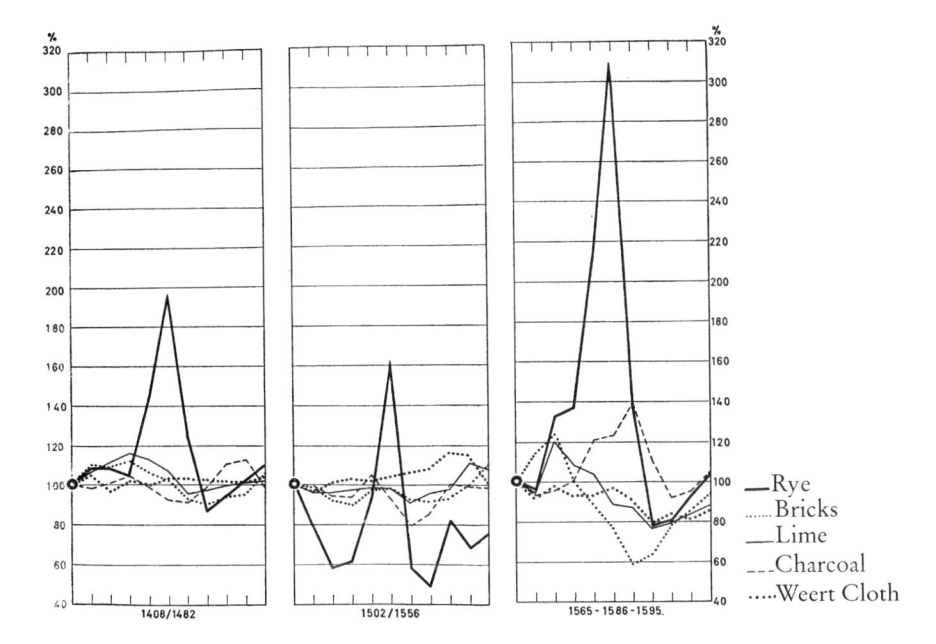

Figure 13.4: *Cyclical evolution in the price of industrial products in Brabant during the three successive phases (15th–16th centuries).*

industrial activities in the Netherlands were gradually reduced to production destined for local or regional consumption, becoming increasingly detached from the great ups and downs in the European economy.

It is essential to distinguish between town and country in the study of income. For the countryside a second distinction must be made between wage earners (labourers or *handwerkers*), the mass of small peasants (who were often employed as part-time labourers as well) and a limited core of wealthier peasants (farmers or people of independent means). For the 15th century we have information regarding only the first category. Famine made the outlook for these poor people very grim. Their income was not only undermined by the drastic increase in grain prices, but also by the appreciable decline in their employment prospects. In itself, a poor harvest meant less demand for labour. Moreover, the more prosperous peasants, their employers, endeavoured to keep their production costs, and in particular the number of labourers employed, to a minimum, all the more so since it was customary in rural areas to provide food for both the day labourers and for piece workers. For their part, those labourers who still had work were inclined to prolong their daily labours and to increase their productivity in order to ensure the good-will of their employers. In such circumstances unemployment increased alarmingly in the rural districts.[16] Hence, during periods of famine in the 15th century, the wages for rural day labourers in the vicinity of Lier reveal a declining trend.

For the urban population a distinction must be made between industrial and commercial incomes. In the 15th century, as we have stated, the evolution of prices for luxury products and other goods of international trade (Rhine wine and spices, for example) was not linked to fluctuations in the price of grains; it is thus plausible to claim that the income of those involved in international trade and finance was affected little if at all by the famine. The industrial sector, on the other hand, in view of the global cyclical behaviour of industrial prices, was severely affected by crises in foodstuffs. Wages and profits therefore should have been affected, too. Nevertheless, the wages for construction workers at Antwerp and at Lier, and for linen weavers at Brussels, did not follow the cyclical movement of industrial prices (Figure 13.5); these are sectors where the corporative grip must have been exceptionally firm during this period.[17]

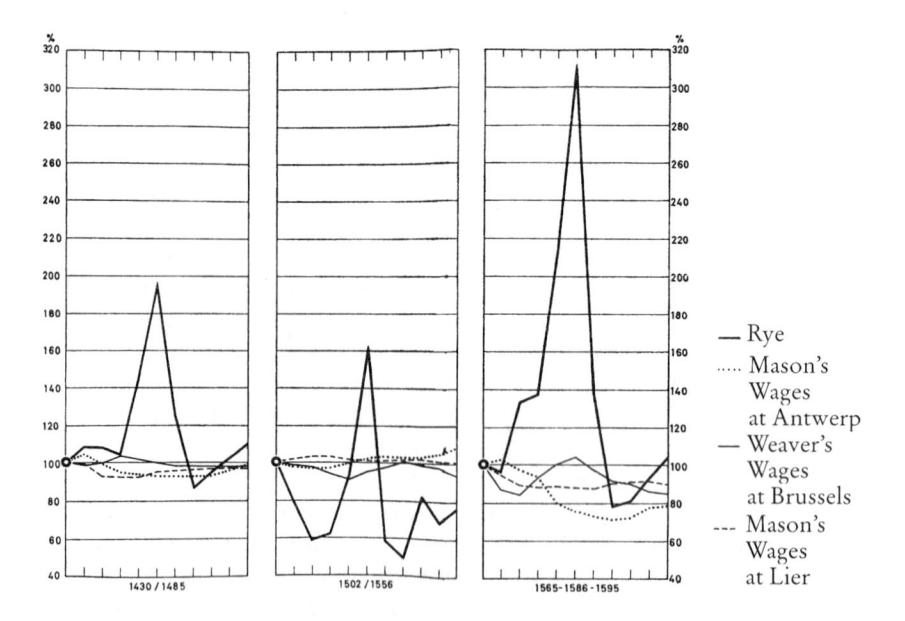

Figure 13.5: *Cyclical evolution in the wages of skilled urban labourers in Brabant during the three successive phases (15th–16th centuries).*

---

[16] Labrousse, *Esquisse du mouvement des prix...* II, pp. 520 ff.

[17] It should nevertheless be noted that the 1433–35 monetary reforms also had an effect on the evolution of wages.

16th Century Expansion: Towards a Flourishing International Economy

The increasing prosperity apparent in the Netherlands, particularly during the first two-thirds of the 16th century, tended to stimulate demand for non-grain agricultural products like butter and cheese. But this could only further aggravate the cyclical variation in grain prices. Indeed, during the worst famine years, the demand for dairy products must have decreased as demand was concentrating solely on bread, which offered a higher caloric content for the same price (Figure 13.2). Thus famines must have led to an increase in the demand for grain during the years of highest grain prices, while during the years of lower prices the demand for grain must have decreased.[18] Nevertheless, the cyclical variation in grain prices showed during the first two-thirds of the 16th century a distinct tendency to decline (Figure 13.1). This clearly proves that supply played a more preponderant role at that time. The area of land under cultivation in such densely populated areas as Brabant was insufficient to fully supply their nutritional needs; supply was also dependent on imports. Recent research has estimated that such imports accounted for up to 23% of consumption for the years 1562–69.[19] As a result, at the time of the great expansion of maritime commerce in the first two-thirds of the 16th century, the cyclical variation of grain prices measurably decreased. Moreover, the maximum cyclical amplitudes nearly always coincided with maritime or political crises, generally of short duration.[20] It is interesting to note that during periods of declining maritime commerce, like the 30s, 40s, and 80s of the 15th century and even more the last third of the 16th century, cyclical oscillations were much greater and generally lasted for more than one year.

A comparison between the cyclical variation in the price of barley and that of wheat leads to equally interesting conclusions. The decline in the cyclical intensity of barley prices during the first half of the 16th century is clearly shown in Figure 13.1. It demonstrates that the prosperity of the masses, traditionally consumers of rye, had increased to the point where even in times of famine they were no longer obliged to resort on a large scale to barley consumption. Further, the preference for wheat over rye during years of lower grain prices became more pronounced.

---

[18] See also: E. Scholliers, *Loonarbeid en honger. De levensstandaard in de XVe en XVIe eeuw te Antwerpen* (Antwerp: 1960), p. 175.

[19] C. Verlinden *et al.*, *Dokumenten voor de geschiedenis van prijzen en lonen in Vlaanderen en Brabant (XVe–XVIIIe eeuw)* (Bruges: 1959), p. XVI.

[20] Amsterdam even more clearly determined European grain prices in the 17th and 18th centuries, see J. Meuvret, 'La géographie des prix des céréales et les anciennes économies européennes', in: *Revista da Economia* IV, 2, pp. 63–9; also 'Les mouvements des prix de 1661 à 1715', in: *Journal de la Société de Statistique de Paris* (1944), pp. 109–19; Ruwet, *Prix, production et bénéfices agricoles...*, pp. 100 ff.

Hence the appreciable decline in the price of rye relative to that of wheat in good years.[21]

An analysis of agricultural products other than grain contributes substantially to the image of prosperity in the first two-thirds of the 16th century. During that period not only cheese, but also butter and eggs, were distinctly more sensitive to cyclical variations in demand. These two products seem to have become established in the dietary habits of the masses. But during periods of famine there is a visible abandonment of dairy products in favour of grain products (Figure 13.2). This phenomenon might imply an intuitive physiological appreciation on the part of consumers for the higher caloric value of grains in comparison to dairy products; but the explanation is perhaps psycho-physiological in nature: for the same money bread seems to fill the belly better than a portion of butter or cheese.

Only the price of meat constitutes an exception to this tendency towards an increasing negative correlation. Nevertheless, the growing cattle markets of Brabant, the intensification of the international cattle trade, and information gleaned from institutional accounts, lead to the conclusion that there was a real increase in meat consumption. Had meat become so integral a part of the general diet that famine scarcely diminished the demand for it, or was its consumption, on the contrary, limited to such a small portion of the population even in the 16th century that the demand for meat remained unaffected? We can offer no definitive answer to this question. Still, the available qualitative information inclines us to support the former hypothesis.[22] The psycho-physiological argument cited above tends to support this conclusion. Meat gave, and still gives today, the impression of substantial and filling nourishment, so that even in times of famine during the generally prosperous first half of the 16th century its consumption was not abandoned in favour of grain.

A study of the price of industrial products reveals a sharp contrast between the 15th century and the first two-thirds of the 16th century (Figure 13.4). In the latter period the construction industry was still sensitive to the rhythm of famines, but the intensity of cyclical depressions was substantially diminished by the general prosperity and by the construction boom. Furthermore, the price of charcoal, normally supported by the growing urban demand for fuel,[23] appears to have been highly

---

[21] See also: A. Wyffels, 'Het kwalitatief en kwantitatief aspekt van het graanverbruik in Vlaanderen in de XVIe en XVIIe eeuw', in: *Cahiers d'histoire des prix, publiés par le centre interuniversitaire pour l'histoire des prix et salaires en Belgique* III (1958), p. 115.

[22] The percentage of meat in the diet, as reflected in the budgetary allocations of the Beguinage Infirmary at Lier, was clearly on the rise until the years of the Revolt.

[23] This increase was particularly high in a great city like Antwerp. Commercial exploitation of the woods owned by the Poor Relief Institution at Lier began only in the early 16th century and was systematically oriented towards sale to Antwerp.

sensitive to the reduced purchasing power typical of crisis years. The price of Weert cloth on the other hand was hardly affected at all by famine: its tendency to rise persisted beyond the crises, providing resounding proof that Weert and its rural surroundings became an important export area during that period.[24] The same is true for the price of flax: it suffered no decline even at the height of the crises, again underlining the growing international importance of the linen industry in Flanders and Brabant.

During the period of commercial expansion in the 16th century there seem to have been close correlation between the maritime commerce of the Netherlands and famine. Famines did not become really critical unless poor local harvests also coincided with commercial crises or with political troubles. Furthermore, cyclical rises in the price of salt had a strong tendency to coincide with those of grains. The numerous wars between France and the House of Habsburg indeed must have had catastrophic effects on the import of French products, such as salt and grain, making the crisis mechanism of famines far more complex than during the previous century.

Comparison of Hondschoote's production of serge and the trade in English cloth further confirms the hypothesis (Figure 13.3). Both bear witness to a negative correlation of their prices with the cyclical fluctuations of grain prices, a correlation which cannot be explained by a fall or rise of real income in the Netherlands and by a declining or rising demand for Hondschoote serge and English cloth in the same area, as both goods were mainly exported or re-exported. The decline in the prices of both goods can be explained only in the light of a production crisis, linked with commercial or political difficulties which in turn exerted cumulative pressure on grain prices in the event of a crop failure.

The cyclical behaviour of short-term interest rates, as represented by the interest rates the government paid, is from this point of view equally suggestive (Figure 13.3). At the rumour of a political or commercial crisis the interest rate dropped significantly. This leads to the conclusion that a lower demand for credit due to the abrupt stagnation of commercial investment more than compensated[25] for the increased governmental

---

[24] The slower growth in the sale of Weert cloth during the crisis years shows that it, too, had relied relatively heavily on the domestic market. Indeed, the cloth purchased by the Poor Relief at Lier for distribution to the poor, and by the Antwerp orphanage to clothe the orphans came chiefly from Weert and neighbouring centres.

[25] A. Friis, 'An Inquiry into the Relations between Economic and Financial Factors in the Sixteenth and Seventeenth Centuries', in: *The Scandinavian Economic History Review* (1953), pp. 193–244, has shown that it was the famine of 1556–57 that plunged the already precarious public finances of Spain and the Netherlands into disastrous bankruptcy in 1557. Nevertheless it would be erroneous to generalize this scenario. The falling interest rates for short-term government loans during the crises of the first half of the 16th century are proof that there was no lack of credit at such times, in fact quite the contrary.

demand for credit and for the pessimism typical of political crises. We can thus conclude that the political and commercial situation was decisive in the crises occurring during the period of Antwerp's expansion. Even if the actual course of the crisis was dominated by famine, the crises remained inextricably linked to commercial and political factors.

With respect to the cyclical movement in the wages of rural labourers the tendency towards a negative correlation between wages and grain prices was manifestly less pronounced in the 16th century. The generally favourable economic circumstances were probably largely responsible for this, the agricultural depression of the 15th century contrasting with the expansionist climate of the first two-thirds of the 16th century. The influence of the expansionist climate on the post-crisis cyclical evolution of wages was equally remarkable. The activity of the labourers, reflected in higher wages immediately after the famine year, was also much greater during the first two-thirds of the 16th century than it had been in the 15th century. It suggests that the demand for day labour had become much more urgent in the 16th century, despite an increase in the population.

The situation of the small peasants was not substantially different from that of labourers. In so far as they hired out as labourers they shared the fate of the day labourers; thus it can be deduced that the cyclical evolution of their wage income improved somewhat in the 16th century in comparison to the 15th, though it does not follow that this income was particularly high. Moreover, the small peasants were in no position to increase their agricultural income. They generally cultivated the poorest soils, so that the deduction of their seed reserve weighed heavily upon their resources, especially in the wake of a poor harvest.[26] Furthermore they had insufficient capital available to profit from the seasonal price rises when bringing their surplus to the market, in case there was a surplus, they could not afford to wait until the end of the following year, just before the new harvest, when prices rose most steeply, to sell their crop. On the contrary, they needed to sell their grain immediately after harvesting when prices were still relatively low. This was in stark contrast to the larger farms and the small number of great landowners who received rents in addition to their income as producers: they could afford to speculate on the seasonal price rises and were consequently able to maximize their profit in years of grain shortages.

Only very approximate information is available regarding the cyclical evolution of income for the wealthier peasants and great landowners: it concerns the cyclical evolution of debts in cash and in kind of the medium-sized to large farms of Lier's Poor Relief Institution. Figure 13.6 shows a negative correlation between grain prices and farmers' debts for the

---

[26] Labrousse, *Esquisse du mouvement des prix...* II, pp. 386 ff., made some suggestive remarks on this subject concerning 18th century France.

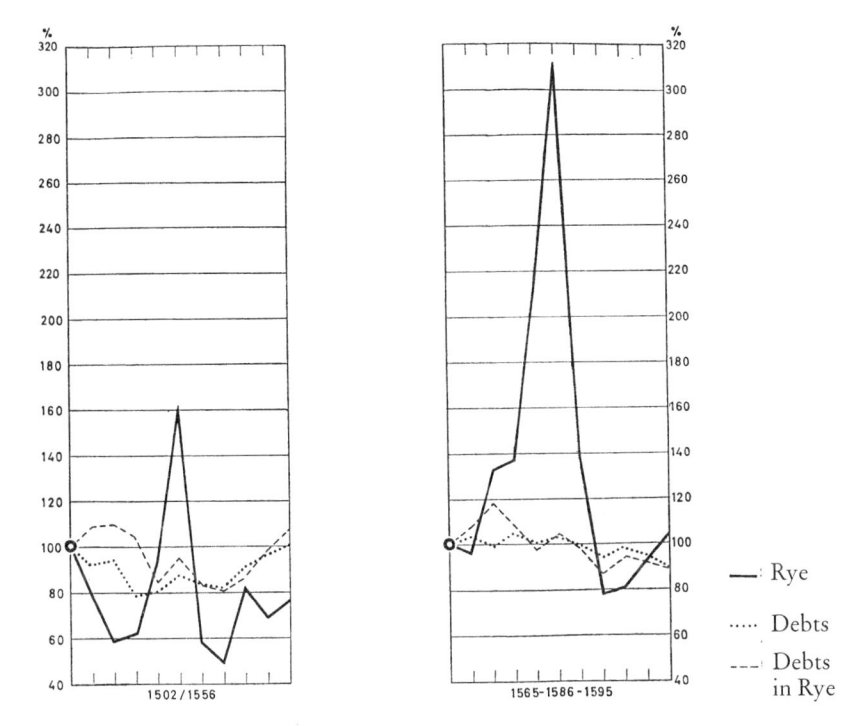

Figure 13.6: *Cyclical evolution of debt for large and medium-sized farms in Brabant during the three successive phases (15th–16th centuries).*

first two-thirds of the 16th century, aside from times of extreme harvest failures and violent price rises. In cases of less catastrophic price rises the farmers seem to have been able to repay their debts more easily, which must have favoured a tendency towards more concentration of wealth in the hands of the larger farmers and wealthy landowners. On the other hand the commercial growth of the 16th century, leading as it did to increasing imports of foreign grain, must have acted as a brake on price rises and must have slowed the tendency towards concentration of wealth. Indeed no obstacles were placed in the path of foreign grain imports, which meant that the farmers of the Netherlands suffered losses in the event of poor harvests, as there was not a sufficient compensatory rise in the price of grain.

With regard to the urban population, the increasing correlation between commercial crises and famine in the 16th century clearly posed a serious threat to commercial incomes derived from international trade. It was, however, possible to compensate for these losses to a certain extent by intensifying the international trade in grain, which offered enticing prospects for handsome profits despite the risks of the moment.

The bargaining strength of the mass of salaried urban workers during the period of strong economic growth in the 16th century is conclusively demonstrated in Figure 13.5. The corporative wage scales became definitively outmoded. The most convincing proof of this is the salary increases that the master-masons and journeymen of Antwerp and the master-weavers of Brussels were able to exact even in mid-crisis. In the unskilled labour sector the same increases took place, though noticeably later than for skilled workers. In fact, the wage increases for unskilled labour took place only after grain prices had returned to normal levels. Were the latter increases then the result of a reduction in the supply of labour brought on by increased mortality, particularly among the poor, during the famine? It is possible. But increased demand for labour probably exerted a more decisive influence. Once the famine was over there was a general resumption of industrial activity, heightened by the need to compensate for the interruption of activity in the preceding years. Unskilled workers, even without craft guild protection, suddenly found themselves more favourably situated and increased their wage demands. Employers were also more inclined to grant wage increases at such a moment.

Cyclical wage movement was substantially less vigorous for Lier than for Antwerp and Brussels, which means that the labour market in small towns remained for a longer time more rigid than the labour market in larger towns. It was only after 1540 that the mass of Lier's wage-earners finally started to break with the corporative tradition of respecting fixed wage tariffs.

The Revolt of the Netherlands: Collapse and Return to a Regional Economy

The Revolt of the Netherlands against Spain (1568–1648) had serious repercussions on the economic and cyclical development. The intensity of the cyclical oscillations of grain prices grew more alarming and most of the crises lasted two years (Figure 13.1). Moreover, the crises appear to have been more closely linked to local grain production. Hence the classic formula: 'a poor harvest followed by a second crop failure will generate a famine,' is particularly apt for this period.[27]

The Revolt also adversely affected the income of the rye-consuming masses. There is a striking discrepancy between the increasing cyclical intensity of rye prices and the relative decrease in the cyclical intensity of wheat prices.[28] The demand for wheat again retreated to within the

---

[27] Meuvret, *Les crises de subsistances...*, pp. 643–99.

[28] Since the prices for barley and oats pertain only to autumn purchases, there is a discrepancy with respect to the prices for rye and wheat, calculated according to an annual average, for the harvest year 1587 due to an abrupt drop in prices in January 1588. In order to retain the homogeneity of the comparison the prices of barley and oats have been adjusted for that crisis.

restricted circle of the more prosperous citizens, whereas during the famine years there was a massive switch to barley on the part of the traditional consumers of rye. A rise in the demand for barley during famines more than compensated for the falling demand of breweries for barley.[29] These curves thus bear emphatic witness to the misery of the period.

The cyclical evolution in the prices of meat and dairy products is entirely consonant with a general decline in prosperity (Figure 13.2). In contrast to the preceding period, the consumption pattern for meat now resembles that for dairy products. In spite of huge reductions in livestock numbers, the price of meat declined drastically in times of crisis. Patently, there was an abrupt decrease in the demand for meat and dairy products in times of famine, and poorer people fell back almost entirely on grain.[30]

Before 1565 a rising price trend for grain did not lead to a significant decline in flax supplies. During the final third of the 16th century on the contrary such a tendency seems to have become predominant. The abrupt and drastic increase in the cyclical intensity of grain prices unquestionably encouraged increased cultivation of grain. The linen industry, by that time entirely export-oriented, was extremely sensitive to variations in its supply of raw materials. The price of flax spiralled higher, always reaching a maximum following record grain prices. A year after the collapse of grain prices a return to flax cultivation again led to lower flax prices. At any rate this switch in time of famine appears to have been motivated less by the short-term profits of grain producers than by the pressing nutritional needs of the small producers. Still, such changes in crop choice are noticeable only during periods of exceptionally violent cyclical intensity. In normal times the influence of the demand for industrial crops remained dominant.

The curves also show a marked return to a regional economy in the cyclical evolution of industrial production during the period of the Revolt (Figure 13.4). The cyclical intensity of the prices of lime and bricks took on alarming proportions at that time and their negative correlation to the prices of grain is noticeably powerful. Even the price of Weert cloth was ominously affected: to the paralysing effects of the war psychosis and the trade embargo, totally disrupting international trade, was added the collapse of domestic consumption. The only exception appears to have been the price of Antwerp charcoal. Here a variety of circumstantial factors played a role: the risk involved in forestry work, resulting in huge wage increases, and the depopulation of the countryside (already appreciable

---

[29] Cf. above, note 11.
[30] The budgetary allocations of the Beguinage Infirmary at Lier also reflect in sharp contrast with the trend of preceding decades, a noticeable drop in expenditures for meat at the end of the 16th century.

in 1580).[31] These factors, both operative during the 1580s and 1590s, were further aggravated by extremely long and severe winters.[32]

The insecurity of the countryside during the turbulent years of the Revolt, reaching a peak around 1586–87 and again towards the mid-1590s, also played a crucial role in the cyclical evolution of income for rural day labourers. Moreover, high mortality caused by the terrible famines and epidemics had catastrophically reduced the supply of rural day labour. The famines of the closing third of the 16th century were the occasion to increase wages substantially, but such increases had only a marginal effect on global rural wage income, as many labourers had died and employment still remained very irregular as a result of the devastation of the countryside by the war.[33]

The aggravation of the cyclical intensity of grain prices during the years of the Revolt presumably led, in the absence of large-scale grain imports,[34] to disproportionate price rises that more than compensated for the diminishing volume harvested, thus better protecting than before the income of the big farmers and great landowners (Figure 13.6). The rapid agricultural recovery, shortly after 1587, was without doubt closely related to this income evolution.

The sensitivity of urban industry to famines during the years of the Revolt also increased strikingly. Wages were catastrophically affected (Figure 13.5). The evolution of nominal wages, already under heavy pressure from price rises at the height of the crises, gives only an imperfect notion of the real circumstances of urban labourers, for there was rising unemployment as well. The heavy mortality resulting from undernourishment and contagious diseases, particularly during the famine of 1586–87, decimated the working population. It was precisely this abrupt drop in the supply of labour that brought on the favourable evolution of wages during the post-1588 economic recovery. Nevertheless, a return to the prosperity of yesteryear was still far away.

The greater cyclical sensitivity of masons' (skilled workers') wages at

---

[31] Very clear in the meteorological chronology published as an appendix to our study *The Growth of the Antwerp Market and the European Economy (Fourteenth–Sixteenth Centuries)*.

[32] On this subject it should be noted that the price of wood at Lier shows a lower cyclical intensity, more in line with the cyclical movement of industrial and dairy products. In severe winters during famine years it was indeed easier for the inhabitants of small centres like Lier, whose links with agrarian circles were more intimate, to furnish themselves with sufficient firewood than for the inhabitants of a great town like Antwerp.

[33] Only a few were inclined to run great risks. Moreover, they were involved only in occasional small projects in more remote agricultural regions and this in no way involved full-time employment.

[34] The rapid growth of the trade in Baltic grain was oriented more towards Spain, Portugal and Italy.

Antwerp in comparison to those at Lier seems to underline the force of general economic factors. The ruin of industry weighed more heavily on a town the size of Antwerp than on the smaller centres where greater continuity in the corporative tradition offered some protection. On the other hand the evolution of the income of the unskilled (urban) labourers of Antwerp as well as of Lier was inextricably linked with the immigration of rural labourers to the towns in search of security. In a smaller centre like Lier the resultant increase in the supply of unskilled labour heightened the cyclical intensity of wage adjustments, better aligning them with Antwerp's.

The pronounced differences between the evolution of the wages of linen weavers at Brussels and the evolution of wages in the construction industry at Lier and Antwerp can be attributed to the still solid position of Flemish and Brabant linen on the international markets, and to a dwindling supply of weavers owing to the depopulation of the countryside.

Figure 13.7, comparing the trimestrial prices of wheat to the number of marriages and conceptions in the small town of Lier from 1582 to 1600,[35] illustrates clearly the catastrophic effects of the famines on the urban population at the end of the 16th century. Meuvret and Goubert's hypothesis linking the short-term demographic evolution to market prices is fully confirmed here.[36] Mortality undeniably reached alarming levels during the hunger years. Many people died of hunger and privation. At the same time malnutrition and poor hygiene left survivors vulnerable to the infectious diseases[37] that ran rampant during the famine or appeared shortly afterwards and further increased mortality.

By increasing mortality while decreasing the birth rate the famines led to some extremely dangerous chronic gaps in the growth of the population. Infant mortality also attained frightening levels. All of this was naturally aggravated by inadequate medical care and poor hygiene. Moreover, social behaviour also exerted a powerful influence on the demographic evolution in times of famine by limiting the number of births, because of delayed marriages.[38]

---

[35] Conception dates were obtained by subtracting nine months from baptism dates.

[36] Meuvret, *Les crises de subsistance...*, p. 643–99; P. Goubert, 'En Beauvaisis: problèmes démographiques du XVIIe siècle', in: *Annales E.S.C.* VII (1952), pp. 453–68; P. Goubert, *Beauvais et le Beauvaisis de 1600 à 1730. Contribution à l'histoire sociale de la France au XVIIe siècle* (Paris: 1960).

[37] Slicher van Bath, *De agrarische geschiedenis van West-Europa*, p. 97.

[38] Goubert, *Beauvais...*, p. 25–84, shows, supported by extensive data, that the number of children from a normal marriage at Beauvais during the 17th century reached a maximum of only eight. Four or more of these would generally die before the age of twenty-one. If the large number of unmarried people, widow(er)s, and childless marriages are taken into account, the proportion of the population actually responsible for reproduction was relatively limited.

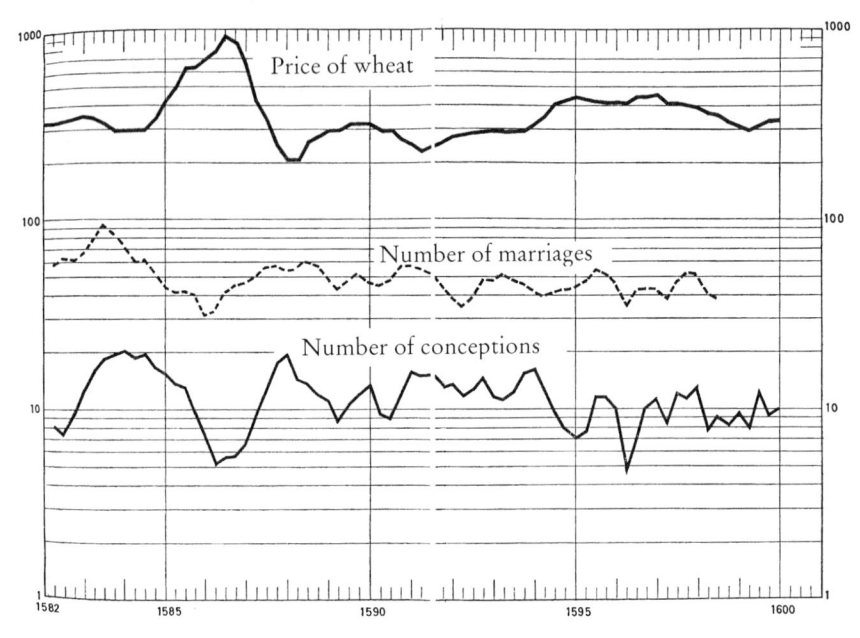

Figure 13.7: *Trimestrial movement in the price of wheat, the number of marriages and conceptions at Lier (1582–1600) (moving averages over three trimesters).*

The famines of earlier periods did not of course have such serious consequences for the urban and rural population as those of the final third of the 16th century. Nevertheless, the famines of 1437, 1482, 1489, 1521 and 1556 also represented crises of very high cyclical variations. Our qualitative sources reveal that they were also accompanied by infectious diseases and the toll they took of the population was by no means negligible. The demographic stagnation of the 15th century seems to be due at least in part to these events.

Conclusion

The classic outline of the crises of the Ancien Régime developed by Labrousse is in general valid for the Netherlands in the 15th and 16th centuries. Nevertheless, certain adjustments are in order. First of all, we have discovered that there are specific characteristics of the three great decades-long phases marking the economic development of our territories. We have, moreover, observed that the advanced character of the economy in Flanders and Brabant rendered the mechanism of these crises more complex than in the case of less advanced regional economies. And above all during the first two-thirds of the 16th century during which the economy of the Netherlands had, boldly for that period, taken on a modern and international flavour, the intensity of commercial expansion, and the appreciable increase of urban, and even rural, prosperity had visible effects on the structure of the crises. The changes thus observed can be best understood in the light of a tendency for the economy as a whole to develop into a more subtle system of interdependences: at once agrarian, commercial, industrial and political.

14

The Economy as a Factor in the Revolt in the Southern Netherlands

It is a pleasant task for me to address this distinguished company about the background to a historical event that was of crucial significance for the subsequent development of the Low Countries. I also feel particularly honoured that the Historical Association should have entrusted me with this commission in connection with the solemn commemoration of the 400th anniversary of the beginning of the Revolt, and I would like to express my sincere gratitude to the Chairman and the Board of the Association for their friendly invitation.

In defining the chronological boundaries of my subject, however, allow me to point out that recent historical research has revealed that the traditional view of 1568 as the year in which the Revolt started[1] requires some modification.[2] The unrest in the Western District in the Autumn of 1566, that took the form of raising a Beggars' army in and around Tournai marching upon Valenciennes, then besieged by the forces of the government – was already the result of an *organized plan of action* drawn up with political intent by Protestant preachers and members of the lesser nobility.[3] The iconoclastic movement of the summer of 1566 was also highly organized and was politically motivated.[4] I should therefore prefer to regard the initial phase of the

---

[1] J. Presser, *De Tachtigjarige Oorlog* (Amsterdam–Brussels: 1948), p. 52.

[2] H.A. Enno van Gelder, 'De Nederlandse Adel en de Opstand tegen Spanje, 1566–1572', in: *Tijdschrift voor Geschiedenis* 43 (1930), pp. 1f. and 138f.; E. Kuttner, *Het Hongerjaar 1566* (Amsterdam: 1964), pp. 213–375; W. Brulez, 'De Opstand van het Industriegebied in 1566', in: *Standen en Landen* 4 (1954), pp. 79–101.

[3] See especially W. Brulez, *ibid.*, pp. 85ff.

[4] M. Dierickx, 'Beeldenstorm in de Nederlanden in 1566', in: *Streven* 19, 2 (1966), pp. 1040–8; also 'De Beeldenstorm en Frans-Vlaanderen', in: *Ons Erfdeel* 10, 2 (1966), pp. 12–20.

Revolt as a period of agitation and disturbance occurring between 1566 and 1568.

I should also like to emphasize from the outset that the initial phase of the Revolt – political circumstances aside – was dominated by a complex of religious, intellectual, social and economic factors affecting developments on two different planes. On a *long term* basis these factors increased tension between the dynamism of 16th-century change and expansion and in the inertia of established structures and institutions; on a *short-term* basis, they resulted in emotionally charged conflict-situations. I would like to develop my argument along these lines and will therefore split it into two parts: the first section dealing with the secular background to the start of the Revolt so far as this was dominated by cultural and economic factors; and the second an enquiry into contemporary conditions of which the Revolt was, in part, an immediate result.

In a long-term view, the Revolt was due among other things to the cultural emancipation of the population and to spectacular economic growth in the Netherlands during the 16th century. Among the élite of Northwest Europe, cultural emancipation was expressed in the triumph of the Renaissance and of Humanism and, before long, also in the breakthrough of the Reformation – which in the early stages marched in step with contemporary cultural regeneration. In this connection we observe with interest that in Italy this same cultural emancipation – which in that progressive country had alrady been achieved in the 15th century – was mainly dominated by increasing individualism and therefore attained its greatest development in the sphere of the arts. In North-west Europe, on the other hand, cultural emancipation was dominated by a growing rationalism and consequently found its strongest expression in Humanism and the Reformation, in other words in the exaltation of critical thinking and the rejection of the *auctoritas* argument.[5]

In the Netherlands, however, the secular process of spiritual emancipation did not stay confined to the circles of the intellectual élite and the religious extremists. It gradually spread to the masses as well. Because of this deeper social penetration, economic factors played a major role. In fact, the growth of the Netherlands economy during the 15th but above all during the 16th century, accelerated the cultural emancipation of the population, including the masses, as a whole. I would therefore like to suggest that the process of cultural emancipation amongst the masses during the 15th – but above all during the 16th – century was determined by increasing prosperity. I base my conclusions on the

---

[5] N.M. Wildiers, *De Kerk in de wereld van morgan*. Verhandelingen van de Katholieke Vlaamse Hogeschooluitbreiding 500 (Antwerpen: 1966) pp. 22–31.

experience that – seen in secular perspective – poverty leads to lassitude, fatalism and acquiescence, whereas better living conditions – by ensuring greater independence – stimulate individualism and rationalism and sharpen the critical sensibilities of the masses.

On the basis of this hypothesis, the breakthrough of Burgundian prosperity into the Netherlands during the 15th century was a new and important milestone along the road to cultural emancipation of the urban population.[6] This prosperity had its foundation in a considerable extension of the urban middle class. In the Southern Netherlands, the declining sector of the traditional cloth industry was gradually replaced by sectors having highly specialized labour requirements and favourable corporative production controls, and by extensive new service sectors.[7]

The spectacular expansion of the Netherlands economy in the 16th century, which had its origins in the international trade of Antwerp, acted as a fresh and powerful incentive towards prosperity, and consequently towards the cultural emancipation of the urban population as well. The growth of the urban middle class resulted in a higher standard of living for a wider range of people. Moreover, the reduction in open and hidden unemployment and the rise in industrial productivity helped to raise *per capita* income.[8] Inventories after death dating from the 15th and 16th centuries, for example, can be used to show how, suddenly, in the 16th century, there was a rapid and tangible increase in the wealth of the middle-class inhabitants of even little towns like Bergues Saint-Winoc.[9]

The tendency towards democratization of education must also be seen in the context of growing urban prosperity. In the course of the 15th century there had already been a remarkable increase in the number of lay schools in Antwerp. In the 16th century educational opportunities for children of the middle class rose spectacularly: by about 1560 there were no fewer than 150 private, non-ecclesiastical schools teaching

---

[6] T.S. Jansma, 'Het vraagstuk van Hollands welvaren tijdens hertog Philips van Bourgondië' ('s-Gravenhage: 1964) pp. 55–73; R. van Uytven, 'La Flandre et le Brabant, terres de promission sous les ducs de Bourgogne?', in: *Revue du Nord*, XLIII, 172 (1961) pp. 281–317.

[7] H. Van der Wee, *Conjunctuur en Economische Groei in de Zuidelijke Nederlanden tijdens de 14e, 15e en 16e eeuw* (Brussels: 1965) pp. 15–9.

[8] H. Van der Wee, 'Das Phänomen des Wachstums und der Stagnation im Lichte der Antwerpener und südniederländischen Wirtschaft des 16. Jahrhunderts', in: *Vierteljahrschrift für Sozial- und Wirtschaftsgeschichte* 54 (1967) pp. 213ff.

[9] N. Six, *De Schepenen van Sint-Winoksbergen. Bijdragen tot de sociaal-ekonomische geschiedenis tussen 1420 en 1540* (M.A. thesis K.U. Leuven) (Louvain: 1968).

Wals ende Diets and *Arithmetica ende Geometrica*.[10] The rapid expansion of the printing industry is linked with this: for the first time in history, the printed word was brought efficiently and systematically within reach of a wider public. Besides manuals for merchants and book-keepers, all sorts of handbooks for craftsmen were published.[11] Antwerp was the indisputable North European centre of this new movement.

The prosperity of the 16th century was not confined to the towns. The successful breakthrough of rural industry also meant a gradual increase in prosperity in the country districts. With the increase in linen weaving, rural industry – which had already gained a foothold here and there in the previous century – expanded enormously in the course of the 16th century.[12] Income from small holdings could now be supplemented by income from industrial work, which meant that the hidden unemployment of the masses was rendered productive. The rise in rural incomes and, in consequence, the increase in rural prosperity was in itself conducive to gradual cultural emancipation. No less important, however, was the emancipating effect of increased contact between urban markets or urban merchants with rural workers. It is not therefore surprising that during this period industrialized rural areas like the Western District proved very receptive to Calvinist agitation and to the psychosis of revolt which characterized the 1560s, whereas agrarian zones like Haspengouw, although poor and backward, proved completely inert and insensitive to the social, religious and political currents of the day.

To summarize: if the emancipation of the masses is an important element of the background to the Revolt in the Netherlands, the long-term development of the Netherlands economy as such cannot be dismissed as a depth-factor either. An economy is a mixture of present and past; it is a synthesis of contemporary activities in which the past is inevitably reflected. In other words, an economy assimilates the present within the framework of a given institutional structure that has grown up historically. This is a definite advantage since it means that the present can profit from the experience of the past. It may also represent a threat since institutional structures always assume a conservative character and thus have difficulty in avoiding rigidity and immobility. In a stagnating economy the structure is a guarantee of continuity; in a growth economy, on the other hand, the institutional structure is a garment that rapidly becomes too tight and old-fashioned and should therefore be forcibly and ruthlessly discarded. Growth seen in this

---

[10] H.L.V. De Groote, 'De zestiende-eeuwse Antwerpse Schoolmeesters', in: *Bijdragen tot de Geschiedenis inzonderheid van het oud hertogdom Brabant* L (1967), pp. 180ff.

[11] A.J.E.M. Smeur, *De zestiende-eeuwse Nederlandse Rekenboeken* ('s-Gravenhage: 1960). See also various articles by H.L.V. De Groote, in: *Scientiarum Historia*, 1960, 1962 and 1963.

[12] E. Sabbe, *De Belgische Vlasnijverheid*, Part 1: *de Zuidnederlandsche Vlasnijverheid tot het verdrag van Utrecht* (1713) (Bruges: 1943).

perspective would mean the unfailing capacity of the economy to adapt the institutional structure by means of creative processes to the changing conditions of the time. We might call this qualitative growth a necessary consequence of growth in quantity.

Quantitative growth (in other words, an increase in the GNP and even a rise in the *per capita* income) was definitely present in the progressive economy of the 16th century Netherlands. Qualitative growth was not entirely lacking but was certainly insufficient, so that existing structures no longer proved adequate to assimilate the expansion that was taking place and a conflict-situation became inevitable. The state bankruptcies of 1557, 1575, 1596, 1607, 1627 and 1647[13] in Spain, for instance, clearly showed that the financial and fiscal institutions of the Habsburg world in the 16th and 17th centuries were no longer able to cope with the powerful expansion of public finances.

The influence of the personality of the sovereign was catastrophic in intensifying the clash between qualitative and quantitative growth. Opportunism, and perhaps rationalism too, in the character of Charles V and his entourage might still – by fortunate improvization perhaps – have solved some of the difficulties. On the other hand, a certain insensitivity to developments in Northern Europe, a failure to take a general overall view, and the wavering and reticent character of Philip II proved insuperable obstacles to the structural institutional changes so vital.

It is not my intention to dispute here the classic theory that political resistance at the beginning of the Revolt was primarily a reaction against the centralizing tendencies of Philip II, in other words a reaction of conservatism and particularism on the part of the provinces of the Netherlands to a more modern view of state as advocated and upheld by the king. It cannot be denied that this factor was present and indeed found tangible expression. Yet at the same time I wish to emphasize that the resistance-psychosis of the day was nourished not only by conservative self-interest but, to an equal extent, by progressive attitudes that were also undeniably present in the Netherlands at the time. There was, in fact, a growing aversion among many aspects of the medieval system of universal Catholicism so brutally maintained through the Inquisition. And there was equally strong opposition to the territoral estrangement of the Crown since in the Netherlands too, the development of the modern concept of state was accompanied by the conviction that king and country should be inseparable. Resistance to the fiscal reforms crystallized not only in the fear that the fiscal burden would be increased and the fiscal privileges of the nobility and the clergy undermined, but perhaps even

---

[13] J.G. Van Dillen 'De Opstand en het Amerikaanse Zilver', in: *Tijdschrift voor Geschiedenis* 73 (1960), p. 36.

more by a general dislike to the idea that the proceeds would largely be used to finance a Habsburg world policy that no longer rang true in the Netherlands.

So, to achieve his policy, Philip II made use of modern centralization techniques, but the policy itself remained permeated with medieval conservatism and outmoded conceptions.[14] This extraordinary situation welded the conservative and the progressive forces of the Netherlands into collective opposition. It is here that we should look for the fundamental explanation of the success of the Revolt in its initial phase. The alliance that came into being between conservative and progressive streams tangibly broadened the basis of the opposition. It did more than that: it gave rapid and decisive support to the current psychosis of embitterment and disaffection. It was precisely this alliance which made it possible to cross the borderline between resistance and revolt.

Fiscal reform was one of the poles around which the alliance really crystallized. If the progressives had had the idea that these measures could contribute towards a progressive policy for the future, they might have put up with it – even to the detriment of their own interests – but the conviction that the new taxes would not benefit the Netherlands at all was bound to intensify their resistance. Moreover, at the beginning of his reign and particularly under Alva, Philip II made the unforgivable blunder of proposing and insisting upon the definitive replacement of the old system of provincial taxes (*bede*) by a new system of permanent taxes on income – and he did this in an extremely clumsy and authoritarian way.[15] Since the new system primarily affected the privileged groups, a bitter reaction could also be expected from them. Conditions were therefore such as to unite the entire population in fierce opposition on this point. Conservative and progressive movements in the Netherlands now joined in common protest against the unfortunate methods that Philip II and his advisers had adopted with a view to stimulating qualitative growth by artificial means. And this emotional reaction no longer took any account of the fact that such growth was urgently needed to achieve

---

[14] For the following passage many thanks are due to Prof. P.W. Klein, Prof. P.J. van Winter, and Dr H.E. van Gelder; the valuable suggestions they made during the debate following my address have been extremely helpful to me in the definitive formulation of this hypothesis.

[15] J. Craeybeckx, 'La portée fiscale et politique du 100e denier du duc d'Albe', in: *Recherches sur l'histoire des finances publiques en Belgique* (Brussels: 1967), pp. 343–74. In this connection, it seems odd that in 1543 Emperor Charles did manage to obtain tithes, and that in 1544–45 the Estates of Flanders and Brabant also succeeded in imposing a similar tax on incomes. By introducing a progressive direct tax in 1577 the Estates-General were actually to go much further with fiscal reforms than Philip II and Alva.

suitable consolidation of the quantitative expansion that had taken place in the economy in the preceding decades.

Opposition to the new tax system, however, brings us right into the sphere of the economic situation, which means that it is time to start the second part of our discussion, in which we shall investigate the trade cycle as a factor at the start of the Revolt.

There are two aspects to be taken into account when discussing this factor. In the first place there are the mid-term waves called Kondratieffs, and alongside these the short-term fluctuations that, in the Ancien Régime, were usually connected with famine crises. It therefore seems advisable to divide the analysis into two subsections.

The Kondratieff movements in the Netherlands economy during the 16th century were most peculiar. Encouraged by the vigorous long-term expansion of the European economy, the upward phases came strongly to the fore while the downward phases tended to be less in evidence. The upward phase of the first Kondratieff lasted from about 1495 to about 1525, the upward movement of the second one from about 1540 to about 1565.[16] In the Southern Netherlands, the outcome of the uncertain period of depression after 1565 was a brutal catastrophe engendered by an exogenous factor, namely military action.

The first upward phase of the Netherlands economy, which occurred between 1495 and 1525, might be described as one of peaceful expansion. The urban economy was clearly dominated by the growing international trade centred on Antwerp, yet this growth concerned transit trade in the first place and did not give rise, therefore, to serious bottlenecks. The growth of agriculture, on the other hand, had a much deeper effect. It was dominated by sharp demographic increase, yet this also did not lead to immediate tension because demographic expansion only filled up lacunae resulting from industrial[17] and agrarian depression of the mid-15th century and from the Flemish war of the 1480s and early 1490s.

The upward movement of the second Kondratieff cycle, which occurred between 1540 and 1565, was more feverish in character, wider in scope, and proceeded less smoothly in the Netherlands. It was mainly characterized by the intensive integration of urban and rural industry into the spectacular expansion of international trade. In the towns it was the highly specialized sectors of craftsmanship that benefited primarily

---

[16] For a more detailed analysis see H. Van der Wee, *The Growth of the Antwerp Market and the European Economy (Fourteenth–Sixteenth Centuries)* II (Paris–The Hague: 1963), pp. 113–244.

[17] Particularly the decline of the 'old draperies'.

from this: the towns became the suppliers of specialized and differentiated fabrics for the whole of Europe. Rural industry concentrated mainly on mass production, including lightweight woollens and linens for which there was a world-wide market.[18] The growing alliance between increasing international trade and internal industrial development was soon to lead to pressure on the labour market. To the extent that this pressure was absorbed by demographic transfer from the country to the towns, by a rising birth rate or by immigration from abroad, an echo-effect of pressure on agrarian production was inevitable.

The conditions required to give new and forcible impetus to the demographic growth of the early part of the 16th century had therefore been met. But there were no longer lacunae from former centuries to be filled, so that the threat of increasing tension between agriculture and acreage assumed substance. Further technical improvements could not provide a solution since in this sector the opportunities for rapid innovation within the framework of the times had been exhausted. For that reason the solution was sought mainly in commerce, that is to say in the maritime sphere where contemporary techniques permitted the expansion of such traffic. It is common knowledge that the grain imports from France, and more particularly from the Baltic, had a decisive effect on the expansion of the shipping trade in the provinces of Holland. My colleague, E. Scholliers, has calculated that grain imports from the Baltic area in the 1560s accounted for 20 to 25% of the total consumption in the Netherlands.[19] Yet the rapid rise in grain prices during the second third of the 16th century proves that grain imports from abroad – even on this scale – could not compensate for shortages in domestic grain production.[20] It goes without saying that when analysing prices for this period the inflation of silver imports from the New World should also be taken into account, but, to my mind, this influence was not the only determinant of the rise in grain prices[21] (see Figure 14.1).

The powerful population surge during the second phase of expansion also had an important side-effect on capital formation. Inasmuch as the new growth settled mostly in the towns, there was an urgent need for more intensive investment in house building, in the urban infrastructure, and in quantitative expansion of production; in other words, savings were mainly used for widening of capital. These investments certainly produced

---

[18] H. Van der Wee, *Conjunctuur en Economische Groei*, pp. 19–21; see also D.C. Coleman, 'An Innovation and its Diffusion: the New Draperies', in: *The Economic History Review* 2nd ser., XXII (1969), pp. 417–29.

[19] E. Scholliers in: C. Verlinden *et al.*, *Dokumenten voor de Geschiedenis van Prijzen en Lonen in Vlaanderen en Brabant: XVe–XVIIIe eeuw* (Bruges: 1959) p. XVI.

[20] Van der Wee, *The Growth of the Antwerp Market*, III, graph no. 52.

[21] *Ibid.*, part II, pp. 416–7.

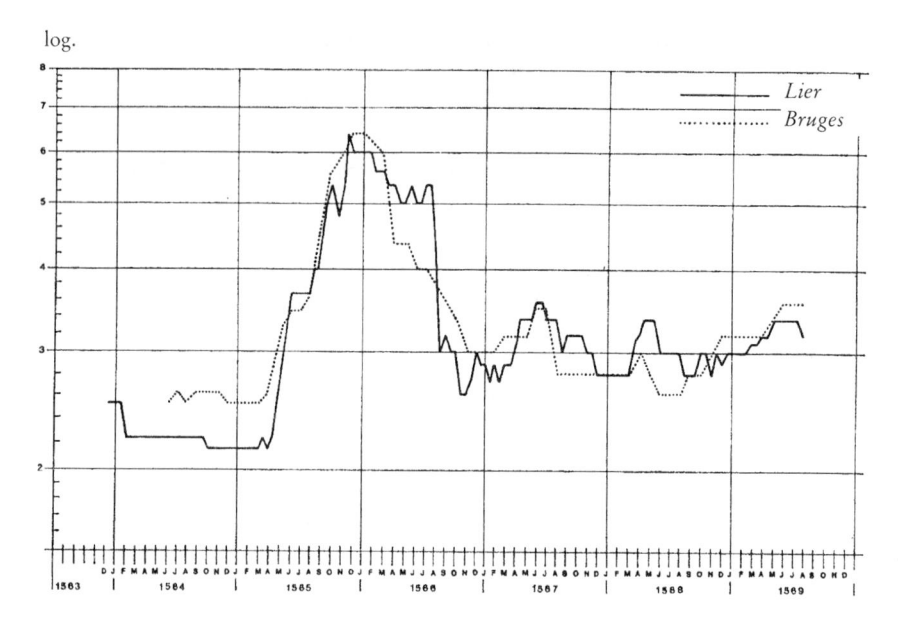

Figure 14.1: *Corn prices (1563–69)*

Lier
Half-monthly market prices of the amount of wheat needed for the making of a loaf of 1½ pound, in Brabant groats (semi-logarithmic scale).

Bruges
Average market prices of a 'hoed' wheat in Flemish groats (semi-logarithmic scale).

the atmosphere of feverish expansion in industrial activity, but they were presumably realized at the expense of more productive investments, the so-called deepening of capital aimed at more rational use of labour or the replacement of manpower with tools. In Antwerp, for example, during the early 1560s, merchants like Daniel de Bruyne put their profits into building craftsmen's houses instead of investing it in the purchase or construction of ships.[22] In this way they indirectly curbed any attempt at solving the growing difficulties in the supply sector.

The expansion was not confined to industrial growth with its demographic and agrarian consequences; it was also strongly felt in the sphere of commerce. It was precisely during this phase that overseas trading in the Netherlands underwent definitive democratization, based

---

[22] *Ibid.*, part II, p. 227.

especially upon the more general application of new participation techniques and the growth of the commission business.[23] This laid the foundations for a new breakthrough of the Netherlands middle class into international trade. We all know of the decisive role played by this creatively dynamic class in the further expansion of the Netherlands economy. However, this growth of the middle class had another, specific, effect: it conflicted inevitably with the Spanish–Portuguese hegemony in intercontinental trade. The commercial history of later decades supplies plenty of evidence that Netherlands merchants were fiercely opposed to this monopolistic structure.[24] Precisely during the second third of the 16th century, Netherlands trade with Spain, Portugal and the Atlantic Islands was characterized by a definitive growth impulse, the climax being reached in the early 1560s.[25] It therefore strikes me as probable that the feelings of frustration experienced by Netherlands merchants in the matter of Atlantic trade can be traced right back to the 1560s, which means that a feeling of opposition to a hostile and outdated structure was also created in this sphere.

One last question remains for me to answer, namely did the short-term development of the economy exercise a tangible effect on the initial phase of the Revolt? My answer is in the affirmative but needs some elaboration. The economic factor did indeed exert an influence *in the short run*, mainly via the circuitous route of Protestantism where it played a momentous role when the Reformation – which had been the inspiration of a select few – suddenly turned into a mass movement on a very wide scale. In this connection it seems necessary to supplement with a further premise my former working hypothesis about the importance of the role played by prosperity in the gradual cultural emancipation of the masses. This is that poverty does not as a matter of course lead to revolt or open revolution. When, on the other hand, in the euphoria of long- or mid-term expansion, prosperity is suddenly seriously threatened by economic malaise or a famine crisis, then it is the middle class – which may be regarded as providing the major sinews of a prosperous society – that is mainly affected. Inevitably this is followed by a bitter desire to find a culprit. Further, in so far as the economic resilience of the middle class has been appreciably consolidated during the previous period of expansion, reaction in the form of stubborn resistance can be maintained for a great length of time.

---

[23] *Ibid.*, part II, pp. 325–6; see also W. Brulez, *De Firma Della Faille en de Internationale Handel van Vlaamse Firmas in de 16e eeuw* (Brussels: 1959), pp. 457–9 and p. 479–98.

[24] Such opposition was justified in theory in two well-known treatises by Hugo Grotius: *Mare liberum* (1609) and above all in *De Jure Belli ac Pacis* (1625).

[25] Brulez, *De Firma Della Faille*, pp. 24 and 261; Van der Wee, *The Growth of the Antwerp Market* II, pp. 223–4.

It is in this perspective that the triumph of Protestantism in our regions must be seen. Notwithstanding the favourable background of a phase of economic upswing, the 1650s were characterized by a climate of increasing political uncertainty, culminating in the abdication of Emperor Charles V in 1555 and in the first great national bankruptcy of 1557.[26] The acute famine of 1556–57 cut even deeper. It not only brought about a serious diminution of the ranks of unskilled labour, but for the first time since the 1520s the real income of the middle class was painfully affected. True, the crisis was of short duration, but the resumption of hostilities on the southern borders in the Spring of 1557, the government's urgent need for money, and the renewed attempts of the king to replace the *bede* system with a more efficient permanent system of taxing income were enough to revive the feeling that prosperity was in jeopardy. Fortunately the fiscal proposals could be turned down, and the Peace of Cateau-Cambrésis, concluded in April 1559, did much to relieve the political tension.

The expansion which Atlantic trade had undergone in the foregoing years suddenly developed into a feverish boom. This had an immediate effect on the internal economy of the Netherlands. Soon there were signs of increasing inelasticity in the labour supply. Wages, which in many towns and villages of the South had already started rising in the 1540s, suddenly rocketed, and actually increased more strikingly even than prices (see Figure 14.2). Flanders and Brabant had apparently more or less full employment and a complete bottleneck prevented any further expansion. There can be no doubt that the tension in the labour market and the consequent wage increase suddenly induced a new and very spectacular atmosphere of prosperity in the Netherlands, based on the intensified bargaining power of the middle class.

The new boom conditions were of crucial significance since the subsequent disillusionment was painful and deep. The first clouds loomed up from England. In the period 1563–64 the British embargo and the Anglo-Netherlands conflict resulting from it created a real crisis in the important Brabant industry of finishing English cloth. The rate reduction of the very popular *daalders* of German origin, a measure that was finally carried through with success in the mid-1560s, involved losses for middle-class incomes: many members of this class had saved up these silver coins and – unlike the big merchants – could not dispose of them abroad at the high rates. Moreover, the official undervaluation of these *daalders* kept German buyers out of the Netherlands and this hampered trade and industry. Confidence in the future appeared seriously undermined, and indeed it

---

[26] For a more detailed analysis of these events, see Van der Wee, *The Growth of the Antwerp Market* II, pp. 213–4.

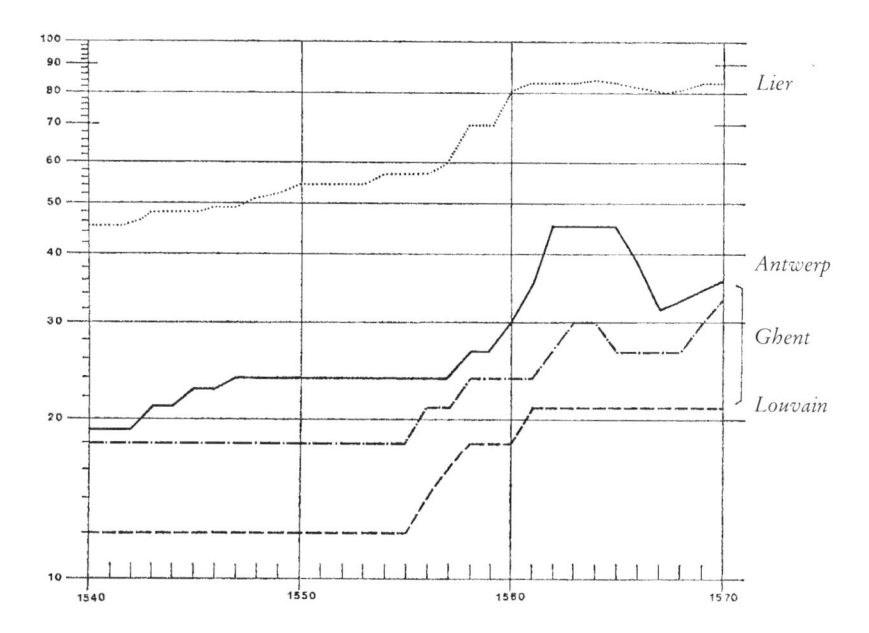

Figure 14.2: *Wages (1540–70)*.

Urban wages in Antwerp, Ghent and Louvain: summer wages of bricklayers in Brabant groats (semi-logarithmic scale).

Rural wages in the neighbourhood of Lier: piece-wages per hundred fagots of fagot makers in the woods around Lier, in Brabant groats (semi-logarithmic scale).

is striking how the building boom – which in Antwerp had been more or less continuous since the beginning of the century – died down at an alarming rate and for good.

To cap it all, in 1564–65 the Netherlands suffered an extremely hard winter. Increased heating costs depleted urban budgets, and this had a negative effect on the demand for industrial products. The situation went from bad to worse when, starting in the Spring of 1565, grain prices showed a tendency to rise and reports of possible closure of the Sound evoked the bogy of approaching famine (see Figure 14.1). Unemployment now made itself felt on all sides. Even the sectors of skilled craftsmanship were affected. This is apparent from the fact that, commencing with the financial year 1564–65, for the first time in many years, skilled labourers were to be found in the Poor Relief lists of Lier. Even more eloquent of unemployment was the wages trend. During a four-year period starting in 1564–65, nominal wages in both town and country fell rapidly and steeply in Flanders and Brabant (see Figure 14.2). As far as I know, trade cycle pressure had never before produced such a phenomenon in the Netherlands, neither in the 14th, the 15th, nor the 16th century. The threat to real incomes was now increased by a fall in nominal incomes.

Fortunately grain prices were already easing off again by the end of December 1565 (see Figure 14.1) and consequently there was no question of a genuine famine. Thus things most certainly did not reach the stage of actual catastrophe.[27] For that reason the years 1564–66 are better seen in the perspective of a serious threat to prosperity as far as the majority of the lower middle class was concerned. Although of material and economic origin, the depression therefore made itself felt rather in the psychological sphere and had an explosive effect on the state of mind of that group.

But two other factors also helped to determine the explosive nature of the psychological reaction. The threat to prosperity in the 1560s and the state of vacuum as regards political authority in the Netherlands (a situation which had become particularly acute since Granvelle's recall in March 1564) coincided for the first time. More important still was the successful dissemination of Calvinist ideas. In most of the larger towns, Calvinist congregations or kindred groups were already active in the 1650s. In the early 1660s this new ideology had also penetrated smaller communities. Although sympathy with the Protestant religion now increased generally, the number of those daring to take the final step in this direction was still comparatively small. When, however, the threat to prosperity and the lack of political authority in the mid-1560s synthesized with the inspired teachings of the Calvinist preachers, the way was suddenly and boldly opened for mass defection from the old order. In a recent work, Riemersma has demonstrated that the economic aspects of the doctrine of the Reformation can hardly account for the sudden enthusiasm of the masses because essentially they confronted the traditional doctrine with little that was new.[28] Nor is there any greater justification for evoking deep religious feeling as a decisive factor since in the Southern Netherlands there is repeated evidence of the dispatch with which the masses abandoned the new religion and reverted to Catholicism.[29] Yet the religion of Calvin and his followers apparently exerted an irresistible fascination upon the

---

[27] *Ibid.*, III, pp. 92–3, graph 40.

[28] J.C. Riemersma, *Religious Factors in Early Dutch Capitalism, 1550–1650*. (The Hague–Paris: 1967), pp. 18–21, 62–6 and elsewhere.

[29] Even the rebellious villages of the Western District, following the defeat of the Beggars' Army near Rijsel on 29 December 1566; Brulez, *De Opstand van het Industriegebied*, p. 100.

imaginations of the middle class just at the critical moment when prosperity was being threatened in the 1560s.[30] The reason lay in the fact that the doctrine of Calvin and his followers *did* hide something new, namely the rejection of the hierarchical solidarity peculiar to Christian society in the Middle Ages, the acceptance of a lay society with broad streaks of rationalism, and the propagation of the principle of *la carrière ouverte au caractère*. Here was an ideology that made a direct appeal to the industrious middle class of trade and industry and at the same time fitted in well with the prevailing mood of frustration and protest.

The preachers played a momentous role in the wholesale changeover to the new doctrine and in the earliest organization of opposition to the existing religious and political order. Yet mass conversion and revolt did not develop primarily from religious inspiration but from the current psychosis of unrest. The fact that the organization of opposition by preachers and nobles could only be successfully carried through when a broad mass-consensus existed, proves how important the role of the middle class during the initial stages of the Revolt should be considered to have been.

However important the role of the middle class in the large-scale dissemination of Protestantism and in the organization of political opposition, it would be unfair to discount entirely the influence of the *unskilled* labourers. With the disabled, the sick, the widowed and the aged, they formed the substratum of the population in which a ferment of revolutionary sentiment permanently smouldered below the ashes of fatalism and resignation. With the growth of towns in the 16th century, moreover, their numbers started increasing again in the Netherlands, a circumstance which must undoubtedly have added to their mass-consciousness.[31] However, although they had become more numerous, I am of the opinion that these needy individuals were still too isolated in the 16th century to be able to assert themselves as a distinct group.[32]

This was no longer the case when the interests of the middle class started to coincide with those of the proletariat. Out of this coincidence of

---

[30] It is really striking, for example, that in Hulst the affluent salt makers who, just at this time, were especially hard hit by the rapid decline of the salt trade in those parts, came to the fore as advocates of the new doctrine and local leaders of the opposition; J. Decavele, 'De reformatorische beweging te Axel en Hulst (1556-1566)', in: *Bijdragen voor de Geschiedenis der Nederlanden* XXII (1968-69), pp. 26-32.

[31] E. Scholliers, 'Vrije en onvrije arbeiders voornamelijk te Antwerpen in de XVIe eeuw', in: *Bijdragen voor de Geschiedenis der Nederlanden* XI (1956), pp. 285-322; E. Scholliers, *De Levensstandaard in de XVe en XVIe eeuw te Antwerpen* (Antwerp: 1960), pp. 65-82, 96-9, 123 f.; Van der Wee, *The Growth of the Antwerp Market*, II, pp. 194-8.

[32] During the 16th century local strikes in particular sectors of unemployment, local famine riots or proletarian unrest never – until the 1560s – developed into a general revolt on the part of the poor – not even on a local basis.

interests was born a common dissatisfaction, a common bitterness, which in the crisis of the 1560s found its first concrete expression in the organization of the iconoclastic revolt and the uprising in the Western District, and which in subsequent years was also of critical significance in the further successful organization of political opposition and war.

Only a few general and rather vague hypotheses have been advanced in the course of this discussion. They have been propounded in the hope of proving that the economy – while not of exclusive significance – was nevertheless an important factor in the start of the Revolt: in the first place as the background to the process of emancipation of the masses, and to the growing obsolescence of the institutional structure; second, as an immediate cause of tensions in the Kondratieff development; and lastly as a concrete reason for the sudden flare-up of feelings conducive to creating unrest under pressure of the threat to prosperity.

15

Nutrition and Diet in the Ancien Régime

The Hunger for Commodities

Food has always been a problem in every human community, though not to the same extent everywhere and in every period. Since the breakthroughs of the industrial and agricultural revolutions it has been chiefly a problem of overproduction in developed countries; but the same cannot be said of the Ancien Régime.

During this earlier period, a 'hunger for commodities' predominated even in the more advanced economies of Europe: agricultural productivity also suffered from a lack of technical knowledge while primitive communications impeded the efficient distribution of agricultural products. Meteorological disturbances and political troubles were translated almost instantaneously into crop failures and desperate food shortages, so that people lived ever in fear of famine. Food supplies consequently remained a primary concern, far outstripping all others. Hence the many municipal and governmental ordinances intended to protect the food supply. And hence, too, the cult of the feast in former times, where the spectre of famine could be forgotten and luxury and plenty enjoyed, at least for a day.

The Menu

The daily menu varied from one social group to another, the more so since the emphasis on indirect taxes imposed an uneven fiscal burden and extended a wide gap in incomes. The tiny majority of the wealthy (chiefly the nobility and the clergy), a goodly middle class (principally merchants and craftsmen) and masses of poor people, especially unskilled or semi-skilled labourers) made up the three income categories of society. Their staple foods were the same, but as income increased there was more variation in the daily menu. For example, the Frisian farmer Rienck Hemmema's farmhands were served only rye bread and beans as their basic diet in the 16th century. The farmer-tenants of the Poor Relief Institution of Lier were treated to a breakfast of rye bread with bacon and Flemish cheese and even a pot of foaming Lier beer before beginning their yearly peat digging in 1531. Upon their return they feasted on white bread (bolted wheat), beer and fresh beef prepared with carrots, mustard greens and salt. In 1518 the masons who had accomplished a difficult task in the headquarters of the Poor Relief Institution at Lier were given a bonus meal of rye bread, beer, Tienen cheese and butter. Four mill specialists from the region of Antwerp who repaired the windmill were served a daily luncheon of rye and wheat bread, fresh beef, butter and eggs, beer, and on one occasion even wine.

The rule of the St James Hospice at Lier, dating from the mid-15th century, allotted each of the twelve brothers, mostly old craftsmen, a daily bowl of good potage – a sort of thick soup made chiefly from beans and peas, and with carrots, turnips, onion, and cabbage when in season. Each brother also received daily a one-pound loaf of currant bread, consisting of two-thirds of wheat flour and one-third of rye flour. In addition a daily ration of 35 grams of butter, 29 grams of Tienen cheese, one egg, and 1.4 litres of good Lier beer was allotted to each. Every Sunday, Tuesday and Thursday evening fresh meat was served, and on the other evenings salt beef or pork. During Lent pickled or smoked herring was substituted for the meat, and a daily ration of 70 grams of figs for the butter and eggs. The brothers were occasionally given an extra portion of salt and pepper.

During the 17th century, the municipal orphanage of Amsterdam served rice with jam, and even stew made with prunes, on Sundays and holidays. Still, these delicacies were reserved for special occasions. During the week an ordinary potage of peas and beans was served, with a portion of salt cod on Wednesday, a strip of stockfish on Saturday, a bit of meat on Thursdays and blood sausage on the other days.

Soldiers were usually better supplied by the army, certainly with respect to quantity. Gaspar Schetz, as Treasurer-General under Philip II, made an estimate of the requirements for reprovisioning the 600-man garrison at the castle of Antwerp. He allowed per soldier per day: 1½ pounds of rye bread, 2 litres of beer brewed from barley, oats and hops, ¼ pound of Dutch cheese, ⅛ pound of butter, salt, ⅕ litre of peas or beans for potage and a portion of salt beef or stockfish. For meal preparation at the garrison several barrels of vinegar and rapeseed oil were ordered. The Spanish soldiers received one litre of wine instead of beer, preferably Spanish, French or Rhine wine. Since the Spaniards did not care for salt meat or stockfish either, they received in their place ¼ pound of bacon, and instead of a potage of peas and beans they received a ration of rice.

In West Frisia an estimate was made in 1648 for the reprovisioning of an expeditionary corps of 3,000 men headed for Brazil. Each soldier was allotted a daily ration of 1½ pounds of rye bread, 102 grams of meat,

68 grams of stockfish, 68 grams of cheese, 68 grams of butter and a goodly ration of oil.

An example of a more extensive menu can be found in the accounts of Our Lady Cathedral of Antwerp in 1555 recording the purchase of white bread, 100 eggs, 4 kilograms of butter, 9 kilograms of ham, 75 litres of beer, vinegar, parsley and all sorts of spices: these were the ingredients for a festive breakfast served to the celebrating priest and his assistants and to the canon of the chapter following the solemn high mass on Trinity Sunday.

The annual budget plan made up by the Antwerp merchant Gerard Gramaye for the nourishment of his household, including servants, on 1 January 1565 is of particular interest. He noted: 1,760 litres of wheat, 2,400 litres of rye, 2 oxen (roughly 350 kilograms of meat), 3 pigs (roughly 150 kilograms of meat), 1,700 pickled herrings, approximately 1,000 smoked herrings, 447 kilograms of butter, 94 kilograms of Dutch cheese, 280 litres of vinegar, 84 litres of oil, some 7,000 litres of Antwerp beer, approximately 2,000 litres of imported beer (primarily from England, Hamburg and Gdansk), 3,265 litres of wine (including French, Rhine, Spanish and Greek wines) and around 36 kilograms of sugar (at that time chiefly from Madeira, the Canary Islands, or the Azores). A stock of dried peas and beans was purchased for potage. In addition a fixed sum was budgeted to purchase salt and spices on the Antwerp market, including: pepper, ginger, cloves, almonds, cinnamon, saffron, mace, cumin, nutmeg, and so on. Lenten fruit, particularly dried figs and raisins, was listed as a separate entry. Finally there followed a global sum for the 'daily marketing', intended for the purchase of milk, vegetables, fruit, mustard seed, honey and foreign cheeses from Parma and Cornwall, as well as exceptional holiday purchases like fish, game and poultry (chickens, geese, rabbits, partridges, '*sneppen, borst van de calve, ossetonge, gesouten salm*' (snipes, breast of veal, ox-tongue, salt salmon), eel, pike, and other freshwater fish). Naturally, we can draw no conclusions from these figures, since it is impossible to arrive at even an approximate idea of how many people the budget was intended to provide for. Together with the family and the regular staff there is the unknown 'guest' factor, which in the home of a merchant like Gramaye was substantial. The sharp contrast between the rich and varied menu of a small group of well-to-do burghers and the poor and monotonous fare of the less fortunate masses, clearly reflected in all the institutional accounts of the period, is striking.

Beer and Wine Consumption

Tea and coffee were introduced at the end of the 17th century, but came into general use in Europe chiefly in the course of the 18th century. Before then beer, mead (a beverage made from honey) and wine were the commonest beverages served at mealtime. Beer had been known in our territories since the dawn of time. To improve its flavour a certain amount of 'grout' (a mixture of berries and herbs) was added to the malt. In the course of the 14th century this grout was superseded by hops. The advantage of hops was not only that they refined the flavour of beer but also that they appreciably extended its shelf life. This dual improvement in quality immediately stimulated beer consumption. The preparation of hop beer presumably began in the Baltic area, Northern Germany and Holland. In towns like Gdansk, Hamburg, Bremen, Haarlem, and later Gouda as well, production soon increased sharply, in the first instance for domestic consumption, but gradually more for a growing export market. In 1374 Hamburg alone had some 450 breweries within its walls. Haarlem also exported hop beer in quantity, to Flanders and Brabant, among other places. In 1408–9 three-quarters of the beer consumed at Lier came from the North: 97% of this came from Haarlem and 3% from Hamburg. English beers also found their way on to our markets. The Southern Netherlands also gradually introduced hop beer technology. In 1474 domestic beer production again accounted for 76% of local consumption, only 23% was still imported from Holland (and that no longer from Haarlem but from Gouda) and only 1% from Hamburg.

The appreciable improvement in the quality of hop beer in a period of increasing prosperity brought annual *per capita* beer consumption in the Burgundian and Habsburg Netherlands to a very high level. Around 1472 this level was approximately 271 litres for Louvain and around 310 litres for Lier; in 1526 it was 256 litres for Diest and around 300 litres for Ninove. At Antwerp in 1543 a level of around 243 litres was reached. Compared to the present situation – in 1958 the average beer consumption per inhabitant per year in Belgium was 115 litres – the Brabantine figures for the 15th and 16th centuries are indeed very high. In Flanders, Artois and Picardy, on the other hand, beer production was, with few exceptions, less successful. In Ostend, Nieuwpoort, Bruges and Ghent the domestic breweries were unable to compete against the Dutch, English and North German beers. The imports of the latter into Flemish towns also remained relatively low in comparison to, for example, the imports into Brabant. In Saint-Omer in the third quarter of the 16th-century average beer consumption was recorded at only 55.6 litres per person per year. The centuries-old contacts between the Flemish ports and the French wine-producing regions were probably at least partially responsible for this difference.

In the late Middle Ages wine was a common consumer product in the Netherlands. It was primarily a beverage of the higher classes, but was not yet considered the luxury product it became in the 19th and 20th centuries.

For example during the 15th and 16th centuries the Saint-Gummarus Church at Lier distributed substantial quantities of wine among the poor who attended any high mass on special occasions. The highest average wine consumption was in Flanders, where imports from France were concentrated at the staple market of Damme. In wealthy, cosmopolitan Bruges the average annual wine consumption per person was around 100 litres in 1420-21, and around 75 litres in 1444. In more industrial Ghent this figure varied from 30 to 44 litres at the end of the 14th century; in Saint-Omer more than 150 years later it was still between 39 and 55 litres.

These averages were appreciably lower in Brabant. This is all the more surprising since substantial amounts of wine were produced in Brabant itself during the Middle Ages: the vineyards around Hoegaarden, Louvain, Wezemaal, Testelt, Aarschot, Langdorp, Diest, and Tienen produced a local wine of passable, if rather low quality. It was exported in considerable quantities to the towns of North Brabant and Flanders. In 1474 at Lier, Brabant wines still accounted for a quarter of the wine imports. In the wine-producing regions around Louvain and Diest, for example, approximately half the wine consumed in 1509 was of local vintage. Nevertheless, the average annual consumption of wine in 1509 at Louvain was only 23.65 litres, and at Diest barely 19.3 litres. In Lier this average was around 17.5 litres in 1474 and in 1543 Antwerp it was 19.2 litres.

The lower figures for Brabant are not attributable exclusively to regional differences from Flanders; they also date from a later period and reflect a general decline in wine consumption in the Netherlands. By 1532 this average had also declined to 25 litres for Bruges itself, for Louvain and Diest the average figures for 1550 had already fallen to 15.13 litres and 16.70 litres respectively and during the 1590s, at the peak of the revolt-crisis, Louvain reached an all-time low of 1.3 litres. Afterwards consumption again rose, though the average still remained around 3 litres in the mid-17th century. By that time wine had become a luxury product in the Netherlands, as indeed it still is today: in 1950-51 in Belgium the average annual *per capita* wine consumption scarcely reached 6 litres.

Brabant's falling wine consumption in the late Middle Ages is also related to the decline of its traditional local wine. The majority of the population switched more and more to beer consumption, especially after the addition of hops had so improved its quality. For their part, the wealthier classes preferred the better wines like the Rhine wine, though its relatively high price limited demand for it. In 1474 two-thirds of the wine consumed at Lier was imported from the Rhine and Mosel regions.

French wines from Poitou, and especially those from Burgundy, were also popular in Brabant, though to a lesser extent. French Bordeaux wines penetrated the northern part of the duchy in the course of the 16th century, winning a definitive place on the markets in the southern parts in the

284   THE LOW COUNTRIES IN THE EARLY MODERN WORLD

17th century only. These wines, too, remained a luxury product in limited demand for the wealthy.

Providing for Life's Necessities

In the late Middle Ages and in Early Modern Times most incomes remained low and the products available relatively limited. Thus for every family a strict and selective budgetary policy was an urgent necessity. An Antwerp orphanage has provided us with details of its expenditures allowing us roughly to determine the breakdown of an Antwerp labourer's budget in the period 1586-1600 (Figure 15.1).

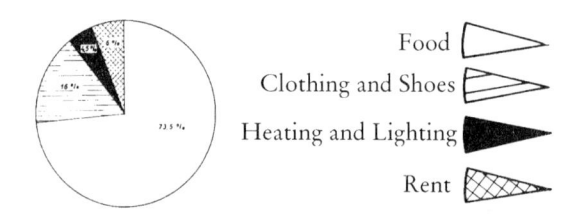

Figure 15.1: *Average distribution of an Antwerp labourer's budget: 1586-1600.*

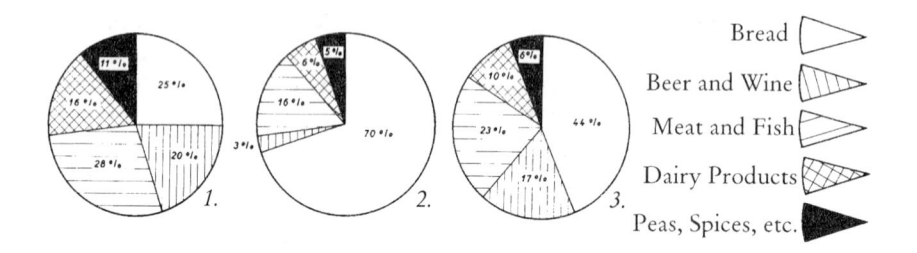

Figure 15.2: *Distribution of the food budget of the Beguinage Infirmary at Lier.*
1. Years of low grain prices (harvest year 1561-62)
2. Years of high grain prices (harvest year 1586-1687)
3. Average for the period 1526-1602

The enormous importance of food in the labourer's budget is immediately apparent. This food budget had, moreover, its own peculiar characteristics. In the Beguinage Infirmary at Lier during the period from 1526 to 1602 the budget was normally distributed as follows: 44% for bread, 16% for grain-based beer, only 1% for wine, 3% for fish, 20% for meat and 10% for dairy products (Figure 15.2). The expenditures for meat were relatively high. This observation is further confirmed in other sources: for example in 1474 at Lier, with a population of approximately 5,300, no fewer than 115 oxen, 531 cows, 595 pigs, 2,040 sheep, 533 lambs and 205 calves were slaughtered. This represents an average annual consumption of 35 kilograms per person. In Germany around 1500 this average was probably much higher, approximately 75 kilograms for Nuremberg and 130 kilograms for Frankfurt-am-Main. Even during the famine years of the 16th century, when all the other expenditures of the Lier Infirmary were drastically reduced in favour of bread, the purchase of meat remained at a relatively high level.

An examination of the calorie distribution, in so far as it can be estimated from the few daily rations known in the Netherlands for this period, offers a preliminary explanation for this surprising observation. In addition to the monotonous diet of grains and legumes, the consumption of meat and fish provided the necessary proteins in the diet. In the daily rations of the St James Hospice (in the year 1450), of the Antwerp garrison (in the year 1568), and of the Frisian expeditionary corps sent to Brazil (in the year 1648) the proteins provided by meat and fish provided 16%, 15% and 17% respectively of the total calories present in these rations. Moreover, in famine years many animals were slaughtered prematurely due to a shortage of fodder. This increased the supply and was assuredly a contributing factor in maintaining meat consumption at relatively high levels even in years of high grain prices.

The greatest portion of the budget was allotted to grain-based products. On average these expenditures, including purchases of beer so closely linked to those of grain, accounted for some 60% on average of the Lier Infirmary budget for the period 1526–1602. This preference clearly shows how limited the food budget actually was. Expressed in terms of money, grains and beer had by far the highest calorie content: no cheaper diet was conceivable. In fact the consumer did not count calories, of course – a modern obsession – but simply filled his belly as full as he could! Nevertheless, if an unskilled labourer at Antwerp around 1500–5 were to devote his entire day's wage to the purchase of rye bread, he would dispose of a total of 24,350 calories. If he devoted it to the purchase of peas he would have 20,700 calories, for Flemish cheese only 11,200 calories, for butter 7,120 calories, for beef no more than 3,940 calories. Consequently the food budget of lower and middle-class families tended to focus on those products with the highest calorie value for the money. In the daily rations of the St James Hospice at Lier in the year 1540, and of the Antwerp garrison in 1568, bread and beer accounted for 66% and 64% respectively of the total calorie intake; bread, beer and peas together for 75% and 70% respectively. Even in times of crop failures and famine,

286   THE LOW COUNTRIES IN THE EARLY MODERN WORLD

Soldiers of the Frisian Expeditionary Corps to Brazil (1648)

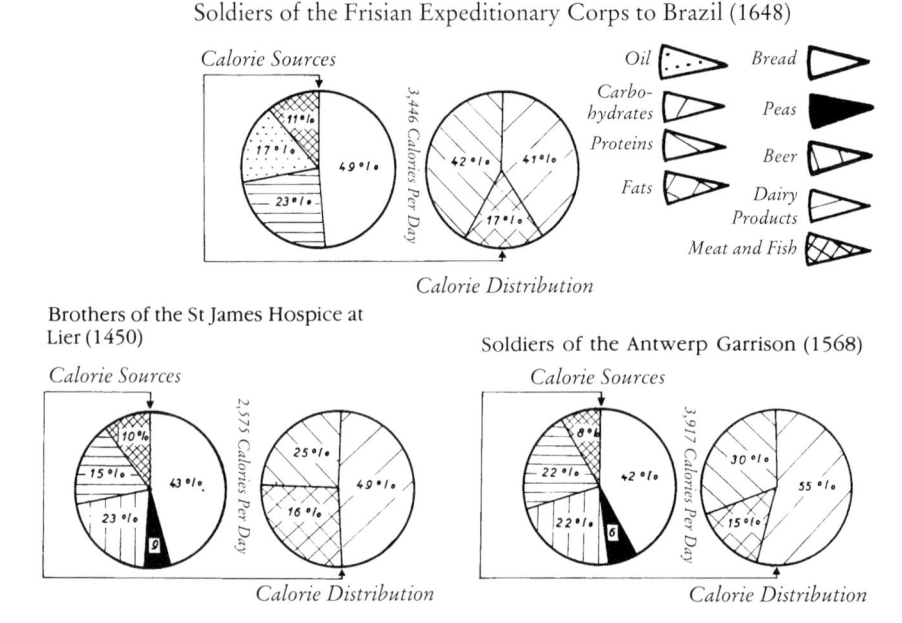

Figure 15.3: *Distribution of the calorie content of various daily rations in the Netherlands.*

grains continued to provide the highest caloric value per monetary unit expended. Therefore budgeted purchases were concentrated even more on grains and beer in such anxious times, and purchases of cheese, butter and spices were sharply curtailed. Increased demand for grain at a time of severe shortage led to even more rapid price increases, to the point where, even devoting virtually the whole of a budget to the basic necessities, it no longer sufficed to provide them.

Finally, a word concerning the remarkably high beer consumption of the 15th and 16th centuries. Beer, as an alcoholic beverage, certainly provided medieval man with the euphoria of a befuddled mind, allowing him to forget the cares of life for a few hours. And water supplies, especially in towns, might be foul-tasting and polluted, so beer might be both tastier and healthier! Furthermore, beer provided some variation in the carbohydrate content and a welcome and flavourful break in the monotony of a grain-based diet. Nor should we forget that tea and coffee were not yet in general use, and beer was still the most common mealtime beverage for the vast majority of families.

Were income and nutrition adequate to provide for the essential dietary needs of the vast majority of the population of the Netherlands during the Ancien Régime? This is a thorny problem and can be answered only approximately. A study of the daily rations of the brothers of the St James Hospice at Lier (1450), of the Antwerp garrison (1568), and of the Frisian expeditionary corps sent to Brazil (1648) points to consumption of 2,575 calories, 3,917 calories, and 3,446 calories, respectively. Keeping in mind that today, for an adult labourer doing normal work, 2,700 calories is considered adequate, and for a soldier 3,500 calories, then the figures cited above can be considered reasonable. A comparison with daily rations elsewhere in Europe leads to similar conclusions, with the reservation that the higher classes appear to have consumed considerably more calories. Finally, taking the income of skilled and unskilled labourers at Antwerp and Lier during the 15th and 16th centuries, we find that in normal years their wages were ample to provide a normal family of five (two parents and three children) with a varied diet of roughly 12,500 calories per day. In times of famine and political unrest, on the other hand, and particularly when unemployement rose to alarming levels, the unskilled labourers and even skilled craftsmen frequently went hungry.

Index

1. Index locorum

Aachen, 18, 65, 93
Aarschot, 8, 205, 283
Africa, 7, 114
   African Coast, 18
   North Africa, 7, 171, 178
   West Africa, 17, 18, 92–4, 100, 103, 181
Alexandria, 96
Alost, 62, 66, 104, 106, 205
Alps, 6, 18, 24, 94, 233
Alsace, 170, 224, 234
America, 35
   North America, 35
Amsterdam, 8, 19, 23, 26, 32–3, 35–6, 39, 108, 140, 145, 147–8, 196–7, 280
Ancona, 105, 109
Antwerp, 17–20, 24–8, 39, 53–5, 65–6, 79, 82, 91–120, 122–3, 127, 130, 136, 138–41, 145, 148–54, 156–8, 160–6, 179–80, 186–97, 216, 220, 226–7, 229, 245, 247, 252, 256, 258–9, 261, 266–7, 272, 275, 280–5, 287
Aquitaine, 173
Armentières, 106, 115, 117, 121, 215, 221
Arnemuiden, 135
Arras, 8, 204, 210, 221
Artois, 6, 49, 178, 203–4, 210, 282
Asti, 185
Athus-sur-Orges, 172
Atlantic Coasts, 19
   Atlantic Islands, 17–8, 273
   Atlantic Ocean, 17
   Atlantic Sugar Islands, 109

Augsburg, 165, 224
Austria, 37, 235
Axel, 106, 131, 133–4
Azores, 18, 95, 283

Bailleul, 215
Baltic, 9, 11–2, 19, 58, 61, 110, 271
   Baltic area, 271, 282
   Baltic lands, 220
   Baltic region, 19, 21, 23, 92, 97–9, 102–3, 107–8, 112–3, 128, 139–40
   Baltic world, 126
   Baltic zone, 139
Banska-Bystrica, 18
Basque Coast, 109
   Basque region, 19
Bay of Bourgneuf, 135
Bayonne, 100
Belgium, 22, 38, 39, 223, 282, 283
Bergen-op-Zoom, 17, 92–3, 96, 116, 120, 128, 150, 179, 192–3
Bergues Saint-Winoc, 106, 204, 266
Besançon, 28, 164
Biervliet, 129–31, 134
Black Sea, 7
Bohemia, 170
Bordeaux, 283
Brabant, 6, 8–9, 11, 14, 17–9, 21–2, 23, 25, 47–60, 62–3, 65–7, 78–9, 90–7, 99, 104, 106–7, 110, 112–3, 120, 127–33, 136–9, 141, 149–50, 158, 169–82, 184–93, 195–6, 204–5, 210–9, 224, 226, 229–35, 237–40, 247–9, 253–5, 261–2, 274, 276, 282–3

288

INDEX

North Brabant, 34, 221, 283
Northern Brabant, 57, 133
South Brabant, 56
Southwest Brabant, 50
Southwestern Brabant, 53, 55, 59, 62
Walloon-Brabant, 56
West Brabant, 96, 107
Western Brabant, 57, 108, 229, 247
Brazil, 35, 280, 285, 287
Bremen, 109, 126, 282
Brenner Pass, 109
Brielle, 131, 132
British Isles, 19
Brittany, 19, 138, 173
Brouage, 135
Bruges, 8–10, 14, 17–8, 20, 26–7, 50, 52–3, 55, 82, 91–4, 96–7, 104, 108–10, 126, 128, 138, 141, 150, 152, 185, 191, 196–7, 204–5, 210, 215, 218–21, 282–3
Brussels, 8, 39, 59–60, 79, 104, 107, 131, 153, 169, 185–8, 205, 209, 218, 229, 247, 258, 261
Burgos, 109
Burgundy, 137, 283

Cadiz, 135
Cahors, 185
Calais, 100, 113, 141, 213–4
Cambrai, 8, 56, 99, 204
Cambrésis, 48, 56, 274
Campine, 11–2, 96, 219
Canary Islands, 18, 95, 109, 281
Castellany of Furnes, 63, 65
Castile, 18, 145, 147–8, 159
Catalonia, 204, 212
Cateau, 274
Châlon-sur-Saône, 93, 145
Champagne, 8, 9, 170, 204
Chieri, 185
Cleves, 118
Cologne, 8, 9, 18, 92, 94, 109–10, 118, 130, 185, 191
Comines, 205, 215
Condroz, 56
Cornwall, 281
Courtrai, 74, 78, 106, 205
Cracow, 93

Damme, 138, 283
Deinze, 74, 78, 79, 205
  Deinze-Tronchiennes, 70, 72, 78, 81
Delft, 127–8, 136, 148
Denmark, 23, 97–8, 107
Deventer, 93

Dieppe, 130
Diest, 8, 104, 139–40, 205, 282–3
Dixmuide, 8, 136, 204
Dinant, 18, 93
Diu, 118
Dordrecht, 9, 92, 108, 127, 137–8, 152
Douai, 8, 139, 204, 221
Dranouter, 106, 215
Drenthe, 11, 23, 54, 57, 62, 97, 136
Duffel, 106, 215
Dunkirk, 113
Dutch republic, 67

Edingen, 104, 106
Eeke, 106, 215
Eeklo, 106
Emden, 109, 112
England, 7–9, 13, 17, 19, 21, 26, 29, 36–7, 39, 52, 91, 102, 105, 108, 112–4, 116, 118, 121, 128–9, 159, 163, 165–6, 170–2, 202, 204, 212, 224, 229, 230, 234, 236–8, 240–1, 274, 281
  Southern England, 224, 226–7, 229–30, 234
English Channel, 113
Estaire, 215
Europe
  Central Europe, 4, 17–8, 25, 31, 37, 63, 80, 93–4, 98, 100, 120, 179, 237
  East Europe, 37
  Eastern Europe, 4, 9, 18, 32, 80, 120, 237
  Northeastern Europe, 103, 108
  Northern Europe, 7, 8–9, 13, 17, 26, 94, 97, 111, 113, 184, 190, 268
  Northwest Europe, 265
  Northwestern Europe, 6–9, 14, 17–8, 21, 26, 100, 110, 151, 190, 194, 217, 237
  Southern Europe, 17, 18, 32, 37, 63, 94, 97, 108, 109, 111, 113, 138, 146, 159, 180
  Western Europe, 4, 7, 32, 48, 49, 52, 69, 137, 145, 202–3, 237, 245
Far East, 7, 19, 35, 93, 94, 103
Flanders, 6, 8–9, 11–2, 19, 21–3, 25, 39, 41, 47–53, 55–62, 66, 69–70, 78–81, 90–2, 99, 104, 107, 113, 127–30, 136, 138, 141, 150, 158, 168, 170–80, 190–1, 203–5, 210–5, 217, 219, 221, 234, 237, 248, 255, 262, 274, 276, 282–3
  East Flanders, 62, 65–6, 219

Eastern Flanders, 59–60, 106
French Flanders, 219, 221
South Flanders, 58
Southeast Flanders, 58, 62
West Flanders, 12, 58
West Quarter of Flanders
  (*Westkwartier*), 21
Western Flanders, 63, 105
Fletre, 215
Florence, 7, 171
Flushing, 113
Franc de Bruges, 63, 65
France, 7–8, 18, 21, 29, 31, 37–9, 87,
  93, 98–9, 103, 105, 109, 117,
  120, 135, 138, 140, 168, 171–2,
  176, 180, 224, 234, 245, 247, 255,
  271, 283
  Central France, 109
  North of France, 6
  Northern France, 19, 92, 97, 99, 139
  Southwestern France, 185
  Western France, 100
Frankfurt, 93
Frankfurt am Main, 285
Frisia, 11, 23, 47, 54, 57–8, 61–2, 64,
  97, 99, 107, 126, 136, 178
  West Frisia, 108, 280

Gdansk, 19, 98, 281–2
Geel, 215
Geldenaken, 8
Gelderland, 56–8, 65, 118, 175, 179
Geneva, 93, 145–6
Genoa, 7, 145, 147–8, 161
Germany, 7–8, 18, 21, 31, 39, 62, 94,
  102–3, 105, 109, 179, 285
  Central Germany, 9, 100, 109, 215
  East German region, 128
  Eastern Germany, 139
  German world, 126
  North Germany, 215
  Northern Germany, 107, 109, 126,
    127, 282
  Northwestern Germany, 235
  Southern Germany, 18, 93–4, 100,
    212
  Western Germany, 109
Gerona, 147
Ghent, 8, 50, 53, 74, 78, 104, 106,
  139, 140, 173, 175, 204, 205, 221,
  282–3
Goes, 131, 134, 135
Gouda, 128, 282
Grammont, 205
Gravelines, 100
Groningen, 11, 23, 54, 57, 61, 62, 97,
  136

Guinea, 94
Haarlem, 8, 126–8, 141, 282
Hageland, 90, 108
Hainault, 6, 9, 12, 21–3, 37, 39, 49,
  51, 55, 57–9, 65, 104, 176, 178,
  204, 221
Hamburg, 109, 112, 127, 148, 164–5,
  281
Hannut, 56
Hanse, 9, 19, 52, 92, 130
  German Hanse, 9–10, 12, 19, 126
  Hanse area, 215
Hanseatic area, 9
Hanseatic ports, 128
Hanseatic territories, 8, 132
Hanseatic towns, 126
Hanseatics, 91, 96, 99, 110, 128, 149
Haspengouw, 90, 108, 139–40, 267
Hauboudin, 106
Herentals, 8, 104, 107, 139, 187, 205
's Hertogenbosch, 60, 64, 96, 130,
  136, 187
Herve, 56
Hesbaye, 56
Hoegaarden, 56, 140, 283
Holland, 6, 8–9, 11–2, 18–9, 21–3,
  32–6, 39, 47, 49, 50–3, 55–9, 61,
  63, 65, 91–2, 99, 107, 110, 113,
  126–30, 135–6, 138, 148, 176,
  178, 271, 282
  North Holland, 64, 99, 108
  South Holland, 99
Holstein, 97, 136
Hondschoote, 12, 21, 105, 109,
  115–8, 121, 221, 255
Hoogstraten, 215
Hoorn, 12, 21, 106, 215
Hugevliet, 130
Hulst, 106, 131, 133–4
Hungary, 18, 220

Iberia
  Iberian Coast, 109
  Iberian Peninsula, 4, 93, 102–3, 105,
    140
Ijssel, 9
Ile-de-France, 8, 203–4
India, 19, 118
  East Indies, 32, 138
  West Indies, 19, 32, 35, 138
Italy, 7–10, 17–8, 21, 27, 31, 92, 98,
  100, 103, 105, 108–9, 115–8, 120,
  126, 128, 140, 148, 161, 162, 212,
  220
  Northern Italy, 6, 109, 204, 234

Java, 36

INDEX

Jülich, 118

Langdorp, 283
Langemark, 205
Languedoc, 204, 212
Leerbeek, 50, 53, 55
Leipzig, 93
Levant, 7, 32, 100, 102, 105, 109, 161, 178
Leyden, 8, 140–1
Liège, 9, 22–3, 37, 39, 47, 53, 56, 59–60, 62, 65, 79, 87, 97, 107, 204
Lier, 8, 50, 53–5, 127–8, 136–7, 139, 187, 205, 229, 247, 252, 256, 258, 261, 275, 279–80, 282–5, 287
Lille, 8, 26, 104, 106, 204, 221
Limburg, 21, 50–3, 59, 94
  South Limburg, 56
  Southern Limburg, 47–8, 59
Lisbon, 96, 100, 109, 120, 135, 151, 156
Lombardy, 185
London, 8–9, 17, 93, 102, 126, 134, 145, 158, 166, 191, 196
Louvain, 8, 53, 55–6, 59, 62, 104, 131, 139–40, 173, 175, 185–8, 191–2, 205, 218, 282–3
Lübeck, 109, 133
Lucca, 154
Lüneberg, 133
Lyons, 18, 93, 95, 100, 145–7, 164
Lys, 8, 205
  Lys area, 205, 211

Maaseik, 12, 56, 106, 215
Maastricht, 50, 59, 62, 65, 106, 215
Madeira, 94, 95, 109, 281
Mansfeld, 18
Marseille, 95, 100, 118
Mechlin, 8, 14, 18, 93, 96, 104, 130–1, 139, 158, 188, 205, 216, 218, 247
Mediterranean, 161
  Mediterranean area, 7, 12, 221
  Mediterranean region, 6, 7, 31–2, 91, 100, 140
  Eastern Mediterranean region, 178
  Mediterranean route, 120
  Southern Mediterranean region, 178
Meerssen, 56
Meldert, 50, 53–4, 56, 59, 62
Menen, 205
Meuse, 6–8, 49–50, 56, 107
Mexico, 181

Middelburg, 9, 26, 135, 138–40, 148, 166
Middle East, 32, 103, 171
Milan, 147
Moerspeye, 134
Mosel, 137, 283
Munster, 87, 197, 224

Naarden, 8
Namur, 47–50, 53, 55, 59, 62, 65, 178
Nantes, 113
Naples, 114
Narva, 108
Netherlands, 29, 49, 92, 94, 97, 101–5, 108–9, 111, 113, 116, 119–23, 128–30, 132, 139–40, 150, 152, 160, 170, 178–81, 191–2, 194, 197, 219–20, 245–7, 250–1, 253, 255, 257–8, 262, 265–77, 282–3, 285–6
  Burgundian Netherlands, 14, 103, 179, 186, 210, 217, 219, 249, 282
  Habsburg Netherlands, 282
  Northeastern Netherlands, 58
  Northern Netherlands, 14, 22, 24, 29, 31–2, 39, 48, 58–9, 61–4, 67–8, 93, 96, 113, 126, 139, 141
  Southern Netherlands, 14, 24, 29–31, 37–9, 41, 53, 59–63, 65–7, 87–93, 96–105, 107–14, 126–7, 138–9, 141, 188, 201, 209, 213–7, 220–3, 226, 241, 266, 276, 282
Neuve-Eglise, 215, 221
Nevele, 62
New World, 17, 19, 21, 25, 100, 105, 109, 181, 221, 271
Nieuwkerke, 106
Nieuwpoort, 113, 282
Ninove, 50, 53, 55, 205, 215, 282
Nivelles, 187
Normandy, 204, 212
North Sea, 32, 37, 98, 138
  North Sea region, 19
Nuremberg, 18, 93, 285

Ostend, 37, 282
Oudenaarde, 104, 107, 205
Overijssel, 6, 11, 23, 47, 54, 56–7, 62, 64, 97, 136

Palermo, 147
Palma, 95
Paris, 37–8
  Paris region, 49
Parma, 281

Pepingen, 50, 53, 55
Peru, 181
Petegem, 53, 55
Piacenza, 28, 145–8, 161, 197
Picardy, 56, 104, 203, 282
Poitou, 137–8, 283
Poland, 220
Poperinghe, 205, 209, 215
Portugal, 21, 98, 100, 109, 135, 138, 181, 273
Posen, 93
Potosi, 181
Prussia, 29, 37
Puerto de Santa Maria, 135
Pyrenees, 94

Ré, 135
Red Sea, 120
Reimerswaal, 131, 134–5
Retie, 215
Rhine, 6–8, 92, 109, 122, 137–9, 149, 179, 249, 252, 283
  Rhine region, 179
  Rhineland, 9, 93, 97, 108, 185
Rome, 121, 147
Rotterdam, 148
Rouen, 113, 130, 156
Roulers, 205
Rupel, 108
Russia, 37

Saaftinge, 132
Saint-Malo, 113
Saint-Omer, 8, 204, 210, 221, 282–3
Saint-Quentin, 100
Saint-Truiden, 49–50, 56, 104, 139
Salland, 64
Sambre, 107
San Lucar de Barrameda, 135
Saô Tomé, 109
Savoy, 146
Saxony, 18, 170
Scandinavia, 7, 23, 108
  Scandinavian world, 126
Scheldt, 6–7, 19, 32, 37, 97, 113–4, 135
Schiedem, 131
Schleswig, 97, 136
Schleswig-Holstein, 23
Schonen, 129–30, 133
Scotland, 26, 202
Seine, 90
Senlis, 90
Setubal, 135
Seville, 19, 100, 109, 148, 197
Sluis, 127
Somme, 90

Spain, 17, 19, 21, 26, 28, 31–2, 39, 55, 58, 82, 98, 100, 103, 108–9, 111, 120, 135, 138, 148, 197, 221, 235, 245, 258, 268, 273
Spires, 108, 139, 140
Steenbergen, 131–3
Stettin, 98
Swabia, 92
Sweden, 29, 108
Switzerland, 109

Termonde, 106, 205, 215
Testelt, 283
Tienen, 8, 50, 53–4, 56, 59, 62, 104, 185, 205, 280, 283
Tolen, 131
Tongeren, 56
Tourcoing, 215
Tournai, 8, 104, 108, 204, 221, 264
Transylvania, 170
Turkey, 114
Turnhout, 50, 53, 55, 107
Tuscany, 162
Twente, 34, 64, 65
Tyrol, 18

United Kingdom, 38
Upper Franconia, 92
Utrecht, 9, 61, 65, 99, 152

Valencia, 224
Valenciennes, 8, 204, 221, 264
Veere, 140
Veluwe, 64
Venice, 7, 94, 96, 100–1, 105, 109, 114, 118, 147, 149, 159, 171
Verviers, 37, 39, 65
Vienna, 37, 100, 224
Vier Ambachten, 106
Vilvoorde, 8, 187, 205

Waasland, 106
Waasten, 185
Walcheren, 96–7, 101, 118, 133, 135, 138, 140
Walem, 215
Wallonia, 21, 39, 41
  Walloon provinces, 97, 107, 108
  Walloon territories, 39
Warneton, 205, 215
Weert, 12, 21, 56, 106, 121–2, 215, 219, 221, 250, 255, 259
Wervik, 205
Westdorpe, 134
Western District (*Westkwartier*), 264, 267, 278
Westphalia, 87, 197, 224

INDEX

Wezemaal, 283

Ypres, 8, 50, 204, 205, 209, 221

Zacatecas, 181
Zeeland, 6, 9, 18-9, 32, 49-51, 56-9, 61, 91-2, 97, 99, 102, 107, 110, 113, 126, 129-30, 132-3, 135-6, 138-40, 148

Zeeland islands, 133
Zeeland-Brabant, 133
Zeeland-Flanders, 99, 102, 113, 132-5, 219
Zele, 58, 60, 62
Zevenbergen, 131, 133
Zierikzee, 131, 134-5
Zoutleeuw, 8, 185, 187, 205
Zuiddorpe, 134

2. Index nominum

Affaitadi, the, 94
Albert, archduke, 188
Albert of Bavaria, 176
Alfer, Bertelmeeus, 191
Alva, duke, 59, 113, 269
Austrian Monarchy, 37
    Austrian rule, 65

Beukels, Willem, 129
Beveridge, William, 225
Burgundian dukes, 14, 16-8, 177, 192
    Burgundian rulers, 15-6, 25, 193
    dukes of Burgundy, 69, 81, 150, 196

Calvin, 277-8
Carolingian rulers, 167
Carus-Wilson, Eleonora, 213
Charlemagne, 9, 168-9
Charles the Bold, 16, 53, 82, 87, 92-3, 179-80, 186, 196
Charles V, 25, 26, 81-2, 117-20, 138, 140, 181, 189, 197, 268
    Charles, 181
    Charles, Emperor, 181, 222, 274
Christensen, Axel, 161
Clement V, 186
Cobergher, Wenzel, 188
Contarini, Tommaso, 149, 154, 159
Coornaert, Emile, 109
Craeybeckx, Jan, 226

Danish kings, 118
de Bruyne, Daniel, 164, 272
De Curiel, Jeronimo, 154
de Gauna, Juan, 135
de Malynes, Gerard, 156, 158, 162, 165
de Roover, Raymond, 150, 159, 191
Della Faille, 109
    Della Faille archives, 164-5
Doorman, 129
Ducci, Gaspar, 158
Duke of Brabant, 171
    dukes of Brabant, 196
Duke of Cleves, Jülich and Gelderland, 149

Edler, Florence, 115
Elizabeth I, 112
English, the, 149
English government, 166

Farnese, Alexander, 113, 114, 233
Flemish counts, 15

François I, 100, 118
French kings, 118
Frescobaldi, the 94
Frisians, the, 7
Fuggers, the, 26, 94, 95, 165

Genoese, the, 28
Germans, the, 149
Goubert, Pierre, 261
Goy, Joseph, 48
Gramaye, Gerard, 281
Granvelle, 276
Gresham, Thomas, 173
Groenenborg, Jacob, 95
Gualterotti, the, 94

Habsburg, 120, 140
    Habsburg Empire, 17, 27, 53
    Habsburg government, 181
    Habsburg Monarchy, 25
    Habsburg rulers, 16, 19
    Habsburgs, the, 17, 20, 28, 81
    House of Habsburg, 255
Hansards, the, 193
Hemmema, Rienck, 279
Henry II Plantagenet, 170
Henry VII, 93
Henry VIII, 102, 121
Hessians, the, 109
Hopkins, 224-6, 234

Isabella, archduchess, 188

Janssone, Harman, 109
Jews, the, 185
Joan of Brabant, 175
John II of Brabant, 172
John III of Brabant, 173, 186
John the Fearless, 81-2

Kitson, Thomas, 163, 195
    Kitson Papers, 163, 195
Klein, Peter, 35
Kondratieff, 270

Labrousse, Ernest, 245, 247, 262
Lapeyre, 159
Le Roy Ladurie, Emmanuel, 48
Lombards, the, 17, 185-8, 196
Louis IX, 171
Louis XIV, 30, 48, 63-4
Louis of Crécy, 173
Louis of Male, 174

INDEX

Margaret of Male, 14
Margaret of Palma, 112
Marius, John, 162, 165
Mary of Burgundy, 187
Maximilian of Austria, 16, 25, 82, 136, 139, 180–1, 187, 233
Medicis, 159
Mellema, 164
Mennher, 164
Meuvret, Jean, 261
Morineau, Michel, 48, 65
Munro, John, 211, 213, 215
Muslims, the, 4

Napoleon, 39

Ottoman Empire, 118

Phelps Brown 224–6, 234
Philip II, 28, 81. 83, 113, 268–9, 280
Philip of St-Pol, 177
Philip the Bold, 174–6
Philip the Fair, 14, 93
Philip the Good, 16, 52–3, 81–2, 177–80, 186–7, 217
Piccamiglio, 159
Portuguese, the, 17–9, 93–5. 100, 145, 180
Pruynen, 95

Requesens, 113
Riemersma, 276
Robrecht of Bethune, 172
Rogers, Thorold, 225
Rug, Robert, 162
Ruweel, Willem, 191
Ruwet, Joseph, 247

Saint Louis, 170

Schets, Gaspar, 280
Schetz, Erasmus, 95, 153, 160
Scholliers, 226, 271
Selby, W., 162
Southern Germans, the, 18–9, 94, 145, 149
Spaniards, the, 19
  Spanish, the, 95, 145
  Spanish Empire, 29
Suleiman I, 100
Suleiman the Magnificent, 118

Tawney, 161

Valois, 20, 120, 140
Van Bombergen, 153
van den Bloke, Jacob, 191
Van der Molen, 115–6, 121–3, 160, 163
  Van der Molen brothers, 115
Van Immerseele, 161, 166
van Marcke, Colaert, 191
Van Rossum, Maarten, 100
Van Uytven, Raymond, 191
Vandenbroeke, Chris, 48, 65, 66
Vanderpijpen, 48, 65–6
Van Rechtergem, 95
Venetians, the, 94, 102
Verlinden, Charles, 223, 226
Vigerszone, Coppin, 127
Vikings, the, 6
Vleminx, 95

Washington, Thomas, 153
Weddington, John, 156
Welsers, the, 26, 94
Wenceslaus of Brabant, 175
William I, 38